Harnessing Dynamic Knowledge Principles in the Technology-Driven World

Mark E. Nissen
Royal Oaks, USA

A volume in the Advances in Knowledge Acquisition, Transfer, and Management (AKATM) Book Series

Managing Director:	Lindsay Johnston
Production Manager:	Jennifer Yoder
Publishing Systems Analyst:	Adrienne Freeland
Development Editor:	Allyson Gard
Acquisitions Editor:	Kayla Wolfe
Typesetter:	Christina Barkanic
Cover Design:	Jason Mull

Published in the United States of America by
Information Science Reference (an imprint of IGI Global)
701 E. Chocolate Avenue
Hershey PA 17033
Tel: 717-533-8845
Fax: 717-533-8661
E-mail: cust@igi-global.com
Web site: http://www.igi-global.com

Library of Congress Cataloging-in-Publication Data

Nissen, Mark E., 1958-
Harnessing dynamic knowledge principles in the technology-driven world / by Mark Nissen.
pages cm
Includes bibliographical references and index.
ISBN 978-1-4666-4727-5 (hardcover) -- ISBN 978-1-4666-4728-2 (ebook) -- ISBN 978-1-4666-4729-9 (print & perpetual access) 1. Knowledge management. 2. Information technology--Management. 3. Organizational learning. I. Title.
HD30.2.N588 2014
658.4'038--dc23
2013027881

This book is published in the IGI Global book series Advances in Knowledge Acquisition, Transfer, and Management (AKATM) (ISSN: 2326-7607; eISSN: 2326-7615)

British Cataloguing in Publication Data
A Cataloguing in Publication record for this book is available from the British Library.

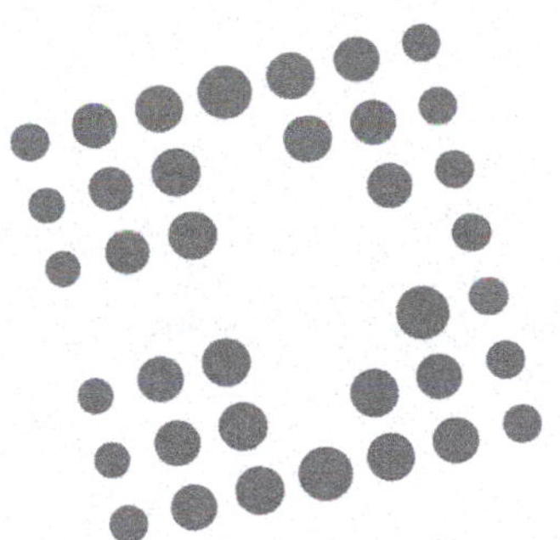

Advances in Knowledge Acquisition, Transfer, and Management (AKATM) Book Series

Murray E. Jennex
San Diego State University, USA

ISSN: 2326-7607
EISSN: 2326-7615

Mission

Organizations and businesses continue to utilize knowledge management practices in order to streamline processes and procedures. The emergence of web technologies has provided new methods of information usage and knowledge sharing. The **Advances in Knowledge Acquisition, Transfer, and Management (AKATM) Book Series** brings together research on emerging technologies and its effect on information systems and knowledge society. **AKATM** will provide researchers, students, practitioners, and industry leaders with highlights on the knowledge management discipline, including technology support issues and knowledge representation.

Coverage

- Cognitive Theories
- Cultural Impacts
- Information and Communication Systems
- Knowledge Acquisition and Transfer Processes
- Knowledge Management Strategy
- Knowledge Sharing
- Organizational Learning
- Organizational Memory
- Small and Medium Enterprises
- Virtual Communities

IGI Global is currently accepting manuscripts for publication within this series. To submit a proposal for a volume in this series, please contact our Acquisition Editors at Acquisitions@igi-global.com or visit: http://www.igi-global.com/publish/.

The Advances in Knowledge Acquisition, Transfer, and Management (AKATM) Book Series (ISSN 2326-7607) is published by IGI Global, 701 E. Chocolate Avenue, Hershey, PA 17033-1240, USA, www.igi-global.com. This series is composed of titles available for purchase individually; each title is edited to be contextually exclusive from any other title within the series. For pricing and ordering information please visit http://www.igi-global.com/book-series/advances-knowledge-acquisition-transfer-management/37159. Postmaster: Send all address changes to above address.

Titles in this Series

For a list of additional titles in this series, please visit: www.igi-global.com

Harnessing Dynamic Knowledge Principles in the Technology-Driven World
Mark Nissen (Naval Postgraduate School, USA)
Information Science Reference • copyright 2014 • 267pp • H/C (ISBN: 9781466647275) • US $175.00 (our price)

Building and Sustaining Knowledge Resources for Competitive Advantage
Michael A. Chilton (Kansas State University, USA) and James M. Bloodgood (Kansas State University, USA)
Information Science Reference • copyright 2014 • 340pp • H/C (ISBN: 9781466646797) • US $175.00 (our price)

Ontology-Based Applications for Enterprise Systems and Knowledge Management
Mohammad Nazir Ahmad (Universiti Teknologi Malaysia, Malaysia) Robert M. Colomb (University of Queensland, Australia) and Mohd Syazwan Abdullah (Universiti Utara Malaysia, Malaysia)
Information Science Reference • copyright 2013 • 423pp • H/C (ISBN: 9781466619937) • US $175.00 (our price)

Knowledge Management and Drivers of Innovation in Services Industries
Patricia Ordóñez de Pablos (Universidad de Oviedo, Spain) and Miltiadis D. Lytras (The American College of Greece, Greece)
Information Science Reference • copyright 2012 • 349pp • H/C (ISBN: 9781466609488) • US $175.00 (our price)

Customer-Centric Knowledge Management Concepts and Applications
Minwir Al-Shammari (University of Bahrain, Bahrain)
Information Science Reference • copyright 2012 • 315pp • H/C (ISBN: 9781613500897) • US $175.00 (our price)

Knowledge Management for Process, Organizational and Marketing Innovation Tools and Methods
Emma O'Brien (University of Limerick, Ireland) Seamus Clifford (University of Limerick, Ireland) and Mark Southern (University of Limerick, Ireland)
Information Science Reference • copyright 2011 • 308pp • H/C (ISBN: 9781615208296) • US $180.00 (our price)

Strategies for Knowledge Management Success Exploring Organizational Efficacy
Murray E. Jennex (San Diego State University, USA) and Stefan Smolnik (International University Schloss Reichartshausen, Germany)
Information Science Reference • copyright 2011 • 350pp • H/C (ISBN: 9781605667096) • US $180.00 (our price)

www.igi-global.com

701 E. Chocolate Ave., Hershey, PA 17033
Order online at www.igi-global.com or call 717-533-8845 x100
To place a standing order for titles released in this series, contact: cust@igi-global.com
Mon-Fri 8:00 am - 5:00 pm (est) or fax 24 hours a day 717-533-8661

Table of Contents

Preface

Knowledge is power. Knowledge represents one of the few bases of sustainable competitive advantage available to the modern enterprise, but knowledge is distributed unevenly through most organizations. Rapid and reliable flows of knowledge across people, organizations, times, and places are critical to enterprise performance. Unfortunately, most leaders and managers have negligible current guidance for assessing and enhancing knowledge flows in practice. A dearth of contemporary research addresses the dynamics of knowledge, which are fundamental to understanding knowledge flows—and in turn both individual and organizational learning and the knowledge-based competitive advantage that they enable.

Epistemology has much to say about the nature of knowledge, but it offers little actionable guidance for the leader and manager; Information Science and information technologies have much to say about flows of information and data, but knowledge is distinct (e.g., it enables action) and exhibits different dynamic behaviors; Knowledge Management has much to say about organizing static knowledge, particularly knowledge articulated in explicit form, but it remains largely silent concerning the dynamics of tacit knowledge; Strategy has much to say about the benefits of competing on the basis of knowledge, but it offers little in terms of how such benefits can be obtained.

Alternatively, Knowledge Flow Theory has been developed to address the dynamics of knowledge—as distinct from information and data—directly. It applies equally well to tacit and explicit knowledge, static knowledge stocks and dynamic knowledge flows, knowledge at the individual and organizational levels. With this, principled techniques enable the practicing leader and manager to analyze and visualize flows of knowledge using a multi-dimensional framework. Such techniques facilitate diagnosing an enterprise's knowledge flows for problems such as bottlenecks, clumping, source inadequacies, and short circuits. Archetypical knowledge-flow patterns associated with well-understood management interventions (e.g., training, mentoring, communities of practice, experience, technology) can be matched with diagnosed problems to generate practical plans and actions for enhancing knowledge flows.

The knowledge of how to diagnose and enhance knowledge flows exists today. It has emerged from the laboratory and begun informing leaders and managers in highly practical ways. Such knowledge, however, remains held by a relatively small and rarefied collection of academics and practitioners, knowledge which itself can enable competitive advantage, particularly over those hipster organizations that have dismissed knowledge management as a fad passé and their primitive counterparts that continue to place hope and money on information technology tools.

Indeed, Knowledge Flow Theory is much more than theory; it is practice—just not common practice yet—informed by actionable principles. This book condenses, consolidates, and collimates such actionable principles into an articulated form that can enable leaders and managers to depart from the prevalent, current, and problematic practices of trial and error, imitation, technology focus, and willful ignorance.

Trial and error represents a well-known approach to organizational knowing and learning: it is known for being very slow and inefficient as well as error-prone. Imitation represents another well-known approach to organizational knowing and learning: it is known for copying the many mistakes of others as well as their occasional successes. Technology—particularly information technology—is necessary but not sufficient: it tends to be expensive and to change rapidly, but it is known for *not* supporting sustainable competitive advantage. Willful ignorance represents a "strategy" adopted at one's peril.

In contrast, our principled approach to organizational knowing and learning can enable leaders and managers to identify and solve problems with knowledge flows. Through such principled intervention, an organization can set the standard to be envied and imitated by its competitors.

This book builds upon theory but targets practice; it takes knowledge known only within a small, rarefied community and shares it with many leaders and managers. It translates what may seem arcane and controversial into managerial guidance that is sophisticated yet practical. It complements the many extant management books on strategy, technology, knowledge, and systems while addressing a well-recognized and significant void. This book provides 30 principles on which to base the most important decisions and actions in an organization: harnessing dynamic knowledge principles for competitive advantage in the technology-driven world. Such a principled approach defines a unique place for and contribution of the book. This book also provides 30 leadership mandates to make actionable the principles and applications presented in this volume. Such integration of principles and applications defines another unique place for and contribution of the book. The book further provides clear and broad application to multiple organizations in the corporate, government, and non-profit sectors, and it takes on cyberspace, cloud computing, virtual environments and worlds, social media, and emerging knowledge phenomena to guide contemporary leaders and managers and to illustrate the broad and powerful applicability of such principles and mandates—tomorrow as well as today.

The overall objective is to inform the practicing leader and manager about the importance of dynamic knowledge and to provide practical but principled guidance for diagnosing and enhancing knowledge flows. The mission is to condense Knowledge Flow Theory—and the principled practice that it informs—and to distill it into an actionable form of immediate relevance and use by enterprise leaders and managers. The principal audience is the enterprise leader and manager (e.g., in business, government, non-profit) with concerns about organizational knowledge and sustaining competitive advantage. The book provides a set of actionable principles to understand the phenomenon of knowledge flows, and it includes many concrete examples to help ground such principles in the realities of practice. The principles explain why dynamic knowledge phenomena behave as they do, and through principles-based reasoning, they inform the leader and manager of ways to harness dynamic knowledge for competitive advantage in the technology-driven world. The application cases explain how organizations from across a very wide range of sizes and domains—from the largest corporations and government agencies to the smallest non-profit clubs and groups—both succeed and fail at harnessing dynamic knowledge; hence, through case-based reasoning, they provide both positive and negative examples for the leader and manager to use in comparison with his or her own organization.

The academic is also likely to take interest in the book for use in teaching (e.g., on knowledge management, information systems, strategy, organization) and for research. The concise and articulated set of 30 principles for knowledge dynamics remains unmatched today in the scholarly literature. Each chapter also includes exercises to stimulate critical thought, learning, and discussion. These exercises are ready for classroom use and allow ample room for instructors to tailor the associated discussions. The references cited in this book point to a rich and integrated literature that remains fragmented largely among several different scholarly fields at present. Such references point to a substantial, growing intellectual basis for understanding knowledge flows and for harnessing the power of dynamic knowledge. Because most dynamic knowledge principles remain timeless, the corresponding references refer to seminal and key works published many years or even decades ago; yet because the technology-driven world changes incessantly, the corresponding references are much more current (at the time of this writing).

The international scholar and business manager is likely to take interest in the book as well. Although the examples and cases reflect in large part the author's principal focus on relatively large, Western organizations, the examples and cases span multiple nations across Europe and North America, and they include small non-profit firms as well as large corporations and government agencies. Further, the intellectual basis of the book builds upon scholarly work rooted in the East and West alike, and the dynamic knowledge principles articulated throughout the book are intended to be quite general, applying equally to the small firm as to the large, in the East as in the West, and to tomorrow as to yesterday. Nonetheless, we acknowledge that the examples and cases do not include everyone and that some people may wish to see others. We welcome such people to build upon the content, concepts, and principles written in this book and to expand our collective repertoire to address just such additional examples and cases.

This book is organized into three major sections. Section 1, "Intellectual Basis," provides the intellectual foundation needed for practical application as addressed in Section 2 of the book, and it enables insightful interpretation of emerging phenomena discussed in Section 3. Each section is comprised of five chapters, and each chapter is organized with a comfortable level of similarity.

The book also includes a relatively large glossary of key terms. Each such term is defined and includes a pointer to the chapter in which it is discussed. Although universal agreement on the definitions contained in this glossary would not be expected at this time, by including such glossary, we make explicit the meaning and usage of key terms used in the book. This helps to promote a common lexicon in the field of Knowledge Dynamics. It also enables one to understand, explicitly, what the various terms in this book are intended to mean. This provides a stark contrast with most books today.

The book further includes an appendix that lists the code of a small, simple, illustrative expert system discussed in the knowledge technology chapter. By including the complete code, the book enables an instructor to leverage the expert system discussion and gives students an assignment to develop a small system of their own. Students can learn much from developing expert systems, particularly when assigned to "knowledge engineer themselves"; that is, when the assignment is for students to make explicit the knowledge that they possess. This helps students to understand better their own tacit knowledge, and it reinforces numerous important principles about knowledge from the book.

To harness the power of dynamic knowledge principles, one must understand how knowledge flows, in its myriad different forms, through the organization; that is, one must understand the dynamics of knowledge flows. The key to such understanding is knowledge: knowledge about knowledge dynamics. Such knowledge represents the focus of this book. Through its principles, the leader and manager can learn to harness knowledge for sustainable competitive advantage in the technology-driven world.

Mark E. Nissen
Royal Oaks, USA

Acknowledgment

As with any undertaking on the scale of a book such as this, the author serves largely as spokesperson for many others who have contributed and helped to refine good ideas. This is certainly the case here. This also explains in part why the words "we" and "our" are used instead of "I" and "my." The book contains myriad literary citations to acknowledge the sources of good ideas upon which it builds. This represents the standard for acknowledgement in academics. Each of the cited authors should feel proud to know his or her work contributes to an endeavor as important as harnessing dynamic knowledge principles for competitive advantage in the technology-driven world. Of course there are others as well. You know whom you are, and I thank all of you, again, warmly. Last and hence first, there could be no book like this without the grace of God, to Whom I am thankful most of all.

Mark E. Nissen
Royal Oaks, USA

Knowledge Flow Principles and Application Cases

For ready reference and as a précis of subsequent chapters, we summarize here 30 knowledge flow principles addressed in detail through Section 1 of the book. Each principle is accompanied by a corresponding implication (**emboldened** for emphasis) for managerial learning and intervention.

1. Knowledge is distinct from information in enabling competitive advantage (see Ch. 1). **Hence, shuttling *information* around via computers, networks, reports and communications does not address the flow of *knowledge*, at least not directly or on the same time scale**.
2. Knowledge is distributed unevenly and hence must flow for organizational performance (see Ch. 1). **Hence, knowledge clumps need to be identified, and knowledge flows need to be enabled through the organization**.
3. Tacit knowledge supports greater appropriability for competitive advantage than explicit knowledge does (see Ch. 1). **Hence, organizational leaders and managers may benefit from an emphasis on tacit knowledge flows**.
4. Knowledge flows must balance exploration through learning with exploitation through doing (see Ch. 1). **Hence, understanding the kinds of knowledge that are important in an organization's particular environment is essential for promoting the most important knowledge flows**.
5. Enhancing knowledge flows requires simultaneous attention to people, processes, organizations, and technologies (see Ch. 1). **Hence, the elements *people, processes, organizations,* and *technologies* operate as a cohesive system and should be addressed as an integrated design problem**.
6. Knowledge enables action directly, whereas information provides meaning and context for such action (see Ch. 2). **Hence, understanding whether flows of data, information, or knowledge are required in a particular situation depends upon what needs to be accomplished (e.g., resolving uncertainty, deriving meaning, enabling action, respectively)**.
7. Data, information, and knowledge flows are interrelated dynamically yet distinct *mental* processes and *organizational* processes (see Ch. 2). **Hence, people play the critical role in flows of data, information, and knowledge**.
8. Flows of knowledge require supplementary flows of information, data, and signals (see Ch. 2). **Hence, every flow (i.e., data, information and knowledge) from signal interpretation through knowledge creation, and back, requires some kind of knowledge**.
9. *Explicitness* represents a very discriminatory dimension for evaluating the uniqueness of knowledge (see Ch. 2). **Hence, moving knowledge through tacit versus explicit flows represents a leadership or management decision in many cases, a decision which has implications in terms of *power***.

10. Information technology supports principally flows of explicit knowledge (see Ch. 2). **Hence, the nature of knowledge represents a critical factor for determining where IT can be expected to enhance knowledge flows**.
11. Knowledge exhibits some properties of inertia such as *tendency to remain at rest* (see Ch. 3). **Hence, knowledge flow processes represent direct focuses of leadership and management action**.
12. Experiential processes contribute principally toward workflows (i.e., doing), whereas educational processes contribute principally toward knowledge flows (i.e., learning; see Ch. 3). **Hence, changes to workflows demand changes to knowledge flows, and vice versa**.
13. Knowledge flows lie always on the critical paths of workflows and hence organizational performance (see Ch. 3). **Hence, knowledge flows should be planned and managed like workflows are**.
14. Time-critical workflows must wait for enabling knowledge flows to run their course (see Ch. 3). **Hence, most knowledge flows must complete their course before critical and dependent workflows can begin**.
15. Explicit knowledge flows very quickly and broadly, but its relatively power is diluted, whereas tacit knowledge flows comparatively slowly and narrowly but at high power (see Ch. 3). **Hence, the dynamic nature of knowledge has great implication in terms of selecting the most appropriate organizational processes to effect knowledge flows**.
16. Information technology is helpful and necessary but not sufficient for knowledge management (see Ch. 4). **Hence, leaders and managers need to employ non-technological interventions to enhance knowledge flows**.
17. People—not information technology—are central to tacit knowledge flows (see Ch. 4). **Hence, one cannot manage tacit knowledge without managing people**.
18. Information technology plays supportive roles in most organizational work routines, whereas people play the performative roles generally (see Ch. 4). **Hence, most IT plays a supportive role in the organization, whereas people play most of the performative roles**.
19. Expert systems, software agents, and like "intelligent" applications address and apply knowledge directly (see Ch. 4). **Hence, "intelligent" applications can play a performative role in the organization**.
20. Simulation technology can enhance knowledge flows across several phases of the life cycle (see Ch. 4). **Hence, simulation represents a different class of IT, one that facilitates learning as well as doing through virtual practice**.
21. Knowing reflects knowledge in action and is required to realize a return on investment (see Ch. 5). **Hence, knowledge must be put to use through action in order to be useful**.
22. Learning reflects knowledge in motion and is required for knowing (see Ch. 5). **Hence, learning both uses and increases knowledge**.
23. Amplifying knowing and learning beyond the individual offers the greatest potential for knowledge superiority (see Ch. 5). **Hence, the impact of leadership and management increases in direct proportion to the reach of knowledge flows through an organization**.
24. To the extent that an individual, group or organization focuses on knowing, then to some extent learning must suffer, and vice versa (see Ch. 5). **Hence, promoting doing can limit learning, and vice versa**.
25. Doing and learning involve action and potential (see Ch. 5). **Hence, an organization's knowledge inventory both enables and inhibits what actions it can take**.
26. Knowledge management involves organizational change (see Ch. 6). **Hence, the leader and manager have much to learn from change-management**.

27. Once one understands a relatively small set of key knowledge flow processes, he or she can analyze any knowledge flows—healthy or pathologic—in any organization (see Ch. 9). **Hence, the leader and manager need to measure the knowledge inventory for every organization**.
28. When estimating the value of knowledge, it is often better to light a candle than to curse the darkness (see Ch. 6). **Hence, knowledge power measurement provides an approach to assessing the relative efficacy of knowledge flowing through various organizational processes**.
29. Culture, trust, and incentives affect organizational learning and hence performance as much as process, technology, and training do (see Ch. 6). **Hence, every organizational process should improve its performance over time, and every leader and manager should measure the dynamic performance of repetitive processes**.
30. Computational modeling is useful for knowing and learning about organizational knowing and learning (see Ch. 6). **Hence, computational models of knowledge flows provide an approach to mitigating the risk inherent in KM programs**.

We also list the nine application cases to which such principles are applied in Section 2 of the book.

1. In the chapter on business organizations, we look first at an advanced-technology company involved with new-product development (see Ch. 7).
2. The discussion turns then to examine an independent production company involved with a feature film (see Ch. 7).
3. The third case involves a technology-transfer project between a university and a microelectronics company (see Ch. 7).
4. In the chapter on government organizations, we look first at a military organization involved with maritime warfare (see Ch. 8).
5. The discussion turns then to examine a federal government agency involved with a knowledge management program (see Ch. 8).
6. The sixth case examines a public service organization involved with large-scale IT integration (see Ch. 8).
7. In the chapter on non-profit organizations, we look first at a national youth soccer organization (see Ch. 9).
8. The discussion turns then to examine a local tennis club (see Ch. 9).
9. The final case examines a nondenominational community church (see Ch. 9).

We list further the set of 30 leadership mandates induced through practical application in Section 2 of the book.

1. Realistic expectations, shared vision, and appropriate people participating full-time represent the preconditions for success that are absent or insufficient most often in KM projects (see Ch. 6).
2. Reliance upon external expertise, narrow technical focus, and animosity toward staff and specialists represent the preconditions for failure that are present or sufficient most often in KM projects (see Ch. 6).
3. Knowledge representation, attention to tacit knowledge, and focus on organizational memory represent unique considerations that merit particular attention in KM projects (see Ch. 6).
4. Knowledge audits can help organizations that do not know what they know (see Ch. 6).

5. In cases where quick results in short conflicts are important, the organization should focus on explicit knowledge flows, but where sustained results in long confrontations are required, tacit knowledge flows offer greater power (see Ch. 6).
6. Knowledge value analysis privileges tacit knowledge appropriately (see Ch. 6).
7. The greater the use of automation at the beginning of a process, the lower the improvement rate (see Ch. 6).
8. Performance improvement reflected by learning curves involves more than just individual knowing and learning (see Ch. 6).
9. Knowledge can be lost and found (see Ch. 6).
10. Trust cannot be bought (see Ch. 6).
11. Using computational models, organizations can be designed and tested virtually in a manner similar to the design of airplanes, bridges, and computers (see Ch. 6).
12. Specialist and generalist knowledge represent (imperfect) economic substitutes for one another (see Ch. 6).
13. Knowledge flow vectors can be used to represent dynamic knowledge requirements (see Ch. 7).
14. It is essential to plan how knowledge technologies will be used by people (see Ch. 7).
15. The learning curve measures knowledge flows through OJT (see Ch. 7).
16. Socialization and acculturation represent viable approaches to enhancing tacit knowledge flows (see Ch. 7).
17. Trans-organizational collectivities (e.g., communities) may have greater influence over employee knowledge, culture, and performance than leadership and management do (see Ch. 7).
18. Knowledge flows critical to enabling critical workflows center on tacit knowledge (see Ch. 7).
19. An organizational process without consistent improvement over time suffers from knowledge clumping (see Ch. 7).
20. Members of a team must learn to work with one another before knowing how to work together on a project (see Ch. 7).
21. Ten unique knowledge flow processes are required for military task force efficacy (see Ch. 8).
22. OJT involves knowledge flowing at two different speeds: knowledge application through doing is fast; knowledge creation through learning is slow (see Ch. 8).
23. Given the time-critical nature of warfare, most tacit knowledge must already be in place when the officer reports first for duty (see Ch. 8).
24. Systematic storytelling can increase the reach of this time-honored and effective approach to sharing tacit knowledge (see Ch. 8).
25. Socialization, teamwork, and acculturation must interconnect to enable healthy knowledge flow circulation (see Ch. 8).
26. Leading by example and evangelism represent viable approaches to enhancing acculturation knowledge flows (see Ch. 9).
27. Once one understands relatively small set of key knowledge flow processes, he or she can analyze any knowledge flows—healthy or pathologic—in any organization (see Ch. 9).
28. The key to self-organization is having people enjoy what they do together (see Ch. 9).
29. The ability of different people to work together on teams is just as important as the individual skills and experiences they bring individually (see Ch 9).
30. Leaders who are concerned about acculturation knowledge flows must address participants' beliefs (see Ch. 9).

Section 1
Intellectual Basis

True knowledge exists in knowing that you know nothing. – Socrates

Let the wise listen to these proverbs and become even wiser. Let those with understanding receive guidance. – Solomon

The intellectual basis of this book centers on Knowledge Flow Theory (KFT), which has become very stable and well established over the years. KFT encompasses a large body of research articulating principles of knowledge dynamics; viz. understanding and explaining how knowledge "moves" through an organization. As understood within such principled rubric, knowledge enables action, action drives performance, and performance supports competitive advantage. Hence, knowledge is on the critical path of organizational action, performance, and competitive advantage through the work that it enables.

To the extent that organizational knowledge does not exist in the form needed for application or at the place and time required to enable work performance, then it must flow from how, when, and where it exists to how, when, and where it is needed. This is the concept knowledge flow. As explained in this book, knowledge flow represents more than just a metaphor: it explains the dynamics of how knowledge moves through an organization.

In the context of organizational performance, where knowledge flow problems such as clotting, poor circulation, or bleeding (metaphorically) may exist, it is important to diagnose such problems and to understand flow principles well enough to identify and implement the appropriate interventions. KFT provides the intellectual basis for diagnosis and intervention of problems with dynamic knowledge. Harnessing dynamic knowledge requires understanding flow principles well enough to identify and correct pathologies. Further, it requires anticipating where and when future flow problems are likely to occur, and it depends upon designing work processes, organizations, technologies, and personnel systems to address such problems before they become manifest. As such, the principles explain why dynamic knowledge phenomena behave as they do, and through principles-based reasoning, they inform the leader and manager on ways to harness dynamic knowledge for competitive advantage in the technology-driven world.

This first section of the book is organized into five chapters. Chapter 1, "Knowledge Power," focuses on how the power of dynamic knowledge can be harnessed. Chapter 2, "Knowledge Uniqueness," addresses how knowledge flows differ from flows of information and data, and it indicates where such differences are important. Chapter 3, "Knowledge Flow," centers on the phenomenology of dynamic knowledge. Chapter 4, "Knowledge Technology," surveys several classes of technologies, and it indicates which kinds of knowledge flows are enabled and supported better and worse by such technologies. Chapter 5, "Knowing and Learning," discusses the concepts *knowing*, which involves knowledge in action, and *learning*, which involves knowledge in motion.

Together, these five chapters provide the intellectual foundation needed for practical application as addressed in Section 2 of the book. The application cases explain in turn how organizations from across a very wide range of sizes and domains—from the largest corporations and government agencies to the smallest non-profit clubs and groups—both succeed and fail at harnessing dynamic knowledge; hence, through case-based reasoning, they provide both positive and negative examples for the leader and manager to use in comparison with his or her own organization. In combination, the KFT principles and application cases enable insightful interpretation of emerging phenomena discussed in Section 3.

Chapter 1
Knowledge Power

ABSTRACT

This chapter focuses on how the power of dynamic knowledge principles can be harnessed for competitive advantage in the technology-driven world. The authors look first at how knowledge enables competitive advantage and then discuss the nature of knowledge flows. The chapter concludes with five knowledge power principles and includes exercises to stimulate critical thought, learning, and discussion.

COMPETITIVE ADVANTAGE

It is difficult to find an organization that is not interested in competitive advantage in today's dynamic, global, highly competitive environment (Matusik & Hill, 1998; Chaharbaghi & Lynch, 1999; Barney, 2002; Fahey, 2002; Teece, 2009). Organizational strategists have long discussed competitive advantage (esp. in economic terms such as earning superior rents, gaining larger market share, raising barriers to market entry, locking out competitors, and locking in customers; see Barney, 1986), but the comparatively recent advent and continuing proliferation of social media applications (e.g., social networking such as via Facebook, microblogging such as Twitter, collaborative projects such as Wikis; see Kaplan & Haenlein, 2010) is changing the nature of competition (Nissen & Bergin, 2013). Nonetheless, numerous empirical studies assess (Castillo, 2003) and provide evidence (Darroch, 2005; Marques & Simon, 2006; Bogner & Bansal, 2007; Holsapple & Jones, 2007; Zack et al., 2009; Holsapple & Wu, 2011; Jayasingam et al., 2012; Nold, 2012) that competitive advantage stems from the intellectual and other assets that an organization is able to appropriate[1] (i.e., assert ownership and control over), in addition to how such assets are used (Holsapple & Singh, 2001) and the process capabilities that it is able to employ dynamically (Teece et al., 1997). The latter part of this point is key: if an organization bases its competitive advantage on some assets that can be obtained readily through the market or other means of imitation, then there is little to prevent competitors from matching its actions and performance (Dierickx & Cool, 1989). Hence any competitive advantage effected by the lead firm is destined to be ephemeral at best.

This is the case especially for information technology (Nissen, 2006). For a period of time in the Seventies, for instance, a few banks offering automated teller machines (ATMs) to customers enjoyed some competitive advantages over those

DOI: 10.4018/978-1-4666-4727-5.ch001

without this technology, but today nearly every bank offers ATMs. Instead of conferring some competitive advantage, now ATM technology represents just another cost of doing business in banking. Computerized reservation systems (CRSs), as another instance, similarly conferred some competitive advantage to the pioneering airlines behind their development and initial deployment in the Eighties, but today nearly every airline uses CRSs. Instead of conferring some competitive advantage, now CRS technology represents just another cost of doing business in air travel. Leading-edge financial investment firms, as a third instance, gained some competitive advantage in the Nineties through computer trading systems for securities such as stocks, bonds and futures, but today nearly every financial investment firm trades securities as such. Instead of conferring some competitive advantage, now this information technology represents just another cost of doing business in securities financial investment. The list of similar instances goes on and continues through cloud computing, mobile applications, tablets, social media and like trends that are current at the time of this writing.

The same applies also to other primary resources such as the traditional economic inputs of land, labor and capital. For instance, in terms of land, for centuries the vineyards of France enjoyed considerable competitive advantage over wine producers in other regions. However, world-class, award-winning wines are produced today in California, South America, Australia and other regions. Fine wines are produced still in France of course, but the land alone is no longer sufficient for competitive advantage over vintners in other fertile regions of the world. As another instance, in terms of labor, for decades following World War II the relatively low cost and high quality of Japanese workers conferred considerable competitive advantage across numerous durable-goods and consumer-electronics industries (e.g., machinery, automobiles, televisions, radios). Then labor-based advantages shifted to places like South Korea, Malaysia, Mexico and other nations. Today China appears to be capitalizing best on the basis of labor. Japanese firms remain competitive still in markets for some goods, electronics and other products, but the labor force alone is no longer sufficient to confer competitive advantage over manufacturers in other industrializing nations.

Such shifting of labor-based advantage is clearly not limited to manufacturing industries. A huge number of IT and service jobs, for two contemporary instances, have moved from Europe and North America to India, Singapore and like countries with relatively well-educated, low-cost work forces possessing technical skills. However, as educational levels and technical skills continue to rise in other countries, India, Singapore and like nations enjoying labor-based competitive advantage today are likely to find such advantage cannot be sustained through the onset of new competitors. As a third instance, in terms of capital, for centuries the days of gold coins and later even paper money restricted financial flows to relatively small geographical regions. Regional concentrations formed where large banks, industries and markets coalesced together, and such regions enjoyed competitive advantage over others that lacked equivalent coalescence. Alternatively, capital can flow all around the world in seconds today. Global commerce no longer requires regional interactions between business people. Regional capital concentrations in places such as New York, London and Tokyo persist still of course, but the capital concentrated there is no longer sufficient for competitive advantage over other capitalists distributed worldwide. Only if an organization is able to combine, integrate and apply its resources (e.g., land, labor, capital, IT) in an effective manner that is not readily imitable by competitors can such organization enjoy competitive advantage that is sustainable over time.

In a knowledge-based theory of the firm, this idea is extended to view organizational knowledge as an asset with at least the same level of power and importance as the traditional economic inputs

(Drucker, 1995; Grant, 1996; Spender, 1996). An organization with superior knowledge can achieve competitive advantage in markets that appreciate the application of such knowledge. Semiconductors, genetic engineering, pharmaceuticals, software, military warfare and like knowledge-intensive competitive arenas provide both time-proven and current examples. Consider semiconductors (e.g., computer chips), which are made principally of sand and common metals. These ubiquitous and powerful electronic devices are designed within common office buildings, using commercially available tools, and are fabricated within factories in many industrialized nations. Hence land is not the key competitive resource in the semiconductor industry. Likewise, people with training and experience in semiconductor design and fabrication are available throughout the world. Hence neither is labor the key competitive resource in this industry. Similarly, even though semiconductor fabrication plants must be custom-designed, require over a billion dollars to build, and become obsolete within a year or few, a great many nations and large corporations can afford to construct such expensive plants. Hence capital fails to qualify too as the key competitive resource here. Yet one semiconductor firm is hugely successful in financial terms such as earnings and market share. This firm knows how to design, fabricate and market semiconductors better than its competitors do. Hence knowledge is the key competitive resource in the semiconductor industry. This knowledge-based competitive advantage has been sustained for several decades now. Similar examples concerning computer operating systems software, networking equipment, Internet search and like knowledge-based products serve to reinforce this point.

Two competitors can possess exactly the same kinds of land, labor, capital and IT, but differ in terms of how such assets are combined in the organization, integrated through work processes, and applied to develop products and services. The one with better knowledge can win, consistently and through time. Consider military combat (e.g., naval warfare), the history of which is replete with examples of "inferior" forces (e.g., in terms of land, labor, capital and technology) winning battles and even wars. For instance, recall the colorful era of wooden sailing ships with fixed rows of cannons along their sides. The outcomes of naval battles in this era were predictable generally on the basis of: a) number of ships in a fleet, and b) number and size of cannons onboard the ships. The countries whose land, labor, capital and technology could produce fleets in greater numbers than those of adversaries fared well consistently in battles at sea.

However, such battles were fought commonly through broadside cannon exchanges between ships from opposing fleets sailing past one another in long, straight lines. "Crossing the T" (i.e., sailing perpendicular to the line of ships from an opposing fleet) represented a tactic (i.e., a set of actions based upon knowledge) that conferred competitive advantage even to a smaller fleet of lesser-equipped ships (e.g., consider the Battle of Trafalgar). Because ships of the day had difficulty shooting forward, the "crossing" fleet faced comparatively little cannon fire. Further, because cannons were relatively inaccurate in those days, the "crossing" fleet also had a long line of opposing ships to target lengthwise, whereas the fleet shooting broadside had comparatively small targets as ships pitched, rolled and sailed on the high seas. Here tactical knowledge conferred competitive advantage even to fleets lacking the materiel advantage based upon traditional resources of land, labor, capital and technology. In our current era of networked sensors, weapons (Alberts et al., 1999) and Cyberspace capabilities (Clarke & Knake, 2010; Kramer et al., 2011), knowledge remains a key competitive resource in military combat.

Even when leveraging knowledge for competitive advantage, however, organizations can suffer the same limitations in terms of sustainability. As with the assets above, for instance, where a competitor can obtain the same kind of knowledge and apply it just as well, then any competitive advantage that may obtain (e.g., via first-mover advantages) is unlikely to be sustainable. Information—and knowledge made explicit—falls generally into this category. When an organization attempts to take advantage of such information or explicit knowledge, it is required to protect it vigilantly or risk losing any advantage it enables. This is the fundamental motivation for keeping secrets (e.g., military, trade, investing) and underlies laws for patent and copyright protection in many countries, as well as espionage and organized intelligence collection. Thus, not all knowledge offers equal potential in terms of competitive advantage. Speaking generally, the more explicit that knowledge becomes, the lower its competitive potential becomes (Saviotti, 1998).

Alternatively, tacit knowledge, particularly knowledge that is specific to a particular person, organization, market or domain, is not as susceptible to loss. Gained principally through experience and accumulated over time, personal and organizational capabilities based upon tacit knowledge are difficult to imitate, even if observed directly by competitors. Consider a virtuoso violinist, for instance, auditioning for a lead role with a symphony orchestra; a competing violinist (e.g., auditioning for the same lead role) can watch every stroke made and note played by the virtuoso, but this does not imply that he or she will be able to achieve comparable virtuosity simply through observation. The same kind of competitive advantage applies to experienced contract negotiators, aviators, golfers, chess players, parents, politicians and many other people whose performance is based principally upon experience-based tacit knowledge.

Likewise with organizational tacit knowledge, which manifests itself through organizational cultures, routines and procedures; simply observing a high-performance organization—say with considerable experience in a particular product or service market—does not necessarily confer comparable capability to a competitor. This is one driver of first-mover competitive advantage, and it helps to explain why it can be so very difficult for second-mover firms to ever catch up.

Contrast such knowledge-based competitive advantage to activities predicated upon keeping explicit knowledge secret; were someone to view the secret recipe for making a soft drink, to discover the top secret keys used to encrypt military communications, to uncover a security trading firm's explicit trade algorithms, or achieve like access to explicit knowledge used to enable competitive advantage, for several instances, then one would not expect for such advantage to be sustainable for long.

Hence relatively inimitable knowledge-based competitive advantage can obtain and be sustained readily on the basis of tacit knowledge, but such advantage is more difficult when predicated upon knowledge in explicit form. Speaking generally, tacit knowledge offers greater promise in terms of competitive advantage than explicit knowledge does due to its greater inimitability. Such inimitability represents a proverbial two-edge sword, however. Even in situations of planned technology transfer between different units of a single firm, for instance, in which management encourages knowledge to flow, such transfers are consistently problematic (Szulanski, 1996). The tacit knowledge is "sticky" (von Hippel, 1994), clumps in the transferring experts and units (Nissen, 2006), and does not flow freely (O'Dell et al., 1998). Further, even where substantial knowledge has been made explicit (e.g., through engineering drawings, standard procedures, lessons learned), in many cases it is not sufficient to write down the work steps and to expect people in different offices, plants, companies or regions to perform at comparable levels (Szulanski & Winter, 2002). We know more than we can tell (Polanyi, 1966).

For instance at the organizational level, despite overt help and cooperation from Toyota, advantages stemming from producing low cost, high quality automobiles via the Toyota Production System have been elusive for numerous other companies attempting to replicate Toyota's success. As another instance, the US Government has encountered similar experiences. Many large contracts to produce major weapon systems (e.g., airplanes, missiles, vehicles) have required defense firms to provide detailed engineering drawings, manufacturing assembly plans and production tools to enable competing firms to build the same systems. The rationale was to introduce a modicum of competition in the defense procurement process. However, "second sources," as they are called, are able rarely to compete on a head-to-head basis. Even after being forced to share abundant explicit knowledge, the lead firm retains its knowledge-based competitive advantage. Tacit knowledge, which resists articulation and transfer, accounts in great part for this phenomenon.

Organizations that develop tacit knowledge—at the individual level as well as across groups, teams and organization-wide—enjoy much greater power of appropriation and lower risk of imitation than organizations relying upon traditional assets do. Further, an organization's level of current knowledge enhances its ability to learn new knowledge. The further behind one organization gets with respect to its competitors in terms of knowledge, the more difficult it becomes to catch up. Notice this represents a dynamic phenomenon. Not only is the *inventory* (i.e., knowledge level) important to enable competitive advantage, but also the *learning rate* (i.e., knowledge flow) is critical to sustaining any such advantage that may obtain. The more you know, the faster you learn. This maxim applies to organizations as well as to individuals (Cohen and Levinthal 1990).

KNOWLEDGE FLOWS

Drawing heavily from Nissen (2006), here we discuss the dynamics of knowledge flows. Like mineral deposits that are rich in some geographical regions and sparse in others, knowledge is not distributed evenly throughout the world or across organizations. Different organizations possess different kinds and levels of knowledge, and we note above how differential knowledge between organizations can establish a basis for competitive advantage. However, we note above also how tacit knowledge is difficult to imitate, even when corresponding knowledge flows are encouraged by management within a single organization. This sticky nature of tacit knowledge is thus a mixed blessing. On the one hand it supports competitive advantage, but on the other it restricts knowledge flows within one's own organization.

To emphasize this important point, consider an organization that develops a knowledge-based competitive advantage through the learning and application of an exceptional team of people in one particular plant, regional office or product line. This organization would seek naturally to exploit such advantage and to capitalize on its knowledge differential over competitors. Keeping this exceptional team of people together and preventing defections to rival organizations represent two objectives management is likely to pursue to prevent knowledge from flowing out of its prize unit.

Capabilities based on the tacit knowledge enabling this organization's competitive advantage will be difficult for competitors to imitate. This contributes toward sustainability of its knowledge-based advantage, but at the same time, this organization seeks to leverage such advantage by transferring key knowledge from its prize unit to other plants, regional offices and product lines. The same attributes of tacit knowledge that make it difficult for competitors to imitate knowledge-based capabilities make it difficult also for other parts of the same organization to imitate. Such organization seeks methods and technologies to promote knowledge flows internally yet prohibit such knowledge from leaking externally. This represents a challenging problem of harnessing dynamic knowledge.

A case study of one successful automobile company in Europe (Loch et al., 2001) illustrates in part this difficulty of promoting internal knowledge flows. The company developed and implemented an effective means of improving research and development (R&D) decision-making through the use of mathematical programming techniques. Despite demonstrating performance benefits of such techniques within the adopting unit, however, the company had little success in terms of diffusing the approach through other units within the firm. The manager responsible for the original advance had contracted with consultants who were external to the company. Although this manager understood the benefits and overall approach of mathematical programming, he did not possess the detailed expertise to implement it in his unit of the company or in other units. Hence the company failed to appropriate the mathematical programming knowledge. Rather, it remained dependent upon external consultants. When such consultants were not retained by the company to extend the decision-making techniques into other units, the corresponding knowledge and expertise left the company along with the consultants. Knowledge flows associated with the mathematical programming techniques ceased then.

It is important to note, the objective of promoting knowledge flows internally within organizations is not restricted to select knowledge that enables competitive advantage. All knowledge required for an organization to perform its work processes and accomplish its mission needs to flow within such organization. Knowledge lies always on the critical path of work; that is, people must know how to accomplish a job before they can accomplish it, and they must know how and when to accomplish it well—generally in conjunction with others—before the corresponding work can be accomplished on required schedules and at acceptable quality levels. Hence even routine knowledge necessary to perform ordinary work processes within an organization must flow across numerous dimensions.

For instance, we note above how knowledge flows between different organizational units are desirable where such knowledge enables competitive advantage. Inter-unit knowledge flows are important also for organizations that seek to maintain consistent work processes, technological environments and product quality levels across units. Whether the products of interest are semiconductors, pharmaceuticals, software applications or government services, knowledge is required to perform the corresponding work processes, and such knowledge must flow between units to ensure consistent performance organization-wide. The case of the automobile company above illustrates well how failure of inter-unit knowledge flows can prevent some units within a single firm from enjoying even benefits demonstrated in other units.

As another instance, knowledge flows across time are necessary also, in addition to flows across different organizations and geographical regions. Consider where one shift replaces another in a factory, processing plant or military watch. Management is interested in using the knowledge gained during a shift by one group to enhance the performance of the other group. Take a network problem, for example, in a global telecommunications firm. Such firms operate 24 hours a day, yet individual employees work generally only eight hours at a time. When an individual customer service agent leaves at the end of a shift, it is important for him or her to convey what he or she knows about the network problem to the person taking over. Otherwise, the agent beginning a new shift may not understand adequately the network status to relate effectively with customers or to steer them toward work-around solutions to current or emergent network problems. Similar examples in other settings (e.g., plant equipment problems in a petroleum-processing operation, health problems of a patient in a hospital intensive-care unit, intentions of commercial aircraft in flight as air traffic controllers change shifts) abound as well. Notice, such knowledge flows—across shift changes—represent dynamics occurring over relatively short periods of time (e.g., hours).

Alternatively, other flows require knowledge to move over extended periods of time. Consider how most organizations expect junior members to develop knowledge and expertise over time. Some aspects of knowledge and expertise can be acquired directly (e.g., through education and training programs), whereas others accumulate indirectly through experience (e.g., working on a particular kind of problem). Some kinds of knowledge are quite general and transferable broadly (e.g., engineering principles and methods), whereas others are specific to a particular company, department and work assignment, and hence more restricted in terms of opportunities for application and transfer. In some cases people can begin at a state of ignorance and incompetence yet develop knowledge and expertise through a process of repeated trial and error (e.g., on-the-job training or OJT), whereas other work contexts require competent performance on the first attempt (e.g., surgery). In still other situations knowledge and expertise apply to individuals (e.g., the examples above), whereas group, team and department interaction requires collections of people to learn how to work together (e.g., basketball teams, software development groups, police SWAT teams).

In every case, considerable time is required for learning (i.e., knowledge to flow). The amount of time allocated for learning represents a management decision. In the typical research university, for example, assistant professors are given six years to establish a positive national reputation, after which they face an up-or-out staffing decision, but the kinds of work they perform (e.g., research, instruction) remain the same for the most part throughout this period (and in many cases for years or even decades beyond). Most research universities have decided that six years of the same work after earning a PhD is enough time to become an associate professor, or not. In a corporate employee-internship program, as a different example, new college hires may be rotated through different departments and jobs every six months. Unlike the research university, here the kinds of work new hires perform change with each rotation. Such organizations have decided that six months of the same work after earning a college degree is enough time for rotation to another job. The US Navy, as a third example in between the two above, rotates its personnel roughly every two or three years. Here all of its people (e.g., junior and senior, enlisted and officers, sailors and staff) change jobs on two- or three-year intervals. This military organization has decided that two or three years of the same work after assignment to a new command is enough time for rotation to another job.

Knowledge flows between people denote a related instance. Of course this transcends the other instances above, for ultimately nearly all tacit knowledge flows in an organizational context take place between people. In the case of inter-unit transfers, people in the different organizations must learn from one another (e.g., about decision-making techniques). In the case of flows between shifts, people on the different shifts must learn from one another (e.g., about equipment problems). In the case of new employees, people must learn from some combination of the work itself (e.g., trial and error, OJT) and other people (e.g., supervisors, mentors, instructors, peers). Hence knowledge flows across different organizational units, geographical regions and points in time involve people and are necessary just to accomplish the work at hand (e.g., ordinary work processes), even where such knowledge may not necessarily lead to competitive advantage. This elucidates a critical point in terms of diagnosing knowledge flow problems. Viewed in reverse, where knowledge fails to flow well, even to enable ordinary workflows, the organization may experience competitive disadvantage, as it fails to perform even its routine work effectively.

Consider the Business Process Re-engineering (BPR) movement in the Nineties, for instance. Conceived originally as an approach for radical change to effect dramatic performance improvements in organizations (Davenport, 1993; Hammer & Champy, 1993), BPR provided a broad-based impetus and set of techniques to enable organizations to perform better with fewer assets. However, the focus of this approach shifted over time from one of superior performance to a cost-cutting mechanism. Profits rose at many companies, and competitors followed suit to avoid being left behind, but in the US alone many tens of thousands of jobs were eliminated through the process. Many of such jobs belonged to knowledge workers and middle managers. After some period of time, it became apparent to several firms that critical organizational knowledge had left the company with the people who were "downsized." Such people had to be rehired—oftentimes as expensive consultants or for far more than their previous salaries. The short-term focus on cost-reduction and job-elimination took place at the expense of longer-term performance and knowledge accumulation.

A similar situation is occurring at the time of this writing for a different reason. A large number of people from the Baby Boom Generation are retiring. Organizations lack the resources and techniques to ensure that Baby Boomer knowledge flows effectively to the Generation X, Y, Millennial and other groups that are performing junior- and mid-level jobs in such organizations. Indeed, the US Government estimated nearly a decade ago that half of its workforce would be eligible for retirement today (Liebowitz, 2004a). This estimate remains relatively accurate (OPM, 2008), yet despite such forewarning, the massive governmental organization remains perplexed regarding how to preserve the corresponding knowledge. This applies in particular to the kind of rich, experience-based tacit knowledge that makes seasoned employees so valuable.

Even within a particular organization, knowledge can be observed to clump noticeably in certain people, groups, locations and points in time. The phenomenon of knowledge distributing itself unevenly across different people has been studied extensively for years (e.g., see Turban & Aronson, 1998). Researchers have examined the nature of expert performance and tried to draw generalizable comparisons with the performance of novices, for instance. Many studies of leadership fall into this category. A whole industry of expert systems was developed in the Eighties around the idea of capturing expert level capabilities and formalizing them in computers. Indeed, knowledgeable people have been painting caves, chiseling stones and writing books for millennia in attempts to share their expertise, and Society has developed many other techniques for experts (and novices) to share knowledge (e.g., stories, mentoring, apprenticeship, university courses, webinars, Utube videos).

Since expert knowledge is generally tacit, it is sticky, and the corresponding clumps remain difficult to distribute. For instance, it is recognized widely that roughly ten years' sustained and dedicated effort is required to become an expert in a particular field, with accumulation of some 10,000 chunks of knowledge corresponding (Turban & Aronson, 1998). Trying to share such expertise encounters the well-understood problem associated with "the fish." Recall the parable of giving someone a fish versus teaching him or her how to fish. In the former case, one feeds the person for a day, but he or she becomes hungry again the following day. In the latter case, the person learns to feed him or herself for a lifetime, but such learning takes time. Ask an expert to solve a problem, and he or she solves the problem. This takes care of the situation until its next occurrence. Now ask the expert to teach an apprentice how to solve the problem. The expert (or simply more knowledgeable person) must be willing and able to share; the novice must be willing and able to learn; and the organization must be willing and able to help them do so. Very few organizations accomplish such individual learning well at present. As a general rule, individual knowledge does not flow well through most organizations.

Even more difficult is enabling knowledge flows at other levels. Because groups, teams, departments, firms and even larger aggregations of people, for several instances, are comprised of individuals, all of the same individual-level problems noted above are present within such organizations. In addition, knowledge is noted to clump in certain organizations as well as specific individuals. Accounts abound of groups, teams, offices, units, ships, crews and like organizations that are practically identical except for the individuals comprising them, yet in which one organization outperforms the others, oftentimes dramatically so. Identifying the sources of performance differences between apparently equivalent organizations is difficult enough, even though it reduces often to some kind of tacit knowledge that is shared within a particular group. Nonetheless, conceiving mechanisms for such shared knowledge to flow between two groups remains very challenging. Because the shared knowledge is tacit, attempting to write it down and disseminate it via books, standard operating procedures, lessons learned, Web portals, workflow systems, wikis, social networking sites, and other approaches relying upon explicit knowledge offers limited efficacy potential. Reading a book or report about how to do something is not the same as having learned to do it tacitly.

This same point pertains to enterprises that are separated across time and space, as well as those separated by organizational boundaries. Think of a new group taking over a work task from a counterpart that has been performing it effectively for some time, or an organization in one geographical region that is able somehow to perform more effectively than its equivalent peer in another region. Knowledge flows are essential for power through competitive advantage, but enabling such flows remains a huge challenge for most organizations. We address such challenge in subsequent chapters.

KNOWLEDGE POWER PRINCIPLES

Five principles developed in this chapter help shed light on developing knowledge power: 1) knowledge is distinct from information in enabling competitive advantage; 2) knowledge is distributed unevenly, and hence must flow for organizational performance; 3) tacit knowledge supports greater appropriability for competitive advantage than explicit knowledge does; 4) knowledge flows must balance exploration through learning with exploitation through doing; and 5) enhancing knowledge flows requires simultaneous attention to people, processes, organizations and technologies.

Principle 1: First, distinguishing knowledge from information is important. One effective operationalization is, knowledge enables direct action (e.g., correct decisions, appropriate behaviors, useful work), whereas information provides meaning and context for such action (e.g., decision criteria, behavior norms, work specifications). As a Gedanken experiment, consider two people tasked to perform a knowledge-intensive activity. These could be captains on the bridge of a ship, surgeons at the operating table, managers at the negotiating table, professors in a classroom, attorneys in a courtroom, or many like situations requiring knowledge. Provide these two people with exactly the same information (e.g., books to read, charts and reports to reference, instruments to monitor, direct views and sounds, advisors to consult, others), but say that one person has twenty years' experience, whereas the other has much less experience (or possibly none). Most informed leaders, managers and scholars would expect differential performance from these two people. Such differential performance can be attributed generally to differences in knowledge. Hence shuttling *information* around via computers, networks, reports and communications does not address the flow of *knowledge*, at least not directly or on the same time scale.

Principle 2: Second, knowledge clumps in particular people, organizations, regions and times of application. Knowledge power through competitive advantage requires knowledge to flow, but tacit knowledge in particular is sticky, difficult to imitate, and slow to move. This same property, which enables knowledge-based competitive advantage to be sustainable, inhibits simultaneously sharing within the organization. Hence knowledge clumps need to be identified, and knowledge flows need to be enabled through the organization.

Principle 3: This gives rise to a third principle, which is focused on differentiating between different kinds of knowledge. In particular, explicit knowledge that can be articulated is distinct in many ways from the kind of tacit knowledge that accumulates, often slowly, through experience. Neither is individual expertise quite the same as knowledge shared across members of a group, team or other organization. Knowledge can also be quite situated, ephemeral and local, meaning a person on the "front lines" cannot always communicate the richness of what he or she knows to someone at headquarters. Yet people at headquarters tend to demand abundant information flows to support decision-making that is made better on location often. Of course, the person on the scene with detailed and local knowledge lacks the high-level integrative understanding of leaders and managers at headquarters often, and the need for functional specialists to share specific knowledge for complex problem solving is known well, but central to the point of knowledge power is, tacit knowledge supports greater appropriability than explicit knowledge does. Hence organizational leaders and managers may benefit from an emphasis on tacit knowledge flows.

Principle 4: Fourth, not all knowledge, not even tacit knowledge, is of equal value, and not all knowledge needs to be shared to effect performance. Indeed, there is a classic tension between exploration and exploitation. Because resources such as time, energy and attention are limited, investing in exploration of new knowledge and opportunities limits necessarily the resources available to exploit the knowledge and opportunities that exist, and vice versa. Further, to the extent that an organization focuses solely on exploitation, for instance, it can develop quickly competency traps (Levitt & March, 1988) and suffer from debilitations associated with single-loop learning (Argyris & Schon, 1978); that is, an organization can learn to do the wrong thing very well and not realize that its competency is suited well to the environment no longer. Likewise, to the extent that an organization focuses solely on exploration, as a contrasting instance, it can see quickly its demise, as competitors capitalize upon current opportunities and take advantage of the organization's time away from task; that is, the organization can prepare itself well for a future environment but fail to survive until such future arrives. Similar tensions arise between learning and doing, sharing and hoarding knowledge, acquiring general versus specialized expertise, and like knowledge-oriented tradeoffs. Hence understanding the kinds of knowledge that are important in an organization's particular environment is essential for promoting the most important knowledge flows.

Principle 5: Fifth, it is known well that organizational personnel, work processes, structures and technologies are interconnected tightly and interact closely (Leavitt, 1965). When seeking to redesign and change organizations to identify knowledge clumps and to enhance knowledge flows, it is important to focus simultaneously upon all of these interconnected and interacting elements, together. Most people can identify quickly a technological "innovation" that failed to produce favorable results when implemented in an organization, for instance. Bringing in people or teams with different backgrounds in terms of education, training, skills and experience represents a similar instance (e.g., conjuring up memories of failed implementation), as does changing work processes or organizational reporting relationships and responsibilities without addressing personnel and technologies. Hence the elements *people, processes, organizations* and *technologies* operate as a cohesive system and should be addressed as an integrated design problem.

EXERCISES

1. Describe briefly a situation of knowledge enabling competitive advantage in an organization with which you are familiar. Explain how knowledge and not other resources is key.
2. Describe briefly how additional knowledge could—but has not—enable improved competitive advantage in the organization of Exercise 1 above. What would have to be done to effect such improved competitive advantage?
3. Describe briefly a situation of knowledge clumping in an organization with which you are familiar. What was done to address the clumping in such situation? What else could be done?
4. Conceive of an experiment or other empirical test to assess the relative value of two different chunks of knowledge that you possess. Describe briefly how the value of knowledge could be measured.

REFERENCES

Alberts, D. S., Garstka, J. J., & Stein, F. P. (1999). *Network centric warfare: Developing and leveraging information superiority* (2nd ed.). Washington, DC: CCRP Publication Series.

Argyris, C., & Schon, D. A. (1978). *Organizational learning*. Reading, MA: Addison-Wesley.

Barney, J. B. (1986). Strategic factor markets: expectations, luck, and business strategy. *Management Science*, *32*(10), 1231–1241. doi:10.1287/mnsc.32.10.1231.

Barney, J. B. (2002). *Gaining and sustaining competitive advantage*. Upper Saddle River, NJ: Prentice Hall.

Bogner, W. C., & Bansal, P. (2007). Knowledge management as the basis of sustained high performance. *Journal of Management Studies*, *44*(1), 165–188. doi:10.1111/j.1467-6486.2007.00667.x.

Castillo, J. (2003). Challenging the knowledge management mystique: An exploratory study on the performance of knowledge managing companies. *Journal of Management Research*, *3*(3), 152–172.

Chaharbaghi, K., & Lynch, R. (1999). Sustainable competitive advantage: towards a dynamic resource-based strategy. *Management Decision*, *37*(1), 45–50. doi:10.1108/00251749910252012.

Clarke, R. A., & Knake, R. (2010). *Cyber war: The next threat to national security and what to do about it*. New York, NY: HarperCollins.

Cohen, W. M., & Levinthal, D. A. (1990). Absorptive capacity: a new perspective on learning and innovation. *Administrative Science Quarterly*, *35*(1), 128–152. doi:10.2307/2393553.

Darroch, J. (2005). Knowledge management, innovation and firm performance. *Journal of Knowledge Management*, *9*(3), 101–115. doi:10.1108/13673270510602809.

Davenport, T. H. (1993). *Process innovation: Reengineering work through information technology*. Boston, MA: Harvard University Press.

Dierickx, I., & Cool, K. (1989). Asset stock accumulation and sustainability of competitive advantage. *Management Science*, *35*(12), 1504–1511. doi:10.1287/mnsc.35.12.1504.

Drucker, P. F. (1995). *Managing in a time of great change*. New York, NY: Truman Talley.

Fahey, J. (2002). A resource-based analysis of sustainable competitive advantage in a global environment. *International Business Review*, *11*(1), 57–77. doi:10.1016/S0969-5931(01)00047-6.

Grant, R. M. (1996). Toward a knowledge-based theory of the firm. *Strategic Management Journal*, *17*, 109–122.

Hammer, M., & Champy, J. (1993). *Reengineering the corporation: A manifesto for business revolution*. New York, NY: Harper Business Press. doi:10.1016/S0007-6813(05)80064-3.

Holsapple, C. W., & Jones, K. G. (2007). Knowledge chain activity classes: Impacts on competitiveness and the importance of technology support. *International Journal of Knowledge Management*, *3*(3), 26–45. doi:10.4018/jkm.2007070102.

Holsapple, C. W., & Singh, M. (2001). The knowledge chain model: Activities for competitiveness. *Expert Systems with Applications*, *20*(1), 77–98. doi:10.1016/S0957-4174(00)00050-6.

Holsapple, C. W., & Wu, J. (2011). An elusive antecedent of superior firm performance: The knowledge management factor. *Decision Support Systems*, *52*(1), 271–283. doi:10.1016/j.dss.2011.08.003.

Jayasingam, S., Ansari, M. A., Ramayah, T., & Jantan, M. (2012). *Knowledge management practices and performance: are they truly linked?* Knowledge Management Research & Practice. doi:10.1057/kmrp.2012.5.

Kaplan, A. M., & Haenlein, M. (2010). Users of the world unite! The challenges and opportunities of social media. *Business Horizons*, *53*(1), 59–68. doi:10.1016/j.bushor.2009.09.003.

Kramer, F. D., Starr, S. H., & Wentz, L. (2011). *Cyberpower and national security*. Dulles, VA: Potomac.

Leavitt, H. J. (1965). Applying organizational change in industry: structural, technological and humanistic approaches. In March, J. (Ed.), *Handbook of Organizations*. Chicago, IL: Rand McNally.

Levitt, B., & March, J. G. (1988). Organizational learning. *Annual Review of Sociology*, *14*, 319–340. doi:10.1146/annurev.so.14.080188.001535.

Liebowitz, J. (2004). *Addressing the human capital crisis in the federal government: A knowledge management perspective*. Amsterdam: Elsevier.

Loch, C. H., Pich, M. T., Terwiesch, C., & Urbschat, C. (2001). Selecting R&D projects at BMW: A case study of adopting mathematical programming models. *IEEE Transactions on Engineering Management*, *48*(1), 70–80. doi:10.1109/17.913167.

March, J. G. (1991). Exploration and exploitation in organizational learning. *Organization Science*, *2*(1), 71–87. doi:10.1287/orsc.2.1.71.

Marques, D. P., & Simon, F. J. G. (2006). The effect of knowledge management practices on firm performance. *Journal of Knowledge Management*, *10*(3), 143–156. doi:10.1108/13673270610670911.

Matusik, S. F., & Hill, C. W. L. (1998). The utilization of contingent work, knowledge creation, and competitive advantage. *Academy of Management Review*, *23*(4), 680–697. doi:10.2307/259057.

Nissen, M. E. (2006). *Harnessing knowledge dynamics: Principled organizational knowing & learning*. Hershey, PA: IGI Global.

Nissen, M. E., & Bergin, R. D. (2013). Knowledge work through social media applications: Team performance implications of immersive virtual worlds. *Journal of Organizational Computing and Electronic Commerce*, *23*(1-2), 84–109. doi:10.1080/10919392.2013.748612.

Nold, H. A. (2012). Linking knowledge processes with firm performance: organizational culture. *Journal of Intellectual Capital*, *13*(1), 16–38. doi:10.1108/14691931211196196.

O'Dell, C., Ostro, N., & Grayson, C. (1998). *If we only knew what we know: The transfer of internal knowledge and best practice*. New York: Simon & Schuster.

OPM. (2008). *An analysis of federal employee retirement data*. Washington, DC: US Office of Personnel Management.

Polanyi, M. (1966). *The tacit dimension*. Garden City, NY: Doubleday.

Saviotti, P. P. (1998). On the dynamics of appropriability, of tacit and of codified knowledge. *Research Policy*, *26*, 843–856. doi:10.1016/S0048-7333(97)00066-8.

Spender, J. C. (1996). Making knowledge the basis of a dynamic theory of the firm. *Strategic Management Journal*, *17*, 45–62.

Szulanski, G. (1996). Exploring internal stickiness: Impediments to the transfer of best practice within the firm. *Strategic Management Journal*, *17*, 27–43.

Szulanski, G., & Winter, S. (2002). Getting it right the second time. *Harvard Business Review*, *80*(1), 62–69. PMID:12964468.

Teece, D. (2009). *Dynamic capabilities and strategic management*. Oxford, UK: Oxford University Press.

Teece, D., Pisano, G., & Shuen, A. (1997). Dynamic capabilities and strategic management. *Strategic Management Journal*, *18*(7), 509–533. doi:10.1002/(SICI)1097-0266(199708)18:7<509::AID-SMJ882>3.0.CO;2-Z.

Turban, E., & Aronson, J. (1998). *Decision support systems and intelligent systems*. Upper Saddle River, NJ: Prentice-Hall.

von Hippel, E. (1994). Sticky information and the locus of problem solving: implications for innovation. *Management Science*, *40*(4), 429–439. doi:10.1287/mnsc.40.4.429.

Zack, M., McKeen, J., & Singh, S. (2009). Knowledge management and organizational performance: An exploratory analysis. *Journal of Knowledge Management*, *13*(6), 392–409. doi:10.1108/13673270910997088.

ENDNOTES

1 As used in this book (e.g., see the Glossary), appropriable knowledge is that which can be taken possession of and put to exclusive use; hence it can provide sustainable competitive advantage, because others cannot take it, not even when observing the knowledge being put to use. This is why tacit knowledge is more appropriable than explicit is: as bound within the minds of people and routines of organizations, it is comparatively difficult to take, and hence the knowledge-based activities that it enables are correspondingly difficult to imitate.

That being said, the adjective "appropriable" and verb "appropriate" are used, unfortunately, with opposite meanings by different authors. Indeed, some people use this term to mean that competitors *can* imitate one's knowledge-based activities, and hence equate appropriability with *explicit* knowledge and *lesser* sustainability in terms of competitive advantage. Alternatively, other people use this term to mean that competitors *cannot* imitate one's knowledge-based activities, and hence equate appropriability with *tacit* knowledge and *greater* sustainability in terms of competitive advantage. Clearly our usage in this book is consistent with the latter: greater appropriability implies lesser imitability and greater opportunity for sustainable competitive advantage.

Chapter 2
Knowledge Uniqueness

ABSTRACT

This chapter focuses on how flows of knowledge differ from flows of information and data. It also outlines where such differences are important. The authors look at the concept knowledge hierarchy and then discuss the role of information technology in knowledge management projects. The discussion turns subsequently to examine knowledge explicitness. The chapter concludes with five knowledge uniqueness principles and includes exercises to stimulate critical thought, learning, and discussion.

KNOWLEDGE HIERARCHY

Many scholars conceptualize a hierarchy of data, information and knowledge. As illustrated in Figure 1, each level of the Knowledge Hierarchy builds upon the one below. For instance, data can reduce uncertainty or equivocality, and they are required to produce information, but information involves more than just data: the data must be in context in order to inform (e.g., so someone can ascribe meaning to a message). Similarly, information can help people make sense of their environments, and it is required to produce knowledge, but knowledge involves more than just information: it enables direct action (e.g., good decisions, appropriate behaviors, useful work; yes, judgment and norms determine what constitutes "good," "appropriate" and "useful"). These three concepts are clearly complementary, yet they are clearly distinct also.

Consider this Gedanken experiment. Say someone sends you an e-mail message. This person prepares the message meticulously to ensure it is correct factually. It is sent via Internet and arrives in your computer mailbox within seconds of being sent. The message suffers from no transmission errors and appears on your screen exactly as it was sent. The message is written in Korean. Is this knowledge (e.g., reading the message enables you to take direct action)? Is it information (e.g., you can ascribe meaning to the message content)? Is it even data (e.g., it reduces uncertainty or equivocality)? Unless you can read and understand Korean, the answer is probably "no." In such case, you would have received visual signals (e.g., symbols on the display screen) that do not even represent data to you. Many otherwise capable intelligence analysts confront this situation daily when searching for clues through communications (e.g., e-mail messages, recorded telephone conversations). Notice here that some knowledge (e.g., of Korean language) would be required to interpret signals into data.

Now say the message is written in a language you can understand (e.g., English). The message

DOI: 10.4018/978-1-4666-4727-5.ch002

Figure 1. Knowledge hierarchy (adapted from Nissen, 2006)

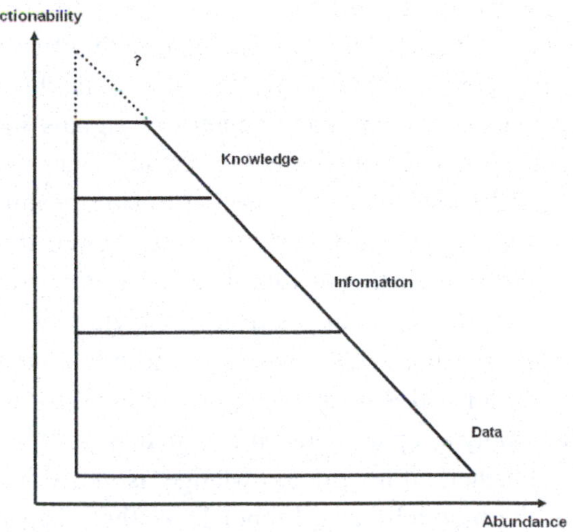

is: "333/33." Is this knowledge, information, data, or simply signals? Unlike the example above, in which a lack of language knowledge precludes even the interpretation of signals from conversations into data, here no such language barrier exists. One can say the message provides data: a person can interpret the signal as a compound symbol with three "3"s preceding a "/" and two more "3"s, but can we say this data symbol represents information or knowledge also? Unless the symbol comes in the context of an answer to a factual question (e.g., how can the repeating decimal number 10.09 be represented by two whole numbers, with five digits in total, and both ending with the digit "3"?) or other, comparable context (e.g., mathematical symbols), the answer is probably "no." The symbol constitutes data but not information or knowledge. In other words, the symbol can reduce uncertainty or equivocality, if the appropriate context is known, but it is unlikely that such symbol alone would enable someone to ascribe meaning to the message (i.e., constitute information). Notice here that some knowledge (e.g., how to place the message into appropriate context) would be required for data in the message to inform its recipient (i.e., for information to flow). Notice too that such contextual knowledge (e.g., mathematical symbols) differs from the kind of language knowledge (e.g., Korean) from above that supports signal interpretation. One should get a sense that different kinds of knowledge (e.g., language, contextual) are required for different kinds of actions (e.g., interpretation, informing) related to the knowledge hierarchy.

Next say the message includes some context in terms of an English-language clause: "your blood pressure: 333/33." Is this knowledge, information, data, or simply signals? Here we are not constrained by a lack of either language or contextual knowledge. Hence one should be able to both interpret the signals and ascribe meaning to the content of the message. Indeed, with such context one can become informed about a blood-pressure measurement; that is, one could say information has flowed. Recall from above such ascription of meaning could not be achieved with the same message sent without context, but what about knowledge? Absent supplementary physiological knowledge, for instance, it is unlikely that the message would enable direct action (e.g., what, if anything, should be done in response to the blood pressure measurement). Hence the message content involves the flow of (signals, data and) information but not knowledge. Notice here the message recipient can interpret the signals (i.e., for data) and ascribe meaning (i.e., for information) to the message but cannot take action (i.e., for knowledge) without additional knowledge (e.g., of human physiology).

Finally say you learn from a physician or health website that systolic blood pressure levels—the number listed first (i.e., before the "/") in blood pressure measurements—above 200 are hazardous, and diastolic levels—the number listed second (i.e., after the "/") in blood pressure measurements—below 60 are dangerous. At this point one can understand the health implications of the message: the person is near death! Such understanding enables one to take action such as deciding whether to consult a doctor. Notice here that a different kind of knowledge (e.g., of human physiology) is required to understand the health implications of the message. Still different knowledge (e.g., of alternate treatment options) is needed to enable action on the basis of the message content. Through the four parts of this e-mail example, it should be clear how knowledge is required for action at every level of the hierarchy and how different kinds of knowledge are associated with different actions at the various levels.

Drawing from Nissen (2002a), we operationalize notionally the triangular shape of this hierarchy using two dimensions—abundance and actionability—to differentiate further between the three constructs data, information and knowledge. Briefly, in this view data lie at the bottom level, with information in the middle and knowledge at the top. The broad base of the triangle reflects the abundance of data, with exponentially less information available than data and even fewer chunks of knowledge in any particular domain. Thus the width of the triangle at each level reflects decreasing abundance as one progresses from data to knowledge. The height of the triangle at each level reflects actionability (i.e., one's ability to take direct action). Converse to their abundance, data are not particularly powerful for supporting action, and information is more powerful than data, but knowledge supports action directly, hence its position near the top of the triangle. Interestingly, some models (esp. those in the trade press) discuss one or more levels "above" knowledge in the hierarchy (e.g., termed wisdom, intelligence, enlightenment, omniscience and the like). This book does not attempt to address "wisdom management" or engage in similar speculation. Indeed, can you imagine someone in an organization with a title such as Chief Enlightenment Officer?

Notice this figure elucidates a conceptual inadequacy associated with knowledge hierarchy: the hierarchy infers that knowledge—positioned at the top—is somehow "more" or "better" than either information or data is. Yet we describe above how knowledge is required for action at every level of the hierarchy (e.g., to interpret signals, ascribe meaning to symbols, understand implications of messages) and how different kinds of knowledge are associated with different actions at the various levels of the hierarchy. If knowledge is required to interpret signals into data, then how is it "more" or "better" than such data? If knowledge is required to ascribe meaning to symbols, then how is it "more" or "better" than the information that results? Hence it is important to interpret the vertical axis of the hierarchy in a value-free manner: knowledge is more actionable than information or data are, but actionability does not imply a separate judgment such as "better."

Further, although knowledge is positioned on the hierarchy at a higher level than data is, knowledge without data is incomplete frequently; that is, knowledge requires data often to enable action. In our blood pressure example above, an experienced and licensed medical doctor would certainly know the health implications of blood pressure and be able to prescribe several alternate treatments for a diversity of patients and measurements, but without the data (i.e., "333/33") to reduce uncertainty (e.g., answer the question, what is the patient's blood pressure?), such physiological knowledge could not be put to use directly to prescribe treatment. The point is, knowledge without data is insufficient for action. Knowledge is necessary for action, but it is not necessarily sufficient. Clearly the interrelationships between knowledge, information and data are more complex than implied by a simple three-layer diagram such as the one presented in Figure 1. Nonetheless, the knowledge hierarchy provides insight into some unique and complementary characteristics of knowledge, information and data.

Indeed, many scholars share this simple, layered view of the Knowledge Hierarchy (von Krogh et al., 2000), but certainly not all scholars do. For instance, some argue for an inverted hierarchy (Tuomi, 1999), in which hierarchical relationships such as those outlined above are reversed to reflect data on the "top" and knowledge on the "bottom." The argument is, knowledge is required to establish a semantic structure to represent information, which in turn represents a prerequisite for creating data. With this inverted hierarchy, there appears to be a contradiction with even the basic order of hierarchical levels. Further, in the inverted view, activities performed at different levels of hierarchy differ also from those above (e.g., "establish semantic structure" and "create data" vs. "interpret signals" and "ascribe meaning"). In other words, the elements of the two hierarchies (i.e., data, information, knowledge) appear to be the same, but transitions from one hierarchical level to another (e.g., data to information, information to data) take on different meanings. Plus, if knowledge is required at the base of this inverted hierarchy to represent information and in turn create data, then one must ask, from where does the knowledge derive? When taken together as contrasting views, the two hierarchies present something of a conundrum.

Perhaps this apparent conundrum can be resolved in part by introducing the concept directionality in terms of knowledge flow. As depicted in Figure 2, the producer or source of knowledge could indeed view the inverted hierarchy as conceptualized above—where knowledge is necessary to produce information, which in turn is necessary for data that are conveyed through signals. We do not invert the hierarchy in Figure 2; rather, we reverse the flow arrow direction to depict flows from top to bottom (i.e., knowledge → information → data) instead of bottom to top (i.e., data → information → knowledge).

For instance, say an experienced attorney is confident that his or her client is innocent of some criminal charge. This attorney seeks to convince members of a jury that the verdict "not guilty" is appropriate in the case. The attorney may use his or her experience-based knowledge of how to persuade jurors in order to outline a set of arguments to make, witnesses to call for testimony, questions to ask, and so forth (i.e., make a case for innocence). One could say here the attorney is using knowledge in a manner he or she hopes will influence the meaning ascribed by jurors (i.e., inform them) to various data produced through court proceedings. Then in turn by making the arguments, calling the witnesses, and asking the questions, data (e.g., words spoken by the attorney, visual appearances of the witnesses, answers to questions) can reach the jurors via signals (e.g., pressure waves of sound through the air, patterns of light reflecting off of people). If jurors ascribe meaning to such data in the manner hoped for by the defense attorney, then they may come to view the defendant as innocent and take consistent action by rendering a "not guilty" verdict.

Alternatively, the consumer or receiver of knowledge could view the hierarchy from the op-

Figure 2. Knowledge flow directionality (adapted from Nissen, 2006)

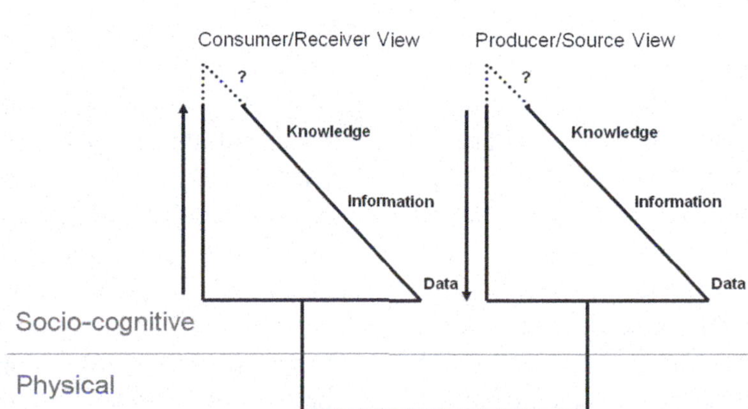

posite perspective outlined above—where data are placed into context to become information, and information enables action through knowledge. Continuing with our courtroom example, say a juror who hears the sound waves and sees the light patterns is able to interpret such signals into data (e.g., words spoken by the attorney, visual appearances of the witnesses, answers to questions). With the courtroom context of such data, a juror would likely be able to ascribe meaning (e.g., the attorney is trying to make a case for innocence) and be informed by the corresponding arguments, testimony and answers. The juror could in turn come to understand how the relevant matters of fact and law in the case interrelate, which would enable action in terms of rendering a verdict. Of course whether or not such verdict coincides with the "not guilty" hope of the attorney becomes a matter of the *juror's* knowledge[1], not the attorney's, but as a consumer or receiver of knowledge, the juror could be viewed according to the former knowledge hierarchy (i.e., in which knowledge is positioned on top). This knowledge-consumer or –receiver view is compatible with, and supplementary to, the knowledge-producer or –source view from above. The key point is, there is directionality to knowledge as it flows from producer or source to consumer or recipient. This concept *directionality* helps explain how both knowledge hierarchies can co-exist, and indeed supplement one another, as they correspond to different directions of knowledge flows (e.g., to or from). We revisit knowledge flow directionality repeatedly in this book.

Figure 2 raises an additional point that is noteworthy to discuss here. Notice the horizontal line separating the two knowledge hierarchies from the signals linking them. Below this line, signals exist in what Alberts and Hayes (2003) refer to as the physical domain. This pertains to all of the layers of standard network models (e.g., OSI, TCP/IP) responsible for transmission of data. Drawing from our discussion above, however, such signals themselves do not convey data. Recall, for instance, the example of the perfectly delivered email message written in Korean; the signals are sent and received without errors, but unless the person reading this message can understand Korean, the result is that only signals are received, not knowledge, information or even data. This phenomenon is explained by Nissen (2006). Everything above the horizontal line exists in what Alberts and Hayes (2003) refer to as the socio-cognitive domains; that is, data, information and knowledge exist in the minds and experiences of people and cultures and routines of organizations, not in networks, computers, databases, social networking sites and other implementations of information technology.

Whenever you hear someone exclaim, "knowledge is in the database," "knowledge is on the shared information repository," "knowledge is on the network," and the like, you should understand that what exists on such (computer) media is in the form of bits, bytes and baud, represented physically by sequences of electromagnetic polarities. No more than receiving an email message written in an unfamiliar language, such media cannot even be interpreted in their native form, and hence are not even data in the context of this discussion; they represent signals. Only after signals are converted and presented in a form that can be interpreted by a person can these media represent data.

INFORMATION TECHNOLOGY

Many knowledge management projects fail to appreciate the distinction between knowledge and information/data. Project after project in practice implements information technology (IT) applications such as databases, data warehouses, document repositories, search engines, Web portals and the like when attempting to support knowledge management. Arguably, however, just looking at the word "data" in the names of many "knowledge management tools," we are not even working at the level of information, much less knowledge.

Moreover, although Internet tools applied within and between organizations provide a common, machine-independent medium for the distribution and linkage of multimedia documents, videos and other communication media, most extant intranet and extranet applications, social media sites, wikis and like implementations focus principally on the management and distribution of information, not knowledge per se (Nissen et al., 2000).

Consider, for an example that builds upon our statement above, a corporate database that is fed by the company's nation-wide point-of-sale (POS) system. The POS system records the specific details of every merchandise item, purchased by every customer, every day. One may overhear expressions such as, "there's a wealth of knowledge in that POS database." But our discussion above should stimulate one to question the veridicality of statements along these lines. Specifically, the POS database—after its electromagnetic signals have been converted into an interpretable form—may contain volumes of data, but the data themselves (e.g., 654321-10987) require something more to enable action. One can argue that meta-data (i.e., data about the data in a database) allow a person (or machine) to piece together the various data elements and values to make sense of database records. The string of symbols comprising a database record such as "28 March 2004 Smith Margarie A 654321-10987 2 socks crew white M 6.99," for instance, could be ascribed meaning as a customer purchase, but even after being informed that some person named Margarie Smith purchased two pair of medium size, white, crew socks for $6.99 on March 28, what action is enabled by such information? Not much without supplementary knowledge. One can argue further that running database queries and performing data-mining analyses across numerous records can reveal insightful patterns (e.g., purchasing habits of customers, sales trends of products) that enable knowledge-based actions (e.g., targeted advertising, coordinated sale-pricing). Yet the wealth of knowledge resides within the analyst performing the queries and mining the data, not the database. The actions are enabled by knowledge learned through analysis, not data stored on disk, network or cloud. This reinforces our distinction above between signals existing in the physical domain and the data, information and knowledge that exist in the socio-cognitive domains.

Along these same lines, groupware (e.g., e-mail, chat, text, wiki, blog, discussion board, social media) offers infrastructural support for knowledge work and enhances the environment in which knowledge artifacts are created and managed, but the flow of knowledge itself remains indirect. For instance, groupware is noted widely as helpful in the virtual office environment (e.g., when geographically dispersed knowledge workers must collaborate remotely). It provides networked tools such as shared, indexed and replicated document databases and discussion threads (e.g., Lotus Notes/Domino applications), as well as shared "white boards," joint document editing capabilities, and full-duplex, high-bandwidth, multimedia communication features. These tools serve to mitigate collaborative losses that can arise when rich, face-to-face joint work is not practical or feasible, but supporting (even rich and remote) communication is not sufficient to guarantee a flow of knowledge (e.g., consider such technologies used by people who are unable to communicate in a common language, convey context, or enable learning).

Consider, for example, video teleconferencing (VTC) and PC-based collaborative applications (e.g., Groove, NetMeeting, InformationWorkspace, Skype). Such applications are heralded often for supporting rich, synchronous, audio and video communication in addition to capabilities for exchanging and working remotely on common documents. The situation in terms of knowledge is similar to that discussed above through the database example, however. On a very basic level, one can turn on the VTC and let it run indefinitely, but unless people are using it to communicate, clearly no knowledge, information or data are flowing (cf. only signals flow). The same can be said for PC-based collaboration tools: people must use them in order for any flows except for signals to take place. Even at a higher level, however, having people use such applications to communicate is insufficient for knowledge, information or data to flow. This follows the same set of reasons articulated above in terms of the e-mail message (e.g., need to understand Korean, context of a message, understanding of its health implications).

Alternatively, because people are connected synchronously via rich communication media, they can interact, ask questions, provide examples, inquire about interpretations, question ramifications, propose implications, and perform other typical actions of interlocutors trying to communicate. If, through such communication, the receiver interprets correctly the symbol "333/33," for instance, then one can say data flows have taken place. Likewise, if the receiver ascribes meaning to the symbol as a blood pressure measurement, as a related instance, then one can say information flows have occurred. Moreover, if the receiver understands the health implications of such measurement and learns of treatment alternatives, as another related instance, then one can say knowledge flows have obtained. The point is, such flows depend upon the people, not the technologies.

KNOWLEDGE EXPLICITNESS

One important dimension of relevance in terms of knowledge uniqueness is explicitness. The distinction between knowledge and information/data is particularly apparent where tacit knowledge is involved. Tacit knowledge is described generally as being implicit within the knower and inherently difficult to articulate (e.g., through writing, drawing, discussing, observing, codifying). Riding a bicycle, playing chess, raising children, interviewing for a job, interpreting tactical patterns in warfare, diagnosing diseases in patients, and recognizing when students are comprehending principles: these all represent examples of activities (i.e., direct actions) that depend upon tacit knowledge for effective performance. In contrast, explicit knowledge is described generally as articulable. Such explicit knowledge exhibits many properties of information that complement yet are distinct from those of tacit knowledge. Notice here we extend our discussion of knowledge uniqueness: not only is knowledge distinct from information and data; different kinds of knowledge (e.g., tacit, explicit) are mutually distinct across multiple dimensions as well.

However, although explicit knowledge can be articulated (e.g., through written text, rendered drawing, verbal speech, visual observation, software programming) and shares properties in common with information, even knowledge made explicit as such enables action (e.g., decisions, behaviors, work). The distinction between explicit knowledge and information is subtle—particularly when compared with tacit knowledge—but informative. Consider a cookbook, for instance. Recipes in a cookbook are comprised generally of two supplementary parts: 1) list of ingredients, and 2) preparation procedure. The former is declarative in nature. It represents a set of symbols (e.g., amounts, units of measure, food items) in the context of preparing a meal. As such it informs the reader about how much of which ingredients go into each dish. In the context of a cookbook, one can ascribe meaning to the list of ingredients, but the list alone is insufficient for most people to use for preparing a meal (i.e., the action of cooking). Hence we would classify the list of ingredients generally as information. Alternatively, the latter is procedural in nature. It represents a sequence of steps for combining and heating different ingredients to prepare a meal. As such it enables the action cooking. Hence we would classify a cooking procedure as knowledge. Nonetheless, such knowledge is explicit, not tacit. It describes explicitly, through writing, which what cooking actions are required and in which order.

Notice in this cooking example that both parts of the cookbook are explicit (e.g., written down in a book) and that both parts are necessary for most people to prepare a meal, but one part informs a reader about ingredients, whereas the other enables cooking actions. Notice too that neither explicit part of a recipe may be necessary for an expert chef, who may, for instance, be capable of preparing consistently fine meals (e.g., principles learned through cooking experience) without ever referring to a written recipe and without ever repeating exactly the same recipe twice. Here we elucidate again the contrast between knowledge made explicit (e.g., in a cookbook) versus its tacit counterpart (e.g., learned through experience).

The contrast in terms of explicitness goes much further. For instance, even where a recognized expert is able to articulate his or her knowledge about actions to take (e.g., how to prepare a meal), such articulation is insufficient often to enable a non-expert to perform effectively. Many colorful images of newly married couples experiencing this phenomenon at the family dinner table may come to the reader's mind here. Reading a book about how to ride a bicycle, as a different instance, can inform a person considerably about riding bicycles and even make explicit the actions required for riding safely (e.g., stay balanced; lean into turns; watch for cars), but it is unlikely that someone who has never ridden a bicycle would be able to do so based solely upon reading a book about it. Nearly everyone with children who ride bicycles can attest to problems they have with watching for cars, even after "expert" parental instruction. The same holds in the organizational environment as well. Even if one can "capture" knowledge (e.g., expertise in an organization) in explicit form such as through writings, where tacit knowledge is involved, one is simply accomplishing the organizational equivalent of telling people how to ride bicycles. The same holds true even if one can organize such expertise through a taxonomy or directory of some sort, and even if one can distribute this organizational expertise broadly, say through a searchable, web-based, document repository or wiki on the corporate intranet. In many cases, not even videos or direct observation are sufficient; to continue this example, watching someone ride a bicycle on video is not the same as experiencing the motion and balance directly, nor is watching the bicycle rider directly.

Even more troubling, in many domains, experts have demonstrated repeatedly great difficulty articulating their tacit knowledge. The saying is, "experts know more than they can tell." This is the principal problem experienced by developers of expert systems (i.e., artificial intelligence applications that include codified expertise) over the past four decades. When someone has developed expertise, particularly through the accumulation of considerable, tacit, experience-based knowledge, it can be exceptionally difficult and time-consuming for another person—or a machine—to develop a comparable level of expertise. This represents a key distinction regarding the explicitness of knowledge flows: tacit knowledge is sticky (von Hippel, 1994), clumps locally and flows slowly (Nissen, 2006). Yet rich, tacit, experience-based knowledge is powerful, oftentimes the most valuable resource that an organization can possess.

Let's reconsider our cooking example from above. An expert chef possesses considerable tacit knowledge about cooking, enough to enable him or her to prepare fine meals without consulting a cookbook. One could argue that such chef has simply memorized the recipes and could make explicit the corresponding knowledge at any time by writing down the steps, by speaking into a tape recorder, or by being filmed while each meal is being prepared. Many television shows continue to feature chefs doing just this. However, most experienced chefs will tell you that their cooking involves much more than simple memorization. They spend long periods of time in schools and apprenticeships, learning by observation, practice and mentoring from master chefs to understand the principles of which kinds of foods combine in a pleasing manner and which approaches to preparing, mixing and heating are most appropriate for various kinds and combinations of ingredients. Many such experienced chefs never measure ingredients using devices such as teaspoons, tablespoons and cups. Nor do they monitor preparation and cooking time with clocks, kitchen timers or thermometers. Rather, they observe ingredients as they are combined and adjust where they deem appropriate. They watch a meal as it cooks, often judging by taste, texture, color and aroma when various ingredients may need to be added and when a meal is ready to be served. This appears to be a different approach to preparing meals (i.e., set of actions enabled by knowledge) than following or memorizing a cookbook.

The action of preparing meals through memorization or by following recipes in a cookbook is enabled by explicit knowledge. In contrast, the action of preparing meals by application of principles and by sight, smell and other senses is enabled by tacit knowledge. Moreover, many experienced chefs would find it difficult to articulate the latter approach to cooking. Even if such an experienced chef is able to write down in a book—or is able to speak into a microphone—guidance such as, "adjust ingredients as necessary to taste," or "heat until the bouquet of the wine wanes," it is unlikely that an inexperienced cook would be able to prepare meals well from such guidance. The key point is, explicitness represents a very discriminatory dimension for evaluating the uniqueness of knowledge.

This brings us back to the knowledge hierarchy. The neat, triangular shape of the knowledge hierarchies depicted above belies some underlying complexity, which merits brief elaboration here. The triangular figures above imply that the abundance of knowledge is considerably less than that of information or particularly data. As we begin to differentiate between ***tacit*** and ***explicit*** knowledge, however, it becomes evident that tacit knowledge (e.g., in people's minds and experiences, in organizational cultures and routines) is very abundant. Explicit knowledge (e.g., as articulated via artifacts such as books, drawings, formulae, software), alternatively, is relatively scarce. Hence an irregular shape at the top of the knowledge hierarchy in Figure 3 depicts the relationship better.

KNOWLEDGE UNIQUENESS PRINCIPLES

Five principles developed in this chapter help shed light on knowledge uniqueness: 6) knowledge enables action directly, whereas information provides meaning and context for such action; 7) data, information and knowledge flows are interrelated yet distinct mental and organizational processes; 8) flows of knowledge require supplementary flows of information, data and signals; 9) explicitness represents a very discriminatory dimension for evaluating the uniqueness of knowledge; and 10) information technology supports principally flows of explicit knowledge.

Figure 3. Knowledge hierarchy with irregular shape for tacit knowledge

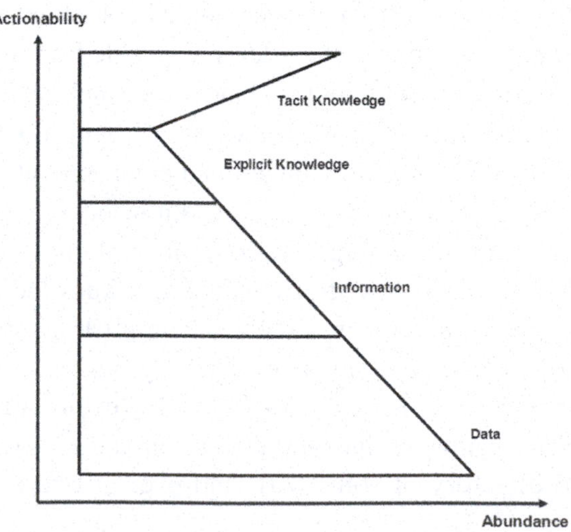

Principle 6: First, distinguishing knowledge from information and data is important. One effective operationalization is, knowledge enables direct action (e.g., correct decisions, appropriate behaviors, useful work). Alternatively, information provides meaning and context for such action (e.g., decision criteria, behavior norms, work specifications). Data reduce uncertainty or equivocality (e.g., supplying parameters to an equation, providing numbers for a formula, specifying states in a relationship). We identify also a fourth level for the knowledge hierarchy above: signals. One can say with confidence, "only signals flow across time and space," not knowledge, information, or even data. Signals (e.g., light reflecting from objects in the world or computer-generated images; sound waves propagating through a room; electrical currents alternating in discrete and analog patterns) are perceived by people and machines. Where they are interpretable, they can provide the basis for data; where uninterpretable, they constitute noise. Where in turn data are provided in context, they can inform. Where information enables direct action, knowledge exists. Hence understanding whether flows of data, information or knowledge are required in a particular situation depends upon what needs to be accomplished (e.g., resolving uncertainty, deriving meaning, enabling action, respectively).

Principle 7: Second, data, information and knowledge are interrelated dynamically, yet distinct from one another, as mental and organizational processes. A number of Gedanken experiments and practical examples can be used to distinguish between the interrelated concepts, but all three involve mental and organizational (not physical) processes. Whether interpreting data from signals, deriving information from data, or learning knowledge from information, such processes take place in the minds of people and routines of organizations, not in computers, networks and databases. Hence people play the critical role in flows of data, information and knowledge.

Principle 8: Third, knowledge flows require flows of information, data and signals. Physically only signals flow. Data, information and knowledge flow via socio-cognitive processes, but such socio-cognitive processes of different people require communication. For knowledge to flow from a producer or sender, information is required to produce data, which are required to encode signals. In reverse sequence, for knowledge to flow to a consumer or receiver, signals must be interpreted into data, which must be placed into meaningful context to inform. Every conversion (e.g., interpreting data from signals; ascribing meaningful information from data; learning knowledge from information) involves some kind of knowledge (e.g., language, context, physiology). Hence every flow (i.e., data, information and knowledge) from signal interpretation through knowledge creation, and back, requires some kind of knowledge.

Principle 9: Fourth, explicitness characterizes an important dimension of knowledge uniqueness. In particular, tacit knowledge can be distinguished along such dimension from its explicit counterpart. One's ability to articulate his or her knowledge provides an operationalization for explicitness: explicit knowledge has been articulated; tacit knowledge has not. Further, some kinds of tacit knowledge can be articulated into explicit form more easily than others can. Some kinds cannot be articulated at all. Most knowledge made explicit loses power in at least two important ways: 1) knowledge made explicit fails often to enable the same levels of performance corresponding to actions enabled by the tacit knowledge from which it is formalized; and 2) explicit knowledge shares many properties with information, which is more difficult to appropriate than tacit knowledge is. Hence moving knowledge through tacit versus explicit flows represents a leadership or management decision in many cases, a decision which has implications in terms of power.

Principle 10: Fifth, IT support is limited principally to explicit knowledge flows—and information/data—but enables large amounts of such knowledge to be organized, aggregated, and disseminated broadly and quickly. Where knowledge is explicit—or can be formalized into explicit form—IT offers great power to enhance the corresponding flows, but where important knowledge is tacit—and cannot be formalized readily into explicit form—IT offers less potential to affect knowledge flows. Hence the nature of knowledge represents a critical factor for determining where IT can be expected to enhance knowledge flows.

EXERCISES

1. Describe briefly a Gedanken experiment that illustrates how knowledge is distinct from information and data in terms of enabling performance. Try to characterize informatively differences between what knowledge enables one to do versus what benefits information and data provide.
2. Describe briefly some tacit knowledge that you possess. Indicate which aspects of such knowledge you feel can be articulated (i.e., made explicit) and which cannot. Why is this the case?
3. Describe briefly how IT can be used to support: a) the sharing of your tacit knowledge described in Exercise 2 above; b) the sharing of your explicit knowledge described in Exercise 2 above; c) the application of your tacit knowledge described in Exercise 2 above; and d) the application of your explicit knowledge described in Exercise 2 above.
4. Describe briefly a KM program with which you are familiar. To what extent does it address explicit versus tacit knowledge? Cite one or two specific examples of each (if applicable).

REFERENCES

Alberts, D. S., & Hayes, R. E. (2003). *Power to the edge: Command and control in the information age*. Washington, DC: Command and Control Research Program.

Nissen, M. E. (2002). An extended model of knowledge-flow dynamics. *Communications of the Association for Information Systems, 8*, 251–266.

Nissen, M. E. (2006). *Harnessing knowledge dynamics: Principled organizational knowing & learning*. Hershey, PA: IGI Global.

Nissen, M. E., Kamel, M. N., & Sengupta, K. C. (2000). Integrated analysis and design of knowledge systems and processes. *Information Resources Management Journal, 13*(1), 24–42. doi:10.4018/irmj.2000010103.

Tuomi, I. (1999). Data is more than knowledge: Implications of the reversed knowledge hierarchy for knowledge management and organizational memory. *Journal of Management Information Systems, 16*(3), 103–117.

von Hippel, E. (1994). Sticky information and the locus of problem solving: Implications for innovation. *Management Science, 40*(4), 429–439. doi:10.1287/mnsc.40.4.429.

von Krogh, G., Ichijo, K., & Nonaka, I. (2000). *Enabling knowledge creation: How to unlock the mystery of tacit knowledge and release the power of innovation*. New York, NY: Oxford University Press. doi:10.1093/acprof:oso/9780195126167.001.0001.

ENDNOTES

1 Epistemological questions such as what constitutes "knowledge"; whether knowledge must necessarily be "true"; if two people can possess conflicting knowledge; how knowledge can be constructed socially versus existing universally; and like topics of philosophical debate are beyond the scope of this book. Speaking generally, we feel that knowledge is viewed most productively in the local context of the person, group or organization seeking to learn or use it. This reflects an interpretivistic epistemology, allowing for the social construction of knowledge, which does not seek to ascribe or guarantee universal truth or objectivity. Most effectively, we operationalize *knowledge* as enabling action; where there is action, there is knowledge to enable it; where there is no knowledge, there is no action. This serves to differentiate knowledge from information and data and to make it visible in the organization through the actions that it enables.

Chapter 3
Knowledge Flow

ABSTRACT

This chapter focuses phenomenologically on the dynamics of knowledge flows. The authors look at the organizational processes responsible for knowledge flows and then discuss knowledge flow patterns. The discussion turns subsequently to examine interactions between knowledge flows and workflows, in addition to timing and obstacles of dynamic knowledge. The chapter concludes with five knowledge flow principles and includes exercises to stimulate critical thought, learning, and discussion.

KNOWLEDGE FLOW PROCESSES

Recall from your high school physics the concept inertia: objects at rest tend to stay at rest; and objects in motion tend to stay in motion. Then of course you have Newton's famous second law: F = ma; that is, force (a vector) equals mass times acceleration (a vector). Combine the concept with the law and note acceleration (i.e., the change in the velocity vector) is related directly to the force applied to an object and inversely to the object's mass. Even such basic principles from physics have been used successfully for centuries to describe, explain and predict the dynamics of objects in the world. They enable a person to analyze nearly any physical object (e.g., within the Newtonian realm), given a set of initial conditions (e.g., starting position, velocity, acceleration), and to predict precisely in which direction, how fast, how far and how long it will move (if at all). Further, for more complex systems of objects and forces, such principles enable the understanding and prediction of intuitive (e.g., ballistic) as well as seemingly random (e.g., chaotic) dynamic patterns. Other factors such as friction, elasticity, energy losses and the like pertain as well, but we can ignore these for now in our present context.

The science addressing physical flows is very advanced. The corresponding principled knowledge enables sophisticated, precise analysis and prediction of dynamic patterns. Unfortunately, the science addressing knowledge flows has not caught up to physics in terms of understanding dynamics, but several knowledge flow principles and discernible patterns are emerging from this science, principles and patterns that enable some degree of description, explanation, prediction and understanding. We begin this discussion by borrowing some concepts from physics for insight through flow metaphors[1]. We delve then into the phenomenology of knowledge flows.

Several principles from physics can be used to conceptualize knowledge flows metaphorically. For instance, knowledge at rest tends to stay at rest. Say some particular knowledge (e.g., a chunk, a fact, a procedure, an association, an inference) is

DOI: 10.4018/978-1-4666-4727-5.ch003

possessed by a single individual, in a particular organization, at a specific location, at a unique point in time. Unless something is done to move such knowledge, it will likely remain confined to that single coordinate (i.e., person, organization, location, time). Looking around most organizations today, such confined, single-coordinate knowledge clearly represents a common case. Hence some kind of metaphorical force is required for knowledge at rest to "move" (we use quotation marks here to indicate knowledge does not represent some tangible physical object that can be rolled around like a ball on the floor).

Further, some aspects of such metaphorical force and the knowledge itself (e.g., organizational analogs to mass, friction, energy) may affect how fast and how far it will move, if at all. Borrowing from Newton, if the "force" is strong and the "mass" is light, then the associated knowledge should flow swiftly and broadly. Moving from metaphor to example, a gifted teacher, for instance, may represent the organizational analog of a strong force. A conceptually simple chunk of knowledge, as a related instance, may represent the analog of light mass. Together the gifted teacher and simple concept may result in rapid and broad knowledge flows. A less skilled teacher and more complex knowledge, as a counter instance, may result in comparatively slow and confined knowledge flows, or even no flows at all. Hence we can argue that knowledge at rest tends to stay at rest and that organizational analogs to forces and masses can affect if, how fast and how far any particular chunk of knowledge may flow. Here the inertia principle and associated flow metaphors appear to apply relatively well in our organizational context.

Alternatively, consider the other part of inertia (i.e., an object in motion tends to stay in motion). In the domain of physics, some force is required to stop a moving object or change its direction. As above, the stronger the force and lighter the mass, the faster an object can be stopped or turned. The organizational analog to this part of the inertia phenomenon is less clear than its counterpart above is, however. On one hand, consider, for example, management trying to stop an outflow of knowledge from an organization resulting from experienced people leaving to join rival firms (e.g., flows set in motion by the defection of a respected employee). Here one can argue that some organizational analog to force (e.g., management action through increased incentives) would be necessary to stop knowledge in motion (i.e., via people leaving the firm), but on the other hand, in our teacher-student learning example, it is unclear whether or how any particular chunk of knowledge learned by one student (e.g., set in motion through classroom interaction) would continue to flow without some additional effort to keep it moving (e.g., to other students). Here the inertia principle and associated flow metaphors appear to break down a bit.

Nonetheless, knowledge can be viewed as exhibiting some aspects of inertia, and it does not appear to flow unless some organizational analog of force makes it move, but if we wish to understand knowledge flows better (e.g., to enable rich description, detailed explanation, precise prediction), then we need to develop principles of dynamics that are based upon more than physical metaphor. Principles can be induced via phenomenology of knowledge flows. Such phenomenology points to the process as a focal concept in our present context of organizations. In other words, the knowledge flow process represents the phenomenological analog to the metaphorical force in a knowledge organization.

We are probably all familiar with processes. They're written generally as gerunds (i.e., ending in "ing"). For instance, as implied by the name, work processes represent the sets of activities responsible for accomplishing work in an organization. Examples from manufacturing organizations include developing new markets for products, designing product components, planning manufacturing sequences, assembling products, supporting customers, accounting for revenues and expenses, managing the organization, and others. Examples from service organizations include developing new markets for services, designing service activities, planning work sequences, delivering services, supporting customers, accounting for revenues and expenses, managing the organization, and others. Work processes are found also in the public sector (e.g., government organizations perform processes to serve constituents; military units perform processes to wage wars), non-profits (e.g., professional organizations perform processes to serve members; churches perform processes to serve congregations), and practically any other kind of organization one can think of (e.g., families perform processes such as grocery shopping, cooking, and raising children). Hence process represents a general concept to describe how work is accomplished in the organizational context. If an organizational process is not performed (or not performed well), then the associated work does not get accomplished (well).

The same relationship holds for knowledge flow processes. If a knowledge flow process is not performed (or not performed well), then the associated knowledge does not flow (well). Examples of knowledge flow processes include educating, training, researching, contemplating, discussing, mentoring, observing, reading, working via trial and error, and others. Through the educating process, for instance, one attends generally some kind of school, completes a curriculum of study, and learns. This last activity is key: where knowledge flows, learning takes place. Hence the phenomenon of knowledge flows involves learning. Continuing with this educating process example, one can view knowledge as moving from instructor to student (e.g., through classroom interaction; through instructor feedback on student points made in class, homework assignments, term papers and examinations; others), but one can view knowledge also as moving in other directions (e.g., through peer interaction with classmates; through the student's individual reading of textbooks and completion of homework assignments; others). Hence several detailed activities (e.g., classroom interaction, instructor feedback, student reading, homework and peer interaction) are involved with the knowledge flow process educating. Detailed activities such as these can be identified readily for other knowledge flow processes (e.g., training, researching, mentoring) as well. Again, some kind of organizational analog to force is required for knowledge to move through an organization. The knowledge flow process—and its detailed activities—provides a phenomenological explanation for how knowledge moves in the organizational context.

KNOWLEDGE FLOW PATTERNS

Knowledge flows are dynamic. As such they form distinctive patterns. Several scholars have worked to model the dynamics of knowledge flows and to help understand such flows by interpreting their patterns. One of the best known models to describe the knowledge flow phenomenon stems from the work of Nonaka (1994) and various colleagues (e.g., Nonaka & Takeuchi, 1995). This model describes a "spiral" pattern of knowledge flows through the organization. It characterizes also recurring patterns of interaction between explicit and tacit knowledge. Recall in Chapter 2 we use the explicit-tacit distinction as one dimension (i.e., explicitness) to help characterize knowledge uniqueness. Here we use the dimension reach—which pertains to the level of social aggregation (e.g., individual, group, organization) associated with knowledge—also to describe different kinds of knowledge flows that are unique and mutually distinct. These two dimensions derive directly from Nonaka's model. Only the names are changed here for clarity (i.e., Nonaka uses the term epistemological to characterize explicitness and the term ontological instead of reach).

Later research by Nissen (2002a) extends Nonaka's two-dimensional model to integrate two complementary dimensions: life cycle and flow time. Life cycle refers to the kind of activity (e.g., creation, sharing, application) associated with knowledge flows. Flow time pertains to the length of time (e.g., minutes, days, years) required for knowledge to move from one person, organization, place or time to another. These four dimensions for characterizing knowledge flows can be employed collectively to visualize the kinds of patterns associated with Nonaka's model. In addition, we elucidate and map below a wide variety of knowledge flows from practice that are otherwise nearly impossible to discern and visualize.

Drawing from Nissen (2005; 2006), in Figure 1 these dimensions are used to delineate one "loop" from the spiral knowledge flow pattern described by Nonaka. Each part of this loop corresponds to one of four knowledge flow processes articulated in the model (i.e., socializing, externalizing, combining, internalizing; note that we express these in gerund form for consistency, which differs slightly from Nonaka's original characterization). The figure illustrates how our four dimensions can be combined to visualize a representative knowledge flow from this well-known theory. The explicitness dimension is shown as the vertical axis with tacit and explicit endpoints. The reach dimension identifies different levels of social interaction (e.g., individual, group, organization) on the horizontal axis. The life cycle dimension is plotted as a third axis labeled with six KM activities (e.g., create, share, apply). To incorporate the flow time dimension, we use arrows of different thickness (e.g., thin for fast flows, thick for slow flows) when delineating various segments of the flow pattern. Notice how the organizational dimension flow time relates directly to the physical concept acceleration discussed above.

We begin at Point A, representing tacit knowledge created by an individual; Nonaka (1994, p. 20) suggests tacit knowledge held by individuals is central to knowledge creation. The socializing flow (A-B) reflects a movement of tacit knowledge across the reach dimension. We depict a representative flow from the individual to the group level in the figure. This kind of socialized flow is classified best as "share" in terms of the life cycle dimension (e.g., Nonaka notes "shared experience" (p. 19) as important to socializing). The externalizing flow (B-C) reflects a movement from tacit to explicit knowledge. We depict a

Figure 1. Multidimensional knowledge flow visualization (adapted from Nissen, 2006)

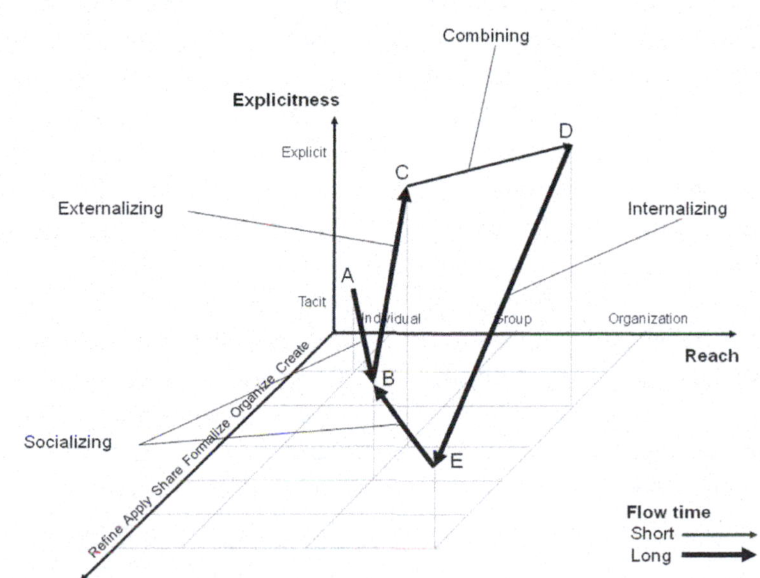

representative flow at the group level in the figure. The formalize life cycle stage corresponds best to this kind of movement (i.e., making knowledge explicit).

The combining flow (C-D) reflects in turn a movement of explicit knowledge across the reach dimension. We depict a representative flow from the group to the organization level in the figure. The organize life cycle stage appears to correspond best to this kind of movement (e.g., Nonaka notes as examples: sorting, editing, recategorizing and recontextualizing explicit knowledge). We also use a thinner arrow to represent this flow, as only explicit knowledge is involved. This is consistent with von Hippel (1994; e.g., tacit knowledge is related to stickiness) and Nissen et al. (2000; e.g., the organize life cycle stage is supported well by IT). Finally, the internalizing flow (D-E) reflects a movement from explicit to tacit knowledge. We depict a representative flow at the organization level in the figure. The refine life cycle stage corresponds best to this kind of movement (e.g., learning organizational routines).

Notice we include also a socializing flow from Points E to B (i.e., tacit knowledge moving from the organization to the group level) to complete the one loop. Individuals and groups learn many organizational routines, cultural norms and objectified ideas (Czarniawska & Joerges, 1996) that remain tacit. This is essentially socializing in reverse, and the term acculturating may be better in terms of characterizing the knowledge flow process. Other loops from the spiral model (e.g., extending beyond the organization level along the reach axis) could be included also, as could various knowledge flows from other models (e.g., life cycle, knowledge transfer), but this single loop is representative, and it provides an illustration of how the four dimensions of our analytic framework can be integrated into a single figure for knowledge flow visualization.

In light of our discussion, the knowledge flows delineated in this figure can be interpreted in part through some organizational analogs to physical principles. For instance, recall only one knowledge flow vector in the figure (i.e., C-D: corresponding to the process combining) is depicted by a thin arrow to denote relatively short flow time. In graphic contrast, all four of the other knowledge flow vectors are depicted by thick arrows to denote comparatively long flow times. One organizational implication is, something is different about the knowledge associated with the combining process. In particular, notice only explicit knowledge is involved. Considering organizational analogs to forces and masses, one could posit here that explicit knowledge corresponds to relatively "light mass" in the context of knowledge flows and hence contributes toward rapid flows (i.e., short flow time).

In contrast, each of the other four knowledge flow processes involves tacit knowledge to some extent, with the socializing flows (i.e., A-B, E-B) involving only tacit knowledge. Accordingly, tacit knowledge would correspond to comparatively "heavy mass" in the context of knowledge dynamics and hence contribute toward slow flows (i.e., long flow time). The key point is, the nature of the knowledge flow process (e.g., combining vs. socializing) and associated knowledge (e.g., explicit vs. tacit) affects how rapidly knowledge will flow (e.g., short vs. long flow time). Similarly, notice only this vector representing the knowledge flow process combining extends outward beyond the group level along the reach dimension. One could posit also that the nature of the knowledge flow process and associated knowledge affect how broadly knowledge will flow (e.g., narrow vs. broad reach) as well. Here we are beginning to develop some principles that may prove useful for describing, explaining and even predicting a variety of knowledge flows.

KNOWLEDGE FLOW AND WORKFLOW INTERACTIONS

Notice several of the knowledge flow processes described in this chapter appear also to involve the performance of work. For instance, many of the activities associated with educating involve work by student and instructor alike. Students engage in "coursework," perform "homework," and "work diligently" to prepare for examinations. In this case of educating, however, all such "work" applies directly and almost solely to the learning process. We say "almost" here to accommodate applied class projects that may result in useful work (e.g., in support of some university sponsor). Nonetheless, while the student is participating in educational activities, he or she is generally not participating in other activities such as working at a fast-food restaurant, at least (hopefully) not at the same time.

Likewise, while such person is busy accomplishing work by flipping hamburgers, he or she has little opportunity for university learning. Here the distinction between a knowledge flow process such as educating and a workflow process such as flipping hamburgers should be relatively clear: learning through the knowledge flow process educating and doing through the workflow process flipping hamburgers represent mutually exclusive activities. Any time and energy devoted to one activity necessarily take away from the other, and vice versa. This explains in part why many students who work part-time while in college take longer to complete their degrees than full-time students do. It may explain in part also why such working students tend to have more spending money than their more-studious counterparts do.

We depict graphically this interaction between knowledge flows and workflows in Figure 2. The vertical axis represents the relative contribution of some process activity toward knowledge flows, and the horizontal axis represents the relative workflow contribution. One vector (i.e., labeled "College coursework") delineates the relative

Figure 2. Knowledge flow and workflow contributions (adapted from Nissen, 2006)

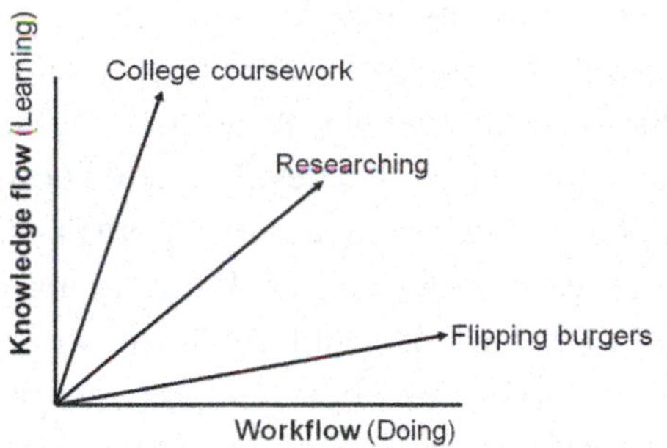

contribution of the educating process activities from above. Another (i.e., labeled "Flipping burgers") delineates the contribution from the work process of flipping hamburgers in a fast-food restaurant. Say that the length of any particular vector represents the amount of time, energy, money or other resources invested in the activity; here we show the two vectors as approximately equal length, indicating, for instance, that roughly the same amount of time is invested in each. Notice the college coursework vector is nearly vertical—but not quite—and the flipping burgers vector is nearly horizontal—but not quite. This depicts graphically the relationship from above: educating contributes principally toward knowledge flows (i.e., learning) and negligibly toward workflows (i.e., doing); working in a fast-food restaurant has inverse contributions with respect to learning versus doing.

The two vectors are depicted as not quite vertical or horizontal, respectively, to illustrate that some useful work can emerge from college coursework (e.g., via practical application project) and that some learning can result from flipping burgers (e.g., cooking techniques). Clearly a great many diverse processes can be depicted graphically in this manner. Such depiction helps elucidate the relative contributions of various process activities toward knowledge flows and workflows. The two examples illustrated here represent relatively pure cases (i.e., contributing almost exclusively toward one flow versus another).

But what about an alternate process such as researching, the activities of which contribute differently? Many people such as professors, attorneys and product development engineers conduct research as their principal job (i.e., doing activity). They also develop new knowledge through research (i.e., learning activity). Clearly there is learning as well as doing taking place. Flows of knowledge and flows of work both obtain through the single process *researching*. Consider the research performed by a university professor, for example. He or she may conduct research to understand some phenomenon (e.g., *dynamic knowledge*) better. Such process activity to improve one's understanding is intense in terms of learning but contributes negligibly toward productive output (i.e., doing). Hence the activity contributes strongly toward knowledge flows and weakly toward workflows. Alternatively, research also provides the intellectual and empirical basis to write papers for publication in academic journals, to write textbooks for use in courses, and to prepare lecture notes for class instruction. Such process activities are more intense in terms of doing but contribute negligibly toward one's own knowledge (i.e., learning). Hence the activities contribute weakly toward knowledge flows and strongly toward workflows.

Taken individually, the learning component of research would plot similarly to the vector in Figure 2 for college coursework, and the doing component would plot similarly to the flipping burgers vector. When taken together, however, the learning and doing components would combine to delineate an intermediate vector such as the one labeled "Researching" in the figure. This method of graphical depiction enables quick visual classification of processes in terms of their relative contributions toward knowledge flows and workflows. We return to utilize such method for classification and visualization later in the book.

KNOWLEDGE FLOW TIMING

Beyond the phenomenology of knowledge flowing through an organization by way of processes, terms such as flow and move imply dynamic action; that is, flows and movements take place through time. Flows of water, for example from the physical world, move through finite and measurable periods of time. Indeed, it can take a particular volume of water several months to make its way down the Mississippi River, for instance, and one can measure the flow time of such water volume (e.g., with a dye marker or empty bleach bottle). Flows of water and other fluids also vary with different conditions of their conduits. Where the banks of a river narrow and the bottom steepens, for instance, the flow rate of river water increases consistently at such points. Flows of electricity take place much faster of course than water flows do, but their flow times are finite and measurable also, and they vary according to the nature of and conditions in the conduit (e.g., conductivity, temperature, size). Flows of electromagnetic radiation (e.g., light, radio waves) are similar (i.e., finite, measurable, vary according to different conditions). Flows of containers along the conveyors of a bottling plant are similar too, as are flows of packages being delivered by mail carriers. They all take place through finite and measurable periods of time and are all affected by various conditions. Knowledge flows are no exception.

Consider, for instance, our example of a student participating in an educational program. Focus in particular on interaction between the professor and the student. The professor presumably knows the material associated with a course, and the student presumably does not (or at least not as well). If this were not the case, then why would such professor teach the course, and why would such student enroll in it? As part of the professor's work process, say he or she prepares for and leads a one-hour class session, in which the student participates. In terms of timing, perhaps several hours are required for the professor to prepare for the class session, and exactly one hour is required to lead it. The knowledge that flows during this period (i.e., as a result of the processes preparing and discussing) does so quite quickly (e.g., in a matter of hours) by knowledge flow standards.

Now consider some related processes that need to be completed before the professor can prepare for a class session. Depending upon the nature and level of material taught in the course, one could argue the professor has to earn a PhD and to research the subject matter discussed in the course, among others (e.g., get a teaching job at the university). The knowledge flows associated with such latter processes take place quite slowly (e.g., in a matter of years) by comparison with those above. Notice the variation associated with time required for knowledge flow processes such as preparation for class and earning a PhD is huge (e.g., many orders of magnitude). The key point is, knowledge flows are dynamic, and such flows can be measured.

Additionally, various knowledge flows are interrelated tightly through precedence relations; that is, some chunks of knowledge must complete their flows before others can begin effectively. Consider further the example of a professor leading class discussion. We note above how the class preparation process must (or at least should) be completed prior to the beginning of class discussion. Otherwise, the professor may come to class prepared poorly for the discussion and hence may fail to anticipate and answer students' questions well. This indicates a precedence relation between these two knowledge flow processes, a relation which we note symbolically: class preparing → class discussing. Flow times for these two processes are noted above as relatively short.

Conversely, flow times for the latter processes such as earning a PhD and researching subject matter are considerably longer. Notice further such latter knowledge flow processes also exhibit precedence relations, between themselves as well as with the former processes. For instance, say earning a PhD is prerequisite to researching effectively the subject matter of a course. Using our notation from above, we could write: earning a PhD → researching subject matter. Notice we highlight these knowledge flow processes with bold font to denote their relatively long flow times. This shows the precedence relation between these two, relatively slow processes.

But the precedence linkage extends farther, as researching the course subject matter is in turn prerequisite to class preparation. Hence our notation could be extended further: earning a PhD → researching subject matter → class preparing → class discussing. Precedence chains as such can be of arbitrary length, depending upon how many different knowledge flow processes are interrelated as prerequisites, for instance. Notice a precedence chain such as this also represents a rudimentary plan; that is, it specifies which flows need to be completed and in which order. Precedence chains also lend themselves readily to computer representation (esp. as graph and tree structures).

With the identification of precedence relations as such, one can begin to make useful inferences about knowledge flow times. For instance, when asked about how much time is required to prepare for a class discussion, the answer would depend clearly upon the states of the prerequisite knowledge flow processes (e.g., earning a PhD and researching subject matter). If such prerequisite processes had completed their flows, as one case (e.g., a professor with a PhD had already conducted research on the course subject matter), then one could answer that class preparation should require time on the order of a few hours to complete. In this case, only the class preparing and class discussing processes would require performance.

If such prerequisite processes had not completed their flows, however, as a contrasting case (e.g., a graduate student had just begun working toward a PhD and accomplished no research to date on the course subject matter), then one may have to answer that class preparation could require time on the order of several years to complete (at the same quality level)! In this latter case, the class preparing and class discussing processes would have to wait for knowledge flows associated with earning a PhD and researching the subject matter to complete. Otherwise, the graduate student could certainly attempt to lead the class, but the quality (e.g., knowledge flow) of the class session would probably be considerably lower than if the experienced professor were to lead it. The point is, by identifying and linking precedence relations between diverse knowledge flow processes, one can develop an understanding of process interrelations and begin to appreciate issues associated with timing and sequencing among various knowledge flows.

KNOWLEDGE FLOW OBSTACLES

Drawing further from our discussion of inertia, we note above one obvious obstacle to knowledge flows: inactivity. Unless a process is performed to move knowledge, there is little reason to believe such knowledge will flow. Building upon research to date on knowledge flows (e.g., Dierickx & Cool, 1989; Nissen, 2002a; Nonaka, 1994), another important consideration pertains to the nature of knowledge. In general, tacit knowledge flows more slowly (i.e., has longer flow time) than explicit knowledge does. Likewise, tacit knowledge flows more locally (i.e., has narrower reach) than explicit knowledge does. Knowledge creation generally requires longer than its application does (i.e., along the life cycle dimension). Hence the various dimensions we use to characterize different kinds of knowledge provide insights into the dynamics of knowledge flows (e.g., flow time).

For instance, where some kind of important organizational knowledge is tacit and clumped within a single person or organization, the leader or manager wishing for such knowledge to flow quickly across many people and across several organizations faces a daunting obstacle. Of course other obstacles to knowledge flows obtain as well: a person must be competent at learning before knowledge creation can take place reliably; a person must be willing to share knowledge before it can be transferred effectively; a person must have internalized knowledge before it can be applied well. A plethora of different obstacles to knowledge flows have been reported and described in the academic literature as well as the management press.

How would a leader or manager work to overcome obstacles to knowledge flows? First, one needs to recognize the need for knowledge to flow. Despite our understanding about knowledge power, not every organization is concerned equally with knowledge flows. Indeed, some organizations may find it important to restrict flows of knowledge. Consider, for example, an organization that bases much of its competitive advantage on keeping secrets within the enterprise. Many commercial firms and military units attempt to compete on the basis of privileged information, trade secrets and explicit knowledge, for instance. In such organizations, there are clearly limits to the kinds of knowledge flows managers are willing to accept, and there are many kinds of knowledge flows managers work actively to prevent. Even for organizations facing limits along these lines, however, effective performance of work processes still depends upon knowledge. To the extent that such knowledge is not located how, where and when it is needed to support workflows, then the knowledge must be induced to flow. Hence the leader or manager is faced with the prospect of trying to restrict some flows of knowledge while trying simultaneously to enhance other flows in a single organization.

Second, one needs to understand the kind of knowledge involved with flows. Using the dimensions of our framework (e.g., explicitness, reach, life cycle) provides a good start. The kinds of managerial, organizational, processual, personnel and technological changes likely to be effective and to induce or enhance knowledge flows depend directly upon the nature of the knowledge. Recall our organizational analogs to inertia, force and mass: a heavy mass requires a proportionately stronger force to effect the same acceleration created by a weaker force applied to a lighter mass. In the organizational context, moving tacit knowledge requires a different, more forceful set of knowledge flow processes than those required for explicit knowledge to flow. For instance, where knowledge is tacit, held individually, and associated solely with creation, there is little point to investing in Web portals with a hope of disseminating such knowledge. The knowledge flow processes associated with such portals (e.g., explicit knowledge dissemination) do not induce tacit knowledge to flow well. Likewise, where knowledge is explicit, distributed widely, and used for application to work processes, there is little reason to collocate people with the hope they will share such knowledge. The knowledge flow processes associated with such collocation have their greatest effect on tacit knowledge.

Third, one needs to understand the timing of and workflow interactions with knowledge. Where work needs to be accomplished in a time-critical, high-quality manner, then generally all of the required knowledge flows must be completed before such workflow begins. Otherwise people performing the work may not be qualified fully (e.g., not know what to do or how to do it well). Further, workflows and knowledge flows alike may have precedence relations between them (e.g., certain work activities must be completed before others can begin effectively; certain learning activities must be completed before others can begin effectively). Project managers and like professionals who plan and schedule work activities for others have developed a robust set of tools and techniques (e.g., Gantt Charts, PERT networks; see Cleland & Ireland, 2002) to identify, align and plan precedence relations among workflow processes. This is from where the term critical path derives, for instance: the sequence of work activities that determine the shortest possible project completion time.

However, few if any such tools and techniques address precedence relations among knowledge flow processes well. This remains the case today, even though precedence relations among such processes must be identified, aligned and planned in a manner comparable to that for workflows. Recall the example above of the university professor preparing for class discussion. The length of time required for such preparation could vary by several orders of magnitude, depending upon which of the prerequisite knowledge flow processes (e.g., earning a PhD, researching the subject matter) had been completed. Moreover, the class preparation workflows must be completed before the work process class discussing can begin fruitfully. Indeed, where workflows depend upon knowledge flows for effective performance, flows of knowledge lie always on the critical paths of workflows. In other words, in nearly every domain of work, people must know what to do and how and when to do it well before they can accomplish a knowledge based activity effectively.

Fourth, one needs to place a relative premium on workflows versus knowledge flows—or vice versa—in the organization. Different processes contribute in different magnitudes toward the relative flows of work and flows of knowledge. We illustrate this concept above through the contrast between process activities such as college coursework, researching and flipping burgers. A related example from the domain of organizations can be seen with formal classroom training versus on-the-job training (OJT; i.e., trial-and-error learning). The former often accomplishes little or no useful work yet achieves focused learning in a relatively short period of time. The latter generally accomplishes useful work directly but has a relatively small and slow learning component. A focus on knowledge flows versus a focus on workflows reflects a leader's or manager's relative concern for learning versus doing, respectively. Indeed, the approach selected by a leader or manager (e.g., formal training, OJT) will contribute differently toward learning versus doing. Hence such approach constitutes an important decision variable for consideration.

Fifth, one needs some kind of model to pull together the various factors, considerations and alternatives associated with workflows and knowledge flows and to help support informed decision-making. Which managerial, organizational, processual, personnel and/or technological changes would be most appropriate in a given situation? This represents the kind of question that most leaders and managers need to have answered. Unfortunately, at present the state of the art has yet to develop a reliable model to support such decision-making well. Even models such as Nonaka's Spiral are purely descriptive and offer little decision support at present. This remains an active topic of current research, however.

For instance, Nissen (2010b; 2011) discusses knowledge power in terms of enabling and supporting competitive advantage, and he links such power to the four dimensions described above. This begins to articulate useful interrelationships between important dynamic knowledge characteristics and to outline heuristics that can inform decision-making. The comparison and contrast above between characteristics of tacit vs. explicit knowledge dynamics elucidate this well. As discussed, tacit knowledge flows relatively slowly and narrowly when compared to explicit knowledge. It can take weeks, months or years for tacit knowledge flows to complete, and they do so generally only with individuals (e.g., OJT), dyads (e.g., mentoring) and small groups (e.g., socializing). Alternatively, once knowledge is articulated in explicit form, and particularly when it is encoded in digital form and placed on a computer network, it can flow around the world in seconds. So why wouldn't leaders and managers strive to commit all knowledge to explicit form?

The answer centers on the comparative power of tacit vs. explicit knowledge. As discussed previously, we know more than we can tell, and reading a book about how to perform some knowledge based action (i.e., learning via explicit knowledge) is not the same as knowing how to perform it (i.e., learning via tacit knowledge). Hence, in a great many circumstances, the power of tacit knowledge exceeds that of explicit knowledge. Hence the leader and manager face a trade space between the speed and breadth of knowledge flows on the one hand vs. knowledge power on the other; that is, explicit knowledge flows very quickly and broadly, but its relative power is diluted, whereas tacit knowledge flow comparatively slowly and narrowly but at high power.

In terms of decision-making heuristics, where knowledge inertia is relatively small (e.g., knowledge to be learned is not particularly difficult or complex), and it is important to distribute such knowledge broadly and quickly (e.g., across all parts of a global organization), it makes sense to focus on explicit knowledge flow processes for sharing. In contrast, where knowledge inertia is comparatively large (e.g., knowledge to be learned is quite difficult and complex), and it is important to sustain high knowledge *power* over time (e.g., for knowledge based competitive advantage), it makes more sense to focus on tacit knowledge flow processes instead.

KNOWLEDGE FLOW PRINCIPLES

Five principles developed in this chapter help shed light on knowledge flows: 11) knowledge exhibits some properties of inertia such as tendency to remain at rest; 12) experiential processes contribute principally toward workflows (i.e., doing), whereas educational processes contribute principally toward knowledge flows (i.e., learning); 13) knowledge flows lie always on the critical paths of workflows and hence organizational performance; 14) time-critical workflows must wait for enabling knowledge flows to run their course; and 15) explicit knowledge flows very quickly and broadly, but its relative power is diluted, whereas tacit knowledge flows comparatively slowly and narrowly but at high power.

Principle 11: First, we note above how knowledge at rest tends to stay at rest. If a leader or manager seeks to have knowledge flow, then something must be done to induce it to flow (e.g., formal training, OJT). Further, knowledge in motion tends to stay in motion in some cases (e.g., via employee defections). If a leader or manager seeks to cease or restrict knowledge flows in such cases, then something must be done to stem the flows. In contrast, if the leader or manager is content with such flows, then no action is required. In other cases, however, knowledge in motion (e.g., student learning through classroom interaction) appears to require additional action just to keep it in motion. If a leader or manager seeks to cease or restrict knowledge flows in such cases, then no action is required to stem its flow. In contrast, if the leader or manager wants such flows to propagate further, then something must be done to continue the flows. The organizational process represents the phenomenological analog to physical force in overcoming knowledge inertia. Hence knowledge flow processes represent direct focuses of leadership and management action.

Principle 12: Second, workflows and knowledge flows interact, and various processes contribute in different magnitudes toward doing versus learning. If a leader or manager is interested in promoting knowledge flows in the organization, then it will be important for him or her to understand how the specific knowledge flows of concern interrelate with workflows of value to the organization. In some cases, workflows and knowledge flows are independent, so one can be changed without affecting the other. In most cases, however, workflows and knowledge flows are interrelated tightly, so altering one will affect the other directly. Hence changes to workflows demand changes to knowledge flows, and vice versa.

Principle 13: Third, the activities associated with organizational processes are responsible for the phenomenon of knowledge flows. Knowledge flow processes represent the organizational analogs to physical forces. The different kinds of knowledge represent the organizational analogs to physical masses. Together the two determine the direction, rate and extent of knowledge flows. If a leader or manager is interested in inducing, enhancing, restricting or ceasing knowledge flows, then he or she should examine the associated organizational processes. Because processes are composed of activities, which have long been the focus of leadership and management attention, such a process focus should be quite natural. Also, there appears to be considerable opportunity for such a process focus to be supported by the same kinds of tools and techniques for the planning, organizing, monitoring and control of work (e.g., Gantt Charts, PERT networks, work/knowledge specifications). Indeed, in every case of knowledge based action, knowledge flows lie on the critical paths of workflows and the associated organizational performance. Hence knowledge flows should be planned and managed like workflows are.

Principle 14: Fourth, knowledge flows and workflows vary in terms of timing. Some workflows require quick, precise and thorough activities that can be performed only by knowledgeable people. In such cases the enabling knowledge flows are prerequisite to their corresponding workflows. Other workflows afford greater tolerances in terms of timing and performance, which can be performed by people who learn over time and by trial and error. In such cases the enabling knowledge flows can be concurrent with (or even follow) their corresponding workflows. Indeed, in many cases such as OJT, the learning associated with knowledge flows takes place through the doing associated with workflows. Before deciding upon and implementing a particular approach to inducing, enhancing, restricting or ceasing knowledge flows, the leader or manager needs to consider how the target flows interact temporally with corresponding workflows of importance. Hence most knowledge flows must complete their course before critical and dependent workflows can begin.

Principle 15: Finally, explicit knowledge flows very quickly and broadly, but its relative power is diluted, whereas tacit knowledge flows comparatively slowly and narrowly, but at high power. In terms of decision-making heuristics, where knowledge inertia is relatively small (e.g., knowledge to be learned is not particularly difficult or complex), and it is important to distribute such knowledge broadly and quickly (e.g., across all parts of a global organization), it makes sense to focus on explicit knowledge flow processes for sharing. In contrast, where knowledge inertia is comparatively large (e.g., knowledge to be learned is quite difficult and complex), and it is important to sustain high knowledge power over time (e.g., for knowledge based competitive advantage), it makes more sense to focus on tacit knowledge flow processes instead. Hence the dynamic nature of knowledge has great implication in terms of selecting the most appropriate organizational processes to effect knowledge flows.

EXERCISES

1. Describe briefly a knowledge flow process in an organization with which you are familiar. Indicate what its constituent activities are and how this knowledge flow process interacts with one or more workflow processes.
2. Describe briefly a critical part of a job you have or have had that requires knowledge. How is such knowledge acquired? To what extent do you devote your time in the organization to learning versus doing (i.e., knowledge flows vs. workflows)?
3. Describe briefly the temporal interaction between the knowledge flows and workflows from Exercise 2 above. To what extent must knowledge flows precede the enabled workflows versus occurring contemporaneously?
4. Describe a clump associated with flows of the knowledge from Exercise 2 above. Indicate the nature of such knowledge. Propose at least two alternate approaches to dissolving the clump and enhancing the corresponding knowledge flow.

REFERENCES

Cleland, D. I., & Ireland, L. R. (2002). *Project management: Strategic design and implementation* (4th ed.). New York: McGraw-Hill.

Czarniawska, B., & Joerges, B. (1996). Travels of ideas. In B. Czarnaiwska & G. Sevon (Eds.), Translating organiztional change, (pp. 13-48). Berlin: de Gruyter.

Dierickx, I., & Cool, K. (1989). Asset stock accumulation and sustainability of competitive advantage. *Management Science*, *35*(12), 1504–1511. doi:10.1287/mnsc.35.12.1504.

Nissen, M. E. (2002). An extended model of knowledge flow dynamics. *Communications of the Association for Information Systems*, *8*, 251–266.

Nissen, M. E. (2004). *Dynamic knowledge patterns to inform design: A field study of knowledge stocks and flows in an extreme organization*. Working paper.

Nissen, M. E. (2005). Toward designing organizations around knowledge flows. In Desouza, K. (Ed.), *New frontiers in knowledge management*. New York: Palgrave McMillian.

Nissen, M. E. (2010). *CyberKM: Harnessing dynamic knowledge for competitive advantage through cyberspace* (Technical Report No. NPS-IS-10-006). Monterey, CA: Naval Postgraduate School.

Nissen, M. E. (2011). Measuring dynamic knowledge flows: Implications for organizational performance. In Schiuma, G. (Ed.), *Managing knowledge assets and business value creation in organizations* (pp. 125–145). Hershey, PA: IGI Global.

Nissen, M. E., Kamel, M. N., & Sengupta, K. C. (2000). Integrated analysis and design of knowledge systems and processes. *Information Resources Management Journal*, *13*(1), 24–42. doi:10.4018/irmj.2000010103.

Nonaka, I. (1994). A dynamic theory of organizational knowledge creation. *Organization Science*, *5*(1), 14–37. doi:10.1287/orsc.5.1.14.

Nonaka, I., & Takeuchi, H. (1995). *The knowledge creating company: How Japanese companies create the dynamics of innovation*. New York: Oxford University Press.

von Hippel, E. (1994). Sticky information and the locus of problem solving: Implications for innovation. *Management Science*, *40*(4), 429–439. doi:10.1287/mnsc.40.4.429.

ENDNOTES

1 We make use of metaphors here and elsewhere in the book, for metaphors can be very useful in terms of generating insight. We use all metaphors with considerable caution, however, for they all break down at some point.

Chapter 4
Knowledge Technology

ABTRACT

This chapter surveys several classes of technologies and indicates which kinds of knowledge flows are enabled and supported relatively better and worse by such technologies. The authors look at common problems associated with the most prevalent and prominent KM technologies and then discuss interactions between such technologies and the knowledge life cycle. The discussion turns subsequently to examine expert systems technology, which addresses knowledge directly. This is followed by a discussion of simulation technology, which enables the development of tacit knowledge through practice in virtual environments. The chapter concludes with five knowledge technology principles and includes exercises to stimulate critical thought, learning, and discussion. As a note, the authors do not consider the kinds of emergent knowledge phenomena enabled via social media technologies here, but they devote the whole of the book's third section to this topic.

KNOWLEDGE TECHNOLOGY PROBLEMS

Have you ever worked with technology in an organization that failed to produce the intended results? Technology—particularly information technology (IT)—forms the foundation of many KM projects in practice and offers great potential in terms of enhancing knowledge flows. As noted repeatedly above, however, few information technologies even address knowledge as the focus or object of flow. Over-reliance on IT has sounded the death knell for myriad KM projects.

Ask yourself why most IT fails to support KM well. We have learned that knowledge is distinct from information. Yet we have learned also that knowledge builds upon information (and vice versa). It appears that flows of information are necessary to support flows of knowledge, but such former flows are insufficient to enable the latter ones. In this way IT to enable flows of information may be necessary to support flows of knowledge, but many KM programs rely naïvely upon such technology as sufficient to effect knowledge flows. IT is capable of transmitting signals (e.g., electrical waves and pulses across networks, photonic patterns from displays, acoustical patterns from speakers), but conversion of such signals into data, information or knowledge takes place within the minds of people receiving such signals, not the electronics of IT systems. To ensure flows of knowledge, one must do more than deliver signals. Thus knowledge flows require more than just IT.

Next ask yourself how some kinds of IT support KM better than others do. Some technologies claim to automate work processes. Many people

DOI: 10.4018/978-1-4666-4727-5.ch004

think of automation as the ultimate in terms of IT evolution. The word processor application automates many document processing tasks such as formatting, spell checking and filing, for instance. The workflow application automates flows of documents through an organization, as another instance. Intelligent software agents can search networks autonomously and retrieve information automatically from distributed and disorganized sources (e.g., the Internet), as a third instance. Related shopping "bots" can identify and select automatically certain products and services based on lowest-price, as a fourth instance.

Nonetheless, people are required still to create the messages that become documents and to complete the work as it flows into their workspaces. People are required also to read and understand documents that are created and to build cumulatively upon the work of others in workflows. People are required further to determine which information retrieved by agents is relevant and to decide whether non-price product and service attributes are sufficiently compelling to override bots' purchase recommendations.

In each of these instances, and as a general rule, the technologies automate some activities within workflows but not all of them. The people in an organization perform most workflow roles requiring knowledge—particularly those involving experience, judgment and like capabilities dependent upon tacit knowledge. This leaves to IT the largely systematic, clerical and procedural roles, for which requisite knowledge can be formalized explicitly (e.g., via computer software). Hence we see again, as in Chapter 2, how knowledge uniqueness and IT are intertwined tightly.

Other technologies such as computer databases and online information repositories are excellent at organizing, storing, manipulating and facilitating the query and retrieval of data and documents, respectively, but we know that even data organized within a database must be placed in context and used to enable direct action to become knowledge. Likewise, even documents organized within a document repository must be read, understood and used for action before they can be considered to represent knowledge. As noted above, such technologies are clearly important in, and in many respects necessary for, supporting knowledge work in the organization, but they are not sufficient to enable knowledge flows. Again, the people in an organization maintain responsibility for most workflow activities requiring knowledge, particularly tacit knowledge.

Moreover, recall the discussion above pertaining to interaction between workflows and knowledge flows. The kinds of KM-prominent technologies described here are largely neutral in terms of supporting processes for learning versus doing. To reiterate briefly, learning has most to do with flows of knowledge, whereas doing has more to do with flows of work. If a particular technology focuses principally on supporting workflows and not knowledge flows, then one should question the value of such technology to a knowledge management effort. For instance, a set of documents from a searchable cloud repository may be used to support knowledge flows (e.g., via a formal training course) or workflows (e.g., via a standard operating procedure) equally well. Hence the key is how a technology is used (e.g., to support learning vs. doing), not the technology itself.

A great many KM programs are meticulous about the technologies they implement, only to then leave people in the organization unguided and uninformed about how such technology can be used to enhance knowledge flows. Indeed, most KM projects that focus on technology miss and neglect the most important resource: people. In our document example above, for instance, it is the person who finds, selects and reads the documents—and the organizational context of his or her activities (e.g., learning vs. doing)—that determines whether the repository is used for learning or working. This point may appear a bit tangential at first look, but it cuts away at the widely perceived primacy and privileged nature of information technologies for knowledge management. For instance, one can make many of the same points about how other "technologies"—such as office chairs, pencil sharpeners, filing cabinets and like common artifacts of both knowledge flow and workflow processes—can be used equally well to support learning as well as doing. Yet what intelligent knowledge manager would base an organization's KM program on "advanced office chair technology"?

Now ubiquitous computer networks share many of these same properties with respect to knowledge. They appear to be present in most KM programs and are in many cases both important and necessary, but networks shunt signals around and connect various other IT applications. To a large extent we can label technologies such as these "infrastructure." As an analogy, trains, depots, tracks, trucks, warehouses and highways support interstate commerce in the US, but they only help to move commercial products around the country—from producers to consumers, for instance. Such commercial infrastructure is important for commerce and can improve the distribution of physical goods, but having them in place, and even using them, does not constitute commerce. Many other processes must contribute also in order to leverage the transportation infrastructure (e.g., product development, marketing, manufacturing, retailing). Likewise with IT infrastructure, it is important to KM and can improve the distribution of information, but much more is required to manage organizational knowledge and the associated work.

Still other technologies such as Web portals and search engines contribute more directly to managing knowledge than infrastructure tools do, but the same caveats apply, and whatever knowledge is embedded in such technologies is principally explicit. For instance, people use Web portals to organize and distribute information and to point to other resources where knowledge can be found, but such portals only point to tacit knowledge (e.g., people, organizational routines). Whatever knowledge they help organize and disseminate (e.g., via electronic documents, graphics, formulae) is explicit (e.g., written down, delineated, formulated) for the most part. Likewise with search engines, people use them to find information in disorganized and distributed sources, but beyond the people who create and maintain the kinds of explicit resources that can be indexed and searched via this technology, there is negligible tacit knowledge involved.

Communication technologies such as e-mail, chat, video teleconferencing, telephone and radio enable people to communicate in a distributed manner, across time as well as space in some cases (e.g., asynchronous tools). Such technologies support conversations and interactions between people and can be used to convey information as well. Communication is important for knowledge flows, and one can argue that it is necessary, but it is not sufficient. Recall the example from above in which the message "333/33" is placed into context as a blood pressure reading. Even when the communication itself is flawless (e.g., no transmission errors, negligible latency, legible message, interpreted correctly by receiver), medical and physiological knowledge are required as well to enable appropriate action based upon such communication. A KM program that includes technologies such as these may be able to improve flows of knowledge, but it cannot guarantee them. Alternatively, "technologies" such as face-to-face meetings, socializing and mentoring often have no prominent place in most KM programs today. Yet many experts identify interpersonal interaction as a central vehicle for learning and the flow of knowledge, particularly tacit knowledge.

TECHNOLOGY AND LIFE CYCLE INTERACTION

Relationships between diverse classes of information technologies and knowledge flows can be understood more systematically in terms of our 4D framework from above. In particular, the life cycle dimension can be used to divide technologies into two broad classes. First, look more closely at the various phases of the knowledge life cycle. We represent these phases as a cycle in Figure 1. As with life cycle models used commonly in the design of information systems and other complex systems—and as with our mutually inverted knowledge hierarchies from above—this dimension gives a sense of directionality to knowledge flows.

Drawing briefly from Nissen et al. (2000) and Nissen (2006), the creation phase begins the life cycle, as new knowledge is generated within an enterprise; similar terms from other models include capture and acquire. The second phase pertains to the organization, mapping or bundling of knowledge, often employing systems such as taxonomies, ontologies and repositories. Phase 3 addresses mechanisms for making knowledge formal or explicit; similar terms from other models include store and codify. The fourth phase concerns the ability to share or distribute knowledge in the enterprise; this includes also terms such as transfer and access. Knowledge use and application for problem solving or decision-making in the organization constitutes Phase 5. A sixth phase is included to cover knowledge refinement and evolution, which reflects organizational learning—and thus a return to knowledge

Figure 1. Knowledge life cycle (adapted from Nissen, 2006)

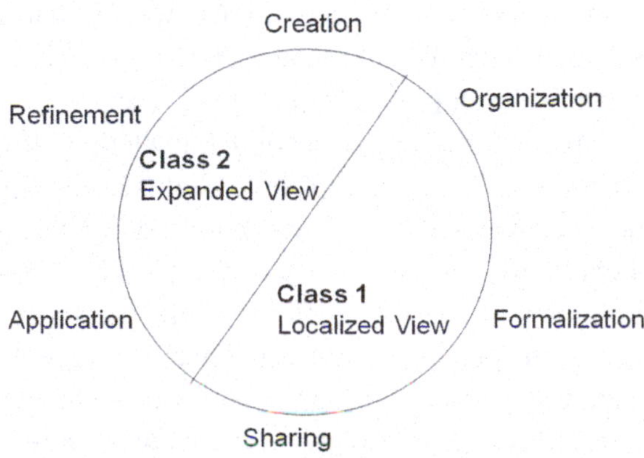

creation—through time. It is important to note, as in the familiar life cycle models used in IT design (e.g., System Development Life Cycle), progression through the various phases of this life cycle model is generally iterative and involves feedback loops between stages. All steps need not be taken in order, and the flow through this life cycle is not necessarily unidirectional.

Notice in the figure the three knowledge activities from above (i.e., organize, formalize, share) that are adjacent on the right-hand side of the cycle. These activities are supported relatively well by extant information technologies. They represent something of a localized view of knowledge management—hence the grouping under the "Class I" heading in the figure. We note such localized knowledge management systems are inherently supportive in nature. This class of implementations to organize, formalize and share knowledge in the enterprise supports people, who perform knowledge flow and workflow process activities. The people in turn also apply, refine and create knowledge in the organization. This represents a common theme that runs through all of the technology examples discussed above.

Alternatively, notice the three activities that are adjacent on the left-hand side of the cycle. In contrast with their counterparts above, these activities are supported quite poorly by most extant information technologies. They represent an expanded view of knowledge management—hence the grouping under the "Class II" heading in the figure. We note such expanded knowledge management systems are inherently performative in nature. This class of implementations to apply, refine and create knowledge in the enterprise performs (e.g., automates) knowledge management activities, either in conjunction with or in lieu of people in the organization.

Unlike the many supportive technology examples discussed thus far in the book, we have said almost nothing about counterpart technologies that perform process activities associated with knowledge creation, application and refinement.

The reason is simple: very few technologies are performative in nature (cf. workflow systems, software agents, shopping bots, expert systems, some software "apps") and capable of doing so. Moreover, in this section we focus principally on the most-prevalent and –prominent technologies used in KM today, making no claims that the discussion is exhaustive or complete. Such discussion is, alternatively, representative of contemporary KM practice. Even the few performative technologies that exist at this time are neither prevalent nor prominent in KM projects. We thus observe a relative abundance of technologies associated with the three supportive phases of the KM life cycle and a dearth associated with the three performative phases.

EXPERT SYSTEMS TECHNOLOGY

From the discussion above, IT plays a supportive role in most KM programs. People play the performative role. This is largely because knowledge is required to perform knowledge work, but few information technologies address knowledge directly. In addition to some automation technologies such as word processing, workflow and software agent applications, which perform certain activities associated with documents and information in the organization, the expert system represents another class of IT that offers performative capabilities. Although far from a "silver bullet" or cure-all for KM programs, the performative capability of expert systems makes them informative to examine in our present context. Many other applications based on artificial intelligence (AI; e.g., software agents, case-based reasoning, intelligent tutoring, qualitative reasoning, Semantic Web) possess similar performative properties and can be considered together as a class, with expert systems representing both exemplar and prototype of such class.

The term expert system was coined in the Seventies within the AI field. As implied by the name, this technology seeks to use computers to emulate the expertise of human experts. The process for developing expert systems relies upon someone, generally other than the expert, conducting interviews and observing expert behavior. This "knowledge engineer" then formalizes the basis of expertise in the computer via heuristic rules, frames, scripts and other techniques for knowledge representation. Returning to our 4D framework, developing an expert system represents a knowledge flow process, through which knowledge moves between two coordinates. It begins as tacit knowledge (i.e., in terms of explicitness), within an individual (i.e., in terms of reach), that is applied (i.e., in terms of life cycle). Through development of an expert system, it moves to explicit knowledge (e.g., heuristic rules of thumb), available beyond the individual (e.g., group), through formalization (e.g., using predicate logic for representation).

Introducing coordinate shorthand to characterize such knowledge movement in terms of our framework, a flow vector can be viewed as extending from one coordinate point to another. In the case of expert system development, one can use the framework to visualize knowledge moving from one coordinate—at which knowledge is Tacit, at the Individual level, and Applied (TIA)—to another—at which knowledge becomes Explicit, at the Group level, and Formalized (EGF). These coordinate points and the corresponding vector are delineated in Figure 2 (i.e., associated with the knowledge flow process labeled "Developing"). We use a relatively thick arrow for such knowledge flow vector, because developing expert systems is often a time-consuming process; that is, the knowledge flow time associated with expert systems development is quite long often.

We include also a second knowledge flow vector associated with expert systems in the figure. This second vector corresponds to using such technology once it has been developed. Notice this latter vector starts from where the former vector terminates (i.e., a precedence relation links expert systems development and use) and is delineated via a relatively thin arrow to depict comparatively short flow time. Notice also that

Figure 2. Knowledge flow vectors for expert system development and use

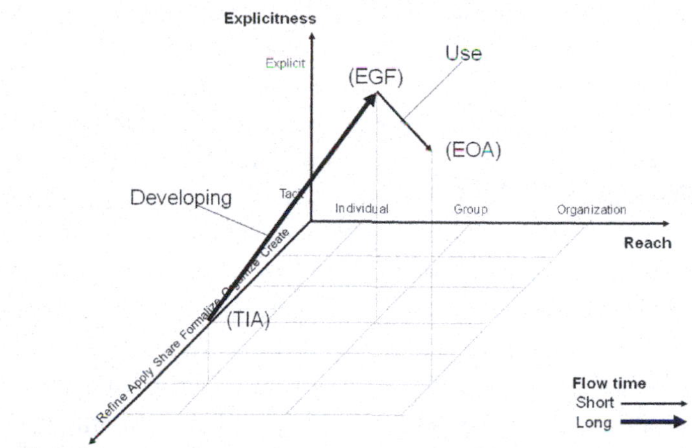

the use vector extends Explicit knowledge out to the Organization level in terms of reach and back to Application in terms of life cycle (i.e., to coordinate EOA). This latter coordinate indicates that knowledge formalized via expert systems, once developed, can be distributed organization-wide for application. Moreover, experience over the past three decades indicates such application often reflects the same level of performance as demonstrated by the individual human experts.

Indeed, where knowledge can be formalized to support computer inference as such, expert systems have demonstrated many times that they are capable of matching, and in many cases exceeding, the performance of human experts. Hence expert systems take on a performative role by employing (explicit) knowledge to enable direct action (e.g., making decisions, enacting communication behaviors, performing analytical work) in the organization. Notice this role is different from those played by most other classes of IT: performative vs. supportive. Further, once developed, expert systems can be distributed broadly across the organization and used simultaneously, in massive parallel, to address many different knowledge-work tasks and problems, by novices. The ability to augment the capabilities of multiple novices, and raise their performance to levels exhibited by experts, represents a powerful contributor to competitive advantage. Contrast this with a single human expert, who at any one time cannot generally work in more than a small number of organizations or on more than a few work tasks and problems.

This is the promise of AI. Unlike most technologies, expert systems address knowledge directly, in addition to information and data. They offer an approach to formalizing tacit knowledge, distributing broadly the associated power for action, and applying it directly through the organization. None of the more-prevalent and –prominent technologies from above offers this capability.

Alternatively, expert systems technology entails difficulty. Many people continue to view AI as over-hyped and unfulfilled even after several decades of active research and commercial work. As noted above, expert systems development can be time-consuming and expensive. Many industrial expert system projects have failed to realize positive returns on investment. Not all experts are able and/or willing to articulate their expertise. Numerous application domains do not lend themselves well to formalization via expert system technology. Hence we reiterate, expert systems technology is far from a "silver bullet" or cure-all for KM programs, but the performative capability of expert systems—and similar "intelligent" applications from the same class of technologies—makes them informative to examine in our present context.

"EXPERT" SYSTEM ILLUSTRATION

It is important to note, one need not be an expert in order to either build or capitalize upon the benefits of expert systems. Indeed, *any* knowledge (e.g., even novice-level) that a person possesses offers potential for formalization into an "expert" system. The key is, one must be able to articulate his or her knowledge in terms that can be encoded into and applied directly by computer. Take, for example, designing an asynchronous (e.g., web-based, interactive, distributed) course on knowledge management. What kinds of technologies should you consider to support such a course? Can such a course even be offered in asynchronous mode? If you are not an asynchronous instructional designer and have never developed an asynchronous course before, you would probably have to call in an expert to assist you. Or you may elect simply to develop the course through a process of trial and error, but what if all of the available experts were busy, and you could not afford the time and expense associated with trial and error? Perhaps you could consult even a relatively simple expert system to point you in the right direction.

Take, as a different example, something from your own professional work that you know how to do better than anyone else. It does not have to be glamorous or sophisticated: just something that no one but you knows how to do well. Say that you wanted to share your expertise. For instance, say your supervisor indicates you will not be eligible for promotion or transfer until someone else can do your job as well as you can. You could spend time mentoring one or more possible personnel replacements to help them learn what you do. You could spend time developing and teaching a training course to help them learn what you do. You could gloat—and wait—as others struggle through trial and error to learn what you do. You could do many different things to help others learn what you do. You—even you—could also develop an expert system and use it to distribute your unique work knowledge in a manner that others—who are not as good as you—can use to perform your job as well as you can.

How could you codify and distribute your own knowledge using an expert system? Shell tools such as KnowledgeWright (KnowledgeWright, 2004), as but one of many instances of applications that facilitate "intelligent" system development, enable you to serve as your own "expert." Even if you do not know a lot about some particular problem area or knowledge domain—and you know nearly nothing about knowledge engineering—you may be able to use expert systems technology to formalize and distribute much of what you do know. By interacting with such a shell or like development tool, you can work to articulate your own knowledge and to formalize it via a rule-based expert system, for one instance. If you are successful, then you could employ the resulting expert system to make decisions and solve problems—automatically and in your absence—that required formerly your personal tacit knowledge and involvement. Plus, many copies of such expert system could be distributed to make decisions and solve problems—again, automatically and in your absence—by people who lack your level of expertise in the area of interest.

As an illustration, we developed a small and simple expert system to help instructors design asynchronous courses. We say, "small and simple," because such system attempts to address only one specific aspect of asynchronous instructional design: content delivery mode. Of the myriad design aspects that should be considered when developing an asynchronous course, our tiny expert system focuses on only this one, very specific consideration. Also, this system does not necessarily represent the knowledge of an *expert*. A "reasonably knowledgeable professional" represents a more-suitable label (but "reasonably knowledgeable professional system" does not roll well off of the tongue or create a clever acronym "RKPS"). Moreover, this system was developed only for illustration and to help elucidate how an expert system works. Hence it lacks both the power and sophistication of a system developed for "industrial strength" application. Nonetheless, the principles of system development and use are roughly the same. More-powerful, production-grade expert and otherwise "intelligent" systems reflect generally only larger scales, not different approaches and techniques.

Figure 3 presents two of the rules used for inference in this simple expert system. They are reproduced directly from the shell application used to develop the systems. Hence their format may appear a bit odd to the reader who is unfamiliar with computer code. Alternatively, the Structured English representation should make the rules intelligible. Briefly, the first rule (i.e., labeled "rule_set(access,/,[") pertains to the kind of computer and network access that may be available to potential students who are interested in taking an asynchronous course. The knowledge embedded within this rule begins on the fourth line (i.e., labeled "rules = [[conditions, value], …") and illustrates some considerations this expert system will include in its reasoning. For instance, the "condition" (i.e., possible state of the world) examined by this rule is "student access." One possible state of the world included in the rule is "modem"; that is, the rule is considering what to do if a potential student will be accessing an asynchronous course via dial-up modem (yes, these are used still, but this is just an example; people yearn incessantly for faster network connections and higher bandwidth; hence the specific names may change over time, but the phenomenon of comparatively fast vs. slow networks persists). This represents the "IF" part of this first IF-THEN rule.

The first "value" (i.e., conclusion based on the condition) in this rule is "low bandwidth." This is a label the system is associating with access via modem (or substitute your own obsolete or previous-generation [e.g., 4GL wireless technology] low-bandwidth connection device). Such association will be used in conjunction with different conditions and values embedded in other rules. The other condition = value pairs considered within this rule include: "DSL or cable" = "high bandwidth"; "T1+" = "high bandwidth"; "other" = "low bandwidth"; and "none" = "no bandwidth". Hence this rule considers technologies ranging

Figure 3. Rules for simple expert system

```
rule_set(access, /, [
  description = "",
  type = single_value,
  rules = [[conditions, value], [student_access = "modem", text("low bandwidth")],
[student_access = "DSL or cable", text("high bandwidth")], [student_access = "T1+",
text("high bandwidth")], [student_access = "other", text("low bandwidth")], [student_access
= "none", text("no bandwidth")]]
  ]).
rule_set(technology, /, [
  description = "",
  type = single_value,
  rules = [[conditions, value], [feasible = "feasible" and access = "low bandwidth", text("use
minimal graphics & interaction via technology")], [feasible = "feasible" and access = "high
bandwidth", text("use full graphics & interaction via technology")], [default, text("current
technology does not appear to support your plan")]]
  ]).
```

from no network access, through low-bandwidth access, to high-speed Internet access via digital subscriber lines, cable modems and T1 connections. All of the conditions, values, technologies and associations reflected by such rules represent the domain knowledge of a professional who is experienced with asynchronous instructional design. This professional's knowledge is made explicit through formalization into rules and is encoded in an expert system.

In short, based on the manner in which a knowledgeable, professional (human), asynchronous instructional designer would reason about how to deliver course content to distributed students (i.e., who cannot participate in face-to-face classroom sessions), this first rule considers several possible states of the world pertaining to network access (e.g., modem, DSL, cable), and it associates connectivity inferences (e.g., high bandwidth, low bandwidth) to the various states. Other rules in this simple expert system are similar, but they consider different conditions and associations gleaned from the (human) instructional design professional. Examples include equipment needs, cost-effectiveness, student demographics and like considerations (not shown).

The second rule shown in Figure 3 represents knowledge used to recommend the approach to and technology for delivery of course content. This rule uses the associations made by other rules as the basis of its conclusions. For instance, as above, knowledge embedded within this rule begins on its fourth line (i.e., labeled "rules = [[conditions, value], …"). Notice the conditions (again, possible states of the world) include labels such as "access," which is considered by the rule above. Specifically, one condition = value pair in this latter rule relates directly to the former rule: "access" = "low bandwidth." This means that our second rule is using as input the output of our first rule. If the first rule were to conclude "access = low bandwidth," for instance, then the expert system would consider such conclusion from Rule 1 as input to make an additional conclusion in Rule 2. Hence one rule can leverage the inference of another and produce relatively complex and sophisticated chains of reasoning. Such leveraging is termed chaining together various rules for inference.

The other condition considered by this latter rule pertains to feasibility. Values associated with both conditions feasibility and access are used by the system in this rule to recommend technology approaches. For instance, the first recommendation within this rule can be interpreted as: IF the project appears "feasible," AND access is limited to "low bandwidth," THEN the recommended design approach and content delivery mode is "use minimal graphics & interaction via technology." In other words, the system recognizes that potential students in this condition have or can obtain network access but that such access is via low-speed connections. Hence the recommendation encourages the course designer to minimize the use of graphics and interaction technologies. Both require much greater bandwidth than text does, and both cause delays for low-bandwidth users.

Because an expert system can perform activities such as decision-making (e.g., selecting course delivery technologies) and problem solving (e.g., designing asynchronous course content for students with low-bandwidth connections) that require knowledge, the system itself can be said to address knowledge and not just information. Notice this differs from sending information to a knowledgeable person (e.g., professional instructional designer) and expecting him or her to use such information for some decision-making or problem solving. By sending an expert system, even an unknowledgeable person can make such decisions or solve such problems. In the case of asynchronous course design, at one time such unknowledgeable person included the author of this book!

SIMULATION TECHNOLOGY

Simulation technology is not new. People have been conducting Gedanken (i.e., thought) simulations for possibly as long as they have walked on Earth. Indeed, the ability to contemplate one or more alternate actions—before selecting and committing to any particular one—and then pursue the one that appears to suit best one's situation probably represents Man's most powerful competitive advantage over other animals. Beyond such thought experiments, people have engaged in iconic simulations also for many millennia. For instance, using small symbols or pieces to represent army, navy and other battlefield forces—before committing such forces to battle—has been an instrumental part of warfare since the ancient Chinese began writing about it thousands of years back. Architects that develop multiple alternate perspectives of different building designs can be viewed as helping clients to visualize alternate possibilities for an edifice of interest—before committing to one particular design—and hence engaging in a type of simulation. The key is, some kind of simulation is conducted using representations of the real world—in advance of committing to decisions affecting outcomes in the real world.

Today of course simulations can be conducted by computer, in addition to the use of thoughts, icons, drawings and like approaches. This enables a great many different elements and complex interrelations to be modeled (e.g., many more than can be accommodated by the minds of most people) via computer. Hence computer simulations can be more complex than those enabled by other approaches. For instance, a battlespace simulation can represent the positions, movements and interactions between millions of people, weapons and related equipment for warfare. Computer simulations can also be conducted very quickly, often on timescales many thousands or millions of times faster than the phenomena of interest in the real world. For instance, in the time it would take for a large office building to be designed and constructed in the physical world, many millions of simulations could take place within a computer's world (i.e., an element of Cyberspace). Simulations are used routinely in the organizational context to facilitate decision-making (e.g., see Law & Kelton, 1982; Turban & Aronson, 1998). Such simulations are conducted generally to support workflows (e.g., associated with waging war, designing buildings, business operations) and hence are associated most closely with doing.

Alternatively, the same technology can be used also to support knowledge flows and hence be associated more closely with learning. This represents the central idea of microworlds (Senge, 1990): simulations that are undertaken for the purpose of learning about certain systems and processes of interest in the world. One key is to simulate the real world with sufficient fidelity that decisions and actions within the simulation produce the same kinds of results and consequences that would be expected in the real world. Another key is to abstract from the details and complexities of the real world and to concentrate on the most important elements and relations. Clearly a tension exists between fidelity and abstraction in simulation models.

Moreover, through simulation a person can learn by trial and error but not suffer the consequences of making real mistakes. For instance, it has long been standard procedure for airplane pilots to have a portion of their training conducted using flight simulators. When pilots train to manage in particularly dangerous or unlikely circumstances (e.g., severe weather, catastrophic equipment malfunctions, unintended uses for aircraft), they do so generally via simulation. Should a pilot "crash" because of a mistake during a simulation, for example, he or she can learn from such mistake, reset the simulator, and try again, as many times as it takes to master the intended piloting skills or maneuvers. When flying aircraft in the physical world, by contrast, one generally has but one "opportunity" to crash and hence zero opportunity to learn from the corresponding catastrophic mistakes. In many circumstances including nuclear accidents, terrorist strikes and epidemic infections, as additional examples, simulation represents the only practical approach to training for such occasions.

Returning to the point about trial and error, this approach to learning is referred to pejoratively often, but trial and error is quite natural for people (e.g., consider how an infant learns most concepts and cause-effect relationships). Without more advanced approaches (e.g., leveraging theory, principles and decision-making tools) at hand, there may be few alternatives. The key to simulation is, one person can repeat the same actions and events many times (e.g., altering his or her approach each time and observing the results) in a relatively short period of time (e.g., hundreds or thousands of repetitions of an event can be simulated within the time required for one unfolding of the corresponding real-world event). Each repetition represents a learning opportunity. Hence a person may be able to learn quite quickly via simulation. This is why we include simulation technology here in a book on harnessing knowledge power: it can support learning activities and enhance knowledge flows.

Indeed, ongoing research includes the use of simulation technology to represent and emulate the performance of organizations that take alternate approaches to enhancing knowledge flows. Hence this approach uses a technology to enhance knowledge flows (i.e., simulation) to help people learn how to enhance knowledge flows. Consider this illustration described by Nissen and Levitt (2004) using simulation technology associated with the Virtual Design Team (VDT) research project (VDT, 2004). Use of this technology has progressed for many years since with the derivative POWer application (POWer, 2013; e.g., see Gateau et al., 2007; Nissen et al., 2008; Nissen, 2010b) and continues actively today. Using a relatively simple work process for exposition, an overview of a correspondingly simple VDT model for IS design is illustrated through the screenshot presented in Figure 4. (This particular screenshot is from the commercial product SimVision™, which emerged from VDT research.)

The organization structure is comprised of three elements: 1) a knowledge worker (i.e., person icon at top of diagram labeled "IS architect") with skills in IS architecture development; 2) a team of software designers (i.e., person icon at top of diagram labeled "IS design team") with skills in software analysis, design and programming; and 3) a project lead (i.e., person icon at top of diagram labeled "IS PM") with skills in project planning, supervision and IS design. The task structure is comprised of two work elements: 1) architecture design (i.e., rectangular icon at middle of diagram labeled "arch design"), and 2) software design (i.e., rectangular icon at middle of diagram labeled "S/W design"). The four milestones shown (i.e., project start, architecture complete, application complete, project finish) serve as markers of progress against schedule but do not involve work. The diagram in this figure illustrates for a small and simple project how models developed in the VDT environment may appear. Of course the diagram itself is clearly static, but by linking to a simulation engine, the extended representation becomes dynamic: time-varying states, conditions and results can be projected for the model. We note here for reference that very large and complex models can and have been developed to capture the scale, richness and detail of numerous diverse organizations in practice (see Kunz et al., 1998). The model discussed here, by contrast, is small, simple and for illustration only.

Now consider the software design work task from the model above. Say that a new technology for developing software architectures is to be used on this project. The problem is, none of the people who will be designing the software architecture is familiar with this new technology. Should management send its software architect to

Figure 4. VDT IS design model (adapted from Nissen, 2006)

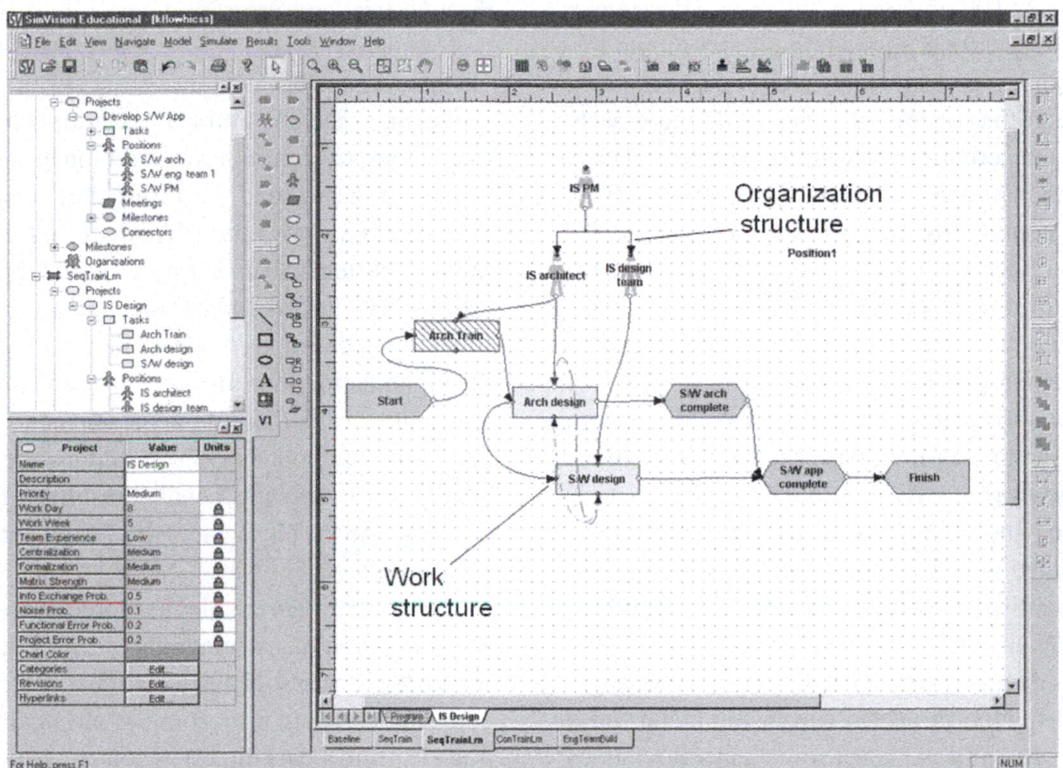

a (formal training) class to learn how to use the new technology, or should it expect this key actor to learn such technology on the job (OJT) while working on the architecture? Drawing from the discussion above, the formal training alternative would contribute principally (if not exclusively) toward knowledge flows and minimally (if at all) toward workflows while the IS-architect actor was away participating in the training course. Alternatively, the OJT approach would contribute symmetrically (i.e., principally toward doing and minimally toward learning).

Notice the inclusion in Figure 4 of a specific task for this knowledge flow activity (i.e., labeled "arch train"). Say the IS architecture actor would require three months' formal training to learn how to use this new tool well. Assume further that any formal training would start at project inception and have to be completed before the IS architecture task could begin. In the case of a formal training course, the IS-architect actor would participate in the course first and then begin work on the architecture itself. In the case of OJT, alternatively, the IS-architect actor would skip such training and begin working (e.g., learning by doing) immediately. Which represents a better approach?

Intuitively, if the IS-architect actor participates in a three-month formal training course, then one would expect the entire schedule for the IS design project to simply extend by a period close to this three-month time span. Alternatively, an experienced leader or manager would expect also for the IS-architect actor to learn valuable knowledge that enables better work performance following the formal training course. Clearly this situation represents a tradeoff that confronts nearly every leader or manager who must balance knowledge flows and workflows in an organization.

After verifying model fidelity and simulating both cases 100 times each, the project duration in the former case (i.e., attending the 3-month formal training course) turns out to be considerably less than that of the latter (i.e., OJT) approach. Although perhaps counterintuitive at first glance, the explanation is consistent with our experience. After completing the training course, the IS-architect actor brings an increase in knowledge and skill to bear on the workflow and performs substantially better on the architecture task than its OJT counterpart does. Further, such performance gain is sufficient to overcome the three-month delay in starting the project while the architect actor is away at school. Simulation of this actor's learning and doing reflects the higher skill level associated with learning from the training class and quantifies the corresponding schedule effect.

We then return to the VDT model, change some factors (e.g., actors' skill levels, course length and difficulty, project requirements), and run it repeatedly until we learn some general relations pertaining to the organization being modeled and simulated. We learn that other conditions could exist in which formal training would represent an inferior alternative. For instance: if the training course requires six months to complete instead of three; if the IS-architect actor lacks sufficient background knowledge to learn effectively through the course; if the new architecture-development tool is similar to the existing technology it replaces; if the architecture-development part of the project is relatively short and minor with respect to the other project tasks; and so forth. The key point is, through running and experimenting multiple times with the simulation model—a virtual trial-and-error approach to learning—we identify several cause-effect relations associated with this system of interest in the real world. We also stimulate knowledge flows pertaining to how a leader or manager can enhance knowledge flows associated with IS architecture development in the project. Such learning would be difficult to accomplish through trial and error, and certainly could not be completed as quickly, in the physical world as via simulation.

Further, such learning is accomplished before having to commit time and money toward a decision (i.e., to send the IS-architect to formal training class or to endure the effects of OJT with the new system). This learning is accomplished also without having to bear the consequences of some faulty decisions made while learning about the organization. For instance, we can learn—in a virtual world—that OJT represents an inferior alternative without having to endure the (cost, quality and) schedule penalty resulting from a decision—in the physical world—to go with such OJT alternative.

This technology enables us moreover to repeat the simulation many hundreds of times, all well within the time associated with either the training course or software project in the physical world. Such learning bears directly upon our knowledge flows at several phases of the knowledge life cycle. For one, we are using simulation to create new tacit knowledge pertaining to the organization and its dynamics. For another, we can use simulation also to share such knowledge by distributing copies of the simulation model to enhance the learning of others. For a third, we are using simulation further to apply such knowledge to decisions regarding whether to send the IS-architects to the formal training course.

KNOWLEDGE TECHNOLOGY PRINCIPLES

Five principles developed in this chapter help shed light on knowledge technology: 16) information technology is helpful and necessary but not sufficient for knowledge management; 17) people—not information technology—are central to tacit knowledge flows; 18) information technology plays supportive roles in most organizational work routines, whereas people play the performative roles generally; 19) expert systems, software agents, and like "intelligent" applications address and apply knowledge directly; and 20) simulation technology can enhance knowledge flows across several phases of the life cycle.

Principle 16: First, we note above how IT plays an important role in supporting knowledge flows. In many cases IT is even necessary for knowledge to flow, but there is more to flows of knowledge than processing and flowing information and data, which is the principal domain of IT. Hence leaders and managers need to employ non-technological interventions to enhance knowledge flows.

Principle 17: Second, we note above how problems abound in terms of KM programs that rely heavily upon IT. Many leaders and managers expect naïvely that IT will improve knowledge flows. Looking at the "I" in IT, however, and understanding the distinctions and relationships between knowledge and information, it should be apparent why such expectations can be considered naïve. In particular, people—not information technology—are central to tacit knowledge flows. Hence one cannot manage tacit knowledge without managing people.

Principle 18: Third, the life cycle involves different kinds of knowledge activities, grouped broadly into classes to represent localized and expanded views of KM. We note above how IT supports activities in these two classes differently. For the localized activities, IT plays a supportive role and does so quite well. For the expanded activities, however, a performative role is called for, but few extant IT applications are capable of—or used for—playing such role. Hence most IT plays a supportive role in the organization, whereas people play most of the performative roles.

Principle 19: Fourth, expert systems, software agents, and like "intelligent" applications address knowledge directly, in addition to information and data. They also enable direct action, and hence can play some of the performative roles called for above. Specifically, once developed, an expert system can apply knowledge directly to perform knowledge work. Expert systems can also be distributed broadly through the organization and used in parallel, even by novices who can sometimes raise their performance to expert levels. Hence "intelligent" applications can play a performative role in the organization.

Principle 20: Finally, we note above how simulation technology can be used to enhance knowledge flows in addition to workflows. By using simulation models to learn about some systems or processes of interest in the real world, one can create new knowledge relatively quickly and safely. Knowledge associated with a simulation model can be shared and applied also, corresponding with multiple phases of the knowledge life cycle. Hence simulation represents a different class of IT, one that facilitates learning as well as doing through virtual practice.

EXERCISES

1. Identify the two kinds of IT that you use most often in your current professional occupation or student activities. Describe briefly how each supports knowledge flows and how each supports information flows. What is the primary distinction between the support of knowledge flows versus information flows?
2. Identify two performative roles that you play in your current professional occupation or student activities and two supportive roles that you play. Describe briefly the impact each role has in terms of how well IT supports your performance.
3. Describe briefly how simulation technology could play a supportive role in your current professional occupation or student activities and how it could play a performative role.
4. Develop a small expert system that codifies your knowledge of this learning module

(i.e., knowledge technology). Download and use an expert system shell tool (e.g., KnowledgeWright) to articulate and formalize a relatively small number (e.g., 25 – 50) of rules into a computer application that could be used by someone without your level of expertise about knowledge technology to make decisions or to solve problems that would otherwise be difficult for such person to accomplish. Feel free to incorporate aspects of the decision-making and problem-solving context of your professional organization into the expert system if that proves helpful to you. Or feel free instead to develop the system in a context-free manner comparable to that of this learning module.

REFERENCES

Gateau, J. B., Leweling, T. A., Looney, J. P., & Nissen, M. E. (2007). Hypothesis testing of edge organizations: Modeling the C2 organization design space. In *Proceedings International Command & Control Research & Technology Symposium*. Newport, RI: Academic Press.

KnowledgeWright. (2004). *KnowledgeWright expert system development shell*. Retrieved 2004, from http://www.amzi.com/products/knowledgewright.html

Kunz, J. C., Levitt, R. E., & Jin, Y. (1998). The virtual design team: A computational simulation model of project organizations. *Communications of the ACM*, *41*(11), 84–92. doi:10.1145/287831.287844.

Law, A. M., & Kelton, W. D. (1982). *Simulation modeling and analysis*. New York, NY: McGraw-Hill.

Nissen, M. E. (2010). *CyberKM: Harnessing dynamic knowledge for competitive advantage through cyberspace* (Technical Report No. NPS-IS-10-006). Monterey, CA: Naval Postgraduate School.

Nissen, M. E., Kamel, M. N., & Sengupta, K. C. (2000). Integrated analysis and design of knowledge systems and processes. *Information Resources Management Journal*, *13*(1), 24–42. doi:10.4018/irmj.2000010103.

Nissen, M. E., & Levitt, R. E. (2004). Agent-based modeling of knowledge dynamics. *Knowledge Management Research & Practice*, *2*(3), 169–183. doi:10.1057/palgrave.kmrp.8500039.

Nissen, M. E., Orr, R., & Levitt, R. E. (2008). Streams of shared knowledge: Computational expansion of organization theory. *Knowledge Management Research & Practice*, *6*(2), 124–140. doi:10.1057/kmrp.2008.1.

POWer. (2013). *Edge center*. Retrieved from http://www.nps.edu/Academics/Centers/CEP/

Senge, P. M. (1990). *The fifth discipline: The art and practice of the learning organization*. New York: Doubleday.

Turban, E., & Aronson, J. (1998). *Decision support systems and intelligent systems*. Upper Saddle River, NJ: Prentice-Hall.

VDT. (2004). *The virtual design team research group website*. Retrieved from http://www.stanford.edu/group/CIFE/VDT/ 2004

Chapter 5
Knowing and Learning

ABSTRACT

This chapter discusses the concepts knowing, which involves knowledge in action, and learning, which involves knowledge in motion. Knowing and learning are tightly interrelated knowledge-based activities, which are connected strongly by the knowledge-based activity doing. The authors introduce each concept separately but weave together many of their dynamic interrelations in the organizational context. The chapter concludes with five knowing and learning principles and includes exercises to stimulate critical thought, learning, and discussion. This chapter builds upon and culminates all of its predecessors to complete the first section of the book.

KNOWING

Here we discuss the concept knowing generally and as a complement to knowledge. We then consider knowing in terms of appropriability and organizational reach.

Knowing and Knowledge

Knowing refers to knowledge in action. This term is used often to differentiate knowledge-based action from the knowledge that enables it. Such differentiation is referred to as epistemology of practice vs. epistemology of possession (Cook & Brown, 1999). The former becomes manifest through what is done. Pragmatism (e.g., as articulated by Dewy) provides a philosophical basis for understanding epistemology of practice. Tacit knowledge practiced in group settings is privileged often in this former view. The latter becomes manifest through what is known. Cartesianism (e.g., as articulated by Descartes) provides a philosophical basis for understanding epistemology of possession. Explicit knowledge possessed by individuals is privileged often in the latter view. Both views can obtain simultaneously and complementarily.

The classic example involves riding a bicycle (Polanyi, 1967). Through the action of riding a bicycle, a person demonstrates his or her knowing how to do so. The knowledge associated with such riding can be tacit as well as explicit. For instance, an effective bicycle rider will certainly be able to balance on two wheels while moving and to turn by leaning into corners, but if one asks such rider in which direction he or she turns the handlebars when falling off balance, it is unlikely that the rider will be able to answer the question (see Cook & Brown, 1999, p. 384). Alternatively, if one asks such rider in which direction he or she leans when turning through a corner, it is very likely that the rider will be able to answer the question.

DOI: 10.4018/978-1-4666-4727-5.ch005

In the former case of turning the handlebars, a rider is able to employ this riding knowledge effectively but unable to articulate it (i.e., the knowledge remains tacit). He or she knows how to balance but cannot explain the process to others. This phenomenon is common across a diversity of knowledge-based activities, and it characterizes well the nature of tacit knowledge. In the latter case of leaning into a corner, the rider is able to both employ and articulate the enabling knowledge (i.e., the knowledge is made explicit). He or she knows how to turn and can explain the process (at least in part) to others. This phenomenon is common across a diversity of knowledge-based activities also, but it characterizes instead the nature of explicit knowledge.

In both cases, the rider is able to demonstrate knowing how to ride a bicycle, and in both cases, the rider has knowledge of how to ride bicycles. In other words, when a person rides a bicycle, he or she knows how to do so, but such person retains knowledge of how to ride even when not riding actively. Knowing and knowledge thus can both obtain simultaneously. Yet they are different: one involves manifest action, whereas the other involves potential for action. We discuss such knowledge-based action and potential in greater depth toward the end of this chapter. Knowing and knowledge are also complementary: the action of knowing cannot obtain without the enabling knowledge; and the enabling knowledge cannot be put to use except through the action of knowing. We discuss such complementation in greater depth also in subsequent sections below.

Additionally, this simultaneous and complementary relationship between knowing and knowledge is dynamic and can be mutually reinforcing. Continuing with the bicycle example, a beginner may find it productive to read a book or like artifact of explicit knowledge about how to ride bicycles. Here theoretical knowledge about riding can reinforce practical knowing through riding. Many similar knowing activities (e.g., flying an airplane, solving differential equations, playing a musical instrument) involve theory as well as practice. Established theory can be learned often through interaction with explicit knowledge sources such as books, for instance. In contrast, practice involves experience with the real world. Nonetheless, books about the real world can serve to inform practice, and practice in the world can serve as the basis for writing books. Hence theoretical knowledge about how to ride can facilitate knowing through riding. Yet the person still needs practice—and hence to experience direct interaction with a bicycle in the physical world—in order to know riding. Likewise, a proficient rider may be able to experiment while riding—for instance, leaning purposefully in a particular direction and noting in which direction he or she turns the handlebars to maintain balance—and make explicit some knowledge that remained tacit formerly.

Recall from above our discussion of simulation technology. Notice that interacting virtually (e.g., via simulation) falls somewhere in between these two cases of theoretical knowledge and practical knowing. As above, theoretical knowledge (e.g., dynamics and balance) is available readily through books, websites, videos and like explicit sources that do not require riding in the physical world, and a beginner in particular can learn much about how to ride bicycles through such theory. However, practical knowing (e.g., leaning one's body)—which requires riding in the physical world generally—can be learned instead through interaction with a simulator, as a person can engage—virtually in a simulated world—in actions that are similar to those associated with riding a bicycle physically. Further, through interaction with a simulator, a person can practice riding without encountering the sometimes mortal hazards (e.g., maneuvering through automobile traffic) and physical limitations (e.g., adverse weather) of riding physically. Nonetheless, even the best simulators are nothing more than sophisticated dynamic models of reality. Using a simulator is never exactly the same as practicing in the real world.

These relationships between knowing and knowledge (e.g., simultaneous and complementary interrelations, mutually reinforcing effects) are not limited to physical activities such as riding bicycles. For instance, they pertain as well to decision-making, speaking in front of people, solving calculus problems, and others. Nor are they limited to individuals. For instance, they pertain as well to groups, organizations and whole societies knowing how to do something and possessing knowledge of how to do it.

An organizational example of this phenomenon pertains to leadership and management. Nearly every organization requires leadership and management (e.g., of people, assets, projects) activities and has people assigned to leader and manager roles. Different people clearly vary in their leadership and management efficacy, but most people would argue that practical experience (i.e., knowing) represents a critical element of being a proficient leader or manager. Likewise, nearly every university offers courses, certificates and degree programs in leadership and management and has students learning about leader and manager activities. Different students clearly vary in their scholastic efficacy, but most people would argue that knowledge learned (e.g., through study) represents a critical element of graduating from a leadership and management program.

Further to the point, many people opine that education in leadership and management (i.e., theoretical knowledge) can enhance a person's leader and manager efficacy (i.e., practical knowing). This accounts in part for the reason that many MBAs, for instance, are able to obtain leadership and management positions in organizations, even when they have little prior leader or manager experience, and why many experienced leaders and managers are encouraged to pursue education in leadership and management to complement their experiential knowledge. Nonetheless, prior experience represents generally a necessary prerequisite for someone without leadership and management education to obtain such employment. This accounts in part for the reason that many organizations select leaders and managers based principally upon leadership and management experience, as opposed to courses, certificates and degrees.

Knowing and Appropriability

Knowing relates further to the appropriability of knowledge. Recall our discussion above, in which we contrast knowledge and information in terms of enabling competitive advantage. Knowledge—particularly tacit knowledge—is difficult to imitate and hence can be used as a sustainable basis of competitive advantage. Information—and most explicit knowledge—in contrast represents a public good that is difficult to keep private over time. Such contrast has to do with the kind of knowledge (e.g., tacit, explicit) and its appropriability. Alternatively, knowing has to do with the use of knowledge—regardless of kind—and its appropriability. Both explicit knowledge about riding bicycles and tacit knowledge about balancing, for instance, can help enable knowing through riding. Likewise, both explicit knowledge acquired via leadership and management education and tacit knowledge derived from leader and manager experience, as another instance, can help enhance knowing through leading and managing.

The key is, where knowledge remains latent in ***stocks*** (e.g., as knowledge inventory; consider explicit and tacit knowledge possessed but not put to use), it offers *potential* for action (Dierickx & Cool, 1989), but where knowledge becomes manifest through ***dynamic*** action (i.e., knowing), the associated action drives performance (Saviotti, 1998). Although latent knowledge stocked in an organization has value, such knowledge also entails an investment in its acquisition and storage (e.g., to create, organize, share). Until an organization can put such knowledge to use, it cannot expect to generate positive returns from its knowledge investment. Hence appropriability depends upon the use of knowledge (i.e., knowing), as well as the type of knowledge (e.g., tacit, explicit) acquired and possessed.

For instance, consider a musician specializing in the piano. Learning to play a musical instrument such as this requires an investment of many years or possibly even decades of time, energy and money into lessons, equipment and practice, in addition to some natural musical ability. Such investment increases a musician's knowledge inventory and enables increasingly better action in terms of playing the piano. The investment increases a musician's potential to play well, but without action, no amount of piano knowledge left stocked as such is likely to generate a return on the musician's investment in piano practice. Even the best piano player in the world, for example, is unlikely to earn a living based upon piano playing knowledge unless he or she performs for or instructs others (i.e., puts knowledge to use through action). Likewise, the organization that invests in knowledge but fails to put it to use will encounter comparable difficulty "earning a living" (e.g., realizing a pecuniary return on its investment). Increasing stocks of knowledge inventory are valuable and necessary to enable productive work in an organization, but performing the associated work processes is what generates returns on organizational investments in knowledge.

Our differentiation above between knowing and knowledge can be viewed in terms of what some call a "knowing-doing gap" (Pfeffer & Sutton, 1999). Although the terms *knowing* and *doing* as discussed here differ from our introduction and preferred usage (We would refer to it as a 'knowledge-knowing gap' or a knowledge 'potential-action gap'.), the discussion merits inclusion here. A "knowing-doing gap" manifests itself in part when organizations know better than to do what they do. For instance, an organization with expertise and experience (i.e., knowledge) in a certain line of work (e.g., marketing, engineering, manufacturing) may repeat past mistakes (i.e., knowing), even though knowledge of such mistakes—and conceivably how to prevent them—may be possessed already by the organization. Such possession could be in terms of management knowledge learned by one or more managers through MBA degree programs (e.g., organizational mistakes that are common across enterprises), direct experience by managers with past mistakes and their corresponding solutions (i.e., tacit knowledge), formal documentation of past mistakes and solutions stored in a lessons learned archive (i.e., explicit knowledge), and others. By any account, such knowledge is possessed by the organization, but it is not put to use through knowing.

Organizational memory (Stein & Zwass, 1995; Walsh & Ungson, 1991) appears to play an important role in explaining gaps like these. Where an organization learns from education or experience, for example, it relies upon storage, access and recall processes to preserve, locate and retrieve the knowledge associated with its experience. Many organizations do not know what they know (O'Dell et al., 1998). Hence managers with problems do not bother to ask managers with solutions before repeating past mistakes. Similarly, many organizations fail to make applicable lessons learned reports easy to locate and interpret. This is despite enforcement of formal procedures for writing and filing them. Also, as with riding a bicycle, reading an explicit document about how to avoid repeating a past mistake may not be sufficient for avoiding such mistake in practice.

A "knowing-doing gap" manifests itself in part also when organizations know how to do something they do not do. For instance, one particular unit of an organization may have demonstrated superior performance pertaining to some important work process, product or service, even though other seemingly identical organizational units remain unable to replicate its high-performance knowing. Such replication could be approached through personnel changes (e.g., assigning people from the high-performance organization to the average ones), organizational routines (e.g., writing work procedures for the average organizations that describe the processes performed by the high-performance one), hiring expertise through external consultants, and like approaches practiced widely under the rubric *knowledge transfer*. Clearly the relevant knowledge needs to flow from one coordinate (e.g., individual person, organizational unit, work location, application time) to another, and such knowledge must be put to use. Hence a "knowing-doing gap" can stem from problems with knowledge flows as well as memory aids.

Knowing and Reach

Knowing can take place at many levels of analysis (i.e., reach), from the individual to groups of organizations. Individual knowing is probably the simplest to understand, because we all do it every day. Indeed, the reader of this text is knowing how to read and understand intellectual material right now. Riding bicycles, playing chess, solving analytical problems, negotiating contracts, searching for information, and many other individual activities require knowledge for action and hence constitute knowing when such knowledge is put to use. Organizational routines such as establishing policies, developing products, training personnel, competing in markets, influencing political-legal-economic environments, attracting capital, and many others require knowledge likewise and hence constitute knowing as well—when put to use—but at a higher level of reach or social aggregation.

Of course no practical organization can function without the individuals and groups of people in it. Yet there is more to what organizations do than can be accounted for by the activities of its individuals and groups at any point in time. For instance, most organizations continue to function effectively even if one individual calls in sick for a day. The same cannot be said generally about the sick individual. As another instance, organizational routines involving many different people can effect useful actions (e.g., product innovation) even when none of the individual participants knows all of the activities of the routine. Organizational routines can also continue long after all of the original individuals have been replaced by other people. This point regarding level of social aggregation is important. Knowing can reach well beyond the knowledge and actions of individuals in an organizational context. Indeed, the power of knowledge put to use for action is said to "amplify" (Nonaka, 1994, p. 20) through increases in organizational reach.

For instance, consider a skilled soccer player, who stands out as a star on his or her team and is possibly even an all-star in whatever league the team participates in. Soccer is a sport that requires considerable investment in knowledge about scoring tactics, physical conditioning, ball-handling techniques and other topics, in addition to some natural athleticism. As with the musician example noted above, such learning and investment increase an athlete's knowledge inventory and enable increasingly better action in terms of playing soccer. The investment increases an athlete's potential to play well. As with the musician example also, however, without action, no amount of soccer knowledge left stocked as inventory is likely to generate a return on the athlete's (cf. a coach) investment in soccer learning.

Additionally, soccer is a team sport. Clearly a skillful individual player is likely to perform well—by putting knowledge to use through knowing—in soccer games, but depending on skill levels of the various other teammates, the superior knowledge and knowing of an individual star may or may not be sufficient for the team to play well. A musical analog to this would follow where an individual pianist (e.g., even a virtuoso) plays as part of a (perhaps mediocre) jazz band or symphony orchestra that exhibits only mediocre performance overall.

Now consider if every player on the soccer team has superior skill at the level of this star. Such a team is likely to play well—again, by putting knowledge to use through knowing—and accomplish more than could be done through a single player. For instance, passing the ball between different players clearly represents a critical part of soccer. No single player is likely to take the ball in an unassisted manner (e.g., without passing) past all players on an opposing team, for example. Likewise with a band or orchestra, an ensemble of skilled musicians is likely to play well—through knowing—and accomplish more than could be done by a single player (e.g., attempting to play many instruments simultaneously). One can see by example how both music and soccer knowledge that reaches beyond the individual can amplify performance through skillful knowing of multiple players.

Nonetheless, our discussion thus far has ignored that a key aspect of organizational performance involves coordination of diverse individuals' knowledge and performance. Even replicating individual knowledge and knowing through multiple players may be insufficient to amplify performance across broader reaches of social aggregation. People as individuals in groups, teams and organizations must know who is responsible for which activities at what times, for example; such coordinative knowledge extends often beyond the individuals' playing skills. Indeed, people need to know how to work with one another and how to coordinate their mutual actions for organizational performance, sometimes even suboptimizing or sacrificing their individual performance in the process.

On the soccer field, for instance, assisting others with the performance of their activities (e.g., helping a teammate to score a goal instead of attempting to score individually) represents a critical part of soccer. Indeed, most goals on winning soccer teams are scored via such "assists" (e.g., passing to the center) from teammates. Sometimes the coordinative knowledge to assist is possessed and shared by a coach or team captain who calls out for passing the ball or assisting in other ways, but at other times the players themselves know how and when to assist (e.g., by having practiced and played together before).

Likewise with jazz bands and other collections of musical performers, many members take turns soloing (e.g., playing accompaniment rhythms to support other soloists instead of attempting to solo individually), thereby enriching the combined performance. As above, sometimes the coordinative knowledge to accompany is possessed and shared by a conductor or band leader who signals for switching the soloing lead or accompanying in other ways, but at other times the players themselves know how and when to switch (e.g., by having practiced and played together before).

Examples from manufacturing organizations pertain as well. For instance, few engineers are able to mass produce the devices they design; few machine operators are able to design the devices they mass produce; and sometimes the coordinative knowledge to design in ways that facilitate manufacturing is possessed and shared by a leader of manager, but at other times the engineers themselves know how and when to design as such (e.g., having designed for and interacted with manufacturing people before).

However, here a noticeable difference between music and soccer (and manufacturing) becomes apparent. Soccer is a competitive sport, in which performance depends upon how well one team competes against another. Hence an additional element of knowing beyond the individual—and even coordinated group action—is notably critical: how to play and compete against others. Similar examples of organizational knowing in a competitive or adversarial manner arise in business, war, politics and like domains. They take on a game-theoretic aspect of analysis.

A business firm, for instance, must know more than designing and mass producing quality devices. To compete effectively in business, the firm needs to also develop products that meet consumer demands (e.g., in terms of product features, quality, price) better than its rival firms do. A military unit, as a similar instance, must know more than operating weapons and coordinating fighting forces. To compete effectively in war, it needs to also battle (e.g., in terms of attacks, defenses, logistics) better than its rival armies and navies do. Political knowing in terms of organizing, fundraising and communicating follows accordingly. Such knowing must be accomplished better by one politician than by rivals in an election or on an issue. In other words, one must consider the knowing by all competitors, and relative performance considerations pertain as much as or more than absolute ones do.

Indeed, any seasoned coach can tell stories about individual, star athletes not knowing how to play well against others on an opposing team, and many teams comprised of star, individual players have failed to win games, even against teams comprised of "inferior" individuals. National sports teams assembled for Olympic and like international events provide a visible example. Experienced leaders and managers have similar stories about high levels of individual knowledge put into action (i.e., knowing) at the team level (e.g., innovation projects, territorial battles, political campaigns) with disappointing results. This same principle applies organization-wide as well, with even greater opportunities for knowledge-based performance to be amplified.

LEARNING

Here we discuss the concept learning generally and as the movement of knowledge. We then consider knowing, doing and learning in terms of knowledge stocks and flows, and we delineate their complementary, dynamic effects on organizational performance and competitive advantage over time.

Learning and Knowledge

Learning refers to knowledge in motion. The concept is used most often to characterize the creation or acquisition of new knowledge, but the movement of knowledge (i.e., flows) between coordinates (e.g., person, organization, place, time) need not be "new" (We use quotation marks here, because the question of whether any knowledge can ever be new remains a topic of epistemological debate.) to the entire world (e.g., knowledge developed through scientific discovery). Rather, such knowledge needs only to be new in the local context of its coordinates (e.g., to an individual or organizational acquirer, at a particular point in space or time).

Classroom instruction represents a clear example at both the individual and group levels. In the majority of circumstances, an instructor knows the subject matter of a course already, but a student acquires "new" knowledge through learning; such knowledge is new to the student but known already by the instructor. A student may, for instance in a business, engineering or information systems course, learn about a particular class of design mistakes that are common across many enterprises and circumstances. In this case, knowledge moves from one coordinate (e.g., instructor, university, classroom, class time) to another (e.g., student, university, classroom, class time). The knowledge flow corresponds to learning at the individual level.

Moreover, this same knowledge can flow across different groups of students (e.g., one group taking the course during the fall semester, then another group taking the course during the spring semester, and so forth) over time. Say a large number of former students, to continue this instance, learn over time to recognize the particular and common class of design mistakes noted above. As these students graduate and become employees of diverse firms that engage in design processes, different departments in many such firms can learn—through the former students—how to address such mistakes. In this case, knowledge moves from one coordinate (e.g., instructor, university, classroom, many class times) to several others (e.g., many students, many enterprises, many design processes, many product-development projects). The knowledge flow corresponds to learning at the individual, group and organizational levels.

Like knowing, learning is action-oriented. A student may know how to learn course material through study, for instance, but he or she is unlikely to learn and perform well (e.g., on an examination) unless such learning knowledge is put to use through homework, for example. Also like knowing, learning is enabled by knowledge. A student of advanced mathematics, for example, needs to learn the fundamental concepts and techniques upon which such advanced coursework builds before progressing to more advanced mathematical concepts and techniques. Indeed, the more that is known in a particular domain, the easier it is to learn something new in that same domain (see Cohen & Levinthal, 1990). Hence learning represents a particular kind of knowing that is focused on moving knowledge between coordinates.

This applies to larger social aggregations (e.g., reach across groups and organizations) also. An organization may know how to learn about producing electronic products, for instance, but it is unlikely to perform well (e.g., in a product market) unless such learning knowledge is put to use through iterative design and prototyping, for example. Also like organizational knowing, organizational learning is enabled by knowledge. A manufacturer of high-performance electronic products, for example, needs to learn the basic product designs and manufacturing methods upon which such high-performance electronics build before progressing to more sophisticated approaches. Indeed, the more that is known in a particular industry, the easier it is to learn something new in that same industry (see Cohen & Levinthal, 1990 again). Hence learning represents a particular kind of knowing that pertains to organizations as well as to individuals.

To reiterate from above, learning—like knowing—can take place at many levels of analysis, from the individual to groups of organizations. Individual learning is probably the simplest to understand, because we all do it every day. Indeed, the reader of this text is learning intellectual material right now. Riding bicycles, playing chess, solving analytical problems, negotiating contracts, searching for information, and many other individual activities require knowledge and hence involve learning. Organizational routines such as establishing policies, developing products, training personnel, competing in markets, influencing political-legal-economic environments, attracting capital, and many others require knowledge likewise and hence constitute learning as well, albeit at a higher level of reach or social aggregation. Learning also plays a central role in the examples from above concerning music, sports, electronics and others. We indicate too how competition in diverse organizational domains such as business, war and politics relies critically also upon learning. Hence learning—like knowing—can amplify knowledge as it reaches beyond the individual level of social aggregation.

LEARNING-DOING TENSION

Here we introduce the concept doing generally as a particular form of knowing. We then consider learning and doing as competing activities, and we interrelate these concepts with organizational exploration and exploitation.

Knowing and Doing

We note above how knowledge put into action represents knowing. We identify doing as one particular form of knowing and learning as another. Doing refers to knowledge-based work. People must know how to do what they do. Hence doing represents one kind of knowing activity. Indeed, when we mention knowing in terms of knowledge-based action, we refer generally to doing, and we use these terms knowing and doing interchangeably often and unless the context requires more precision in our language. Nonetheless, as noted above, learning represents knowledge-based action—and hence knowing—also, so the comparison of learning and doing is technically more precise than that of learning and knowing is. Again, we use these terms knowing and doing interchangeably often and unless the context requires more precision in our language.

Learning and Doing

This discussion builds upon the tension between knowledge flow (learning) and workflow (doing) introduced previously. Because people's time and energy are constrained generally, a tension exists between knowing in terms of learning and knowing associated with doing. To the extent that someone spends all of his or her time learning, little time is left for doing. This is why most people do not get paid a salary for attending school, for instance. Likewise, to the extent that someone spends all of his or her time doing, little time is left for learning. This is why most people do not attend school while working, as a related instance. To the extent that someone combines learning and doing, then a compromise on both doing and learning can obtain. The specific mix of these two knowing activities (i.e., learning and doing) represents an important decision—the criteria, demands and efficacy of which will vary from context to context.

Where successful performance is generating rich rewards, for instance, and a stable environment provides negligible threat or reason for change, then learning activities may be de-emphasized appropriately with respect to their doing counterparts. In the case of an individual leader or manager, for example, he or she may be leading or managing effectively in an organization and receiving frequent promotions and salary increases as rewards. Such leader or manager may see little value in pursuing graduate education in leadership and management, for instance in this situation. Indeed, he or she could envision legitimately the associated educational coursework detracting from his or her leader or manager performance and conceivably even jeopardizing proximate rewards. A similar example pertains to a manufacturing firm with a successful product that is earning high margins for the company and has growing market share in its competitive arena. Such firm may see little value in augmenting research and development (R&D) efforts to enhance this product, for instance in this situation. Indeed, it could envision legitimately the associated R&D investment reducing margins and a redesigned product conceivably jeopardizing market share.

Alternatively, where current performance is viewed as unsuccessful, the environment is unstable and threatening, or similar conditions suggest an individual or organization may not be satisfied with current goal achievement, then learning activities may be re-emphasized appropriately with respect to their doing counterparts . A leader or manager who is passed over repeatedly for promotion, or is not receiving salary increases, provides an example at the individual level. An employee who has been laid off, or whose skills appear no longer to be valued highly by employers, provides a similar example. A manufacturer that is not earning margins on products, or that is losing market share, provides an example at the organizational level. The firm whose technology becomes dated, outmatched or even obsolete provides a similar example.

This tension between learning and doing can be characterized in terms of exploration vs. exploitation (March, 1991). On the one side, individuals, groups and organizations can spend time and energy exploring new opportunities, seeking new knowledge, and experimenting with different approaches to current activities. Such exploration is focused on learning and can lead to innovation and improved performance over time through new customers and markets, new product discoveries, and new work processes. Without such exploration, performance over time tends to remain static and may decline eventually, as markets become depleted, existing knowledge falls behind the state of the art, and work processes ossify.

Consider an individual pianist, for instance, who learns to play only one song. He or she may become exceptionally proficient at playing that specific song, but experience suggests that playing only this one musical piece may become quite boring over time to the individual musician, and audiences are unlikely to pay repeatedly to see the same performance again and again. A similar observation likely applies to the individual soccer player, as a related instance, who learns only a single skill (e.g., taking penalty kicks). Over time the individual player is likely to become bored with practicing and performing the same skill repeatedly, and he or she may not be able to remain with a competitive team if other players know multiple skills. The leader or manager who fails to keep pace with advancing information technology may similarly not find much excitement through working with dated systems, and he or she may not remain employable if such systems are replaced by newer technology. Other comparable examples apply here too.

This observation likely applies further to bands and orchestras as well as individual musicians. This explains in part why most players, groups and symphonies invest considerable time and energy into learning and practicing a diversity of songs and musical scores. Likewise with the soccer team that learns only one way to get the ball downfield into an opponent's area (e.g., a long-ball kick). It is unlikely to succeed by using repeatedly the same approach, again and again, against opposing teams. The same can be said for a business, military or political organization that focuses exclusively on one technology, tactic or issue, respectively, that becomes dominated by another in a corresponding market, battle or election. This phenomenon relates to the concepts competency traps (Levitt & March, 1988) and core rigidities (Hargadon & Fanelli, 2002), which describe how organizations can become exceptionally proficient at certain work processes that fail to ensure performance (e.g., in product markets) over time. In short, they overemphasize exploitation of extant knowledge and underemphasize exploration to learn new knowledge. Competency traps and core rigidities can afflict individuals, groups, organizations, nations and whole societies.

On the other side, individuals, groups and organizations may not benefit from devoting all of their time and energy toward exploration; rather, they can spend time and energy exploiting current opportunities, using existing knowledge, and fine tuning institutionalized approaches to current activities. Such exploitation is focused on doing and seeks current performance by tapping existing customers and markets, delivering existing products, and routinizing extant work processes. Without such exploitation, current performance can suffer and decline, as market opportunities are missed, existing knowledge is not applied productively, and work processes are not accomplished effectively. Here we re-emphasize the need for a pianist to perform (i.e., put knowledge into action) in order to generate returns on investments made in knowledge. The same applies to the musical group or orchestra as well as the soccer player or team. The same can be said also for exploitation in business, warfare, politics and other knowledge-based endeavors. Without exploitation of existing knowledge, few organizations (or organisms) are viable. Given limited time and energy, however, a focus on exploration requires some reduction in focus on exploitation, and vice versa. The specific mix of exploration and exploitation employed represents an important decision. Moreover, a tension between learning and doing (i.e., exploration and exploitation) persists at all levels of reach or social aggregation. Selecting a specific mix of the two foci represents a context-dependent decision to make, whether by individuals, organizations or entire societies.

Knowledge Stocks and Flows

We note above also how knowledge in action (i.e., knowing, but more precisely doing) relates most closely with exploiting extant knowledge stocks or inventories and how knowledge in motion (i.e., knowing, but more precisely learning) relates more closely with knowledge flows associated with exploration. In particular, doing is enabled principally by stocks of knowledge, and generally greater inventories of knowledge enable correspondingly greater performance through action. This relationship is illustrated by our examples from music, sports, electronics and other domains, but these examples illustrate further how doing requires learning—often in substantial amounts over extended periods of time—for the accumulation of such knowledge stocks. This pertains to musicians learning to play instruments, athletes learning to play sports, managers learning to supervise employees, warriors learning to fight battles, politicians learning to raise funds, and quite generally to nearly every knowledge-based activity.

Three important ramifications obtain: 1) the more the learning, the greater the knowledge inventory; 2) the greater the knowledge inventory, the better the doing and hence performance through action; and 3) the greater the knowledge inventory, the faster the learning. Hence learning and doing are interconnected tightly in a mutually reinforcing manner. Such mutually reinforcing processes contribute to the sustainability of competitive advantage based on knowledge. Specifically, the farther ahead one competitor can get in terms of knowledge, the faster such competitor can learn and increase knowledge accumulation. This makes it increasingly difficult for rival competitors to catch up should they fall behind.

The dynamic effect on knowledge and performance is illustrated in Figure 1. Here we include three axes. The cumulative stock or inventory of knowledge is represented by the vertical axis. Time is represented by the horizontal axis. The third axis represents organizational performance. As above, flow time of knowledge is represented by the thickness of arrows used to delineate flow vectors in the figure. Say some important, new organizational knowledge is developed (i.e., through learning), in a particular domain, somewhere in an organization. Developing such knowledge adds to the stock level for this domain as denoted by the point labeled "C_1" in the figure. By developing new knowledge as such, this point is positioned above the origin in the figure (i.e., $C_1 > 0$). Knowledge stocked to this level enables the organization to accomplish some new, corresponding knowing activity (i.e., through doing). Accomplishing this new activity effects initial organizational performance at the level labeled "A_1" in the figure. Notice this vector is represented by a relatively thick arrow. This denotes proportionately slow flow of knowledge as the knowledge-enabled action is accomplished for the first time.

Figure 1. Amplifying dynamic organizational knowledge and performance

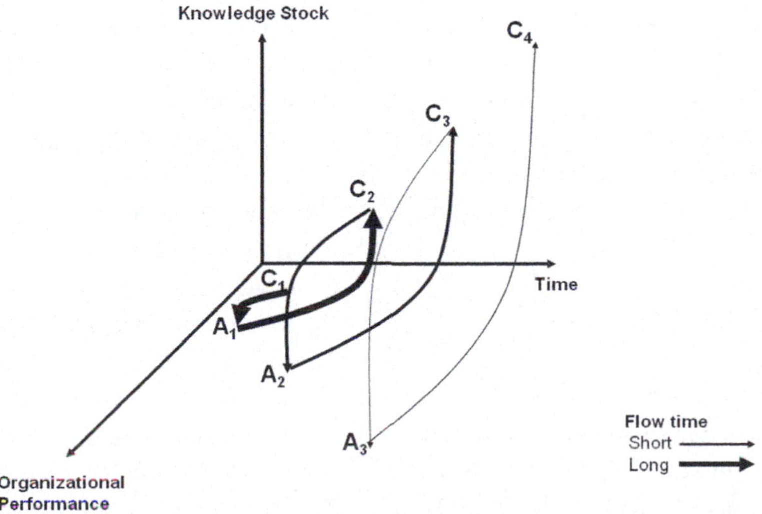

Now as the organization puts this new knowledge into action (i.e., doing), say that it learns through the experience and develops additional new knowledge (i.e., learning). This additional knowledge adds further to the stock level as denoted by the point labeled "C_2" in the figure. Notice this latter point is positioned higher up along the *Knowledge Stock* axis than the former point is (i.e., $C_2 > C_1$). Knowledge stocked to this higher level enables the organization to perform its activities more effectively as denoted by the point labeled "A_2" in the figure. Notice this latter point is positioned farther out along the *Organizational Performance* axis than the former point is (i.e., $A_2 > A_1$). Notice also that the flow vector is represented by a thinner arrow. This denotes relatively faster flows of knowledge that result from the increased knowledge stock.

This pattern continues: greater knowledge and better performance (i.e., at the levels denoted by points C_2 and A_2, respectively) lead to progressively faster learning (e.g., thinner flow vector arrows) and commensurately greater accumulation of knowledge stock (e.g., at the level denoted by point C_3); this greater knowledge stock enables proportionately better performance (e.g., at the level denoted by point A_3), faster learning (e.g., even thinner flow vector arrows), and greater accumulation of knowledge stock (e.g., at the level denoted by point C_4); and so forth. A competitor with lower knowledge inventory or stock than possessed by our focal organization is unlikely to perform as well, will likely learn less rapidly over time, and so forth, being left ever farther behind. This helps to delineate how a knowledge-based competitive advantage can be sustained over time.

PATH DEPENDENCIES

The dynamic cycle of learning (i.e., focused principally on knowledge flows) and doing (i.e., focused principally on knowledge stocks) is discussed above in terms of mutual reinforcement and highlighted in terms of enabling competitive advantage to be sustained through time. Innovation, for instance, involves applying current knowledge to enable novel action (Hargadon & Fanelli, 2002). Aside from good luck and serendipitous discovery, a person, group or organization must acquire knowledge generally in some domain before expecting realistically to become innovative in that domain. Hence learning represents a necessary precursor to doing through the action of innovation. At the same time, innovation provides opportunities to increase the range of potential actions. A person, group or organization can learn from failure as well as success to improve the process of innovation, for instance. Hence doing through innovation can augment powerfully actions associated with learning how to innovate. Learning and doing represent important, complementary enablers: the more the learning, the more the doing opportunities; and the more the doing, the more the learning opportunities.

Consider, for instance, a group that forms to market a new financial product. Say the members of this group are experienced with marketing consumer products but inexperienced with financial products. This group must acquire knowledge in the financial domain before expecting realistically to market such latter product effectively. Hence learning represents a necessary precursor to doing through the action of marketing financial products. At the same time, the doing of marketing provides opportunities to increase the range of potential actions. The marketing group can learn from failure as well as success to improve the process of marketing the new financial product, for instance. Here doing through marketing a new financial product augments actions associated with learning how to market such product. In this example, the more the doing through marketing the new financial product, the more the learning opportunities; and the more the learning about such marketing, the more the doing opportunities.

However, learning and doing also represent important, complementary inhibitors. This phenomenon goes by several names (e.g., "skilled incompetence," "single-loop learning"; see

Argyris & Schon, 1978). The learning that has been accomplished at any point in time determines what knowledge an individual, group or organization possesses at that time. Hence the potential range of actions available for doing is limited by the knowledge possessed. Whereas such knowledge enables a certain set of actions that require knowledge that was learned previously, this same knowledge also inhibits another set of actions that require knowledge that was not learned previously. Economists characterize this in terms of opportunity cost; that is, what one forgoes by making one particular choice instead of another.

Likewise, the doing that is performed over any period of time influences what knowledge an individual, group or organization learns. Hence the universe of experiences available for learning is limited by the actions undertaken. Whereas such doing effects a certain set of actions from which learning through experience can obtain, it also inhibits learning from another set of actions that have yet to be experienced. Building upon our discussion above, learning and doing are essential for the development and sustainment of core competencies, which can enable and sustain competitive advantage, but they suffer from potential to develop and sustain core rigidities also, which can erode or even preclude competitive advantage.

Consider further the new financial product instance from above. The learning that has been accomplished at the time of product launch determines what knowledge the group possesses at that time. Hence the potential range of actions available for marketing is limited by the new-product knowledge possessed. Whereas such knowledge enables a certain set of marketing actions that require the product knowledge that was learned previously, it also inhibits another set of actions that require knowledge that was not learned previously. Likewise, the doing that is performed over any period of time influences what knowledge the group learns. Here the universe of marketing experiences available for learning is limited by the actions undertaken toward the new financial product. In this example, such doing effects a certain set of marketing actions from which learning through experience can obtain, but it also inhibits learning from another set of actions that have yet to be experienced. Hence learning and doing are path-dependent: each is linked closely with the time-based behavior of the other.

With this, we establish links between knowing and learning, exploitation and exploration, doing and learning, and action and potential. Each of these links appears to be dynamic, with some involving mutual reinforcement (e.g., knowing and learning, action and potential) and others illuminating tension (e.g., exploration and exploitation, learning and doing). By understanding such dynamics, one can harness better the power of knowledge in an organization.

KNOWING AND LEARNING PRINCIPLES

Five principles developed in this chapter help shed light on organizational knowing and learning: 21) knowing reflects knowledge in action and is required to realize a return on investment; 22) learning reflects knowledge in motion and is required for knowing; 23) amplifying knowing and learning beyond the individual offers the greatest potential for knowledge superiority; 24) to the extent that an individual, group or organization focuses on knowing, then to some extent learning must suffer, and vice versa; and 25) doing and learning involve action and potential.

Principle 21: First, knowing reflects knowledge in action. It is knowledge manifested through practice and involves doing (i.e., knowledge-based work). In most circumstances it is insufficient to simply know something. Whether to convince someone else that you know, to accomplish some objective associated with knowledge, or to otherwise make knowledge useful, some kind of action is required. Hence knowledge must be put to use through action in order to be useful.

Principle 22: Second, learning reflects knowledge in motion. It represents the action associated with acquiring "new" knowledge (e.g., through scientific discovery or knowledge moving from one coordinate to another). Learning requires knowledge and is action oriented, so it constitutes a form of knowing, but the focus on acquiring knowledge distinguishes learning quite generally from other knowing activities (esp. doing). Hence learning both uses and increases knowledge.

Principle 23: Third, knowing and learning both take place at multiple levels of analysis. Individuals, groups, organizations, groups of organizations and so forth can know and learn, but whereas individuals can know and learn without being affiliated with groups or organizations, groups and organizations require individuals for knowing as well as for learning. Individuals are indispensable to groups and organizations, but there is more to groups and organizations than the collection of associated individuals. The phrase, "the whole is greater than the sum of its parts," applies well here. Indeed, performance effects of knowledge flows can be amplified as they reach broadly through the organization. Hence the impact of leadership and management increases in direct proportion to the reach of knowledge flows through an organization.

Principle 24: Fourth, learning and doing are interrelated. Doing requires knowledge, which must be learned. Learning involves doing focused on acquiring new knowledge. Doing can also involve learning. Doing contributes to learning, and learning contributes to doing. Further, learning and doing involve tension and require decisions. Learning is associated with exploration and focuses on knowledge flows. Doing is associated with exploitation and focuses on knowledge stocks. Both serve important purposes, but constrained time and energy impose some degree of tradeoff between them. To the extent that an individual, group or organization focuses on one, then to some extent the other must suffer. Hence promoting doing can limit learning, and vice versa.

Principle 25: Finally, doing and learning involve action and potential. Doing reflects knowledge put to use through action, which requires knowledge to be acquired before such use. Learning reflects knowledge acquisition, which increases the potential range of actions enabled. Learning from experience (i.e., from action) represents a primary contributor to new knowledge and stems directly from doing, but doing is inhibited by what has been learned, and learning is inhibited by what experiences have been known. Hence an organization's knowledge inventory both enables and inhibits what actions it can take.

EXERCISES

1. Describe briefly how a group within an organization with which you are familiar can exhibit knowing independently from, or over and above, the collective knowing of the individuals comprising the group. Provide an example. Does it matter whether what is known constitutes tacit versus explicit knowledge?
2. Describe briefly how the group from Exercise 1 above can exhibit learning independently from, or over and above, the collective learning of the individuals comprising the group. Provide an example. Does it matter whether what is learned constitutes tacit versus explicit knowledge?
3. Describe an event from your own life in which the amount of your prior knowledge influenced how well you learned something new. Be specific. How could you tell whether you learned better because of the prior knowledge?
4. Describe an event from your own life in which the nature of your prior knowledge inhibited you from learning something new. Be specific. How could you tell that your learning was inhibited?

REFERENCES

Argyris, C., & Schon, D. A. (1978). *Organizational learning*. Reading, MA: Addison-Wesley.

Cohen, W. M., & Levinthal, D. A. (1990). Absorptive capacity: A new perspective on learning and innovation. *Administrative Science Quarterly*, *35*, 128–152. doi:10.2307/2393553.

Cook, S. D. N., & Brown, J. S. (1999). Bridging epistemologies: The generative dance between organizational knowledge and organizational knowing. *Organization Science*, *10*(4), 381–400. doi:10.1287/orsc.10.4.381.

Dierickx, I., & Cool, K. (1989). Asset stock accumulation and sustainability of competitive advantage. *Management Science*, *35*(12), 1504–1511. doi:10.1287/mnsc.35.12.1504.

Hargadon, A., & Fanelli, A. (2002). Action and possibility: Reconciling dual perspectives of knowledge in organizations. *Organization Science*, *13*(3), 290–302. doi:10.1287/orsc.13.3.290.2772.

Levitt, B., & March, J. G. (1988). Organizational learning. *Annual Review of Sociology*, *14*, 319–340. doi:10.1146/annurev.so.14.080188.001535.

March, J. G. (1991). Exploration and exploitation in organizational learning. *Organization Science*, *2*(1), 71–87. doi:10.1287/orsc.2.1.71.

Nonaka, I. (1994). A dynamic theory of organizational knowledge creation. *Organization Science*, *5*(1), 14–37. doi:10.1287/orsc.5.1.14.

O'Dell, C., Ostro, N., & Grayson, C. (1998). *If we only knew what we know: The transfer of internal knowledge and best practice*. New York: Simon & Schuster.

Pfeffer, J., & Sutton, R. I. (1999). Knowing 'what' to do is not enough: Turning knowledge into action. *California Management Review*, *42*(1), 83–108. doi:10.2307/41166020.

Polanyi, M. (1967). *The tacit dimension*. Garden City, NY: Anchor Books.

Saviotti, P. P. (1998). On the dynamics of appropriability, of tacit and of codified knowledge. *Research Policy*, *26*, 843–856. doi:10.1016/S0048-7333(97)00066-8.

Stein, E. W., & Zwass, V. (1995). Actualizing organizational memory with information systems. *Information Systems Research*, *6*(2), 85–117. doi:10.1287/isre.6.2.85.

Walsh, J. P., & Ungson, G. R. (1991). Organizational memory. *Academy of Management Review*, *16*(1), 57–91.

Section 2
Practical Application

Cogito ergo sum. – Descartes

We have much to say about this, but it is hard to explain because you are slow to learn. – Anonymous letter to the Hebrews (5:11 [NIV])

The practical application part of this book builds upon the Knowledge Flow Theory presented in Section 1. Knowledge Flow Theory provides the intellectual basis for diagnosis and intervention of problems with knowledge flows. As such, the principles explain why dynamic knowledge phenomena behave as they do, and through principles-based reasoning, they inform the leader and manager on ways to harness dynamic knowledge for competitive advantage in the technology-driven world. They provide the intellectual foundation needed for practical application as addressed in Section 2 of the book.

Knowledge flow application provides tools and techniques for diagnosing problems with knowledge flows and for identifying appropriate leadership and management interventions. Notice this deductive approach mirrors that of medical practice. A theoretical basis supports principles used to diagnose pathologies and to identify appropriate interventions. Some medical diagnostics and interventions are quite general and apply across several broad classes of patients, whereas others are very specific and employed only in particular settings. The same applies to knowledge flow diagnostics and interventions. Hence, we include general as well as specific tools and techniques for practical application.

The application cases explain further how organizations from across a very wide range of sizes and domains—from the largest corporations and government agencies to the smallest non-profit clubs and groups—both succeed and fail at harnessing dynamic knowledge; hence, through case-based reasoning, they provide both positive and negative examples for the leader and manager to use in comparison with his or her own organization. In combination, the KFT principles and application cases enable insightful interpretation of emerging phenomena discussed in Section 3.

This second section of the book is organized into five chapters. Chapter 6, "Knowledge Assessment," focuses on tools and techniques for identifying problems with flows of knowledge and includes a general set of management interventions that apply across several broad classes of organizations. Chapter 7, "Application Cases in Business," concentrates on knowledge flow diagnosis and intervention in the private, for-profit sector. Chapter 8, "Application Cases in Government," concentrates on knowledge flow diagnosis and intervention in the public sector, including the military. Chapter 9, "Application Cases in Non-Profits," concentrates on knowledge flow diagnosis and intervention in the private, not-for-profit sector. Chapter 10, "Forward!" includes guidance for learning from this book and for continuing to develop new knowledge about principled organizational knowing and learning. Together, these five chapters illustrate the practical application needed to inform organizational leaders and managers.

Chapter 6
Knowledge Assessment

ABSTRACT

This chapter focuses on assessing organizational performance with respect to knowledge flows. The authors look at several theoretical and practical bases for assessment and then discuss knowledge measurement, value analysis, and learning curves in some detail, including examples for illustration. The discussion turns subsequently to examine computational modeling of knowledge flows, which includes a detailed example for practical illustration. The chapter concludes with five knowledge flow assessment principles and includes exercises to stimulate critical thought, learning, and discussion.

THEORETICAL AND PRACTICAL BASES FOR ASSESSMENT

In this section, we review several theoretical and practical bases for knowledge assessment. We select only a few, diverse, representative approaches for discussion, leaving more comprehensive research for the interested reader to pursue via the references cited here.

Change Management Approaches

In terms of theory and practice alike, KM is not as unique as many people assert. For instance, KM is viewed by numerous scholars as fundamentally oriented toward managing change (Davenport et al., 1998). Business Process Re-engineering (BPR) research has addressed several important questions pertaining to managing change. For example, we have the benefit of results such as "tactics for managing radical change" (Stoddard & Jarvenpaa, 1995), revelations of "reengineering myths" (Davenport & Stoddard, 1994), insight into implementation problems (Clemons et al., 1995; Grover et al., 1995), measurement-driven process redesign methods (Nissen, 1998), and many others. Research on BPR has also produced numerous analytical frameworks such as those articulated by Andrews and Stalick (1994), Davenport (1993), Hammer and Champy (1993), Harrington (1991) and Johansson et al. (1993). Many cases of large-scale change have been studied (e.g., Goldstein, 1986; Kettinger et al., 1995; King & Konsynski, 1990; Stoddard & Meadows, 1992; Talebzadeh et al., 1995) as well. Hence KM has much to learn from BPR.

Preconditions for Success

Here we describe one BPR assessment approach—which is quite applicable to KM—centering on "preconditions for success" (Bashein et al., 1994). Through research on numerous re-engineering projects, three obstacles to large-scale change are

DOI: 10.4018/978-1-4666-4727-5.ch006

noted (pp. 7-8): 1) lack of sustained management commitment and leadership; 2) unrealistic scope and expectations; and 3) resistance to change. Examine any KM project today, and you are very likely to encounter these same obstacles. Hence the preconditions for success developed from investigation of BPR projects are very likely to apply also to KM projects. Eight preconditions for KM success are summarized in Table 1 for reference. Most such preconditions are likely to be self-explanatory and intuitive.

Experience to date suggests preconditions 2, 5 and 7 (i.e., Realistic expectations, Shared vision, Appropriate people participating full-time) represent the ones that are absent or insufficient most often in KM projects. In terms of expectations (i.e., Precondition 2), KM is not a "silver bullet" and will not cure all organizational ills. However, enhancing knowledge flows can enable sustainable competitive advantage, which provides a substantial source of power. Hence realistic expectations—particularly in terms of how much progress can be made and how quickly—are key to successful KM implementation. In terms of vision (i.e., Precondition 5), not everyone views KM in the same manner or can envision equally well how organizational knowledge can flow better through change. Yet all involved knowledge workers need to change their behaviors (e.g., in terms of sharing, searching, learning). A common vision can provide necessary cohesion to their disparate change activities. In terms of staffing (i.e., Precondition 7), successful change requires thought and action, planning and doing, patience and persistence. Talented people need to be assigned to conceive, plan and implement KM projects. They need to both commit and devote themselves to such projects as well.

We use this to induce our first leadership mandate from the practical application section of this book. Mandate 1. Realistic expectations, shared vision, and appropriate people participating full-time represent the preconditions for success that are absent or insufficient most often in KM projects.

Table 1. Preconditions for KM success (adapted from Nissen, 2006)

Precondition	KM Implication
1. Senior management commitment	Change of any magnitude requires commitment by senior managers. KM should be considered change of substantial magnitude.
2. Realistic expectations	Expecting too much, too fast, can deflate support for change. Change takes time to implement and refine in KM as in other areas.
3. Empowered and collaborative workers	People doing organizational work are the ones who will make KM work or not. Knowledge workers need some empowerment for exploration and learning, not just exploitation and doing.
4. Strategic context of growth and expansion	Enthusiasm and optimism can pervade a change project and contribute to toward its success, whereas negativity and pessimism can kill it. Setting goals for growth and expansion, through sustained competitive advantage, can facilitate KM change.
5. Shared vision	A vision of how knowledge flows can be enhanced must be conceived and shared broadly in order for empowered people to understand how to change.
6. Sound management processes	The better-organized an enterprise is to begin with, the better its chances for successful change via KM.
7. Appropriate people participating full-time	Successful change requires talented people devoting their attention and effort toward enhancing knowledge flows. Assigning slack, part-time resources is unlikely to produce successful KM change.
8. Sufficient budget	Successful change costs money and requires time. Competitive advantage enabled by knowledge is not free. The KM budget should reflect this reality.

Preconditions for Failure

We include also nine preconditions for KM failure in Table 2. These represent "negative preconditions," which can affect adversely a KM project if present. As with the preconditions for success above, most such preconditions are likely to be self-explanatory and intuitive. Experience to date suggests preconditions 10, 12 and 17 (i.e., Reliance upon external expertise, Narrow technical focus, Animosity toward staff and specialists) represent the ones that are present and sufficient most often in KM projects. In terms of reliance (i.e., Precondition 10), many organizations that stand to benefit from enhanced knowledge flows lack the expertise necessary to plan and implement a successful KM project. Hiring external consultants represents a common tactic used by such organizations, but external expertise is expensive generally, and the corresponding knowledge leaves the organization often before it can be absorbed to sustain whatever KM changes are conceived and/or implemented.

In terms of focus (i.e., Precondition 12), a narrow technical emphasis pervades most KM projects still. This precondition is discussed at length in the chapter on knowledge technology above. Successful KM projects require more than just technology. People, organizations, work processes and technologies must all change—together—in a co-evolutionary manner to enhance knowledge flows. This applies in particular to flows of tacit knowledge. In terms of animosity (i.e., Precondition 17), most leaders and line managers remain very busy and are proud consistently of the organizations they lead and manage. Staff members and specialists are viewed often with contempt and animosity by such leaders and managers, who may perceive them as disruptive at best and as threats at worst. Middle management represents

Table 2. Preconditions for KM failure (adapted from Nissen, 2006)

Precondition	KM Implication
9. Wrong sponsor	Some characteristics of a "wrong sponsor" include: too low in management ranks, too technically focused, getting ready to retire or change jobs, and lacking credibility and leadership.
10. Reliance upon external expertise	Reliance upon external talent may be necessary to initiate a KM program, but such talent leaves the organization, often before the requisite expertise can be absorbed. This leaves the KM project without sufficient knowledge for sustainment.
11. Cost-cutting focus	People do not react well to change when they feel threatened. A focus on downsizing effectively killed the BPR movement in the Nineties.
12. Narrow technical focus	People, organizations, work processes and technologies must all change—together—for successful KM. A single-minded focus on technology is hazardous.
13. Consensus management	Collaboration without leadership is problem-prone. Tough decisions about KM alternatives are required but are unlikely to be resolved well by consensus.
14. Unsound financial condition	Many organizations attempt KM out of desperation. When management is desperate, then realistic expectations, patience and sufficient budget are unlikely.
15. Too many improvement projects under way	Successful change requires focus. If everyone in an organization changes simultaneously everything they do, then chaos is likely. Organizations are advised to focus on one or perhaps a few KM initiatives at any one time.
16. Fear and lack of optimism	This is the counterpart to the cost-cutting focus above. People associated with change need to believe they are working to improve their own work environment in addition to that of others.
17. Animosity toward staff and specialists	Many leaders and line managers view specialists with contempt and perceive change efforts as disrupting their work processes. Middle management is the place in which resistance to change is likely to be greatest on a KM project.

the place in which resistance to successful KM implementation is likely to be greatest.

We use this to induce our second leadership mandate from the practical application section of this book. Mandate 2. Reliance upon external expertise, narrow technical focus, and animosity toward staff and specialists represent the preconditions for failure that are present or sufficient most often in KM projects.

KM-Specific Factors

Unlike the preconditions for success and failure above, which derive from the literature on change management, other sets of success factors have been developed specifically for KM projects. For instance, Jennex and Olfman (2004) survey research on KM systems (e.g., including but not limited to IT) and identify factors such as incorporation of KM into everyday work tasks, senior management support, and employee training. Other factors cited in this survey include user commitment and motivation, knowledge representation, organizational and cultural issues, leadership and top management support, attention to tacit knowledge, promoting a culture of knowledge sharing, focus on organizational memory, and others.

Clearly several such factors (e.g., commitment and motivation, leadership and top management support, promoting a culture of knowledge sharing) are included in the preconditions from above. Others (e.g., knowledge representation, attention to tacit knowledge, focus on organizational memory), however, are unique to KM and merit additional attention. In terms of knowledge representation, this highlights an important issue. AI researchers and practitioners have worked for decades on how various kinds of knowledge can be represented. Recall we include in the knowledge technology chapter above an example of using heuristic rules. Representing knowledge is particularly difficult where such knowledge is tacit. Many organizations satisfice by mapping where (e.g., in which people) such tacit knowledge resides; this reflects an emphasis on transactive memory (e.g., who knows what; see Wegner, 1995), but much work remains to be accomplished in this area.

In terms of tacit knowledge, we devote considerable attention to this phenomenon throughout the book. Such tacit knowledge flows differently than its explicit counterpart does. The appropriability of tacit knowledge also provides a sustainable basis for competitive advantage. Hence tacit knowledge merits separate treatment. In terms of organizational memory, we devote attention to this phenomenon in the book also, but we do so in the context of knowledge stocks or inventories. It is important to re-emphasize that such inventories complement knowledge flows in a complex, dynamic manner. Hence organizational memory represents one of several important success factors and must be addressed in concert with knowledge flows.

We use this to induce our third leadership mandate from the practical application section of this book. Mandate 3. Knowledge representation, attention to tacit knowledge, and focus on organizational memory represent unique considerations that merit particular attention in KM projects.

Related research has addressed KM readiness (Holt et al., 2007). Readiness in this context is equivalent to preconditions for success. The focus of this work is on KM implementation. Over 30 instruments (i.e., guidelines for assessment) are identified for evaluating an organization's readiness for change. Then using a survey of KM practitioners, these researchers identify measures such as pessimism, affective commitment and normative commitment as statistically significant indicators of KM readiness. Notice such measures pertain to how people perceive a KM project. This is consistent with several of the preconditions above, and it reinforces the importance of leadership and management. Related research by Kulkarni and Freeze (2004; 2006) develops a different instrument for measuring KM capability via five levels, and it differentiates between absolute and relative capabilities.

We also find tips for KM project benchmarking (Carpenter & Rudge, 2003), patent analysis (Hansen, 1995), value chain analysis (King & Ko, 2001), knowledge re-use (Markus, 2001), balanced evaluation (Wolf, 2011), strategic cost management (Silvi & Cuganesan, 2006), strategic management (Snyman & Kruger, 2004), and other useful techniques introduced and employed over the past couple of decades.

Knowledge Audit

Other practical research involves the knowledge audit (Liebowitz et al., 2000). This represents a diagnostic activity focused on identifying problems with potential to be addressed via KM. Such problems include: inability to keep abreast of relevant information; "reinventing the wheel"; and not knowing where to go for expertise. Notice each of these problems involves "how-to" knowing (e.g., how to keep abreast of information, how to avoid task duplication, how to locate experts). As outlined by the authors (p. 3), "a knowledge audit assesses potential stores of knowledge and is the first part of any knowledge management strategy." Notwithstanding this assertion, however, if the kinds of preconditions for success from above are absent from a project, or the kinds of preconditions for failure are present, one would be advised well to address such preconditions before investing in a knowledge audit. Six steps associated with a knowledge audit (p. 5) are summarized in Table 3. They are intuitive but easier said than done.

Table 3. Steps of a knowledge audit (adapted from Nissen, 2006)

Step
1. Determine existing and potential knowledge sinks, sources, flows, and constraints.
2. Identify and locate explicit and tacit knowledge.
3. Build a map of the stocks and flows of organizational knowledge.
4. Perform a gap analysis to determine what knowledge is missing.
5. Determine who needs the missing knowledge.
6. Provide recommendations to management regarding necessary improvements.

These researchers also present a survey instrument for auditing knowledge. It includes some of the items summarized in Table 4. It should be clear that such a survey is intended principally for external consultants who do not understand the knowledge inventories and flows of an organization. However, we note above that many organizations do not know what they know. An instrument such as this can be used by internal organizational stakeholders—in conjunction with employees' knowledge of what knowledge is important and of who knows what—to identify key aspects of knowledge within the organization.

Table 4. Sample knowledge audit survey questions (adapted from Nissen, 2006)

Question
What categories of knowledge are required for your job?
Which knowledge categories are available currently?
How is this knowledge used?
Who else uses this knowledge?
Who are the experts in terms of this knowledge?
In what form is the knowledge of these experts?

We use this to induce our fourth leadership mandate from the practical application section of this book. Mandate 4. Knowledge audits can help organizations that do not know what they know.

An unintended additional benefit involves stimulating people in the organization to think more about the knowledge that is important to them. For instance, by completing a survey along these lines, many people in an organization may think explicitly about knowledge and flows that had never surfaced beyond implicit understanding and tacit execution. Nonetheless, many people find such surveys time-consuming to complete and difficult to answer. Yet the results can provide a rough gauge of knowledge in an organization.

Still, surveys are likely to be most valuable to external consultants who do not understand the organization well.

To summarize the approaches described in this section, assessing knowledge flow performance is addressed by theory and practice alike. Most work along these lines involves the development of preconditions for success and failure, evaluation of readiness or capability factors, and knowledge audits. In each case, one is trying to identify problems with knowledge flows and to match such problems with the capabilities of KM projects. In each case also, one is striving to address the management of change. A KM project involves substantial change, which must be managed to enhance the likelihood of success. The key problem with all of the approaches in this class is, they describe what to do but not how to do it. In other words, preconditions, readiness factors, knowledge flow measurement, audit steps and like approaches are prescriptive and articulated at a high level, but they are difficult to operationalize and implement.

KNOWLEDGE MEASUREMENT AND ANALYSIS

Research and practice of a different nature departs from these high-level, non-operationalized approaches via a focus on measurement. Here we discuss knowledge measurement and analysis approaches to quantifying knowledge in the organization.

Knowledge Power Measurement

Recent research by Nissen (2010b; 2011) employs the four-dimensional model discussed in Part I to measure knowledge flows. Specifically, the four dimensions described in Part I of the book (i.e., knowledge explicitness, reach, life cycle, flow time) are used to represent characteristics of a particular knowledge flow, and knowledge power is used to represent its efficacy in terms of effecting knowledge-based action. This produces a five-dimensional model as depicted in Figure 1. The figure is roughly identical to that discussed in Part I above; the addition of a fifth, power dimension reflects the only substantive difference.

Figure 1. 5D knowledge flow model

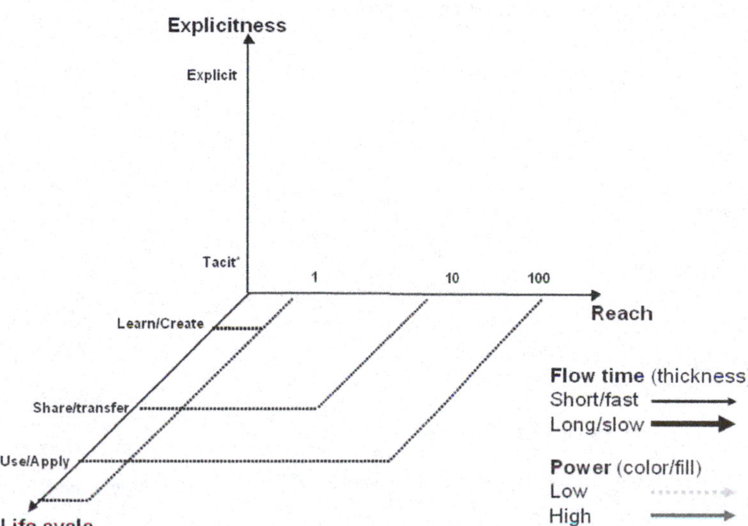

Briefly, like the fourth dimension flow time, the fifth dimension power is represented in terms of line style used to delineate knowledge flow vectors. Knowledge that flows with relatively low power—this corresponds very closely with relatively low performance levels of activities enabled by the knowledge—is delineated through orange, dotted lines, whereas knowledge flows exhibiting high power—and hence enabling high performance—are delineated via purple, solid lines. Measurements can be made using ordinal, interval or ratio scales. This gives us a 5D vector space to examine dynamic knowledge. As with the 4D model discussed above, such 5D space and examination scheme are completely general: they can be applied to any dynamic knowledge in any organizational domain (e.g., acquisition, command and control, software engineering).

As an example of its use and application, consider Figure 2, which illustrates an important knowledge flow desired by some organization. Point A represents some individual in the organization who learns something new (to that organization) or creates entirely new knowledge. In terms of the 5D space, this represents tacit knowledge that is created by an individual (i.e., 1 person); hence its position at the bottom-back corner of the diagram. In the procurement domain, for instance, consider that such new knowledge could pertain to a technique for reducing the acquisition time for an important information system (IS) needed in the field. Because information technology (IT) advances so quickly—outpacing the ability of many procurement organizations to develop and field them responsively—the organization views this new knowledge created at Point A as important, and it would like to see such knowledge shared with and applied by all 100 people in that organization who work with IT. Similar conditions and desired knowledge flow could be found in terms of a novel marketing technique, Cyberspace defense tactic, leadership insight, and like application domains.

Such application by 100 people in the organization is represented by Point B. The thin, purple, solid vector connecting Points A and B represents the desired knowledge flow: the organization wishes for such knowledge to flow quickly and with high power (e.g., enabling all 100 people at Point B to work, within one day, at the same performance level as the individual at Point A). This represents a 5D knowledge flow. The question mark "?" in the figure next to this knowledge flow vector indicates that such flow is *desired* by

Figure 2. Knowledge creation and application needs

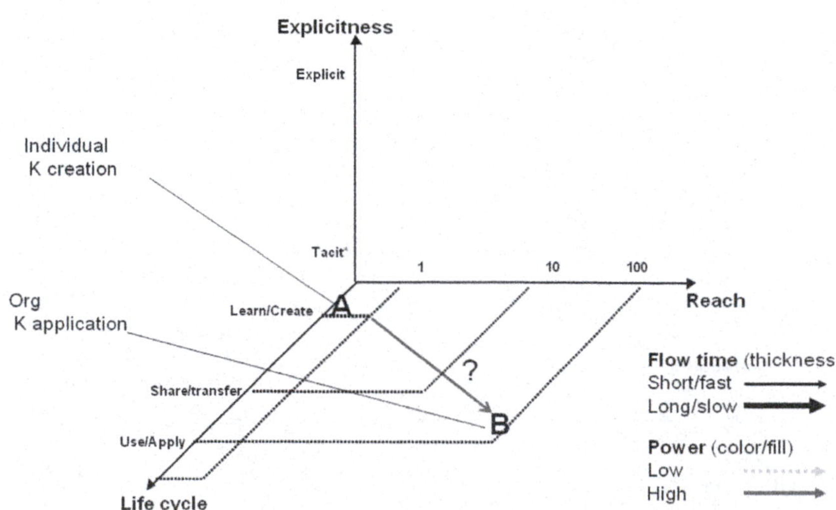

the organization, but it is unclear which if any organizational process will enable this fast, powerful knowledge flow through the tacit knowledge plane.

This leads to Figure 3, which depicts a "Ridge" or obstruction that prevents knowledge from flowing directly, quickly and powerfully from Points A to B as desired by the organization. Practically, this means only that the organization lacks a process for such direct, quick and powerful knowledge flow. Indeed, most organizations do lack such process (Nissen, 2006). Some other approach to sharing and applying the important IT acquisition knowledge is required.

Figure 4 delineates two, alternate, archetypical knowledge flows corresponding to processes that are within this organization's capabilities. We say "archetypical," for most organizations employ these classic processes routinely, and because they present a vivid contrast in terms of how dynamic knowledge flows. One knowledge flow is depicted in terms of a low-power (i.e., orange, dotted line) but relatively fast (i.e., thin lines) vector series; this first flow is associated primarily with explicit knowledge and utilizes one or more IS for knowledge articulation and distribution in explicit form. The other is delineated via a high-power (i.e., purple, solid line) but comparatively slow (i.e., thick line) vector; this second flow is associated primarily with tacit knowledge and utilizes one or more human-centered approaches to learning (e.g., group interaction, mentoring, personnel transfer).

In some greater detail, the first knowledge flow consists of three vectors. The first is represented by the vertical line arising from Point A. This depicts the individual at Point A articulating his or her new, tacit knowledge via an IS so that it can be shared electronically. Such articulation (e.g., consider writing a procedure, developing a training course, posting to an intranet or social networking site) tends to be somewhat time-consuming; hence the relatively thick line. Articulating knowledge in explicit form tends to dilute it in terms of power also (e.g., reading a book about how to accomplish important acquisition tasks is not the same as having direct experience accomplishing them personally); hence the orange, dotted line.

Once articulated in explicit form as such, however—particularly via IS—the knowledge can be shared very broadly (e.g., organization-wide) and very quickly (e.g., within seconds); hence the thin horizontal line at the top of the diagram.

Figure 3. Knowledge flow obstruction

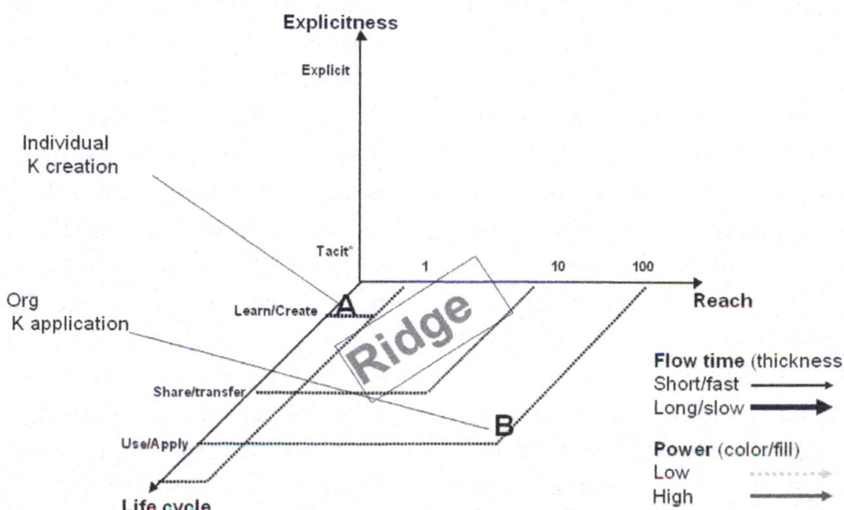

Figure 4. Alternate archetypical knowledge flows

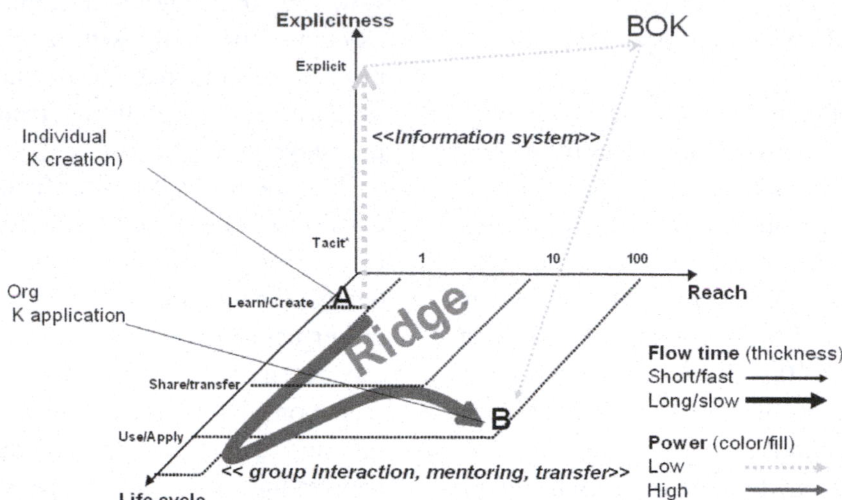

One could consider this flow as an addition to the organization's express body of knowledge (BOK; standard operating procedures [SOPs]; techniques, tactics and procedures [TTPs]; work instructions; lessons learned; and many similar approaches to articulating knowledge are common across a wide array of diverse organizations), which we note at the top-right of the figure. Such explicit BOK can then be accessed and applied quickly (hence the thin line) in turn by all 100 people in the organization. This articulated, explicit knowledge remains relatively diluted and less powerful, nonetheless, so application at Point B would not support the same performance level as at Point A; hence the orange, dotted line descending down to Point B. We can measure these five dimensions of knowledge and relate them to the corresponding knowledge-based performance of people in the organization. Indeed, by correlating such knowledge measures with performance metrics, we can develop a model capable of analyzing, visualizing and even predicting process performance based upon knowledge flow patterns.

Alternatively, the second vector consists of a single line, although it curves and bends through the tacit knowledge plane at the bottom of the figure. This depicts the individual at Point A applying his or her new, tacit knowledge and then sharing it with some number of other people (say, 10 as illustrated in the figure) through one or more techniques such as extended group interaction, mentoring or personnel transfer to work directly with different coworkers across the organization. Once each of these people (again, say 10 as illustrated in the figure) has learned the new, tacit knowledge, then all of them continue the process and share it using similar techniques with others. Through such process, 100 people (i.e., 10 people each sharing with another 10) learn this new, tacit knowledge to the extent necessary for powerful application at Point B. This latter knowledge flow is depicted by a thick vector to indicate that it occurs comparatively slowly, but such vector is delineated by a purple, solid line to show that the corresponding knowledge has high power and enables knowledge-based action at the same performance level as the individual who created it at Point A. As above, we can measure these five dimensions of dynamic knowledge and develop a model capable of analyzing, visualizing and even predicting process performance based upon knowledge flow patterns.

Of course, many combinations of these archetypical knowledge flows are possible too, and the processes noted above are for purposes of illustration; clearly many other processes can be employed as well. Nonetheless, nearly all knowledge flows will reflect some aspects of these two, archetypical dynamic patterns, and this 5D space enables one to understand, visualize and analyze every knowledge flow in any comprehensible organization. This provides a novel, vector basis for 5D measurement of dynamic knowledge. Moreover, through empirical analysis and calibration of specific knowledge flowing through any particular organization (e.g., individual to individual, individual to group, group to group, group to organization, organization to organization, organization to group, group to individual), one can correlate 5D dynamic knowledge flows with work performance. Through this technique, the power of knowledge flowing through organizations can be measured in terms of dynamic knowledge, related to work performance, and predicted via knowledge flow model.

A specific example drawn from the Cyberspace domain illustrates application of the technique and elucidates key insights. The central idea pertains to how new knowledge pertaining to countering a novel cyber attack (e.g., "zero day exploit") can flow best from one individual in the organization (i.e., the innovator who discovers this new knowledge) to be applied quickly and well by numerous others (e.g., 100 people). The example uses simulation to quantify knowledge power differences corresponding to alternate knowledge flows, with the principal distinction pertaining to explicit versus tacit flows along the lines delineated in Figure 4 above. We outline the example only briefly here; the interested reader can peruse the details (Nissen, 2010b).

Succinctly, in the knowledge-based environment of computer network defense, exploitation and attack (CNDEA), knowledge is critical to discovering and countering attacks on an organization's networked infrastructure and computing assets, and time is of the essence, as damage increases exponentially with the time that malware, logic bombs, service disruptions and other cyber threats infect and permeate through one's network. Hence we assess the power of knowledge in terms of the amount of time that a friendly organization is able to penetrate and disrupt the network of an adversary organization that is attacking. Notice that this is an inherently empirical assessment of knowing; that is, it measures knowledge in action.

As with any simulation model, many assumptions are necessary, and it is important to conduct sensitivity analysis to assess how much influence such assumptions have on model results. Three key assumptions here include: 1) explicit knowledge flows much more quickly (10x) than its tacit counterpart does; 2) tacit knowledge flows with much greater power (10x) than its explicit counterpart does; and 3) ten groups of ten people each comprise this organization. Analysis reveals that results are relatively insensitive to variations in these assumptions (Nissen, 2010b).

Two alternate approaches to distributing this important, individual knowledge are contemplated: 1) through tacit knowledge flows associated with the kind of socialization process discussed in terms of the 5D model above (e.g., where an individual embeds him or herself in a group, and through dialog, observation, explanation and other techniques such as mentoring and apprenticeship, he or she helps the other group members to learn the corresponding knowledge); and 2) through explicit knowledge flows associated with the kinds of externalization and combination processes discussed in terms of the model above (e.g., where an individual formalizes his or her knowledge through some means of articulation such as written, multimedia documents, and he or she distributes this explicit knowledge through electronic means such as an intranet web portal with document repository and search capabilities). In each example, we simulate and compare the relative knowledge flow time, reach and power associated with these two techniques.

Succinctly, as expected, results indicate that the key knowledge spreads much more quickly via explicit knowledge flows. This is delineated via the top line in Figure 5 (labeled "ECum PR"), which rises quickly to over 200 units (e.g., consider 200 hours that the adversary's network is disrupted) of knowledge power. The tacit knowledge power is delineated via the bottom line (labeled "TCum PR"), which increases more slowly until Time Period 10, when all ten people in the individual's group learn to apply his or her key counterattack knowledge with equal efficacy. At this point, since tacit knowledge exerts much greater power than explicit knowledge does, it catches up quickly. Then looking at the subsequent ten time periods in Figure 6, the tacit knowledge flow dominates its explicit counterpart in terms of knowledge power, rising to more than 1300 power units, as compared to just over 400 for the explicit knowledge flow.

Two key implications follow. 1) Explicit knowledge flows can extend the reach of knowledge more quickly than tacit flows can, so group level knowledge and power accumulate more quickly through the former than the latter; where quick results are important to organizational leaders and managers, decision makers would emphasize explicit knowledge flows. 2) Alternatively, tacit knowledge flows carry greater power than explicit flows do, so group level knowledge and power accumulate to higher levels over time through the former than the latter; where high knowledge power levels are important to organizational leaders and managers, decision makers would emphasize tacit knowledge flows. In cases where quick results in short conflicts are important, the organization should focus on explicit knowledge flows, but where sustained results in long confrontations are required, tacit knowledge flows offer greater power over time.

We use this to induce our fifth leadership mandate from the practical application section of this book. Mandate 5. In cases where quick results in short conflicts are important, the organization should focus on explicit knowledge flows, but where sustained results in long confrontations are required, tacit knowledge flows offer greater power.

Knowledge Value Analysis

Knowledge Value Analysis (KVA; see Housel et al., 2001) is rooted in Complexity Theory and Thermodynamics. This approach employs principles such as information entropy to measure the return on knowledge (i.e., return on investments in productive assets such as employees and technol-

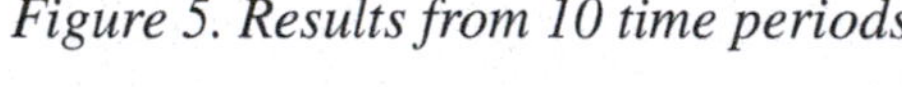
Figure 5. Results from 10 time periods

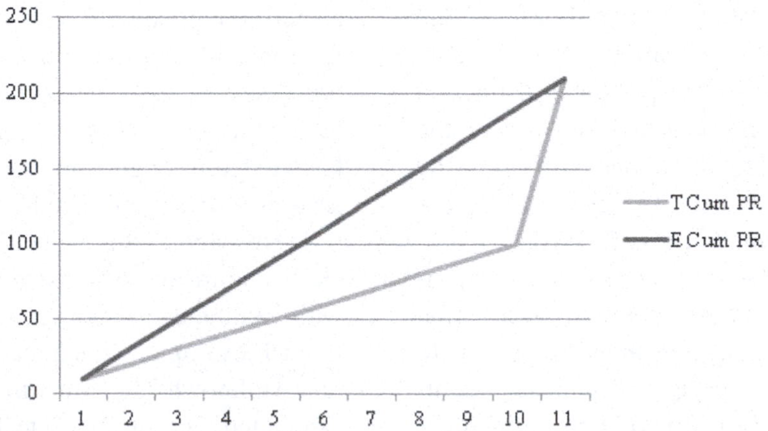

Figure 6. Results from 20 time periods

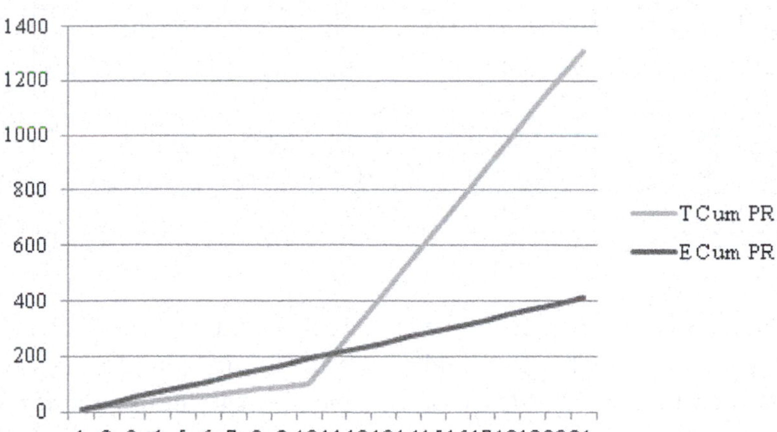

ogy at the sub-corporate level). "KVA provides a methodology for allocating revenue and cost to company's core processes based on the amount of change [i.e., change in entropy] each produces" (Housel & Bell, 2001, p. 92).

The idea is to identify the relative returns of processes that employ resources (e.g., employees and technology) to produce their outputs. This is accomplished via a ratio: return on knowledge (ROK). ROK is a surrogate for return on investment. The revenue allocated to a given process (and its resources) is the numerator in a ROK calculation. The cost to use those resources to produce the process outputs is the denominator. Providing leaders and managers with such information can help them to make resource-allocation decisions using logic similar to that of ratio analysis in managing investment portfolios.

The authors describe KVA (p. 100) as, "an analytic tautology. … [It assumes that] all of the knowledge required to execute processes is known and … is a surrogate for the economic value it produces." To estimate the amount of knowledge contained within an organizational process, this approach prescribes assessing how much time is required by an "average person" to learn how to produce the outputs of a process. The assumption underlying this prescription is, the amount of time it takes for the average learner to acquire a given amount of knowledge is proportional to knowledge. Here the concept knowledge is used as a surrogate for the (change in information entropy and) value added by a process. Hence learning time is argued to be value-proportional.

Notice this is a knowledge flow proposition that involves the knowing activities of both learning and doing. If some activity requires a relatively long time to learn, then it would be considered more valuable than an alternate activity requiring less learning time. This would clearly privilege tacit knowledge—which flows more slowly than explicit knowledge does—and encourage investments in the associated processes. This is consistent with our discussion above on the appropriability of tacit knowledge and its contribution toward competitive advantage.

We use this to induce our sixth leadership mandate from the practical application section of this book. Mandate 6. Knowledge value analysis privileges tacit knowledge appropriately.

The example summarized in Table 5 can help us to appreciate this approach. This example is adapted from Housel and Bell (2001), in which book the KVA method is explained in great detail. Briefly, the first column (i.e., labeled "K Area") lists three areas (i.e., labeled simply "A," "B"

Table 5. KVA example (adapted from Nissen, 2006)

K Area	Learning Time	Knowers	IT %	Auto K	Total K	K %	Revenue	Expense	ROK
A	20	855	80	13680	30780	34.2	82.7	75.0	110%
B	45	600	60	16200	43200	48.0	116.1	175.5	66%
C	35	255	80	7140	16065	17.8	43.2	49.5	87%
Total					90045	100.0	242.0	300.0	

and "C") of knowledge that are deemed to be important in this organization. Such areas could include knowledge of customers, knowledge of internal operations, knowledge of management procedures, and like areas that would clearly vary across organizations. These represent the important things to know about—at a high level of abstraction—in the organization. The second column (i.e., labeled "Learning Time") lists the amount of time (in months) required for the "average person" to become proficient in each knowledge area. For instance, the average person requires roughly 20 months to become proficient at the tasks associated with Knowledge Area A, 45 months for Area B, and so forth. The third column (i.e., labeled "Knowers") lists the number of people associated with each knowledge area. For instance, 855 people participate in tasks associated with Knowledge Area A, 600 with those in Area B, and so forth.

The fourth column (i.e., labeled "IT %") lists the estimated fraction of knowledge embedded within IT artifacts for each knowledge area. For instance, say that estimates indicate 80% of knowledge in Area A is embedded in IT, 60% in Area B, and so forth. The estimate represented in this column is not intuitive and requires some explanation. It represents a fraction that is used to calculate the amount of knowledge embedded in IT automation. This latter amount is listed in the fifth column (i.e., labeled "Auto K") for each knowledge area. For instance, 13680 knowledge units are associated with Knowledge Area A, 16200 with those in Area B, and so forth. Figures in this column are calculated as the product of estimates in columns 2 – 4 (e.g., in Area A: 20 months learning time x 855 knowers x 80% IT fraction = 13680 knower-months). The sixth column (i.e., labeled "Total K") lists the total knowledge associated with each knowledge area. This represents the sum of automation knowledge (i.e., calculated in column 5) and human knowledge. For instance, 30780 knowledge units are associated with Knowledge Area A, 43200 with those in Area B, and so forth. Figures in this column are calculated as the sum of automation knowledge and product of columns 2 – 3 (e.g., 13680 knower-months of automation knowledge + [20 months learning time x 855 knowers] = 30780 knower-months).

The seventh column (i.e., labeled "K %") lists the fraction of total knowledge associated with each knowledge area. For instance, 34.2% of total knowledge is associated with Knowledge Area A, 48.0% with Area B, and so forth. Figures in this column are calculated as the ratio of total knowledge in each area to the total knowledge summed across all areas (e.g., 30780 knower-months for Area A divided by 90045 knower-months for the total organization = 34.2%). The eighth column (i.e., labeled "Revenue") lists the revenue allocated to each knowledge area on the basis of its knowledge. For instance, of the $242.0M total revenue for the organization in the period of interest, 34.2% (i.e., $82.7M) is allocated on the basis of knowledge to Knowledge Area A, 48.0% (i.e., $116.1M) to Area B, and so forth. Figures in this column are calculated as the product of the knowledge fraction from column 7 and the total revenue summed in column 8 (e.g., 34.2% for Area A x $242.0M total revenue for the organization = $82.7M for Area A). The ninth column (i.e., labeled "Expense") lists the expense incurred by each knowledge area (e.g., as recorded via activity-based costing). For instance, of the $300.0M total expense for the organization in the period of interest, $75.0M is incurred for Knowledge Area A, $175.5M for Area B, and so forth.

Finally, the tenth column (i.e., labeled "ROK") lists the "return on knowledge" computed for each knowledge area on the basis of the revenue allocation in column 8. For instance, the return on knowledge is shown at 110% for Area A, 66% for Area B, and so forth. This is calculated as the ratio of knowledge-allocated revenue from column 8 to expense from column 9 (e.g., $82.7M allocated revenue for Area A divided by $75.0M expense = 110% ROK). The intent of this final calculation is to show the relative contribution of the three knowledge areas to the organization's economic value. For instance, a relatively high ROK for Knowledge Area A (i.e., 110%) would be interpreted as indicating this area contributes well to the economic value of the organization. Not only does it contribute relatively better than Knowledge Area B (i.e., 66% ROK) and Area C (i.e., 87%) do, but it contributes more via allocated revenue than its expenses.

One could make an argument that knowledge associated with Area A contributes to an economic profit for the organization, whereas knowledge associated with Areas B and C contribute instead to economic losses. A manager might seek in turn to: a) exploit further the knowledge associated with Area A, b) explore ways to ameliorate the knowledge clumps inhibiting performance in Areas B and C, or c) both. In one case described separately by the authors (Housel, 2004), the billing process of a telecommunications company showed the lowest return of the multiple processes examined via KVA, but because the case company represented a new subsidiary, and because it was stuck for the time being with the current billing process, the executive group decided to invest in a customer-relationship management system to boost sales. So the numbers alone need not lead to a given knowledge investment decision any more than they do with financial investment decisions made by portfolio managers.

This approach offers a technique to conduct an analysis (e.g., as outlined in the example) for any organization that maintains records and has people willing to make the estimates required to complete a table such as the one above. However, the approach has several problems. One problem of course stems from the inherent subjectivity and possible inaccuracy of estimates required for columns 2 – 4 of the table, in addition to the potential difficulty of obtaining expenses for each knowledge area. For instance, many organizations do not use activity-based costing and do not collect expenses by knowledge area. However, other expenses (e.g., General & Administrative, Operations, Management) are reported routinely or can be derived from financial statements.

Another problem lies in the possibility of excluding from the analysis one or more important knowledge areas. Even relatively informed leaders and managers may be unaccustomed to conceptualizing their organizations in terms of knowledge areas. Hence they may overlook important areas when asked to help build a ROK table. However, skilled interviewers offer techniques for ameliorating some limitations along these lines (Housel, 2004), and incorporating a knowledge audit or knowledge power measurements may enhance this technique further.

Identifying an "average person" in the organization can be challenging as well. Say a bright, fast-learning person in Area A and a comparatively dim, slow-learning person in Area B are required to learn essentially the same knowledge. If Person A learns such knowledge in, say, 1 month, whereas Person B requires, say, 6 months to learn equivalent knowledge, then KVA would value the knowledge in Area B at six times the value of its counterpart knowledge in Area A, despite our ex-ante understanding that knowledge in both areas is equivalent.

Perhaps the most substantial problem with this approach is that it reduces to an allocation formula. Where someone has resources to invest among competing process activities, this approach provides a mechanism for making such allocation. However, the approach does not claim any superiority over other allocation formulae (e.g., strategic importance, expected return on investment, expected risk/return ratio). Moreover, as noted above, the logic of basing investment allocations on the amount of time required for "average people" to learn various activities is not entirely cogent. This approach does provide a means to measuring the putative value of knowledge, but the ideas remain a bit inchoate. Further, the approach is still gaining acceptance theoretically. Its employment in practice to date has been positive but limited.

Learning Curves

Similar to the approaches above with their foci on measurement, learning curves provide a technique that blends theory with practice to measure knowledge flows. Learning curves are very well-accepted and –established, both theoretically and empirically, and they have been used for many decades to measure knowledge flows. Born during the World War Era in the aerospace industry, formal techniques were developed to assess organizational learning in terms of the time required to repeat aircraft-assembly tasks successively (Wright, 1936).

Briefly, a general relationship can be observed and measured between the cumulative number of times a task is repeated and the time required to perform each repetition. This relationship has been observed and validated across myriad industries and types of tasks (Yelle, 1979). It appears to represent a fundamental behavior in terms of organizational learning (Argote et al., 1990). In words, this relationship indicates that the unit time required to perform a task declines as a predictable percentage with each doubling of task repetitions. Mathematically the relationship is logarithmic and expressed often as:

$$Y = Ax^b$$

where:

Y is the unit time required to complete a task after x repetitions.

A is the time required to complete a task the first time.

x is the cumulative number of task repetitions.

b is the learning factor (generally: $-1 < b < 0$)

Consider a task that requires 100 hours to complete the first time (i.e., Y = A = 100; x = 1; terminological note: the first time a task is accomplished is termed repetition 1, even though technically it has yet to be "repeated"), with a learning factor (i.e., b = -0.3219) that reflects a common improvement rate. Improvement rates such as this are expressed often in percentage terms (e.g., 80%). Improvement rates can be equated to learning factors (e.g., at 80% improvement: b = -0.3219 = log .80 / log 2) and are considered widely to be more intuitive. For instance, the second time this "100-hour" task is performed (i.e., x = 2), the learning curve would predict the time required to be only 80% of that of the first (i.e., Y = 80% of 100 = 80). The next time the cumulative number of repetitions doubles (i.e., x = 4), the learning curve would predict the time required to be only another 80% (i.e., Y = 80% of 80% of 100 = 80% of 80 = 64), and so forth. Notice after only eight repetitions (i.e., x = 8) that the unit time declines to approximately half the time required at first (i.e., Y = 51). In other words, at an 80% improvement rate, only eight repetitions are required for performance of a task to double!

Several general rules of thumb have been developed through experience with learning curves over the years. One is that the greater the use of automation at the beginning of a process, the lower the improvement rate. The reason is that automation generally improves a process via quantum jump, so cumulative improvement following such jump is very moderate. For instance, whereas an 80% improvement rate is common for people performing manual tasks (e.g., assembling airplanes), the improvement rate corresponding to highly automated tasks (e.g., numeric controlled machining) would be only 95% (i.e., b = -0.0740) or so. Notice, the faster the rate of improvement, the lower the percentage used to depict it. For instance, an 80% improvement rate reflects faster learning than a 95% rate does. The exponents are clearly different (cf. b = -0.3219 vs. -0.0740), with larger negative values corresponding to faster improvement. A helpful way to think about this relationship is in terms of how much time is saved on each repetition. For instance, at an 80% improvement rate, each doubling of repetitions saves 20% in terms of time, whereas at a 95% rate, each doubling saves only 5%. Recall our discussion above of the tension between learning and doing. The learning rate quantifies the slope of the learning-by-doing (e.g., OJT) vector. The faster the learning (i.e., larger negative value of the exponent b), the larger the learning component.

We use this to induce our seventh leadership mandate from the practical application section of this book. Mandate 7. The greater the use of automation at the beginning of a process, the lower the improvement rate.

Figure 7 delineates 80% and 95% learning curves for further comparison. Notice both curves start at the same point (i.e., x = 1, A = 100) and decrease logarithmically with cumulative repetition. The 80% curve decreases much faster than the 95% curve does. For instance, the former curve reaches the 80-hour point in terms of unit time on the second task repetition (i.e., x = 2), whereas the latter curve does not cross this point until the 21st repetition (i.e., x = 21). Notice also that both curves decrease more rapidly

Figure 7. Learning curves at 80% and 95%

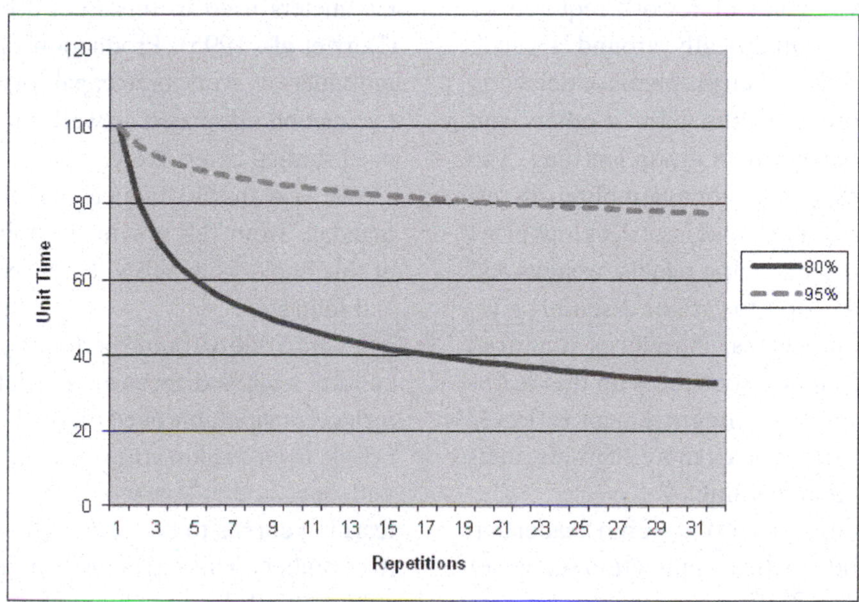

in the beginning than they do as the number of repetitions increases. Mathematically, the second derivatives of these functions with negative values for exponents (i.e., $b < 0$) indicate this must be the case. In words, the more that performance of a task improves through repetition, the less room that remains for subsequent improvement. This makes intuitive sense, given that people tend to make more mistakes when first learning a task than after having mastered it. The learning curve quantifies such intuition.

Another rule of thumb pertaining to learning curves involves the nature of "learning." Recall from above that we describe the use of such curves to depict organizational learning. This includes but is not limited to the learning of people accomplishing a task (see Epple et al., 1991). In the case of aircraft assembly, for instance, people riveting aluminum panels improve individually as they develop increased competence: using the rivet gun, timing and sequencing the holes and rivets they insert, positioning and moving their bodies, and like factors associated with individual learning all provide representative examples. Groups of individual riveters learn also, for instance, how to work simultaneously on a large panel without getting in one another's way, how to decrease the amount of rework required by inserting rivets symmetrically around a panel, how to communicate when problems or delays on one person's work affect the work of others, and like factors associated with group learning. The assembly unit responsible for assembling aircraft panels learns too, for instance, as it develops plans for building and sequencing panels, assigns and trains individual people to various assembly jobs, improves work processes, introduces improved tools, and like factors associated with unit learning. Hence performance improvement reflected by learning curves involves more than just individual knowing and learning.

We use this to induce our eighth leadership mandate from the practical application section of this book. Mandate 8. Performance improvement reflected by learning curves involves more than just individual knowing and learning.

Factors other than cumulative repetition can affect organizational learning as well, and learning curves can be adapted to accommodate many such factors. For instance, calendar time spent in a particular industry or line of work can substitute as a proxy for cumulative number of repetitions (Ingram & Simons, 2002). Assuming that people and organizations follow similar organizational processes and learning trends, then an organization that has been doing some set of tasks for a longer period of time than another one has would be expected to perform better at such tasks. The learning curve can quantify this dynamic using the same logic and logarithmic form as discussed above in terms of learning rate. Using a 90% learning rate, for example, one firm that had been in a line of business for twice as long as another firm has would expect an approximate 10% performance advantage. Clearly the larger the time difference between any two such firms, and the larger the learning rate, the greater the performance benefits accruing to the first mover or incumbent. Knowledge dissipation or forgetting can be quantified through learning curves also, as another instance, with additional parameters used to represent a dissipation rate (Darr et al., 1995). Production rate, technology introduction, workforce capability and other factors can be integrated as well. Such factors have been studied extensively.

We use this to induce our ninth leadership mandate from the practical application section of this book. Mandate 9. Knowledge can be lost and found.

A third rule of thumb pertains to organizational culture, trust and incentives. Such latter factors reflect considerable need for further study. Where people in an organization share knowledge freely with one another, one would expect generally for learning curves to be steeper (i.e., learning rates to be higher). This has been demonstrated empirically through laboratory work on organizational knowledge- and information-sharing tasks (Powley & Nissen, 2012). Knowledge sharing as such as can have multiple effects. It can increase an individual's learning rate, as other, perhaps more experienced people provide guidance, assistance and support to augment the trial and error of OJT. Individuals sharing knowledge about process flaws and opportunities can similarly improve a group's learning rate, as better methods and tools are developed for multiple workers to employ. The same phenomenon can apply at the organization level also. Conversely, where the organization culture does not exhibit knowledge sharing, one would expect generally for slower learning. Hence organizational culture represents an important determinant of success for a KM project.

In terms of trust, this relates directly to knowledge sharing. Knowledge is power, and sharing knowledge requires time and energy. Knowledge sharing also takes time and energy away from the task at hand (e.g., workflows). For someone (or some group or some organization) to share knowledge willingly, he or she (or it) should feel confident that such sharing will not be detrimental to his or her (or its) success. This is a matter of interpersonal trust. Inter-group and inter-organizational trust follow similar logic. For people in or in charge of a group to share knowledge willingly, they should feel likewise that the time and energy required to do so will be worth the corresponding monetary and opportunity cost. This is partly a matter of motivation and goals and partly a matter of incentives. This applies well to groups and organizations as well as individuals. Where trust between individuals, groups and organizations is relatively high, one would expect generally for faster learning. Hence trust represents also an important determinant of success for a KM project.

In terms of incentives, these become important to ameliorate the negative impacts of organizational cultures and conditions of trust that inhibit knowledge sharing. In most cases, the knowledge manager cannot control the organizational culture that he or she inherits in an ongoing organization. Likewise, in most cases, the knowledge manager cannot control the trust that exists within an organization, but given that organizational culture and trust are important in terms of knowledge flows, the knowledge manager should seek to address any problems that may manifest themselves along these lines. Incentives represent an approach to trying to shift organizational culture and/or promote trust.

Where one finds a culture that does not involve knowledge sharing, for instance, individuals, groups and organizations can be incentivized to share more. The use of incentives is discussed thoroughly through a large literature in Economics. Such use has both pros and cons, and a combination of pecuniary and intrinsic rewards can be employed for incentivization. Where one finds an organization in which people exhibit low levels of trust, as another instance, incentives may represent an approach to promoting trust. However, trust cannot be bought, so the use of incentives is challenging in this regard. In many respects, it should be clear how organizational culture and trust are related closely. For instance, a culture of knowledge sharing can promote trust, and trust can promote a culture of knowledge sharing. Incentives can be employed to promote both, but such employment of incentives entails risks as well as opportunities.

We use this to induce our tenth leadership mandate from the practical application section of this book. Mandate 10. Trust cannot be bought.

In terms of assessing knowledge flow performance, learning curves can be used both predictively and descriptively. In the former sense, one can project the learning expected to occur by parameterizing a learning curve. For instance, where one had insight or information to expect an 85% learning rate would obtain for a particular group of tasks, curves such as those plotted above could be projected for such tasks. Many major corporations (e.g., in the aerospace industry) do this routinely in the pricing of aircraft and like products years or sometimes even decades before they have been built. The key is to predict accurately at what rate of improvement the organization will progress. Beyond heuristic rules of thumb (e.g., 80% for manual labor, 95% for automated processes), one must rely intensively upon empirical data to estimate improvement rates.

In this latter, empirical sense, one can measure the learning that occurs by fitting a learning curve to performance data. For instance, where one tracks the time required to complete a group of tasks (e.g., by unit or through time), the associated data can be plotted graphically and fitted via regression or like statistical technique to assess the learning rate. The same major corporations that use learning curves to project product prices also track process improvement rates to assess how well the organizational learning progresses relative to plan. For instance, consider the data presented in Table 6.

The data in this table reflect performance across 32 repetitions of some task, with performance measured in terms of the time required for each repetition. For instance, the first time the task was performed (i.e., Repetition = 1), it required 95 hours to complete (i.e., Time = 95 hours). The next time it required 85 hours (i.e., Repetition = 2, Time = 85); the third attempt took 65 hours, and so forth. When these performance data are analyzed via linear regression (e.g., taking the logarithm of both the Repetition and Time values transforms these into linear series), a curve is fit with properties very close to those of the predicted 80% learning curve. Specifically, the estimated slope is 80.2%. Clearly an 80% improvement rate represents a good estimate in this case. The plot comparing the data and regression is presented in Figure 8 for illustration.

There is little reason why this kind of projection and measurement cannot be accomplished in every organization that engages in repetitive tasks. The problem of course is, some tasks are more repeatable than others are (cf. R&D vs. assembly-line work), and without some kind of benchmark for comparison, it can be difficult to distinguish

Table 6. Improvement data

Repetition	Time
1	95
2	85
3	65
4	64
5	62
6	58
7	52
8	53
9	48
10	45
11	47
12	43
13	45
14	41
15	43
16	39
17	41
18	38
19	38
20	37
21	36
22	38
23	37
24	34
25	36
26	34
27	36
28	33
29	35
30	33
31	34
32	35

between "good" and "bad" improvement rates in practice. For instance, 90% improvement for numeric controlled machining is good, whereas 85% improvement for manual assembly work is bad, even though the former rate of improvement

Figure 8. Performance data and regression fit lines

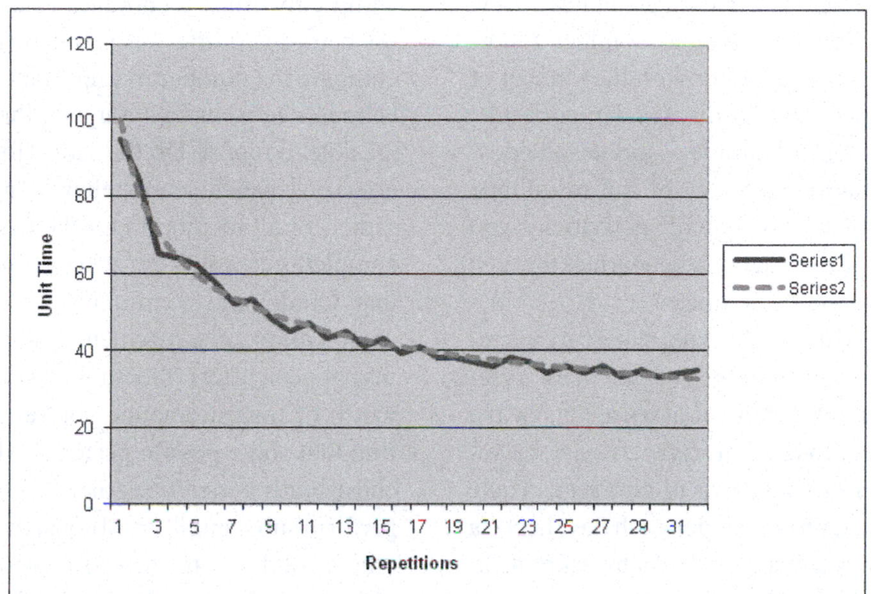

is less than the latter is. Nonetheless, nearly every task has some repetitive component, and the learning curve can provide a useful tool for assessing the learning corresponding to its performance.

Even software development, for instance, every implementation of which is heralded as unique, involves cumulative learning. It is common to have some software developers working at up to 30 times the productivity of others (STSC, 2000), for example. Hence learning via performance improvement is clearly present in the software domain. The question becomes, what is the appropriate unit of repetition for measuring such learning? Clearly the software project or implementation represents an unsuitable unit, for each one is unique in some respects. Rather, finer-grained activities such as determining system requirements, designing software architectures, using specific development tools, coding certain algorithms, and the like involve considerable repetition.

The power of measurement is so important that our point above bears repeating: There is little reason why this kind of projection and measurement cannot be accomplished in every organization that engages in repetitive tasks. When one measures repetitive task performance, one gains the ability to measure the inherent knowledge flows (i.e., learning), which is powerful analytically and extremely useful for leadership, management and decision-making. Where one person, or team, or organization exhibits greater learning (for the same or similar activities) than another, for instance, measurement provides analytical and graphical evidence of such difference and begs the questions, why? and how can we get the underperformers to learn more quickly? These are very important questions, particularly as we recall the dynamics of knowledge-based competitive advantage and how faster organizational learning can sustain (or overcome) first-mover and like advantages that may obtain.

Moreover, no organization is exempt. As with our software example above, every organization has processes that involve at least partially repetitive activities, the performance of which should improve consistently and continually over time (e.g., according to a learning curve percentage). How long does it take your gardener to mow the lawn? Measure him or her with a stopwatch. How long does it take an attorney to prepare a court brief? Measure him or her with a calendar. How long does it take a manager to conduct a staff meeting? Measure him or her with the number of yawns suppressed by subordinates. Humor aside, as with our software example—and despite possibly large variation in terms of the magnitude and complexity of "repeated" activities—you will be surprised by what can be learned through measurement along these lines.

Even in the Military domain, where measurement is encouraged broadly but practiced infrequently, measurement has (or at least can have) a prominent place. Take an aircraft carrier at sea, for instance. Dozens to hundreds of aircraft can take off from and land on the carrier each day; hence a repetitive activity with potential for measurement. Different aircraft are flown by different pilots, in different weather conditions, at different times of the day, but every landing gets measured. Every pilot is measured subjectively (e.g., was the landing "OK"?) and objectively (e.g., which arresting wire did the plane hit?). There are safety, normative, cultural and other reasons behind these, admittedly crude measurements, but carrier leaders, managers, aviators and others feel that the corresponding information is useful; they pay attention to the measurements; and they take corrective actions based upon knowledge inferred from them. One would think that the quality and safety of carrier aircraft landings would be extremely difficult to measure, but even this crude measure provides useful insight. An ancient Chinese proverb reads, "It is better to light a candle than to curse the darkness." A corollary prescription in this book reads, "Measure repetitive activities."

Staying in this military domain for the time being, maintaining situational awareness (SA; e.g., understanding an organization's current circumstances, threats and options) represents a fundamental imperative and constitutes the bulk of myriad people's time and energy as they stand tactical, operational and other watches. Most people will exclaim that SA cannot be measured, and so few if any people even try. Well, here's another, admittedly crude technique. Talk to watchstanders before and after each watch (i.e., shift), and compare the number of important environmental elements (e.g., tracks, targets, threats) that they are able to report. Do the same (for all members) after one watch team relieves another. Do the same (for all members) for the first team when it completes its watch the next day, and the day after that. Crude (and seemingly subjective as well as objective) as a measurement technique such as this may appear, after collecting a week's or a month's worth of measurements, you're highly likely to find that some people perform substantially and consistently better than others do; that some teams perform substantially and consistently better than others do; that some times of day (e.g., Midnight, Dawn, Noon, after dinner) lead to consistently better or worse performance across all people and teams; that some watch leaders generate higher performance levels (even from the same group of people) than others do; and so forth. Most leaders and managers would find use for such information, and most would even view it as knowledge, upon which they could take corrective action. The same goes for maintaining "SA" regarding the status of a telecommunication company's network across areas or shifts, maintaining "SA" of hospital patients' health across wards or shifts, maintaining "SA" of college students' test performance across courses and semesters. Indeed, the list of applications is long, and the technique is powerful.

KNOWLEDGE FLOW COMPUTATIONAL MODELING

Computational modeling represents an extension of simulation, which we discuss in the knowledge technology chapter, and a simple example of which we use to illustrate the measurement of knowledge power above. Computational models are used extensively in the physical sciences to represent the dynamics of phenomena such as fluid flows, heat transfers and resilience of structures, for instance. Comparable models are used also in the social sciences to represent the dynamics of money flows, economic transfers and communication structures, for instance. Models from the former sciences provide a basis for designing physical artifacts (e.g., airplanes, bridges, computers) by representing such artifacts via models and simulating their dynamic behaviors under various conditions. Models from the latter sciences provide a basis for making decisions about social systems (e.g., finance, trade, broadcasting) by representing such systems via models and simulating their dynamic behaviors under various conditions.

In both cases, most of the design and analysis can be accomplished via computer, through iterative conceptualization, scrutiny and refinement of virtual prototypes. A great many alternate, virtual prototypes can be designed and analyzed—via computational models—in relatively short periods of time without incurring the expenses and potential risks associated with using physical prototypes. For instance, nearly all modern aircraft are designed and tested virtually before a single piece of metal, plastic or other structural element is made and long before any person is asked to risk his or her life in an untested airplane. Even before well-accepted wind-tunnel testing of scale models, the virtual equivalents of full-scale designs are conceived, analyzed and refined iteratively via computer.

The key is to develop computational models that reflect well the structures and behaviors of the artifacts and systems they represent. With high-fidelity representations and simulations, the designer can attain considerable confidence that the behaviors obtained via simulation in a virtual world will mirror those of a physical or social system implemented in the real world. In the case of aircraft, to continue this instance, sophisticated computational models represent dynamic flows of fluids (esp. air at high speeds) in three spatial dimensions. The behaviors of such represented fluid flows match exceedingly closely the behaviors of physical fluid flows in comparable conditions (e.g., along a wing section or through an engine nozzle). When designers have conceptualized, analyzed and refined an aircraft via computational analysis to the point at which it satisfies their requirements, they can begin the development and testing of a physical prototype. The same approach holds too for the design of bridges, buildings, computers and many other physical artifacts.

This approach is used as well for designing some social systems, but the models generally lack the same level of sophistication and precision as exhibited by those representing physical artifacts. Micro-theory and analysis tools for designing physical artifacts rest on well-understood principles of physics (e.g., involving continuous numerical variables, describing materials whose properties are relatively easy to measure and calibrate, including physical behaviors that remain invariant across physical locations and times), and analysis of such physical systems yields easily to differential equations and precise numerical computing (Nissen & Levitt, 2004; 2005). In contrast, theories describing the behavior of organizations and other social systems are characterized generally by nominal and ordinal variables, with poor measurement reproducibility, and verbal descriptions reflecting significant ambiguity. Unlike the mathematically representable and analyzable micro-behaviors of physical systems, the dynamics of organizations are influenced by a variety of social, technical and cultural factors; are difficult to verify experimentally; and are not as amenable to numerical representation, mathematical analysis or precise measurement. Moreover, quite distinct from physical systems, people and social interactions—not molecules and physical forces—drive the behavior of organizations and many other social systems. Hence such behaviors are fundamentally non-deterministic and difficult to predict at the individual level. Thus, people, organizations and business processes are qualitatively different than bridges, semiconductors and airplanes are.

It is irrational to expect the former to ever be as understandable, analyzable or predictable as the latter. This represents a fundamental limitation of the approach.

Within the constraints of this limitation, however, we can still take great strides beyond relying upon informal and ambiguous, natural language, textual description of organizational knowledge flows (e.g., the bulk of extant theory). For instance, the domain of organization theory is imbued with a rich, time-tested collection of micro-theories that lend themselves to qualitative representation and analysis. Examples include Galbraith's (1977) information processing abstraction, March and Simon's (1958) bounded rationality assumption, and Thompson's (1967) task interdependence contingencies. Drawing from this theory base, symbolic (i.e., non-numeric) representation and reasoning techniques from established AI research are employed—in addition to time-proven methods of discrete-event simulation (e.g., approximating aggregate behaviors via statistical distributions, Monte Carlo techniques)—to develop computational models of dynamic organizational knowing phenomena. Once formalized through a computational model, the symbolic representation is "executable," meaning it can emulate the dynamics of organizational behaviors.

We use this to induce our eleventh leadership mandate from the practical application section of this book. Mandate 11. Using computational models, organizations can be designed and tested virtually, in a manner similar to the design of airplanes, bridges and computers.

POWer

In terms of computational modeling of knowledge flows, probably the most advanced application is associated with POWer (i.e., Projects, Organizations and Work for edge research; see Gateau et al. 2007). POWer researchers have spent roughly a decade building upon groundbreaking work by the Virtual Design Team (VDT) at Stanford, which is focused on computational modeling of knowledge-based project work with the goal of designing project organizations in a manner analogous to that described above for physical artifacts (see Nissen & Levitt, 2004; 2005). Using an agent-based representation (Cohen, 1992; Kunz et al., 1998), micro-level organizational behaviors have been researched and formalized to reflect well-accepted organization theory (Levitt et al., 1999).

The POWer modeling environment has been developed directly from Galbraith's information processing view of organizations. This information processing view has several key implications (Jin & Levitt, 1996). One is ontological: knowledge work is modeled through interactions of tasks to be performed, actors communicating with one another and performing tasks, and an organization structure that defines actors' roles and constrains their behaviors. In essence this amounts to overlaying the task structure on the organization structure and to developing computational agents with various capabilities to emulate the behaviors of organizational actors performing work.

By building upon VDT, the POWer modeling environment also benefits from extensive fieldwork in many diverse enterprise domains (e.g., power plant construction and offshore drilling, see Christiansen, 1993; aerospace, see Thomsen, 1998; software development, see Nogueira, 2000; healthcare, see Cheng & Levitt, 2001; military operations, see Looney & Nissen, 2006; others). Through the process of "hindcasting"—predicting known organizational outcomes using only information that was available at the beginning of a project—computational models of operational enterprises in practice have demonstrated dozens of times that emulated organizational behaviors and results correspond qualitatively and quantitatively to their operational counterparts in the field (Kunz et al., 1998). Further, the POWer modeling environment has been validated repeatedly and longitudinally as representative of both organization theory and enterprises in practice. This affords considerable confidence in the simulation results.

Moreover, POWer is designed specifically to model the kinds of knowledge work and information processing tasks that comprise the bulk of knowledge flow processes. In particular, building upon Knowledge Flow Theory (e.g., as articulated in Part I of this book), POWer methods and tools have been extended to reproduce increasingly fine-grained behaviors of knowledge in action and motion (i.e., knowing and learning). This includes knowledge flow processes and tools such as direct experience, formal training, transactive memory, mentoring and simulation, in addition to commonplace approaches such as Web portals, knowledge maps, communities of practice, and even technologies enabling the kinds of emerging knowledge phenomena discussed in Part III of this book.

Practical Illustration

As an example of assessing knowledge flows through computational modeling, here we employ the POWer modeling environment to represent work processes associated with a high-level technology development project. This illustration is described by Nissen et al. (2008). The key KM question of interest here is, to what extent should the organization focus on developing specialist knowledge within its two functional areas of design and manufacturing versus promoting generalist knowledge across functional areas? Notice both path dependence and tension between exploitation versus exploration in this question. Where people develop deep specialist knowledge, it limits the variety of problems that can be addressed, but such knowledge is highly detailed and hence powerful within its narrow domain. Where people develop broad generalist knowledge, in contrast, it enables them to address a wide array of diverse problems, but such knowledge is neither particularly detailed nor powerful within any given domain. Further, given limited time, energy and like resources for learning and doing, an investment in learning specialist knowledge restricts one's ability to become a generalist, and vice versa.

Many economists view decisions such as this in terms of whether two alternatives represent complements or substitutes. Where two alternatives are complements, productivity from using one is limited without using the other also. The complementation between one's left and right shoes represents a classic example. Where two alternatives are substitutes, alternatively, productivity from using one is unchanged when switching to another. The substitution between a single dollar bill and four quarter coins represents an example. Classical microeconomic theory (e.g., see Pindyck & Rubinfeld, 1998; Samuelson, 1974) imposes a number of relationships over the manner in which complements and substitutes affect one another as well as the marginal productivity associated with their use. In terms of complementation or substitution of specialist and generalist knowledge, such relationships are described in part by Postrel (2002).

Figure 9 presents a screenshot (This particular screenshot is from the commercial product SimVision™, which emerged from VDT research along with POWer.) delineating two primary tasks (i.e., design and manufacturing), each performed by a corresponding organizational unit (i.e., design actor and manufacturing actor). The two milestone markers shown in the figure (i.e., "Start" and "Finish") are used to denote progress, but such markers neither represent tasks nor entail effort. The tree structure shown in the top-left of the figure displays several of the different ontological elements of the model (e.g., tasks, positions, milestones). The table shown in the bottom-left displays numerous program-level parameters (e.g., team experience, centralization, formalization), which are all set to empirically determined "normal" values for product development work. Values for such parameters are held constant (i.e., controlled) across simulations of alternate cases and scenarios.

Figure 9. POWer baseline product development model (adapted from Nissen, 2006)

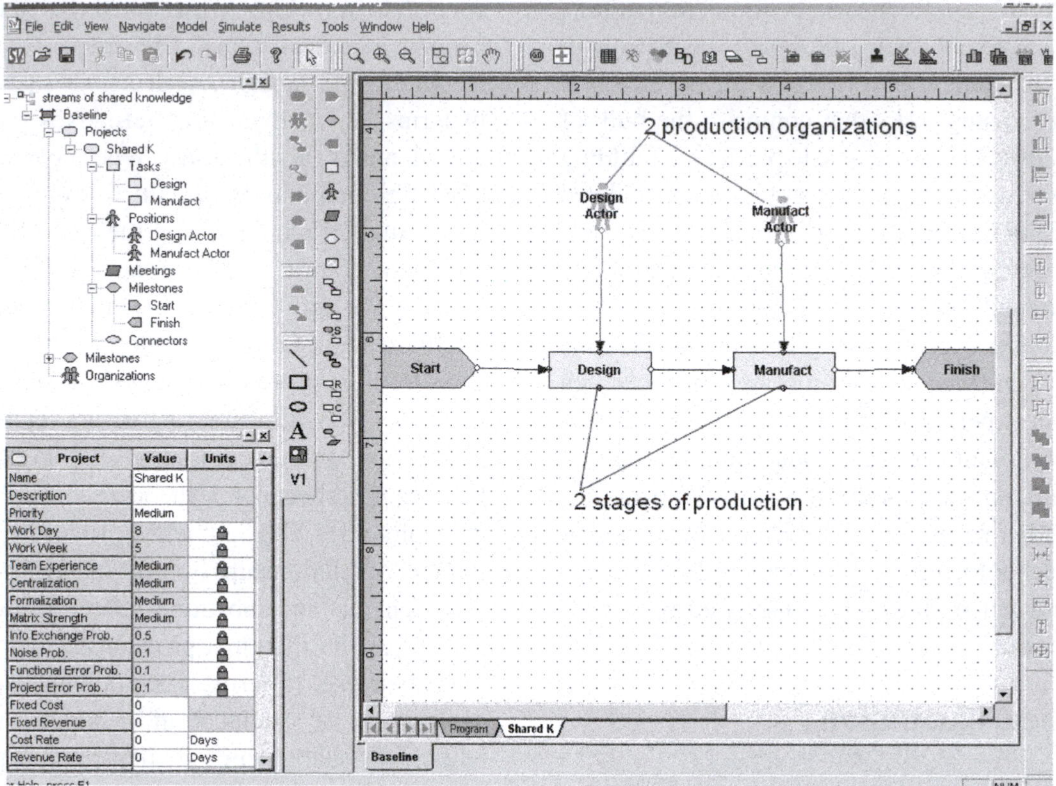

To analyze this computational model, it is parameterized to reflect "medium" specialist knowledge and "medium" generalist knowledge. We are interested in learning how varying the relative levels of specialist and generalist knowledge will impact organizational performance on the project. To develop insight into the dynamic behavior of this project organization, we examine a multitude of different conditions. Indeed, we conduct a full-factorial computational experiment, with knowledge representing "low," "medium," and "high" levels for all combinations of specialist and generalist settings. Examining each case individually provides us with precise control over which factors can vary and hence excellent insight into causality. Examining exhaustively all combinations of specialist and generalist knowledge levels provides us with insight into the entire design space associated with these KM variables of interest, and using consistently the output measure project duration enables us to employ a common metric to assess relative performance. These benefits all accrue from analyzing computationally a virtual prototype of the project organization. Moreover, using empirically determined and validated "normal" settings to depict the behavior of a representative technology project provides us with confidence that results of our simulations bear resemblance to those of operational organizational projects in the field. This benefit accrues from employing the general and validated modeling environment POWer.

Computational results for the product development model are summarized in Table 7. The values listed in the table reflect simulated project duration and are expressed in workdays. For instance, notice the result in the table's center (highlighted in bold font for emphasis): a project staffed with actors possessing medium levels of Specialist manufacturing knowledge (S) and medium levels of generalist knowledge (G) is projected by the model to require 216 workdays to complete. This reflects a nominal 200 days of work specified (i.e., work volume), along with 16 days of additional problem solving (e.g., internal communication, delay and exception handling associated with noise, uncertainty and errors). The additional 16 days' problem solving time reflects empirically determined relationships between model parameters (e.g., levels of S and G) and organizational performance.

Table 7 reports full-factorial results of nine simulation runs, with both the S (i.e., specialist knowledge) and G (i.e., generalist) parameters varying across three levels: low, medium, and high. Notice the simulation results vary in understandable ways across the three levels of both specialist and generalist knowledge. For instance, holding the parameter G constant at the medium level of generalist knowledge, performance in terms of project duration ranges from 264 days when specialist knowledge is low, to 178 days when specialist knowledge is high. The greater the level of specialist knowledge (i.e., holding the level of generalist knowledge constant), the better the organizational performance in terms of project duration, and vice versa. This indicates the marginal product of such knowledge is positive (i.e., consistent with classical microeconomic theory).

This same monotonic relationship is evident at the other levels of generalist knowledge (i.e., low G, high G) as well. Likewise, holding the parameter S constant at the medium level of specialist knowledge, performance in terms of project duration ranges symmetrically from 264 days when generalist knowledge is low, to 178 days when generalist knowledge is high. The greater the level of generalist knowledge (i.e., holding the level of specialist knowledge constant), the better the organizational performance in terms of project duration, and vice versa. This is consistent with classical microeconomic theory also and is evident too at the other levels of specialist knowledge (i.e., low S, high S).

Table 7. Computational model results

Parameter	Low S	Medium S	High S
High G	226	178	141
Medium G	264	**216**	178
Low G	310	264	226

Project Duration in workdays

The symmetry reflected in the results of Table 7 corresponds to the microeconomic case of perfect substitution: specialist and generalist knowledge can be substituted—unit for unit—to maintain performance at some arbitrary level (e.g., along an isoquant). For instance from the table, where specialist knowledge (S) is low, but generalist knowledge (G) is medium, performance (264 workdays) is the same as where specialist knowledge (S) is medium (i.e. one unit higher), but generalist knowledge (G) is low (i.e. one unit lower). Other instances of such substitutability can be identified readily through different combinations of knowledge types S and G (e.g., low S, high G <--> high S, low G [226 days], high S, medium G <--> medium S, high G [178 days]).

With this the computational model indicates specialist and generalist knowledge represent substitutes for one another. It is important to note here, this result reflecting perfect substitution reflects an emergent property of the computational model, not an explicit behavior; that is, nowhere in the development of the POWer environment or this computational project model do we specify behaviors of perfect substitution. Rather, the nature of interactions between POWer actors, tasks, organizations and environmental settings lead dynamically to this result. In a sense this provides some additional validation of POWer behaviors (i.e., from classical microeconomics).

We use this to induce our twelfth leadership mandate from the practical application section of this book. Mandate 12. Specialist and generalist knowledge represent (imperfect) economic substitutes for one another.

Clearly this relatively simple computational model excludes several factors and aspects of the world that would complicate the analysis and alter the symmetry of results. Nonetheless, we are able to model computationally actions associated with knowing in an organizational context. We are able to observe the dynamic behaviors of actors possessing and using different kinds of knowledge at different inventory levels. We are able to compare the relative dynamic performance of the organization associated with each case. This provides considerable insight that is useful for assessing knowledge flow performance.

KNOWLEDGE FLOW ASSESSMENT PRINCIPLES

Five principles developed in this chapter help shed light on knowledge flow assessment: 26) knowledge management involves organizational change; 27) knowledge inventory can be used to assess an organization's readiness to perform its work processes effectively; 28) when estimating the value of knowledge, it is often better to light a candle than to curse the darkness; 29) culture, trust and incentives affect organizational learning, and hence performance as much as process, technology and training do; and 30) computational modeling is useful for knowing and learning about organizational knowing and learning.

Principle 26: First, KM projects involve change. There is much to learn from the literature on change management in this regard. For instance, the leader and manager can assess an organization's preconditions for success as well as preconditions for failure. KM-specific factors such as knowledge representation, attention to tacit knowledge, and focus on organizational memory are important too and can be evaluated and addressed by the leader and manager. We find also how perceptual measures such as pessimism, affective commitment and normative commitment are important in KM projects as well. Hence the leader and manager have much to learn from change-management.

Principle 27: Second, knowledge inventory can be used to assess an organization's readiness to perform its work processes effectively. The knowledge audit represents an approach to discovering and documenting sources, uses and sinks of knowledge in an organization. Generally executed via some kind of survey instrument, the knowledge audit is performed often by consultants and like professionals from outside the organization, but there is little reason why an organization should not be able to audit itself. In addition to articulating explicitly certain aspects of knowledge inventories and flows, conducting a knowledge audit can produce positive effects simply by inducing people within the organization to think about what knowledge is important, how it is used, and how it flows. Alternatively, knowledge audits consume precious time and energy. Perhaps the greatest potential in terms of a knowledge audit lies in the prospect of measuring knowledge inventory. This construct offers potential to assess an organization's readiness to perform its work processes effectively. Hence the leader and manager need to measure the knowledge inventory for every organization.

Principle 28: Third, knowledge power can be estimated and measured. The 5D model introduced above, combined with Knowledge Flow Theory, provides an approach to measuring, analyzing and visualizing the dynamics of knowledge flows through an organization. With empirical analysis, one can leverage characteristics of organizational knowledge flows to predict the corresponding knowledge power effected via action. Although the 5D model and knowledge power analysis remain comparatively novel in terms of development and application, the technique reflects metaphorically the concept candle lighting: when in an environment without light, it is often better to light a candle than to curse the darkness (ancient Chinese proverb). Hence knowledge power measurement provides an approach to assessing the relative efficacy of knowledge flowing through various organizational processes.

Principle 29: Fourth, culture, trust and incentives affect organizational learning—and hence performance—as much as process, technology and training do. Learning rates can be measured and projected, and through the well-accepted and –established learning curve, the knowledge flow component of experiential knowing (i.e., learning) can be measured and related mathematically with the workflow component (i.e., doing). Several general rules of thumb provide guidance for application of learning curves. These include the well-studied roles of automation, calendar time, production rate, technology introduction and workforce capability, in addition to less-understood factors such as organizational culture, trust and incentives. Nonetheless, such latter factors can affect organizational learning and hence performance as much as the former ones do. Every organizational process involving repetition should experience performance improvement through learning at multiple levels of reach (e.g., individual, group, organization). Where such improvement may not obtain, this signals a problem with knowledge clumping and calls attention to the associated knowledge flows. Hence every organizational process should improve its performance over time, and every leader and manager should measure the dynamic performance of repetitive processes.

Principle 30: Finally, computational modeling can be used to learn about organizational knowing and learning. Computational models are used extensively in the physical sciences for the design of artifacts, and their use in the social sciences is increasing. Through advanced computational models that describe dynamic behaviors of knowledge flows in the organization, one can represent, simulate and analyze—virtually—many different organization designs to assess the relative strengths and weaknesses of alternate approaches to enhancing knowledge flows. By analyzing knowledge flows in different organization designs (e.g., alternate structures, workflows, personnel characteristics, technologies), one can gain insight into how different dynamic knowledge patterns affect organizational performance. One can gain insight also into how the knowing and learning that take place within an organization react to different leadership and management interventions (e.g., OJT, training, mentoring, simulation). This represents a risk-mitigation strategy for addressing the change aspect of KM projects: before deciding upon a specific KM approach and implementing a particular set of organizational, work, personnel and/or technological changes, one can assess computationally the relatively efficacy and efficiency of each alternative. Hence computational models of knowledge flows provide an approach to mitigating the risk inherent in KM programs.

EXERCISES

1. Use the preconditions for success and failure from above to analyze a major change that took place in an organization with which you are familiar. Can you identify any lessons to be learned through such analysis?
2. Describe how you would use simulation (even building simple models such as Excel spreadsheets) to assess the knowledge power associated with any two or more knowledge flow processes in your organization. How would you determine the inputs required, and what insights or other benefits would you expect from the analysis?
3. Explain if or how your performance conducting a KVA analysis to assess multiple organizational processes would be expected to improve through repetition or over time. Understanding that every process is different, and hence no two KVA analyses would represent exact repetitions, how would this affect your answer?

4. How could the knowledge flow analysis discussed in the practical illustration of computational modeling above be extended to increase the realism and fidelity of the simulation? How would you go about representing and simulating such increased realism and fidelity in the model?

REFERENCES

Andrews, D. C., & Stalick, S. K. (1994). *Business reengineering: The survival guide*. New York, NY: Yourdon Press Computing Series.

Argote, L., Beckman, S. L., & Epple, D. (1990). The persistence and transfer of learning in industrial settings. *Management Science*, *36*(2), 140–154. doi:10.1287/mnsc.36.2.140.

Bashein, B. J., Markus, M. L., & Riley, P. (1994). Preconditions for BPR success: And how to prevent failures. *Information Systems Management*, *11*(2), 7–13. doi:10.1080/10580539408964630.

Carpenter, S., & Rudge, S. (2003). A self-help approach to knowledge management benchmarking. *Journal of Knowledge Management*, *7*(5), 82–95. doi:10.1108/13673270310505403.

Cheng, C. H. F., & Levitt, R. E. (2001). Contextually changing behavior in medical organizations. In *Proceedings of the 2001 Annual Symposium of the American Medical Informatics Association.* Washington, DC: AMIA.

Christiansen, T. R. (1993). *Modeling efficiency and effectiveness of coordination in engineering design teams.* (Unpublished doctoral dissertation). Department of Civil and Environmental Engineering, Stanford University, Palo Alto, CA.

Clemons, E. K., Thatcher, M. E., & Row, M. C. (1995). Identifying sources of reengineering failures: A study of the behavioral factors contributing to reengineering risks. *Journal of Management Information Systems*, *12*(2), 9–36.

Cohen, G. P. (1992). *The virtual design team: An object-oriented model of information sharing in project teams.* (Unpublished doctoral dissertation). Department of Civil Engineering, Stanford University, Palo Alto, CA.

Darr, E. D., Argote, L., & Epple, D. (1995). The acquisition, transfer, and depreciation of knowledge in service organizations: Productivity in franchises. *Management Science*, *41*(11), 1750–1762. doi:10.1287/mnsc.41.11.1750.

Davenport, T. H. (1993). *Process innovation: Reengineering work through information technology*. Boston, MA: Harvard University Press.

Davenport, T. H., De Long, D. W., & Beers, M. C. (1998, Winter). Successful knowledge management projects. *Sloan Management Review*, 43–57.

Davenport, T. H., & Stoddard, D. B. (1994). Reengineering: Business change of mythic proportions? *Management Information Systems Quarterly*, *18*(2), 121–127. doi:10.2307/249760.

Epple, D., Argote, L., & Devadas, R. (1991). Organizational learning curves: A method for investigating intra-plant transfer of knowledge acquired through learning by doing. *Organization Science*, *2*(1), 58–70. doi:10.1287/orsc.2.1.58.

Galbraith, J. R. (1977). *Organization design*. Reading, MA: Addison-Wesley.

Gateau, J. B., Leweling, T. A., Looney, J. P., & Nissen, M. E. (2007). Hypothesis testing of edge organizations: Modeling the C2 organization design space. In *Proceedings International Command & Control Research & Technology Symposium*. Newport, RI: Academic Press.

Goldstein, D. K. (1986). *Hallmark cards*. Boston: Harvard Business School.

Grover, V., Jeong, S. R., Kettinger, W. J., & Teng, J. T. C. (1995). The implementation of business process reengineering. *Journal of Management Information Systems*, *12*(1), 109–144.

Hammer, M., & Champy, J. (1993). *Reengineering the corporation: A manifesto for business revolution*. New York, NY: Harper Business Press. doi:10.1016/S0007-6813(05)80064-3.

Hansen, P. A. (1995). Publicly produced knowledge for business: When is it effective? *Technovation*, *15*(6), 387–397. doi:10.1016/0166-4972(95)96599-O.

Harrington, H. J. (1991). *Business process improvement: The breakthrough strategy for total quality, productivity, and competitiveness*. New York, NY: McGraw-Hill.

Holt, D. T., Bartczak, S. E., Clark, S. W., & Trent, M. R. (2007). The development of an instrument to measure readiness for knowledge management. *Knowledge Management Research & Practice*, *5*(2), 75–82. doi:10.1057/palgrave.kmrp.8500132.

Housel, T. J. (2004). *Where to invest in information systems: A CRM case study* (Working paper). Monterey, CA: Naval Postgraduate School.

Housel, T. J., & Bell, A. H. (2001). *Measuring and managing knowledge*. Boston, MA: McGraw-Hill.

Housel, T. J., El Sawy, O., Zhong, J. J., & Rodgers, W. (2001). Measuring the return on knowledge embedded in information technology. In *Proceedings International Conference on Information Systems*. IEEE.

Ingram, P., & Simons, T. (2002). The transfer of experience in groups of organizations: Implications for performance and competition. *Management Science*, *48*(12), 1517–1533. doi:10.1287/mnsc.48.12.1517.437.

Jennex, M. E., & Olfman, L. (2004). Assessing knowledge management success/effectiveness models. In *Proceedings Hawaii International Conference on System Sciences*. Hawaii, HI: IEEE.

Jin, Y., & Levitt, R. E. (1996). The virtual design team: A computational model of project organizations. *Computational & Mathematical Organization Theory*, *2*(3), 171–195. doi:10.1007/BF00127273.

Johansson, H. J., McHugh, P., Pendlebury, A. J., & Wheeler, W. A. III. (1993). *Business process reengineering: Breakpoint strategies for market dominance*. Chichester, UK: Wiley.

Kettinger, W. J., Guha, S., & Teng, J. T. C. (1995). The process reengineering life cycle methodology: A case study. In Grover, V., & Kettinger, W. (Eds.), *Business Process Change: Reengineering Concepts, Methods and Technologies*. Hershey, PA: Idea Publishing.

King, J. L., & Konsynski, B. (1990). *Singapore tradenet: A tale of one city*. Boston: Harvard Business School.

King, W. R., & Ko, D. G. (2001). Evaluating knowledge management and the learning organization: An information/knowledge value chain approach. *Communications of the Association for Information Systems*, *5*(14), 1–27.

Kulkarni, U., & Freeze, R. (2004). Development and validation of a knowledge management capability assessment model. In *Proceedings of the Twenty-Fifth International Conference on Information Systems*. IEEE.

Kulkarni, U., & Freeze, R. (2006). Measuring knowledge management capabilities. In *Encyclopedia of Knowledge Management*. Hershey, PA: Idea Group. doi:10.4018/978-1-59140-573-3.ch079.

Kunz, J. C., Levitt, R. E., & Jin, Y. (1998). The virtual design team: A computational simulation model of project organizations. *Communications of the ACM*, *41*(11), 84–92. doi:10.1145/287831.287844.

Levitt, R. E., Thomsen, J., Christiansen, T. R., Junz, J. C., Jin, Y., & Nass, C. (1999). Simulating project work processes and organizations: Toward a micro-contingency theory of organizational design. *Management Science*, *45*(11), 1479–1495. doi:10.1287/mnsc.45.11.1479.

Liebowitz, J., Rubenstein-Montano, B., McCaw, D., Buchwalter, J., Browning, C., Newman, B., & Rebeck, K. (2000). The knowledge audit. *Knowledge and Process Management*, *7*(1), 3–10. doi:10.1002/(SICI)1099-1441(200001/03)7:1<3::AID-KPM72>3.0.CO;2-0.

Looney, J. P., & Nissen, M. E. (2006). Computational modeling and analysis of networked organizational planning in a coalition maritime strike environment. In *Proceedings Command & Control Research & Technology Symposium*. San Diego, CA: Academic Press.

March, J. G., & Simon, H. A. (1958). *Organizations*. New York: Wiley.

Markus, M. L. (2001). Toward a theory of knowledge reuse: Situations and factors in reuse success. *Journal of Management Information Systems*, *18*(1), 57–93.

Nissen, M. E. (1998). Redesigning reengineering through measurement-driven inference. *Management Information Systems Quarterly*, *22*(4), 509–534. doi:10.2307/249553.

Nissen, M. E. (2006). *Harnessing knowledge dynamics: Principled organizational knowing & learning*. Hershey, PA: IGI Global.

Nissen, M. E. (2010). *CyberKM: Harnessing dynamic knowledge for competitive advantage through cyberspace* (Technical Report No. NPS-IS-10-006). Monterey, CA: Naval Postgraduate School.

Nissen, M. E. (2011). Measuring dynamic knowledge flows: Implications for organizational performance. In Schiuma, G. (Ed.), *Managing Knowledge Assets and Business Value Creation in Organizations*. Hershey, PA: IGI Global.

Nissen, M. E., & Levitt, R. E. (2004). Agent-based modeling of knowledge dynamics. *Knowledge Management Research & Practice*, *2*(3), 169–183. doi:10.1057/palgrave.kmrp.8500039.

Nissen, M. E., & Levitt, R. E. (2005). Knowledge management research through computational experimentation. In Schwartz, D. (Ed.), *Encyclopedia of Knowledge Management*. Hershey, PA: Idea Group. doi:10.4018/978-1-59140-573-3.ch008.

Nissen, M. E., Orr, R., & Levitt, R. E. (2008). Streams of shared knowledge: Computational expansion of organization theory. *Knowledge Management Research & Practice*, *6*(2), 124–140. doi:10.1057/kmrp.2008.1.

Nogueira, J. C. (2000). *A formal model for risk assessment in software projects.* (Unpublished doctoral dissertation). Department of Computer Science, Naval Postgraduate School, Monterey, CA.

Pindyck, R. S., & Rubinfeld, D. L. (1998). *Microeconomics* (4th ed.). Upper Saddle River, NJ: Prentice-Hall.

Postrel, S. (2002). Islands of shared knowledge: Specialization and mutual understanding in problem-solving teams. *Organization Science*, *13*(3), 303–320. doi:10.1287/orsc.13.3.303.2773.

Powley, E. H., & Nissen, M. E. (2012). If you can't trust, stick to hierarchy: Structure and trust as contingency factors in threat assessment contexts. *Journal of Homeland Security and Emergency Management*, *9*(1), 1–19. doi:10.1515/1547-7355.1986.

Sameulson, P. A. (1974). Complementarity: An essay on the 40th anniversary of the Hicks-Allen revolution in demand theory. *Journal of Economic Literature*, *12*(4), 1255–1289.

Silvi, R., & Cuganesan, S. (2006). Investigating the management of knowledge for competitive advantage: A strategic cost management perspective. *Journal of Intellectual Capital*, *7*(3), 309–323. doi:10.1108/14691930610681429.

Snyman, R., & Kruger, C. J. (2004). The interdependency between strategic management and strategic knowledge management. *Journal of Knowledge Management*, *8*(1), 5–19. doi:10.1108/13673270410523871.

Stoddard, D. B., & Jarvenpaa, S. L. (1995). Business process redesign: Tactics for managing radical change. *Journal of Information Management Systems*, *12*(1), 81–107.

Stoddard, D. B., & Meadows, C. J. (1992). *Capital holding corporation - Reengineering the direct response group*. Boston: Harvard Business School.

STSC. (2000). *Guidelines for successful acquisition and management of software intensive systems (version 3.0). Hill AFB*. UT: Software Technology Support Center.

Talebzadeh, H., Mandutianu, S., & Winner, C. F. (1995). Countrywide loan-underwriting expert system. *AI Magazine*, *16*(1), 51–64.

Thompson, J. D. (1967). *Organizations in action: Social science bases in administrative theory*. New York: McGraw-Hill.

Thomsen, J. (1998). *The virtual team alliance (VTA): Modeling the effects of goal incongruency in semi-routine, fast-paced project organizations*. (Unpublished doctoral dissertation). Department of Civil and Environmental Engineering, Stanford University, Palo Alto, CA.

Wolf, P. (2011). Balanced evaluation: Monitoring the success of a knowledge management project. *Historical Social Research (Köln)*, *36*(1), 262–287.

Wright, T. (1936). Factors affecting the cost of airplanes. *Journal of the Aeronautical Sciences*, *4*(4), 122–128.

Yelle, L. E. (1979). The learning curve: Historical review and comprehensive survey. *Decision Sciences*, *10*(2), 302–328. doi:10.1111/j.1540-5915.1979.tb00026.x.

Chapter 7
Application Cases in Business

ABSTRACT

This chapter concentrates on knowledge flow visualization and analysis in the for-profit business sector. The authors look at an advanced-technology company involved with new-product development. The discussion turns then to examine an independent production company involved with a feature film. The third case involves a technology-transfer project between a university and a microelectronics company. In each case, they draw from secondary data sources for background. This should prove helpful to the reader who is interested in following up to consider more details than presented in this volume. The authors draw also from their own research and professional experience to fill in missing information, and they apply principles and techniques of this book to contribute new insights through examination of knowledge flows in the cases. Each application case concludes with exercises to stimulate critical thought, learning, and discussion. In conjunction with the principles articulated in Section 1 of the book, the application cases explain how organizations from across a very wide range of sizes and domains both succeed and fail at harnessing dynamic knowledge; hence, through case-based reasoning, they provide both positive and negative examples for the leader and manager to use in comparison with his or her own organization.

ADVANCED TECHNOLOGY COMPANY AND NEW PRODUCT DEVELOPMENT

We draw from Massey et al. (2002a; b) for background of this case. We first summarize important events and issues for context. Visualization and analysis of key knowledge flows follow, with interpretation of leadership and management interventions discussed subsequently. The section closes with exercises pertaining specifically to this application case.

Context

An advanced-technology company in the communications and networks industry faces intense competition. In its technology-intensive competitive arena, product innovation represents a key determinant of performance. Just keeping up with the rapid pace of technological advance is required to avoid falling too far behind competitors, and pulling ahead of competitors requires sustained introduction of innovative products that have market appeal and make business sense. Indeed, the

DOI: 10.4018/978-1-4666-4727-5.ch007

company's strategy centers on innovation. Managers view winning and keeping new customers as the principal means of attaining and sustaining competitive advantage. This competitive backdrop is common across most advanced-technology companies today.

We learn further from the case that management is dissatisfied with the company's performance. The intensity of competition appears to be increasing, and rival firms are beating this company to market with successive new products. When looking for the next new product for the company to introduce, most of the concepts center on extensions and revisions to existing products, as opposed to new-product innovations. The inventory of new products appears to be plentiful, but the inventory of innovations appears to have reached zero. A researcher in the case adds, "some malaise [is present] in product development" at the company (Massey, 2004). Management is justifiably concerned that the company has lost its ability to innovate. Loss of innovation prowess would sound the death knell for an advanced-technology company such as this.

Through in-depth analysis of the problem, management learns the dearth of innovation does not stem from the knowledge of its people. On the contrary, company personnel appear to possess abundant, relevant knowledge necessary for new-product development, and many ideas for new products can be identified. However, such ideas remain stagnant generally, as the process for developing new products is ineffective. The organization does not provide the kind of guidance and support through its routines that people as individuals and in groups need in order to leverage new-product ideas into new product innovations. In other words, the individuals' knowledge appears to be adequate for the task environment, but knowledge embedded in the organization's routines does not. In particular, the problem centers on two issues: 1) new ideas do not flow well to become innovative products; and 2) concept-selection decisions do not reflect shared criteria learned through organizational experience.

Knowledge Flow Analysis

Knowledge flows are critical to both issues. With the first issue, individual knowledge created in terms of new ideas does not move to organizational application through product innovation. We depict the knowledge flow associated with this first issue in Figure 1. The first vector (i.e., labeled "Issue 1") represents our interpretation of problems with knowledge flows in the advanced-technology company; that is, we are not aware that either managers in the company case or researchers reporting the case originally visualized and analyzed knowledge flows in this manner. Rather, we illustrate through the case how knowledge flow principles and analytic techniques can be applied to new-product development in an advanced-technology company such as this. Following 5D vector space notation introduced above, this vector is represented as a thin, solid, purple line to emphasize management's goal for such knowledge to flow quickly and with high power, but we include a question mark ("?") to indicate that it does not yet flow as delineated; that is, the vector depicts the manner in which management would like the knowledge to flow. One can think of the vector in terms of a knowledge flow requirement elucidated via analysis.

We use this to induce our thirteenth leadership mandate from the practical application section of this book. Mandate 13. Knowledge flow vectors can be used to represent dynamic knowledge requirements.

This first issue pertains to knowledge clumping at the individual level. Specifically, the Issue 1 vector points from one knowledge flow coordinate (i.e., tacit, individual, create) to another (i.e., tacit, organization, apply). Using our coordinate shorthand, this would be depicted as (TIC → TOA). Individual people are developing new ideas that offer potential for new-product innovation, but the knowledge associated with such ideas is not flowing to enable application at the organization level and generate innovative new products. Individual knowledge creation is arguably very

Figure 1. Advanced-technology company knowledge flows

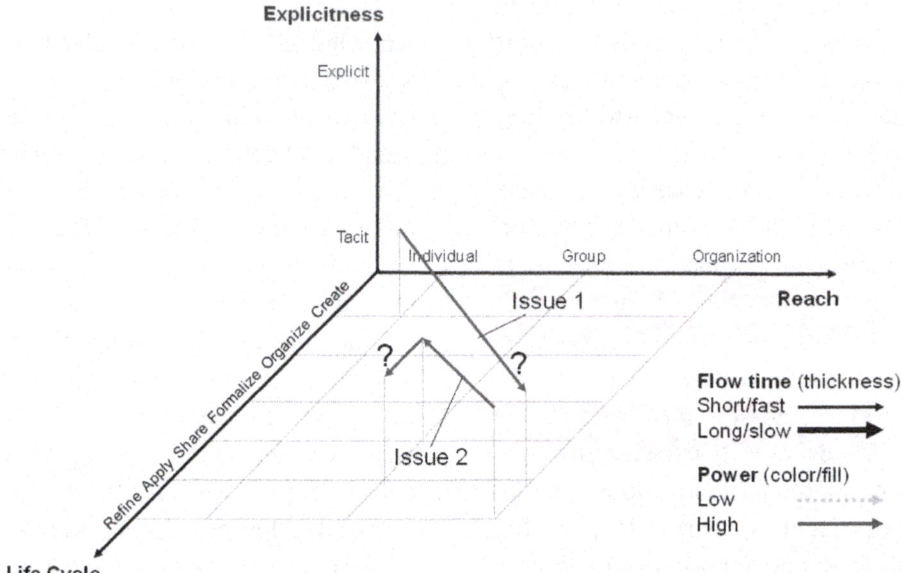

tacit. Hence this vector corresponding to Issue 1 is rooted as such (i.e., TIC). New-product innovation involves tacit knowledge as well. When such tacit knowledge is embedded within organizational routines, imitation becomes very difficult, and competitive advantage through appropriation can obtain. Hence this vector corresponding to Issue 1 is headed as such (i.e., TOA). Notice the vector points toward the application stage along the life cycle dimension. Until such knowledge can be applied, its potential cannot become manifest. This is part of the "knowing-doing gap" (aka 'knowledge-knowing gap' or knowledge 'potential-action gap').

With the second issue, organizational knowledge about concept selection is not shared with groups of decision makers responsible for prioritizing new ideas. We depict the knowledge flow associated with this second issue in the same manner used for Issue 1 in Figure 1. Using our coordinate shorthand, this would be depicted as (TOR → TGS). This second issue pertains to knowledge clumping at the organizational level. The organization has considerable experience in this industry and has learned over time—through both success and failure—which product attributes (e.g., in terms of technology, marketing, business) are important, but the knowledge associated with such attributes is not explicit and does not flow to the group level to provide a consistent basis for evaluating alternate new-product concepts. Organizational learning refined over time is arguably very tacit. Hence this vector corresponding to Issue 2 is rooted as such (i.e., TOR). Knowledge flowing as required for sharing would enable decision-making groups to know the important evaluation criteria. Hence this vector corresponding to Issue 2 is headed as such (i.e., TGS). Notice this vector points toward the share stage along the life cycle dimension. It does not point toward knowledge application. As above, until such knowledge can be applied, its potential cannot become manifest. Hence we include a second ray of this vector pointing to knowledge application at the group level (i.e., TGS → TGA). Also as above, this vector is represented as a thin, solid, purple line to emphasize management's goal for such knowledge to flow quickly and with high power, but we include a question mark ("?") to indicate that it *does not yet flow* as such; that is, the vector depicts the manner in which management would like the knowledge to flow. One can think of the vector in terms of another *knowledge flow requirement* elucidated via analysis.

Leadership and Management Interventions

To intervene in the situation and address the issues reported above, the leadership and management develop a conceptual model of its new-product development process. Recognizing the problem with idea-translation, it focuses in particular on the front end of this process. The goal is to analyze such conceptual model and use it to redesign the process in a manner that enhances the movement of ideas from the minds of individual employees to organizational routines that develop innovative new products reaching customers. Management thinks it important to ensure that whatever new process may emerge from the redesign will be consistent with: a) organizational resources that are available; b) enterprise goals; and c) organizational culture. The importance of fit with resources is clear in terms of not jeopardizing the enterprise's financial performance, but where new-product innovation represents the firm's core strategy, one may question the prudence of worrying about resources when survival appears to be at stake. The importance of fit with goals should be clear and self-explanatory. The importance of fit with culture may require some explanation. In many cases of process change, the organizational culture represents a major cause of problems and source of resistance to changing routines. In this case, the company appears to be trying to maintain its culture and fit an improved new-product development process within such culture. As with the point above about resources, where organizational survival appears to be at stake here, one may question why the company does not address the culture too. (Cultural change is far from trivial, but it is far from impossible too.)

Management is interested also in establishing a set of processes that can filter quickly many new-product ideas and that could apply consistently evaluation criteria with marketing, technology, business and human-factors perspectives. One proposal for changing the organizational routine for new-product development is to establish a relatively permanent team of experts (e.g., in marketing, technology, business and human-factors) to screen new ideas and to facilitate their translation. However, management dismisses this proposal because of the high cost associated with maintaining such an expert group. Most of the other proposals center on requiring individual people who generate new ideas to evaluate and develop such ideas themselves. However, very few individuals who generate new ideas know all of the functions required to accomplish effectively such evaluation and development. Three alternatives are proposed to address this lack of knowledge: 1) train all employees in all functions and require them to evaluate formally their own ideas; 2) assign experts to screen ideas; and 3) capture and formalize expert knowledge via IT. The company selects the third alternative for implementation.

This "EPSS" IT (i.e., from the class electronic performance support systems) is described in the case (p. 50).

EPSS technology could create an electronic version of a human subject-matter expert. ... It could provide efficiencies in process oversight and administration as well as electronic repositories of the intellectual property associated with idea generation. ... It may be considered an electronic infrastructure that captures, stores, and distributes individual and corporate knowledge to enable individuals to achieve desired levels of performance in the fastest possible time and with a minimum of support from others. ... The goal of the software environment is to provide access to integrated information, knowledge, learning experiences, advice, and guidance at the 'moment of need'.

This IT is described further in terms of "enabling performance in the context of work." Notice enabling work represents a fundamental element of knowledge, and this IT implementation is focused on enhancing knowledge flow to application. This is consistent with the Issue 1 vector delineated above. The IT implementation in the case is called "Virtual Mentor" (p. 51) and said to automate "each phase of the intervention process" and support "the performance of those individuals who are working within the process." The company assigns a cross-functional team of experts to design and develop this system, which provides (performative) support to decision-makers as well as individual idea generators. This is consistent with the Issue 2 vector delineated above.

In terms of knowledge flows, the company invests in expert systems style IT to make explicit and distribute formerly tacit knowledge about developing new-product ideas. Figure 2 includes vectors delineating the new knowledge flow associated with this IT approach. One vector is rooted in individual knowledge of the cross-functional experts who design and develop the system. This root reflects tacit knowledge refined through years of individual experience (TIR). The first flow represented by this vector depicts the sharing of such individual knowledge among experts assembled into a group (TGS). The case is unclear on how long this process takes, but sharing tacit knowledge as such is expected to occur at a relatively slow pace and carry high power. Hence we use a relatively thick, solid, purple line to represent the corresponding vector. Shorthand for this first vector is thus (TIR → TGS). It is labeled "Sharing" in the figure.

The second flow depicts the formalization of tacit shared knowledge (TGS) into explicit form suitable for capture in the EPSS (EGF). Comparable in many respects to knowledge formalization associated with expert systems development, this flow is expected to occur at a relatively slow pace also and is delineated accordingly using a relatively thick line for the corresponding vector, but notice this associated vector rises above the tacit plane, moving knowledge to an explicit coordinate (i.e., TGS → EGF). It is labeled "Formalization" in the figure.

Figure 2. IT Approach to management intervention (diluted explicit knowledge power)

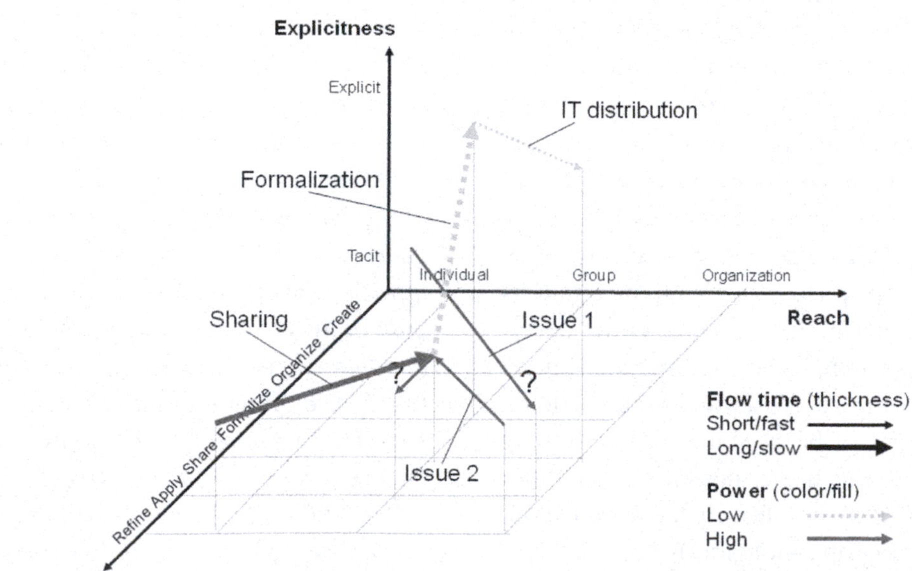

There is considerable uncertainty regarding the power associated with this formalization process, however. Recall from our discussion above how the power reflected via explicit knowledge is diluted generally when compared to its tacit counterpart. Hence we delineate this knowledge flow using a dotted, orange line to illustrate power dilution as theorized. Alternatively, recall further how many expert systems are able to function performatively, effectively substituting for human capability and performing in many cases at or above levels achievable by people. In such case, we would have used solid, purple lines to delineate the undiluted power corresponding to these two vectors, despite their position well above the tacit plane. Figure 3 illustrates this alternate interpretation of these explicit knowledge flows reflecting undiluted power. The case remains unclear, and our expectation would be for diluted knowledge power, despite the implementation of expert systems. Nonetheless, we wish to raise the potential for high power, even through explicit knowledge flows, stemming from the performative capability of many expert systems.

The third flow depicts the organization-wide sharing of explicit knowledge embedded in the IT implementation (i.e., EGF → EOS). With knowledge formalized in explicit form and embedded in IT as such, the corresponding flow is expected to occur at a comparatively fast pace. Hence we use a relatively thin line to represent the corresponding vector. It is labeled "IT distribution" in the figure. Through development and implementation of this EPSS system, we understand from the case that the organizational routine changes to incorporate this new IT application and to support knowledge flows. The same comment pertaining to diluted versus undiluted power applies here and is reflected (i.e., as dotted, orange vs. solid, purple lines, respectively) in the two alternate figures above (i.e., Figure 2 and Figure 3).

Notice, at the organizational level, the knowledge associated with this routine is explicit and resident within the system. Hence Figure 2 (and Figure 3) depicts only knowledge flows associated with developing and distributing the EPSS, but it does not yet depict how the EPSS is used by

Figure 3. IT Approach to management intervention (undiluted explicit knowledge power)

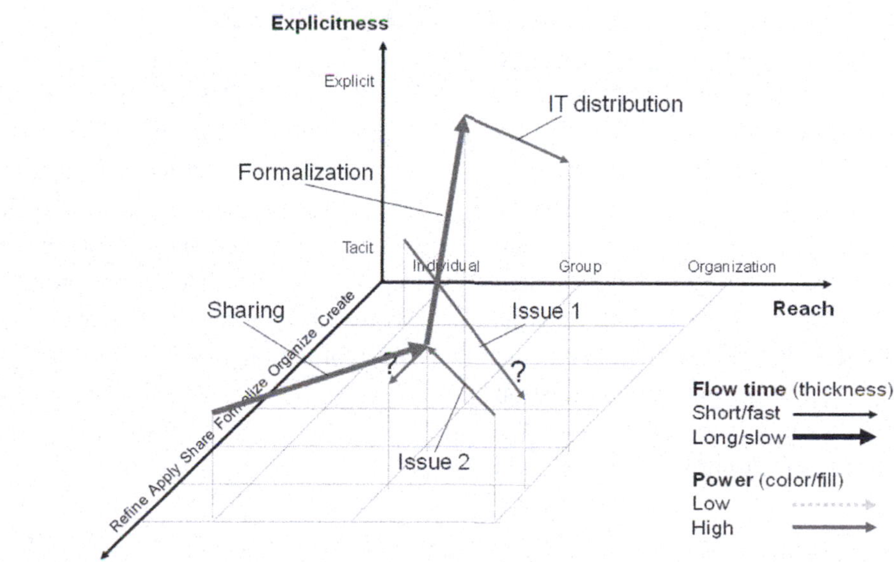

people to move knowledge created through idea generation (TIC) to product innovation (TOA). In other words, this knowledge flow does not depict how individual employees, groups or the organization as a whole would learn to use and interact subsequently with the IT application in the performance of their work processes. Recall, for instance, how the knowledge flow requirements depicted in Figure 1 reflect tacit knowledge flows and how the Issue 1 vector points to knowledge application at the organization level; even with the undiluted (i.e., solid, purple line) IT distribution flow in the alternate Figure 3 above, knowledge moves no farther than the share stage along the life cycle axis, so some additional flow remains for it to reach the application stage. Presumably, formal training courses, mentoring and individual OJT would be required for this human-centered flow. Such latter, human-centered flows are not delineated in the figure, nor do we include the corresponding discussion here, leaving this question instead as an exercise below for the reader.

We use this to induce our fourteenth leadership mandate from the practical application section of this book. Mandate 14. It is essential to plan how knowledge technologies will be used by people.

This application case describes an advanced-technology company that addresses problems with its knowledge flows through performative IT. Discussion of the case enables us to visualize and analyze several of the key knowledge flows associated with this company, both in terms of requirements and interventions. Clearly many additional details are pertinent to the case, which the interested reader can pursue through the source material. The case highlights several of the principles developed in earlier parts of this book, and it provides generalizable insight into application of knowledge flow principles to other cases. We leave such principles and application as exercises for the reader.

EXERCISES

1. Identify and describe three principles from earlier parts of the book that apply to this case. Can you induce additional principles from this application case that are not articulated in the earlier parts above?
2. Delineate vectors to describe knowledge flows corresponding to how idea-generators and decision-makers in the Advanced-Technology Company would learn and use the IT application described in the case.
3. Comment briefly on other approaches the company could take to address its knowledge flow problems. What relative advantages and disadvantages apply to your suggestions when compared with the approach described in the case?
4. Describe briefly how your learning from this case can be related to an organization with which you are familiar. Include a knowledge flow diagram such as the one presented in the figures above.

INDEPENDENT PRODUCTION COMPANY AND FEATURE FILM PROJECT

We draw from DeFillippi and Arthur (1998) for background of this case. We first summarize important events and issues for context. Visualization and analysis of key knowledge flows follow, with interpretation of leadership and management implications discussed subsequently. The section closes with exercises pertaining specifically to this application case.

Context

An independent production company in the motion-picture industry is engaged in a feature film project. In its competitive arena, producing a film that appeals to audiences and generates box-office financial returns is important to principals in the filmmaking project (e.g., Producer, Director, Financiers). Such principals have an equity stake in the organization, but the company itself represents a "temporary enterprise" (p. 127), which forms solely for the production of a single film and is expected to dissolve after project completion. In contrast to such stakeholders, financial returns deriving from a particular film project are not particularly important to the many other people involved with the film (e.g., screen-writers, make-up artists, camera people), who are temporary employees paid for services rendered.

Many aspects of the motion-picture industry and its constituent companies are similar to those observable in advanced-technology industries and firms. For instance, both organizational contexts are project-based. In the advanced-technology company from above, for example, each new-product innovation—which is developed and taken to market by a team of people—represents a separate project. Likewise in the independent production company of this case, each new film—which is produced and distributed by a team of people—represents a separate project.

As another instance, the work in both organizational contexts requires knowledge-based skills and experiences of diverse specialists to be integrated together. In the advanced-technology company from above, for example, each new-product innovation requires scientists, engineers, marketers, manufacturers, accountants and managers to work together to bring a new-product idea—through innovation and development—to market. Likewise in the independent production company of this case, each new film requires actors, directors, screenwriters, camera people, make-up artists, accountants and producers to bring a new-film idea—through production and distribution—to the box office.

As a third instance, people in both organizational contexts must learn to work together in cross-functional teams, and the efficacy of work-flows depends critically on such group learning. In the advanced-technology company from above, for example, cross-functional specialists are assigned often—as teams—to successive projects to exploit previous group learning. Likewise in the independent production company of this case, specialists from diverse professions and guilds are recruited often—as teams—for successive films to exploit previous group learning.

Alternatively, many aspects of the motion-picture industry and its constituent companies are dissimilar to those observable in advanced-technology industries and firms. For instance, company longevity does not represent a consistent concern across the two organizational contexts. In the advanced-technology company from above, for example, one new-product innovation—which is expected to generate financial returns to the firm—is insufficient for the company to be successful. Rather, a stream of new-product innovations is required. By contrast with the independent production company of this case, each new film—which is expected to generate financial returns to the principals—is sufficient for the company to be successful. Any subsequent new films involving the firm's participants will be produced by a different independent company.

As another instance, people's learning is expected to have different contributors and beneficiaries across the two organizational contexts. In the advanced-technology company from above, for example, each new-product innovation provides an opportunity for participants on the project team to learn and acquire experience, and this same company expects (or at least hopes) to retain such participants and hence benefit from their increased experience on the next project. By contrast with the independent production company of this case, each new film provides an opportunity for participants on the project team to learn and acquire experience also, but this same company has little expectation (or even desire) of retaining such participants and hence benefiting from their increased experience on the next project.

As a third instance, people's allegiance and sense of professional identity aligns to different kinds of organizations across the two contexts. In the advanced-technology company from above, for example, people identify largely with their employer and expect (or at least hope) to maintain their employment relationship across projects. People identify also with professional organizations (e.g., societies of accountants, engineers, managers), but such latter organizations can be viewed as subsidiary to the employers paying salaries. By contrast with the independent production company of this case, people identify only loosely with the employers paying for their efforts and do not expect (but perhaps hope) to maintain their employment relationship across projects. Rather, people identify principally with professional organizations (e.g., guilds for screen actors, writers, camera people), and such latter organizations can be viewed as primary over employers.

Experience is paramount in the motion-picture industry. On film projects generally, budgets are very tight, and schedules are very demanding. People are hired based largely on their experience and are expected to perform well immediately when called to do so. There is negligible slack time or margin for learning through trial and error, but experienced people learn exactly through trial and error (e.g., this is the central process for gaining experience). A make-up artist with a dozen films' worth of experience is expected to outperform—and would be more desirable than—one working on his or her first production, but such experienced make-up artist worked on his or her first film at some point in time, and he or she was probably less desirable at the time than a more-experienced person would have been. Because experience is valued so highly, and film-production organizations have such short time horizons, entry into the industry is very difficult for most people. Even low-wage employment through a menial job can represent someone's "big break" in the film business.

Further, the role played by schools and colleges is minimal in this industry. Some skills and techniques can be learned and refined through formal education (e.g., acting schools, theater and film degrees), but the majority comes through direct experience (i.e., OJT). Mentoring plays an important role also. Many junior people, who take on relatively menial and insignificant jobs (e.g., "runners" who deliver script changes to various sets and who fetch coffee for more-senior people), do so principally for the opportunity to observe how professionals work and to get some tips from experienced practitioners during breaks and unplanned idle periods. Also, the tension between learning and doing is biased in an extreme manner toward the latter in the film business, which focuses heavily on exploitation over exploration. Yet success of the industry as a whole depends critically upon learning and exploration over time.

Knowledge Flow Analysis

Knowledge flows are clearly important at the individual level. Individuals must acquire experience-based knowledge to gain employment, and their value to employers increases in rough proportion to their increases in knowledge. This importance of knowledge is similar to that experienced by individuals in most organizations (e.g., independent film companies, advanced-technology corporations, government agencies, non-profit firms). A person seeks to learn through work experience and requires experience to work (and hence learn). People are willing often to begin working at jobs that do not take full advantage of their potential, in part to acquire the experience necessary to qualify for jobs that do take such full advantage, and in part to pay the bills while learning.

In Figure 4 we delineate individual learning through experience as a cycle of tacit knowledge moving iteratively between creation (i.e., learning), application (i.e., doing), and refinement (i.e., learning). This cycle vector is labeled "Individual OJT" in the figure. As a person works, he or she contributes in large part to workflows through individual knowledge application (TIA), but this person contributes to knowledge flows also through learning associated with refinement of individual knowledge (TIR). This is represented by the classic learning curve. Additionally, such person can learn through work variation and experimentation, which contributes to knowledge flows through individual knowledge creation (TIC). This becomes manifest often through OJT or trial and error. The pattern continues then with subsequent flows through recurring application, refinement and creation of knowledge.

We use this to induce our fifteenth leadership mandate from the practical application section of this book. Mandate 15. The learning curve measures knowledge flows through OJT.

The cyclic vector is represented using relatively thick, purple, solid arrows to depict correspondingly slow yet powerful knowledge flows. This is consistent with evidence of experience-based learning at the individual level. Notice we could use a similar cyclic vector to depict individual knowledge flows in the advanced-technology case above, for instance, to represent the learning and knowing of an engineer, marketer, accountant or like individual in the technology organization. Likewise, we use this cyclic vector here to depict individual knowledge flows in the present case, for instance, to represent the learning and knowing of a screen-writer, camera person, accountant or like individual in the film organization.

Knowledge flows are clearly important also at the group level. Individuals must acquire experience working with other people in groups, and such knowledge is requisite to gainful employment in the motion-picture industry. Moreover, in addition to learning how to work in groups generally, employers value individuals' experience working with specific people. In the case we learn that collections of specific people are recruited—as teams—repeatedly to work on successive film

Figure 4. Film company knowledge flows

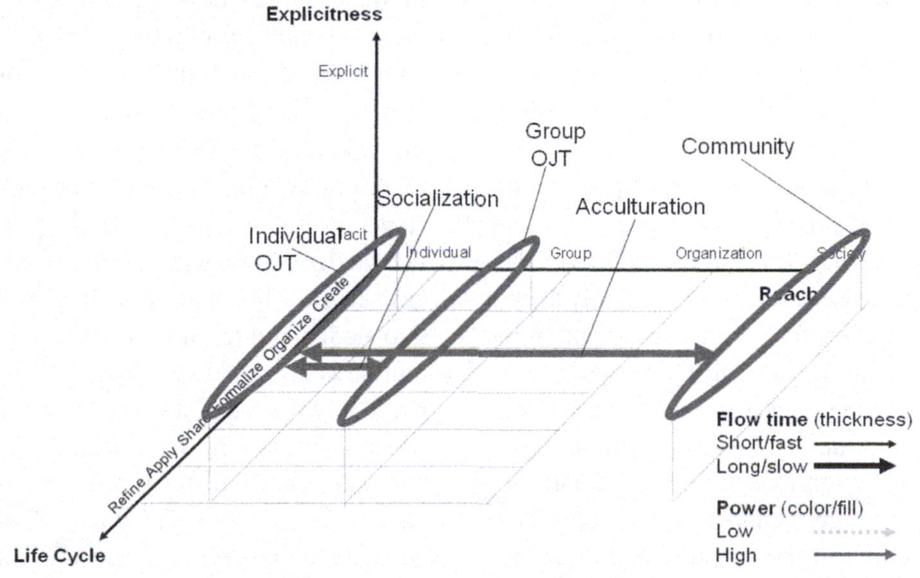

projects. Here knowledge of how to work with specific people, in addition to knowledge of how to perform specialist work activities, is valued, and the value to employers increases in rough proportion to increases in both group (e.g., working with other people generally) and team (e.g., working with specific people) experience.

In the present case, the group represents a clear unit of analysis for knowledge flows. Each individual in every group would have knowledge flows that are described well by the cyclic pattern shown and discussed above in Figure 4, but each collection of individuals (e.g., group, team) would have its own knowledge flows as well. Using the same logic as above for representing individual-level knowledge flows that iterate between knowledge creation (TIC), application (TIA), and refinement (TIR), we can depict group-level learning in comparable fashion. This latter vector is labeled "Group OJT" in the figure. As people in a group work together, they contribute in large part to workflows through collective knowledge application (TGA), but this group of people contributes to knowledge flows also through learning associated with refinement of collective knowledge (TGR). This is represented also by the classic learning curve. Additionally, such group of people can learn through work variation and experimentation, which contributes to knowledge flows through collective knowledge creation (TGC). OJT or trial and error applies at the group level as well as to individual knowing and learning. The pattern continues then with subsequent flows through recurring application, refinement and creation of knowledge.

As with Individual OJT above, this Group OJT cyclic vector is represented using relatively thick, purple, solid arrows to depict correspondingly slow yet powerful knowledge flows also. This is consistent with evidence of experience-based learning at the group level. Notice we could use a similar cyclic vector to depict group knowledge flows in the advanced-technology case above, for instance, to represent the learning and knowing of a new-product team comprised of an engineer, marketer, accountant and like individuals in the technology organization. Likewise, we use this cyclic vector here to depict group knowledge flows in the present case, for instance, to represent the learning and knowing of a film-production team comprised of a screen-writer, camera person, accountant and like individuals in the film organization.

Further, we learn from the case about other knowledge flow interactions between individuals and groups. For instance, some relatively ignorant individuals (e.g., inexperienced, junior people) join groups to work on film projects and to gain experience. Such individuals come to the organization with little knowledge to contribute to the group. The Runner represents one example made clear in the case, but the group may contribute substantial knowledge to the individual in terms of socialization. This is in addition to individuals sharing specialist knowledge (e.g., via mentoring). Here knowledge flows principally from group to individual, remaining in the tacit plane (e.g., TGS → TIS).

As another instance, some highly knowledgeable people join groups to lead film projects and to share experience. Such individuals come to the organization with substantial prior knowledge to contribute to the group. The Screenwriter and Producer represent two examples made clear in the case, but the group may contribute negligible knowledge to such individuals through interaction. Here tacit knowledge flows principally from individual to group (e.g., TIS → TGS). These represent extreme instances in which knowledge flows are unidirectional principally. Alternatively, knowledge flows bidirectionally in the general case (e.g., when individuals and groups share knowledge and learn mutually). We depict such mutual sharing between individuals and groups using a two-headed arrow to represent the bidirectional knowledge flow vectors. This is labeled "Socialization" in the figure, after the process characterized well by Nonaka (1994). The two-headed vector is represented using relatively thick, purple, solid arrows to depict correspondingly slow yet powerful knowledge flows. This is consistent with evidence of sharing tacit knowledge through work activities.

Notice we do not include knowledge flows at the organizational level in Figure 4. Although knowledge is clearly being applied through organizational knowing that becomes manifest via workflows on a film project, and the film-production organization clearly learns through its experience with a film, we understand from the case that such organization disbands at project completion. Hence the organization does not represent a particularly insightful unit of analysis in terms of dynamic knowledge flows. In contrast, such organization represents a very insightful unit of analysis in terms of pre-existing knowledge stocks and workflows. Further, the organization-level knowledge flows taking place during the short time horizon of a film-production company do so relatively quickly (e.g., on the order of weeks and months) with respect to counterpart flows at the individual and group levels (e.g., on the order of years and decades). We know from the case, for instance, that an independent production enterprise can start, work and dissolve well within one year, whereas people comprising some of the teams recruited to work on any particular feature film may have worked together for over a decade.

Alternatively, we do include knowledge flows at the trans-organizational level in Figure 4. Such flows pertain to the guilds and like professional societies. Knowledge flows associated with societies like these transcend film companies, production studios and like economic organizations that employ workers. Such flows transcend also the group-level collectivities that perform project work on films. The knowledge flows associated with these societies involve professional interaction and knowledge exchange at a trans-organizational level. This phenomenon could be characterized well by the term community of practice that describes similar aspects of the process (e.g., see Brown & Duguid, 1991).

The case does not provide much insight into the inner workings of guilds and like societies, but we interpret some recurring patterns of knowledge flows at the community level that are comparable to those described above for individual- and group-level flows. Hence we represent such patterns using the same kind of cyclic vector to depict recurring flows at other levels of reach. This is labeled "Community" in the figure. Likewise, the case does not provide much insight into exchanges between individuals and communities, but we interpret some mutual sharing patterns of knowledge flows between individuals and societies that are comparable to those described above for socialization through individual-group sharing. Hence we represent such patterns using the same kind of two-headed vector to depict bidirectional flows between these two levels of reach. This is labeled "Acculturation" in the figure. Other knowledge flows could be delineated for this film-production case as well (e.g., leveraging a new idea for a film into the film production), but we leave these for the reader as exercises below.

We use this to induce our sixteenth leadership mandate from the practical application section of this book. Mandate 16. Socialization and acculturation represent viable approaches to enhancing tacit knowledge flows.

Leadership and Management Implications

Many business firms organize at least some aspects of their work along project lines. Such organizations include aerospace companies, computer firms, software development enterprises, military task forces, and others. As such, the kinds of knowledge flows discussed and delineated in connection with this case generalize well to corresponding project work beyond the focal firm of the case. Leadership and management implications include, for instance, the importance of group-level experience and learning—in addition to individual-level experience and learning—on project performance. Indeed, the group represents the critical unit of analysis in project work. Implications include also, as another instance, the provision of some idle time or similar slack resources for learning (e.g., through experimentation, trial and error). Learning by observation and mentoring are noted too as important contributors to knowledge flows in the case, but many project organizations focus exclusively on exploitation of existing knowledge to drive workflows, at the expense of exploration to gain new knowledge through learning. Where the company-level organization endures and organizes its work through successive projects, firm-specific, longitudinal learning across time can be as or more important to competitive advantage as knowing within any single project is.

Additionally, some business firms organize all of their work along project lines. In the extreme case exemplified by independent film production, the organization exists solely for the performance of a single project. Similar organizations include architecture-engineering-construction consortia, military task forces, and political campaign offices. Such organizations have little express concern for cross-project learning. (Implicit concern is another matter.) Any learning from the organization's current project accrues to some other organization that comes into being after the focal enterprise has dissolved. Hence a leader's or manager's relative emphasis on learning versus doing should depend necessarily on the time horizon of the organization with respect to that of any particular project. Where the two time horizons converge, an emphasis on recruiting experienced people and on exploiting extant knowledge to enable workflows is in order. Alternatively, where the two time horizons diverge, an emphasis on developing firm-specific expertise in people and on exploring new knowledge for appropriation may be more in order.

Finally, the importance of guilds, unions, professional societies, communities of practice, and like trans-organizational collectivities can vary considerably in terms of knowledge flows. We learn from the case, for instance, that such collectivities play a central role in the professional identity, allegiance and career-long learning of individuals. To the extent that such trans-organizational collectivities are important to employees of an organization, such communities may have greater influence over employee knowledge, culture and performance than leadership and management do. In other instances, collectivities are non-existent or play a lesser role (e.g., social interaction). Membership in professional engineering societies represents an example in which management is likely to have greater influence over employees than trans-organizational collectivities do. In either case, trans-organizational collectivities can play an important role in terms of knowledge flows, a role that has managerial implications.

We use this to induce our seventeenth leadership mandate from the practical application section of this book. Mandate 17. Trans-organizational collectivities (e.g., communities) may have greater influence over employee knowledge, culture and performance than leadership and management do.

This application case describes a film-production company that organizes around a single project and that dissolves following project completion. Discussion of the case enables us to visualize and analyze several of the key knowledge flows associated with this company, both in terms of individual and collective phenomena. Clearly many additional details are pertinent to the case, which the interested reader can pursue through the source. The case highlights several of the principles developed in earlier parts of this book, and it provides generalizable insight into application of knowledge flow principles to other cases. We leave such principles and application as exercises for the reader.

EXERCISES

5. Identify and describe three principles from earlier parts of the book that apply to this case. Can you induce additional principles from this application case that are not articulated in the earlier parts above?

6. Delineate vectors to describe knowledge flows corresponding to how an individual with a new idea for a film in the Independent Production Company would know and learn to leverage such idea into a motion-picture production.
7. Comment briefly on other knowledge flows that are likely to be important to the company. What potential clumps and approaches to enhancing knowledge flows can you envision and suggest, respectively?
8. Describe briefly how your learning from this case can be related to an organization with which you are familiar. Include a knowledge flow diagram such as the one presented in the figure above.

MULTINATIONAL ELECTRONICS MANUFACTURER AND TECHNOLOGY TRANSFER PROJECT

We draw from Daghfous (2004) for background of this case. We first summarize important events and issues for context. Visualization and analysis of key knowledge flows follow, with interpretation of leadership and management implications discussed subsequently. The section closes with exercises pertaining specifically to this application case.

Context

A multinational microelectronics manufacturing company is engaged in a technology transfer project. Customers include telecommunication firms that use these products in global-positioning systems, signal-modulation equipment and cellular-communication devices. This company is effective at present in its competitive arena. Superior knowledge embedded in the company's electronic products enables it to compete well. However, some of its core technologies have become dated with respect to the state of the art. In particular, the company identifies several internal problems centered on automated testing equipment for one of its principal products.

This testing equipment had been designed nearly 25 years earlier by engineers who have long since left the company. The equipment—although perhaps state of the art in its day—performs at a level that is noticeably deficient. Its yield is comparatively low with respect to testing equipment that employs more-current technologies. The system is somewhat unreliable also, breaking down and requiring maintenance more frequently than expected. The equipment software and algorithms are documented poorly too. The original engineers took the associated design with them in terms of tacit knowledge when they left the company. As a result, current engineers must resort often to a process of trial and error, along with deliberate experimentation, to learn about the equipment's myriad idiosyncrasies. The computer code used to automate the testing process via this equipment is written in an archaic and arcane software language that is known by only a couple of the company's employees. Several key parts of the automated test equipment have only a single vendor, leaving the company exposed to the risks of critical reliance upon a single source.

The company maintains a relationship with a university nearby. Through periodic interaction, company engineers and officers have become aware of advancing software and testing technologies that offer potential to improve the dated, automated test equipment described above. A small project forms around the objective of transferring the associated technology from the university to the company. This project begins with university researchers visiting the company frequently and interacting with engineers and operators to learn about the production process and existing automated test equipment. The university researchers report company personnel as very knowledgeable about the current process and equipment. This high knowledge level is seen to enhance the researchers' ability to learn about the company processes in the early stages of the project (p. 79), but this same knowledge level is seen also to inhibit company engineers' ability to learn about the university's technology during these early stages.

The university team develops new technology for automated testing, but they do not start with a clean slate. Most of the existing software algorithms are used in the new technology. However, they are rewritten in a more-contemporary computer language. This modern language is one taught in universities and trade schools and is expected to be both easier for people to learn and known by a broader cross section of people. The university team also solicits input from current operators of the existing test equipment, input that is used to tailor the design of the new equipment to help satisfy operator wants and needs. After demonstration in the laboratory, the university team works with company personnel to implement the new technology in the production process. At first the new technology operates in parallel with the old. This phased-implementation approach is a technique used commonly to reduce the risk of changing from one technology to another.

The new technology demonstrates some aspects of superior performance (e.g., increased yield), but its implementation proceeds more slowly than expected, and it evidences numerous problems. Considerable learning through trial and error is required for company engineers to integrate the new technology into the production process. Problems with new technology—particularly technology incorporating software—are to be expected generally in a project such as this. The new technology also produces some organizational changes. Several skills of operators are needed no longer to use the new technology, so such employees find their corresponding knowledge becoming obsolete. Other skills necessary to operate the new technology are absent from the company staff, so employees find themselves with a requirement for new learning. A combination of experienced and inexperienced (i.e., with respect to the old equipment) people is assigned to work on both the old and new equipment. As the production process transitions from parallel use of both systems toward sole reliance upon the new technology, the company fires some employees with obsolete skills and hires some new people to fill knowledge gaps remaining in the workforce.

Company personnel experience other difficulties associated with adoption of the new technology. In addition to the technical and process-integration problems noted above, the heavy workload of employees constrains their ability to master the new system. Production quotas and efficiency norms are enforced by company supervisors, and negligible time is made available for employees to learn. This also limits the amount of experience-based feedback provided to the university project team. In this output-oriented environment, the day-to-day demands of the production job take clear priority over the technology-transition tasks required to implement, learn about, and refine the new automated test equipment. Indeed, we learn from the case, "experimentation was viewed by the project coordinator as non-value added unless it directly contributed to the bottom-line" (p. 76). We learn also that most knowledge sharing within the company is accomplished through informal discussion. A newsletter is circulated among employees to highlight and comment on lessons learned of interest, but no systematic process exists to collect, store and disseminate such lessons (p. 77). The company is ISO-9000 certified, which indicates it has and employs considerable process documentation, but we learn from the case that such certification has not been extended to incorporate the processes associated with the automated test equipment discussed here.

Knowledge Flow Analysis

Knowledge flows at several levels in this case, and we learn of factors that both enhance and inhibit various flows. Knowledge flows clearly at the individual level, both in operation of the old test equipment and in implementation of the new. Operators of the old equipment, for instance, clearly apply knowledge to use the technology to support production workflows. To the extent that such technology is documented poorly, this suggests such knowledge is tacit and developed principally through processes of OJT and trial and error. This pattern of individual tacit knowledge flowing through creation (e.g., learning to use the system), application (e.g., knowing to use the system) and refinement (e.g., learning improved uses of the system) is similar to the "Individual OJT" cyclic vector described above in the case of film production. We include and label accordingly this same cyclic vector in Figure 5 to represent the knowledge flow pattern associated with operating the old automated test equipment. A similar pattern would apply well also to the company engineers who learn about, troubleshoot and improve the new technology over time and while on the job.

The case makes clear that knowledge flows at the organization level within the company too. The company's production process, for instance, has depended upon the old test equipment for 25 years, and it continues to function even long after the designers of this technology have left the company and even though such technology was not documented well. Hence the organization's knowledge of how to produce and test its micro-electronic products transcends and subsumes the knowledge of its individual employees. This is the nature of organizational routines, which are characterized best as tacit knowledge flowing at the organization level. Such routines are considered widely to involve learning over time, as new knowledge is acquired, put to use, and refined through an iterative cycle. Hence the same kind of cyclic knowledge flow vector from above applies well to these organizational routines too. One such vector is labeled "Organizational routines" accordingly and included in the figure.

Figure 5. Technology transfer knowledge flows

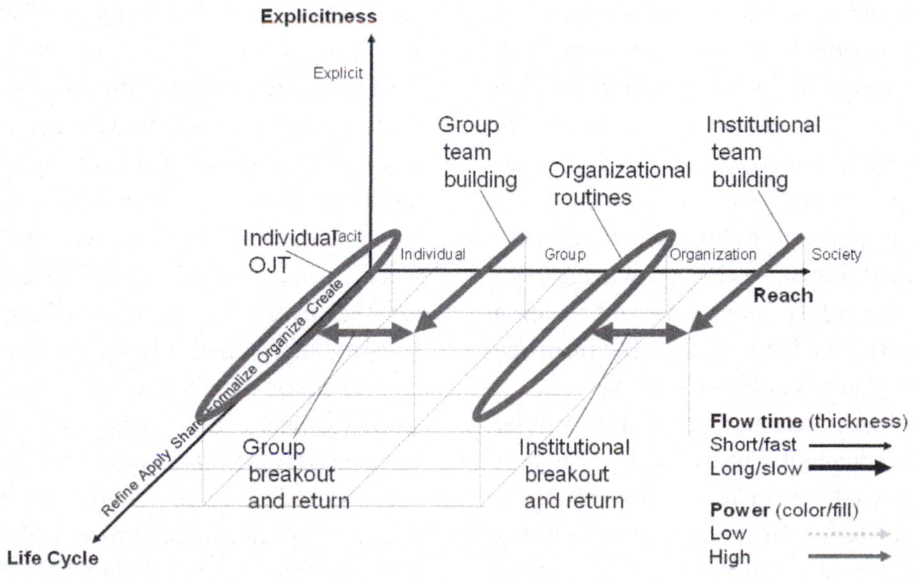

One pattern of interest pertains to the shifting skills required for operators. At one point in time (e.g., before introduction of the new test equipment), operators required knowledge about the existing automated test equipment, and the company valued such knowledge. At a later point in time, however, some such knowledge had been made obsolete by the new technology, and the company valued no longer the obsolete knowledge. In terms of knowledge at the individual level, some employees were compelled to develop new knowledge pertaining to the new test equipment. Such new knowledge was applied and refined in the kind of cycle delineated in Figure 5 for individual OJT.

However, other employees apparently did not acquire new knowledge and were forced to leave the company. Such new knowledge had to be acquired by other (e.g., current or replacement) employees. For these individuals, their personal knowledge inventories would either reflect the new knowledge or not. For the organization, however, refinement of knowledge could be reflected by a partial substitution of new knowledge for old. For some period of time, both elements of knowledge would exist concurrently, but after implementation of the new test equipment, much of the old knowledge would flow out of the organization along with the people leaving the company. Still, some of the old knowledge would remain within the company, as tacit knowledge possessed by employees who had been reskilled (i.e., learned to use the new equipment). Hence we learn that some knowledge (e.g., pertaining to the new equipment) is valued more highly than other knowledge (e.g., pertaining to the old equipment) is, and we learn that such valuation is dynamic, shifting from one kind of knowledge to another over time.

One can identify vectors delineating similar patterns in the university. Individual researchers in the university lab, for instance, develop, apply and refine knowledge through iterative learning and knowing during technology design and development. This kind of knowledge flow would be represented well by the cyclic vector labeled "Individual OJT," even though it pertains to "research" accomplished in the laboratory environment and an educational context. The university has organizational routines of its own, as another instance, pertaining to admitting, educating, graduating and placing research students. This kind of knowledge flow would be represented well by the cyclic vector "Organizational routines," even though considerable variation is likely in terms of how any individual student progresses through the educational process. Knowledge and skills in the university can also ebb and flow in terms of novelty, obsolescence and value.

Some interesting knowledge flows pertain to inter-organizational patterns in the case. In addition to the business-as-usual flows within the company, and counterpart standard-practice flows within the university, an unusual set of knowledge flows pertain to the technology-transfer project. For instance, we understand from the case how individual engineers from the company and individual researchers from the university would meet in groups and interact periodically, essentially forming a project team. Notice this is the same kind of project team described in the advanced-technology and film-production cases above. As such, the group represents the focal unit of analysis for project work.

The corresponding group-level knowledge flows could be represented using patterns similar to those delineated in the advanced-technology and film-production cases above, but instead of process-level descriptions (e.g., how groups of actors, screen-writers and camera people work together over time) as in the film case, here we learn about how individual researchers, engineers and others on a team learn from one another and work together to implement new technology in the company *as a one-shot occurrence*. In other words, this technology-transfer case can be viewed as a single occurrence, not a process. Hence in Figure 5 we illustrate a series of knowledge flow vectors.

The first group-level vector delineated in the figure is rooted in tacit knowledge creation at the group level (TGC). This depicts people from the company and university learning how to work together in a group. This first vector is headed to tacit knowledge sharing at the group level (TGS). This depicts engineers and operators in the company sharing with university researchers their undocumented, experiential knowledge pertaining to the existing test equipment and production process. It reflects also researchers from the university sharing with company participants their knowledge pertaining to automated test equipment in general along with that pertaining to the new-technology implementation. This first vector is labeled "Group team building" in the figure and delineated as such (i.e., TGC → TGS). It should be clear that no single best way of representing knowledge flows is likely to exist, and different people are bound to represent the same knowledge flow phenomenon in different ways. This is true of all representational tasks (e.g., in IS design, free-body dynamics, architectural sketches) and does not detract from the technique. Indeed, it is known well that comparing different views of the same phenomena can lead to rich knowledge flows!

Once the project team members learn to work as a group and begin sharing knowledge with one another, the case describes an iterative series of flows between individuals performing their separate knowledge-based activities and group activities that both build upon and guide past and future such activities, respectively. For instance, group work and knowledge sharing in the early stages of the project led to independent laboratory research at the university. We can depict this with a vector from group sharing to individual application in the tacit plane (i.e., TGS → TIA). A comparable vector could depict knowledge flowing later in the project, as engineers and operators in the company follow group interaction with individual activities to learn about the new test equipment. Once the individual (e.g., researcher, engineer) returns to individual work, he or she is essentially back on the cyclic pattern of OJT (e.g., recurring knowledge creation, application and refinement). Of course knowledge flows from individuals back to the group as well. University researchers return from the lab to share results and ideas with company teammates, and company engineers and operators return from the production line to share results and ideas with research teammates. Hence the knowledge flows between the group and individuals would be represented best as bidirectional. They are labeled "Group breakout and return" in the figure and depicted using a two-headed arrow (i.e., TGS ←→ TIA) between the group sharing and individual cyclic patterns.

As with the project work represented in the cases above, the group also applies knowledge to accomplish work (i.e., TGA). By iterative problem solving, the group refines its understanding of problems (TGR), and it develops new knowledge about how the test equipment technology affects the production process (TGC). Hence it cycles through a pattern of knowledge creation, application and refinement. To avoid clutter in the diagram, we omit a group-level, cyclic vector to depict this iterative knowledge flow. We omit also interactions between the group-level knowledge flows and ongoing organizational routines in both the company and university. Clearly the introduction of new technology in the company affects its organizational routines associated with production testing, for instance, and clearly the research project is part of the university educational routine. This case is relatively rich in terms of including a diversity of knowledge flows. The point is not to see how many different knowledge flows can be represented on a single diagram. Rather, we use the diagram to highlight the most-interesting ones in our present context of application to business firms.

One of the more-interesting knowledge flows pertains to inter-organizational knowledge exchanges. Such flows take place between the university and the company and differ from the kinds of trans-organizational flows discussed above in the context of guilds, professional societies and communities of practice. The flows in our focal case here manifest themselves deliberately between two distinct organizations, whereas those above occur amorphously between a web of companies, societies and other organizational forms. In other words, the inter-organizational technology transfer represents the point of the focal case and takes place between two organizations. The trans-organizational flows from above, by contrast, are more informative in terms of interaction between individuals and (trans-organizational) communities. In essence we have an organizational dyad here, which represents the organizational counterpart of group interaction at the individual level. By symmetry and analogy with the individual-group interaction described and delineated above in this focal case, we use an equivalent set of single- and two-headed vectors to depict inter-organization knowledge flows. These vectors are labeled "Institutional team building" and "Institutional breakout and return," respectively, in the figure.

Leadership and Management Implications

This application case illustrates a variety of knowledge flows, at several levels of reach, within and between multiple organizations. For instance, we find individual knowledge flows within the microelectronics company and within the university. We find also group-level knowledge flows within the project team, in addition to flows between the project group and individual team members in both the company and university. As another instance, we find organizational knowledge flows within the microelectronics company and within the university. We find also inter-organizational knowledge flows between the company and university, in addition to flows between the technology-transfer dyad and separate organizational participants (i.e., the company and the university). The knowledge manager would have a rich variety of flows to evaluate in a case such as this, and enhancing knowledge flows to overcome the clumping evident in the case could be very fruitful, particularly for the company striving to learn and apply the university's knowledge about the advanced test equipment.

This application case illustrates also how all of the important flows pertaining to a work process of interest involve tacit knowledge. Negligible knowledge is articulated in terms of documentation. The key knowledge is possessed by individual people and is embedded in organizational routines. Looking first at the company, for instance, the key workflows center clearly on producing and testing the company's microelectronic products. Knowledge flows critical to enabling such workflows center on tacit knowledge (e.g., individual OJT, organizational routines) that is created, applied and refined over time within the company. Looking next at the university, as another instance, the key workflows center clearly on developing new test equipment technology. Knowledge flows critical to enabling such workflows center on tacit knowledge (e.g., individual OJT, organizational routines) that is created, applied and refined over time within the university.

We use this to induce our eighteenth leadership mandate from the practical application section of this book. Mandate 18. Knowledge flows critical to enabling critical workflows center on tacit knowledge.

The technology-transfer project represents another important focus of workflows. Clearly such workflows are enabled by knowledge flows associated with creating, sharing and applying new knowledge about advanced test equipment. Hence this case illustrates also how knowledge flows enable workflows and indeed lie on their critical paths. Without knowledge of producing and testing the company's microelectronic products, the workflows would not get accomplished or would not get accomplished well. Without knowledge of developing new test equipment technology in the university, the workflows similarly would not get accomplished (well).

The case illustrates further some important dynamics of knowledge flows. One dynamic pertains to individual knowledge that is created, applied and refined through a recurring pattern over time. A similar dynamic applies at the organizational level. This pattern is noted in the other cases above and instantiates the learning curve, as the performance of individuals as well as organizations improves over time and through repetition. Hence the knowledge manager should expect always performance improvement over time. Where such improvement does not obtain, knowledge clumping is likely to manifest itself.

We use this to induce our nineteenth leadership mandate from the practical application section of this book. Mandate 19. An organizational process without consistent improvement over time suffers from knowledge clumping.

Another dynamic pattern pertains to the group interaction of project participants. Upon group formation, members must learn to work with one another before knowing how to work together on the project. This takes time and energy, and the associated phenomenon is documented well in the literatures on teams as well as projects. The knowledge manager should allow for and encourage such group-level knowledge flows before expecting group-level workflows that are dependent upon such learning.

We use this to induce our twentieth leadership mandate from the practical application section of this book. Mandate 20. Members of a team must learn to work with one another before knowing how to work together on a project.

A third dynamic pertains to the creation, application, refinement and eventual obsolescence of knowledge. Knowledge associated with the dated test equipment, for instance, completed the whole cycle, but it did not disappear from the company. Much of the tacit knowledge possessed by individual workers flowed out of the company when such workers were fired, but much of such knowledge also remained within the company, possessed by workers who were not fired as well as embedded within organizational routines. Nonetheless, the value of such knowledge decreased appreciably over time, and in particular following introduction of the new test equipment. The knowledge manager should expect the value of all knowledge to vary over time and should seek out techniques for its valuation.

A fourth dynamic pertains to inter-organizational knowledge flows between participants in the technology-transfer dyad. Some knowledge flows were sustained even before the technology-transfer project began, as the university and company enjoyed an ongoing relationship. When the project began, knowledge flows of a more-focused and specific nature commenced. Although the case does not elaborate, one can envision knowledge flows returning to their original state following completion of the project, and through continued interaction between the university and the company, perhaps another project would start one day. The key point is that the original knowledge flows between the company and the university were relatively modest in magnitude and importance. Yet they led to a substantial technology-transfer project that benefited both organizations. Hence even small, seemingly inconsequential knowledge flows can serve to catalyze large, critical ones through a dynamic described best at present via metaphor (e.g., priming the pump). The knowledge manager should recognize inter-organizational—also inter-group and inter-individual—knowledge flows for their potential in terms of a dynamic priming effect.

EXERCISES

9. Identify and describe three principles from earlier parts of the book that apply to this case. Can you induce additional principles from this application case that are not articulated in the earlier parts above?

10. Delineate vectors to describe knowledge flows corresponding to how some knowledge became obsolete, decreased in value, and flowed out of the company as described in the case.
11. Comment briefly on other approaches the company could take to address its knowledge flow problems. What relative advantages and disadvantages apply to your suggestions when compared with the approach described in the case?
12. Describe briefly how your learning from this case can be related to an organization with which you are familiar. Include a knowledge flow diagram such as the one presented in the figure above.

REFERENCES

Brown, J. S., & Duguid, P. (1991). Organizational learning and communities-of-practice: Toward a unified view of working, learning, and innovation. *Organization Science*, *2*(1), 40–57. doi:10.1287/orsc.2.1.40.

Daghfous, A. (2004). Organizational learning, knowledge and technology transfer: A case study. *The Learning Organization*, *11*(1), 67–83. doi:10.1108/09696470410515733.

DeFillippi, R. J., & Arthur, M. B. (1998). Paradox in project-based enterprises: The case of film making. *California Management Review*, *40*(2), 125–139. doi:10.2307/41165936.

Massey, A. P., Montoya-Weiss, M. M., & O'Driscoll, T. M. (2002a). Performance-centered design of knowledge-intensive processes. *Journal of Management Information Systems*, *18*(4), 37–58.

Massey, A. P., Montoya-Weiss, M. M., & O'Driscoll, T. M. (2002b). Knowledge management in pursuit of performance: Insights from Nortel networks. *Management Information Systems Quarterly*, *26*(3), 269–289. doi:10.2307/4132333.

Nonaka, I. (1994). A dynamic theory of organizational knowledge creation. *Organization Science*, *5*(1), 14–37. doi:10.1287/orsc.5.1.14.

Chapter 8
Application Cases in Government

ABSTRACT

This chapter concentrates on knowledge flow visualization and analysis in the public sector. The authors look at a military organization involved with maritime warfare. The discussion turns then to examine a federal government agency involved with a knowledge management program. The third case examines a public service organization involved with large-scale IT integration. In each case, the authors draw from secondary data sources for background. This should prove helpful to the reader who is interested in following up to consider more details than presented in this volume. They draw also from their own research and professional experience to fill in missing information, and they apply principles and techniques of this book to contribute new insights through examination of knowledge flows in the cases. Each application case concludes with exercises to stimulate critical thought, learning, and discussion. In conjunction with the principles articulated in Section 1 of the book, the application cases explain how organizations from across a very wide range of sizes and domains both succeed and fail at harnessing dynamic knowledge; hence, through case-based reasoning, they provide both positive and negative examples for the leader and manager to use in comparison with his or her own organization.

MILITARY ORGANIZATION AND MARITIME WARFARE

We draw from Nissen (2002b) for background of this case. We first summarize important events and issues for context. Visualization and analysis of key knowledge flows follow, with interpretation of leadership and management implications discussed subsequently. The section closes with exercises pertaining specifically to this application case.

Context

The military of a large industrialized nation is comprised of several services (e.g., Army, Navy, Air Force). It conducts many military endeavors using a composite organization called the Joint Task Force (JTF). The JTF integrates units from multiple services under a common commander to accomplish a substantial undertaking (e.g., requiring months or years to accomplish). Many joint operations include also coalitions of military

DOI: 10.4018/978-1-4666-4727-5.ch008

forces from allied nations; these are referred to often as "Coalition Task Forces," but we include them under the single JTF moniker here.

In many respects the JTF reflects a project organization. Work tasks and people are organized around a specific product or service of the organization; in this case, the "product" or "service" pertains to accomplishing objectives of warfare (e.g., defending territory, countering threat, projecting power). Such project organization is similar to the business case above involving new-product development. In other respects the organization of a JTF is virtual. Diverse people and units come together to compose a temporary organization focused on achieving limited objectives. After the mission is accomplished or abandoned, the organization disbands. Such temporary organization is similar to the business case above involving feature-film production. In still other respects the JTF reflects a matrix organization. While diverse units are organized under a JTF Commander, they continue an enduring affiliation with their home organizations. Such matrix organization is similar to the business case above involving technology transfer. Unlike the matrix from organization theory, however, people in the Military have only one boss at a time.

The organization of a task force is relatively large (e.g., 10,000 people, possibly many more for a very large undertaking) and hierarchical in nature. The JTF is organized functionally for division of labor; relies upon standardized procedures for coordination; employs large technical and support staff organizations; utilizes centralized decision-making; and maintains a unified chain of command. In these respects it represents a classic machine bureaucracy (Mintzberg, 1980), but this military organization also depends heavily upon professionalism for quality and reliability of its work processes. It is steeped in tradition too, with very strong cultural norming forces at every level. Direct supervision, through many hierarchical levels of management, abounds as a mechanism for coordination. Close attention to detail even by senior-level leaders and managers—many refer to this as "micromanagement"—abounds also. "Because lives are at stake," one senior officer in the case says, "commanders and officers at every level immerse themselves in the details of plans and operations."

Military organization and culture are unique in many ways. For one, the organization has few avenues for lateral entry. With only rarefied exceptions (e.g., doctors, lawyers, specialists), people at all of its 20+ ranks come into the organization at its lowest levels. Managers, executives and other leaders are developed exclusively from within. The same applies to supervisors, professionals and skilled laborers. As a result, negligible mixing of backgrounds and experiences beyond the military organization takes place. Within the uniformed services, all people in leadership positions have worked within the Military throughout their entire careers. In the case of top leaders (e.g., Admirals and Generals), such military careers can span 30 years in duration. All military personnel are expected to serve for 20 years before retirement. This exerts considerable and homogenizing norming forces on personnel.

The culture is also bifurcated along status lines. Officers and enlisted represent separate and distinct castes of personnel with little informal interaction between them. Throughout military history, officers have represented broadly the white-collar work force, with enlisted representing blue-collar workers. The role of technology in warfare is shifting more enlisted jobs to white-collar status, however. A great many weapons and systems of war today are computer-based, increasingly autonomous, and linked via multiple, interconnected networks. The Military also rotates all personnel regularly (e.g., nearly one third of the Navy changes jobs each year). This precludes long-term group working relationships from forming naturally, and it promotes the kind of culture associated often with itinerant workers.

The JTF organization is sophisticated technologically. This is evidenced in part by its ability to plan, coordinate and execute continuous, sustained, geographically distributed work activities around the clock and around the world. JTF network and communication technologies enable it to transfer information very rapidly across great distances. For instance, reconnaissance images obtained by satellite and unmanned vehicles are sent to operational planners and decision makers in near-real time half way around the world. Today new technologies are being developed to enable control of missiles in flight to pass automatically from one organization and location to another (e.g., geographically distant submarines, ships, airplanes, shore installations), as the cycle of target acquisition, tracking, attack and monitoring collapses to a matter of minutes or even seconds. Yet the JTF is also risk averse. It relies upon considerable redundancy and can fall back upon manual operations for nearly every work task. With so much of its capability and technological sophistication dependent upon Global Positioning System satellites and Cyberspace operations, for two current instances, prudence dictates that this must be so.

In many respects, the Military represents a *total institution*: "place[s] of residence and work where a large number of like-situated individuals, cut from the wider society for an appreciable period of time, together lead an enclosed, formally administered round of life" (Goffman, 1961, xiii). In particular, when units are deployed overseas for months or even years at a time, people spend all day, every day, working, living and socializing with fellow employees (e.g., shipmates). Military commanders organize people's entire day, specifying (albeit in general terms): when they awaken; what they eat; what work they do; what clothes they wear; how their hair is cut; what kinds of fashion accessories are permitted; with whom they can socialize and eat meals; where they work, eat and sleep; if, when and for how long they may be allowed to leave the physical confines of the unit (e.g., base, ship, encampment); and when they are to sleep. To people outside this kind of environment, military life appears widely as constrained and limiting, but many people within such environment relish the structure and praise the organization.

The JTF environment is hazardous. Military units are designed and trained to go into Harm's way. Injuries and deaths are anticipated in every JTF operation, even during routine peacetime training exercises, but not all military jobs entail mortal or physical hazard, at least not all of the time. Indeed, many jobs reflect the kinds of professional office work found in most business and government organizations. Examples include staff meetings, planning sessions, report writing, e-mail communications, website development and inventory management, along with myriad leadership, management and supervisory activities. Numerous other jobs involve the kinds of skilled and manual labor observable in service and manufacturing industries. Examples include engine maintenance, machine shop work, painting, building repair, electronic diagnostics, equipment service, janitorial and cooking tasks, along with myriad other professional and manual jobs. Alternatively, a great many military jobs are perilous by design. Examples include: flying in supersonic aircraft that are catapulted off of—and have to land in turn on—the decks of ships at sea; parachuting into hostile territory; servicing operational nuclear reactors; exchanging artillery fire; defusing explosive ordnance; and myriad other hazardous jobs found rarely outside the military environment.

The JTF environment is time-critical also. The speed of some weaponry reduces decision and reaction cycles to minutes and sometimes even just seconds. Yet such time-critical cycles are set against a backdrop of long days (e.g., 14-hour shifts are common), weeks (e.g., 7-day workweeks prevail at sea) and months (e.g., JTF deployments can extend to a year or more). Hours, days, weeks, and even months may pass without significant events in some units, but any one event (e.g., attack by missile, aircraft or submarine) can have mortal consequences, hence people seek to stay alert and vigilant always.

Geographical dispersion depicts another key aspect of the JTF environment. Military units on land and at sea can cover thousands of square miles and operate halfway around the world from their home bases and ports. Yet such units are very interdependent and required to coordinate their plans and actions across great distances in both space and time. They even use a common time zone (i.e., termed *Zulu Time*) worldwide to facilitate such coordination. Communication in the field, at sea and in the air is clearly wireless, and requirements for security are strict. Radio represents the time-proven method of choice for distributed, synchronous communications. Sophisticated frequency-hopping and encryption technologies enable widespread wireless communication to be secure. E-mail, chat, video teleconferencing and other electronic communication technologies are employed also, with satellites used extensively for transmission cross large distances.

The military task environment further tends to be quite Spartan. Units in the field may move daily and set up tent camps in the evenings. Soldiers in the field may have to dig holes in the dirt in which to sleep. Showers are a luxury in many areas, and many days in the field may pass without a hot-cooked meal. Naval warships have an industrial look and feel to them, providing a stark contrast to life onboard a cruise ship. Many aircraft have strict size and weight restrictions for crewmembers and passengers due to cramped space, but above all, the work of a JTF is mortally serious. Mistakes can cause losses to life and materiel. Successes can cause losses to life and material too. The only difference is whether such losses are to an adversary's forces or to one's own units.

The focal JTF of this case includes two large naval formations: 1) a carrier battlegroup (aka carrier strike group in current parlance) and 2) an amphibious ready group (aka expeditionary strike group in current parlance). The battlegroup includes a full-size aircraft carrier, which is large enough to launch and recover fixed-wing jet aircraft (e.g., fighter, attack, surveillance), and a host of support vessels (e.g., cruisers, destroyers, submarines) to make up an ensemble for conducting offensive and defensive maritime and air operations. The ready group includes a smaller carrier, which is used to launch and recover rotary-wing aircraft (e.g., attack, anti-submarine, transport) and amphibious-landing craft, along with its own complement of support vessels. The primary mission of the battlegroup is power projection and to establish military superiority (esp. air and maritime). It is designed and trained for strike, intercept, anti-submarine and maritime-interdiction missions. The ready group is employed principally for invasion purposes. It is designed and trained to get Marines ashore for expeditionary warfare. The joint operations of this task force include also several Air Force squadrons and a number of Army units, along with a coalition of military forces from multiple allied nations.

The task force conducts an operation called DELTA WATCH (a pseudonym) in international waters, with operating areas extending hundreds of miles from East to West and nearly a thousand miles from North to South. Adjoining international waters are territories of several different countries—allied, neutral and (potentially) hostile. Each country represents a sovereign nation. Each has its own air, land and naval forces in the area. In all, the operating area may have several hundred *contacts* (e.g., aircraft, ships, submarines)—identified on tactical and operational displays as "friendly," "hostile" and "unidentified"—at any one time. Contacts include civilian and commercial planes and ships, in addition to their military counterparts. Identifying, interrogating, keeping track of, and responding to such a large number of contacts exceeds the bounded rationality of any single individual. Hence people work via watch teams to monitor and make sense of the JTF environment.

Knowledge Flow Analysis

Tacit knowledge gained through cumulative military experience is prized in the Joint Task Force. People are assigned to specific jobs based on the experiences they have accumulated over their military careers. Leaders appear to value experience over education, training, intelligence and like performance-relevant attributes. Personnel rotation and experience on the job (i.e., OJT) represent the central processes behind JTF knowledge flows. Tacit knowledge moves along with each person who is assigned to a new job every two or three years, and each person acquires new knowledge through experience associated with his or her job assignments, but formal training in specialized military schools is quite prevalent also. Nearly every military employee goes through one or more formal schools (e.g., Officer Candidate School, Basic Training) before the first job assignment. Many people are sent to specialized schools (e.g., electronics, warfare, leadership) in between job assignments as well, and some military specializations (e.g., aviation, nuclear power, SEAL) require extensive training.

We learn from the case that Table 8 summarizes the knowledge deemed to be most critical by JTF organization participants. The table identifies also how JTF participants obtain such knowledge. For instance, *situational awareness* (see Column 2 of the table) is noted as essential to performing effectively in the Battle Watch Unit (i.e., listed in Column 1 of the table). The Battle Watch Unit is in charge of the Joint Operations Center—the "nerve center," from which the entire task force operation is directed and monitored. This center is equipped with numerous computers and displays connected to networks of various kinds, along with other communication and work artifacts such as telephones, radios, video teleconferencing equipment, maps, charts, televisions and white boards. Situational awareness involves developing deep understanding of the external task force environment (e.g., with the ability to anticipate and counter adversaries' actions).

Seven knowledge flow processes are included in the table as the source of knowledge that enables situational awareness: 1) OJT (i.e., tactical military experience); 2) formal training (e.g., in specialized military schools); 3) IS use (e.g., understanding how to use information systems, the kinds of information available through each, limitations such as inaccuracy and latency associated with such information); 4) information synthesis (i.e., synthesizing numerous different sources of knowledge and information into a coherent understanding of the operational environment); 5) teamwork (e.g., developing a shared understanding of the operational environment among the team of 6 – 10 people assigned to a particular Battle Watch); and 6) mentoring (e.g., when a senior officer with Battle Watch experience works with a junior officer to help him or her learn while working).

The other areas of critical knowledge listed in the table include warfighting, which pertains to executing tactical combat processes, and task force planning, which pertains to planning future combat engagements. Knowledge in these areas of

Table 8 Critical task force knowledge

Organization	Critical Knowledge	How Knowledge Is Obtained
Battle Watch	Situational Awareness	OJT, training, IS use, information synthesis, teamwork, mentoring
Operations	Warfighting	OJT, Training, intelligence operations
Training	Warfighting	OJT, Training, mentoring
Intelligence	Warfighting	OJT, Training, assignment
Planning	Task force planning	Evaluation, mentoring
Chief of Staff	Task force planning	OJT, command
JTF Commander	Task force planning	OJT, Training

warfighting and task force planning is developed through several of the same flow processes listed in the table for situational awareness. In particular, OJT and training are prominent in both areas. We also note four additional processes: 7) intelligence operations (e.g., formal reports and briefings developed by the Intelligence organization); 8) assignment (i.e., transferring knowledge along with people from one organizational unit to another); 9) evaluation (e.g., understanding alternate battle plans and courses of action by evaluating their relative advantages and disadvantages); and 10) command (e.g., the Commander articulating explicitly and distributing widely his primary battle goals, key intelligence needs, and time tables). There is clearly more to the command process than this, and such activities could be considered to fall within the rubric communicating command intent, but the key ideas pertain regardless. Including OJT, training and the other processes noted above in connection with situational awareness, we identify a total of ten unique flow processes associated with critical JTF knowledge.

We use this to induce our twenty-first leadership mandate from the practical application section of this book. Mandate 21. Ten unique knowledge flow processes are required for military task force efficacy.

The case presents some figures to support visualization of knowledge flows. Figure 1 delineates the ten knowledge flow processes in terms of four dimensions from our theoretical discussion above: explicitness, reach, life cycle and flow time. Here the life cycle dimension is reflected only to highlight knowledge sharing (in bold print) versus non-sharing (normal print) activities. For instance from the table, and using our coordinate shorthand, OJT (TICY) is plotted at the Tacit level of explicitness, Individual level of reach, Create level of life cycle, and Years level of flow time. As another instance, formal training (EOSM) is plotted at the Explicit level of explicitness, Organization level of reach, Share level of life cycle, and Months level of flow time. The fourth coordinate parameter represents flow time as one of six, discrete orders of magnitude:

Figure 1. Knowledge flow visualization (adapted from Nissen, 2006)

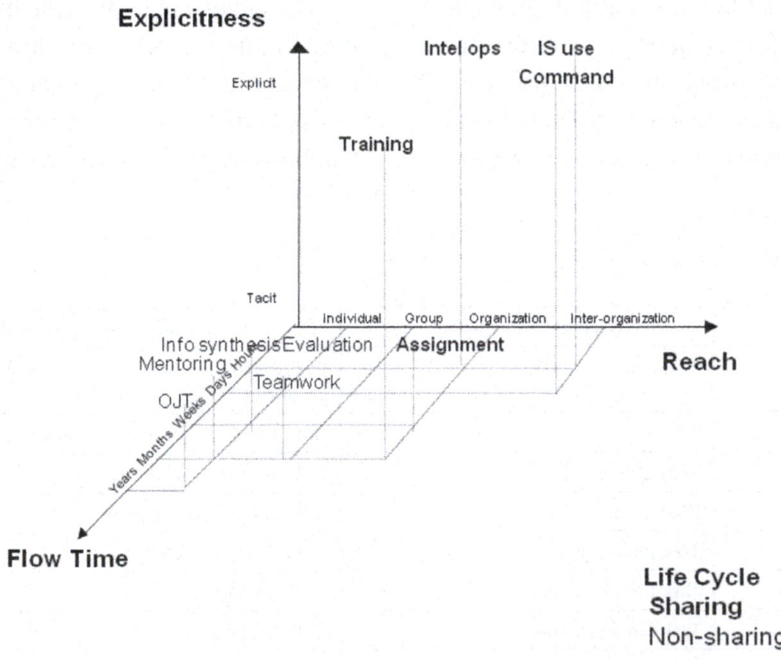

H – hours, D – days, W – weeks, M – months, Y – years, and C – decades. The other eight table entries are plotted in similar fashion.

The figure provides a visual representation and reveals two distinct clusters among the ten JTF knowledge flows. For instance, as an overall pattern discernible in the graph, one can observe some correspondence between flow time and the other dimensions. The knowledge flow processes plot roughly along a diagonal from the bottom-left-front corner (i.e., highly tacit, narrow organizational reach, long flow time) to the top-right-rear corner (i.e., highly explicit, broad organizational reach, short flow time). From this rough pattern in the figure, relatively fast knowledge flows (e.g., with flow times on the order of hours and days) correspond principally to explicit knowledge, broad reach, and knowledge sharing activities (e.g., associated with processes such as IS use, intelligence operations and command) in the JTF organization. IT plays a central, performative role (e.g., organizing, storing and disseminating knowledge) in—and in many cases enables—such fluid (i.e., fast) knowledge flows. Alternatively, the relatively slow knowledge flows (e.g., with flow times on the order of months and years) correspond mainly to tacit knowledge restricted to individuals and small groups (e.g., associated with processes such as OJT, mentoring and teamwork). IT plays a minor, supportive role (e.g., providing information, facilitating remote conversations, summarizing work tasks and results) in such sticky (i.e., slow) knowledge flows.

Figure 2 delineates an alternate view of JTF knowledge flows. We include the same axes as above for explicitness and reach but use life cycle here instead as the third axis; relatively long versus short flow times are differentiated by the thickness of arrows depicting knowledge flows, and comparatively high versus low knowledge power is delineated via respective purple, solid or orange, dotted lines. This is comparable to the knowledge flows delineated in the figures above for the business application cases. Here we focus in detail on the dynamics of two knowledge flows noted as predominate in the case: OJT and formal training. We also depict graphically dynamic interactions between the OJT and training flows.

Figure 2. Knowledge flow trajectories

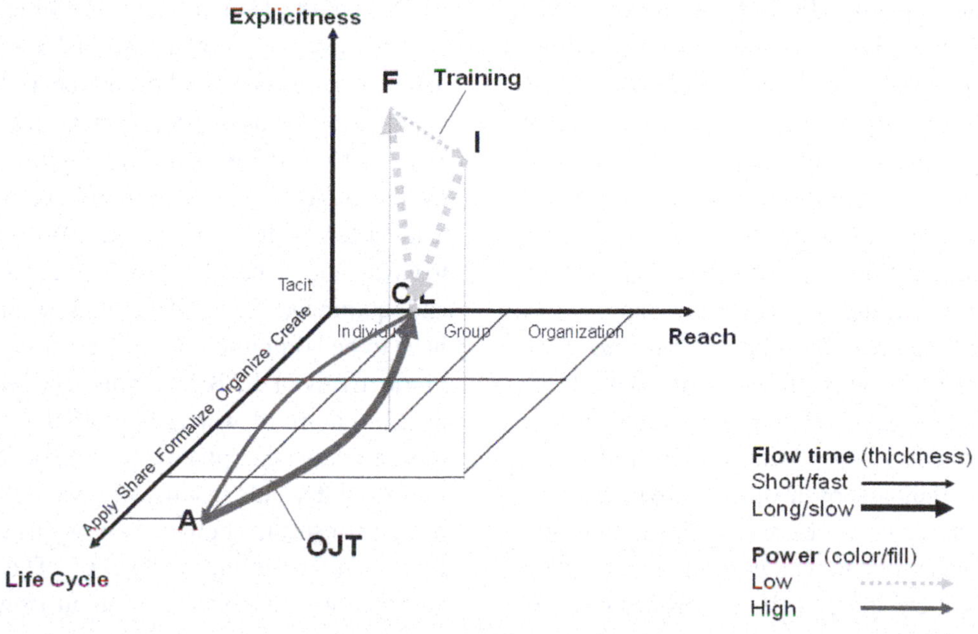

Specifically, the OJT process is delineated as a cycle of two knowledge flow modes in the tacit plane of the figure. The cycle connects points C (TICY) and A (TIAD) corresponding to knowledge creation and application, respectively. Notice the flow represented by this cycle reflects tacit, individual knowledge flowing at two different speeds (i.e., requiring months or years vs. hours or days) along the life cycle axis. Drawing from our discussion above, we depict the flow leading to knowledge creation at point C using a relatively thick line (i.e., slow flow) and the flow corresponding to knowledge application at point A using a relatively thin line (i.e., fast flow). This reflects some elaboration of the archetypical cycles used to represent similar flows in previous cases. As above, such knowledge flowing through the tacit plane is represented using purple, solid lines to depict high power.

The formal training process is delineated by its own cycle that intersects with OJT but arises from the tacit plane in the figure. Beginning at the same, shared point C (TICY), which reflects the accumulation of knowledge through experience (i.e., the OJT process cycle), working knowledge is formalized, say by a group of experienced military people, through course development into an explicit state at point F (EGFM). As above, we use a relatively thick line to represent this as a time-consuming process, and we include an orange, dotted line to suggest some power dilution that occurs through such knowledge formalization.

Distribution of the formalized knowledge for classroom instruction in military schools is shown as a subsequent flow to point I (EOSM), through which explicit training material is shared very quickly and organization-wide. Also as above, we depict this vector via a thin, orange, dotted line to represent the relatively fast yet diluted flow of formalized knowledge. Learning by individual students is denoted by a third knowledge flow vector to point L, which we depict as an individual process of knowledge creation (e.g., for each student completing the classroom course). We use a thick, orange, dotted line here to suggest that the classroom training of students is time-consuming and that such students' knowledge remains diluted—even after completing the training courses—relative to that of the military experts who developed the courses. Notice that the training cycle intersects with its OJT counterpart again at point C. This depicts students as they would leave military schools and return to apply knowledge on the job. The interrelated cycles continue interacting over time, as many former students return—generally years later—to these military schools and serve as instructors; many former instructors attend—often years later—to other military schools to participate as students.

We use this to induce our twenty-second leadership mandate from the practical application section of this book. Mandate 22. OJT involves knowledge flowing at two different speeds: knowledge application through doing is fast; knowledge creation through learning is slow.

Leadership and Management Implications

This application case illustrates a variety of knowledge flows, at several levels of reach, within and between multiple organizations. For instance, the case identifies several flows of knowledge that have to be completed before the Battle Watch work process can begin productively. All Battle Watch officers, for example, require substantial tactical warfare experience before being assigned to a Battle Watch job. Knowledge flows pertaining to naval indoctrination, training on combat tactics and equipment, and leadership experience likewise have to be completed before an officer can work productively in the Battle Watch. Given the time-critical nature of warfare, all of this knowledge must already be in place when the officer reports first for duty. This instantiates a set of important timing constraints between knowledge flows and their corresponding workflows. The leader or manager who is concerned about flows of work in the JTF should be concerned vitally about the enabling flows of knowledge that are prerequisite.

We use this to induce our twenty-third leadership mandate from the practical application section of this book. Mandate 23. Given the time-critical nature of warfare, most tacit knowledge must already be in place when the officer reports first for duty.

This application case illustrates also how some knowledge flow processes are preferred—tacitly if not explicitly—over others. For instance, in terms of interactions between OJT and formal training, people in the case are asked why more JTF personnel are not sent to military schools (e.g., to learn to work together in teams to perform Battle Watch work processes). The common response from the case is simply, they are needed to work. When someone is sent ashore for training, the organization gets little or no work out of him or her until the training course has ended. This instantiates a general preference in the JTF organization for the knowing activity of doing over that of learning. Even though the knowledge flow component associated with OJT is small, this represents the method of choice in terms of JTF knowledge flows. Here training, despite its relatively large knowledge flow component, is used sparingly because it makes so small a workflow contribution.

The case illustrates further how a wide variety of knowledge flows can be classified and visualized to identify patterns through similarities, differences and interrelationships. For instance, we note above how relatively fluid knowledge corresponds principally to explicit movements, across broad organizational reach, generally in the Class-I part of the life cycle (e.g., knowledge organization, formalization, sharing). Sticky knowledge, in contrast, corresponds more to tacit movements, with narrow organizational reach, but enabling action in the Class-II part of the life cycle (e.g., knowledge application, refinement, creation).

This leads to our induction of a new principle. For instance, where the leader or manager is interested in rapid knowledge flows across broad organizational reach—and can accept the likely dilution of knowledge power—this visual pattern suggests that such knowledge should be articulated first in explicit form. Such principle appears to cross multiple domains, as we can identify common application in the Cyberspace domain, for example (Nissen, 2010b). Alternatively, where the leader or manager is interested in powerful knowledge flows—and can accept the likely slow and narrow knowledge flows—this visual pattern suggest that such knowledge should flow tacitly through the organization. Other knowledge flow patterns may be visualized and interpreted through similar analysis.

EXERCISES

1. Identify and describe three principles from earlier parts of the book that apply to this case. Can you induce additional principles from this application case that are not articulated in the earlier parts above?
2. Delineate vectors to describe knowledge flows corresponding to how a team of people performing the Battle Watch would work together to learn and do situational-awareness activities as described in the case.
3. Comment briefly on other approaches the JTF could take to address its knowledge flow problems. What relative advantages and disadvantages apply to your suggestions when compared with the approach described in the case?
4. Describe briefly how your learning from this case can be related to an organization with which you are familiar. Include a knowledge flow diagram such as the one presented in the previous figure.

FEDERAL GOVERNMENT AGENCY AND KNOWLEDGE MANAGEMENT PROGRAM

We draw from Liebowitz (2004b) for background of this case and augment such background with information gleaned from various agency reports (e.g., Bran, 2002) and websites (e.g., NASA, 2004). We first summarize important events and issues for context. Visualization and analysis of key knowledge flows follow, with interpretation of leadership and management implications discussed subsequently. The section closes with exercises pertaining specifically to this application case.

Context

A medium-size agency of the US Federal Government enjoys considerable prestige and undertakes bold, unprecedented, scientific missions. It relies critically upon the technical expertise of its workforce. Employees are expected to exhibit unselfish teamwork through participation on interdisciplinary and cross-functional teams, task forces and groups. Experience is prized in this agency, but technical expertise is essential. Most people in the organization have educational and professional backgrounds in science and engineering, including many advanced degrees (e.g., M.S., Ph.D.). Technical proficiency represents a necessary factor, but it is not sufficient. Experience is seen as making the difference between mission success and failure. This is the case in particular because each mission is unprecedented and involves novel combinations of technical challenges. Hence the technical work is non-routine in nature and inherently risky; this provides a partial contrast with the military case above, the work of which is inherently risky also, but the nature of which is highly routine.

With experience prized as such, the agency requires a sizeable cadre of relatively senior employees to manage projects, lead interdisciplinary activities and organize technical specialists. As described in the case, over a period of several decades, the agency has developed a well-balanced organization comprised of senior, mid-grade and junior personnel. However, the balance is shifting rapidly at the time of the case. Senior personnel are retiring in greater numbers. Mid-grade personnel do not demonstrate many of the desirable work behaviors that have been important in the past. Junior personnel represent a continually decreasing proportion of the agency workforce. In short, the level of experience and expertise is decreasing in the agency, and imminent retirements portend to exacerbate this effect. (This shift continues today, where a bimodal distribution of senior and junior people persists.)

In great part to address such effect, the agency has undertaken a major initiative to mitigate problems stemming from its "graying workforce" (p. 254). This initiative includes some technical emphasis imparted from government superiors: "The Administration will adopt information technology systems to capture some of the knowledge and skills of retiring employees" (p. 254). However, the agency's strategy emphasizes now human capital to an extent greater than any time in recent history. Indeed, we learn from the case that agency KM representatives assert, "80 – 90% of knowledge management is people, process, and culture versus technology" (p. 255).

A KM task force organizes and develops a set of organizational goals (e.g., improved productivity through embedding KM processes into daily work; capture, share and generate knowledge; increase sense of community; increase collaboration) and knowledge-sharing tenets (e.g., integrate knowledge sharing into everyone's job; share the message that with creativity comes failure; educate people about what types of knowledge are valuable; enhance the recognition and reward system to promote learning and knowledge-sharing behaviors).

In terms of organizational changes, several knowledge-specific positions are created and staffed. For instance, a Knowledge Management

Officer is appointed to spearhead the KM project. A number of Knowledge Stewards are matrixed into the KM project from their home units and assigned a variety of duties (e.g., leading and coordinating KM activities within their home units; conducting knowledge-capture sessions; enlisting and coordinating case studies about unsuccessful as well as successful projects). Knowledge Retention Managers are responsible for a related but different set of duties (e.g., facilitating sessions to elicit and capture lessons learned; documenting and posting lessons learned via an online repository system; developing documents to describe "good practices" in the organization).

Several techniques employed for capturing and sharing knowledge involve technology. For instance, the agency maintains an intranet, which includes information such as lessons-learned documents and summaries of good practices. It maintains a library also, which catalogs and makes available multimedia resources such as videos of project managers recalling lessons learned. An expertise locator (i.e., a knowledge map) is maintained and distributed also. People are encouraged actively to use and update this system, which summarizes employees' areas of expertise and experience. This represents an important enabler of the organization's *transactive memory* (i.e., who knows what; e.g., see Weick & Roberts, 1993). The organization further encourages people to participate in online communities of practice.

Several techniques employed for capturing and sharing knowledge involve people and processes. For instance, the organization strives to incorporate factors such as *continued learning* and *knowledge sharing* into its formal reward system. It strives also to recruit retirees as part-time consultants and mentors (e.g., working one day weekly). Despite some drain on productivity, the organization encourages formally mentoring and shadowing. Mentoring involves a relatively experienced person providing guidance to a less-experienced counterpart. Shadowing involves one person with a particular job or area of expertise spending a week or so with someone who performs a different job or possesses expertise in a different area (e.g., to learn what they do and observe how they do it). Additionally, knowledge-sharing fora are set up, and formal storytelling workshops are facilitated. Further, audits are conducted to identify "knowledge gaps" (p. 258). Focused mini-courses are developed to address such gaps deemed critical and at risk of imminent loss.

Knowledge Flow Analysis

This application case is informative in comparison with several of those discussed above. For instance, the government agency engages in project-oriented work. Most of the cases above involve project work as well. Knowledge is critical to this agency, particularly experience-based tacit knowledge. Tacit knowledge plays a critical role in most of the cases above too. The agency recognizes some knowledge flow problems and establishes management initiatives to identify and dissolve the knowledge clumps. We discuss management initiatives for each case above also. Alternatively, the focal case here is engaged in a major KM project. This constitutes a project within a project: a project-based organization, while undertaking a portfolio of mission projects, endeavors simultaneously to pursue a KM project as well. Hence this case focuses on knowledge management directly.

We learn from the case how the agency pursues a combination of organizational, personnel, processual and technological initiatives. This conforms directly to one of our dynamic knowledge principles from above. One can perceive also how the agency has satisfied several preconditions for success (e.g., senior management commitment, appropriate people participating full-time, sufficient budget) and has attempted to avoid many preconditions for failure (e.g., wrong sponsor, reliance upon external expertise, narrow technical focus). However, the informed reader must wonder about other preconditions for success (e.g., realistic expectations, strategic context of growth and expansion, shared vision) that may have been overlooked or that may simply not apply in this case. Likewise, the informed reader must question other preconditions for failure (e.g., consensus management, unsound financial condition, too many improvement projects under way) that appear to be present in the case. Although all such preconditions (i.e., developed in the evaluation chapter above) derive from expertise acquired through re-engineering projects and the associated radical change, the kind of KM project undertaken at this government agency reflects in many ways large-scale change. Hence one can argue that much of this re-engineering expertise would apply well to the case.

One noteworthy knowledge-sharing approach described in the case involves knowledge capture via lessons learned. Recall that a Knowledge Retention Manager is responsible in part for facilitating sessions with experienced people to elicit and capture lessons learned from recent technical projects. Such role is one of an intermediary, as it bridges a chasm between an expert's tacit knowledge and an online repository. By interviewing an expert, the Retention Manager is performing a role very similar to that of a Knowledge Engineer described above in the section on expert systems, and through its use for retention, organization and distribution, the repository is performing a role somewhat similar to that of an expert system. However, a key difference lies in the respective supportive versus performative natures of repository and expert systems. Whereas the repository system is employed to *support* people who want to learn lessons from past projects, an expert system is used to *perform* key tasks in lieu of people.

We delineate some key knowledge flows pertaining to the lessons-learned approach in Figure 3. Notice this figure is very similar to the one from above from the JTF application case. In particular, the figure includes a two-part OJT vector (points A-C: TIC ← → TIA) depicting the experience-based, tacit knowledge flows associated with the development of individual expertise. This vector delineates the gradual accumulation of expertise via experience that is required before someone can be considered an expert. The other, three-part,

Figure 3. Lessons-learned knowledge flows

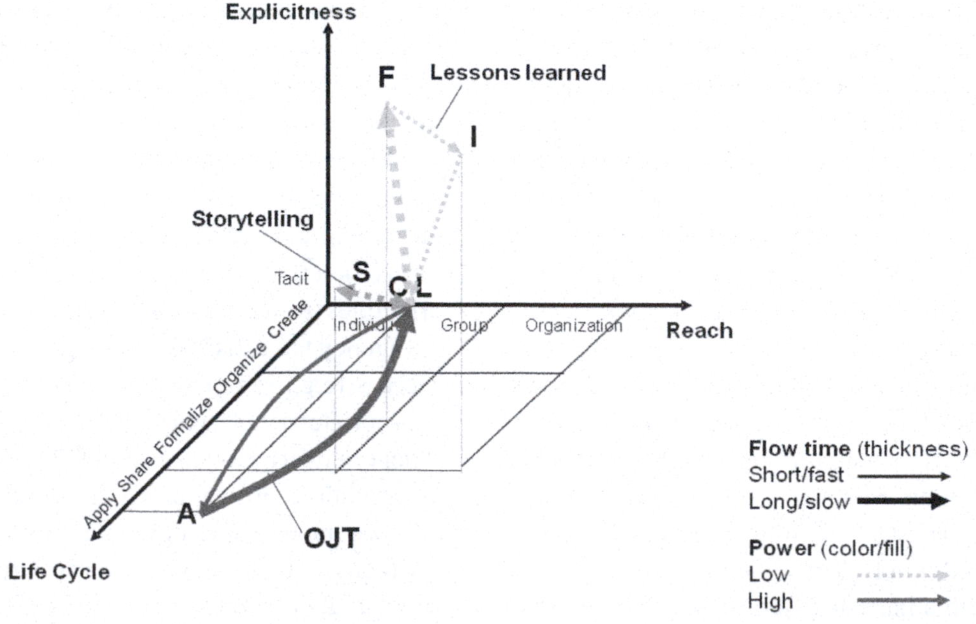

lessons-learned vector is quite analogous to the kind of formal training process involved with JTF knowledge flows. The first ray of this vector (points C-F: TIC → EGF) arises from the tacit-knowledge plane through a process of formalization. This represents the interviewing, storytelling, writing and documentation activities associated with articulating lessons learned (CALL, 2012). It is depicted as a group activity, for an intermediary works with one or more experts to accomplish such activity. Once formalized and organized in an online repository, the lessons-learned documents and related media (e.g., possibly including video and other multimedia formats, immersive simulation technology, expert systems tutorials and like components in addition to static, textual documents) can be disseminated very quickly and organization-wide. This is represented by the second ray of the vector (points F-I: EGF → EOS) associated with knowledge sharing at an organizational level of reach. The third vector (points I-L: EOS → TIC) represents individual learning accomplished by a person reading or interfacing via alternate media with the lessons learned. As with formal training, such person is acquiring new knowledge (i.e. new to him or her), which must be learned, internalized and made tacit for high-performance application to a project endeavor. Hence the lessons-learned approach shares much in common with formal training.

One key difference, of course, pertains to individual, instructorless learning of the former approach as opposed to classroom participation of the latter. Another key difference stems from the likely volume and labeling of lessons learned documents and media. Particularly when compared with formal training courses, a great many lessons-learned documents and media are likely to exist and may require considerable search efforts to find. Thus, it may be relatively more difficult to tell whether any particular lessons-learned document or media is relevant to a specific task at hand. Yet gaining knowledge via most lessons learned approaches is comparatively much quicker than completing many classroom training courses; hence the thinner arrow delineating the corresponding knowledge flow in this figure.

Nonetheless, lessons-learned documents and media can make explicit many events, considerations, actions, inactions, decisions and factors that experts consider to be relevant to a project's relative successes and failures. When read by another person who lacks the experience of the experts, such person may learn from past successes and failures and hence improve his or her performance on the basis of the knowledge associated. Of course, lessons-learned documents and media entail several drawbacks as well. For instance, such documents and media can reflect only a tiny fraction of the experience-based tacit knowledge possessed by the experts. Although creating and reading someone's lessons learned may help fill a knowledge gap and in turn improve performance, the gap does not get filled completely; hence the orange, dotted line representing diluted power corresponding to this knowledge flow vector.

For example, one would still expect the expert to perform the task better than the novice does, even after the novice has read—perhaps repeatedly—the lessons-learned documents or interfaced thoroughly with alternate media. As another instance, reading about how to perform some knowledge-based activity is only a partial substitute for performing the activity; the same applies to interfacing with alternate lessons-learned media. This reflects the distinction from above between knowledge and knowing. For example, recall the discussion above pertaining to reading a book about riding bicycles (i.e., knowledge) versus experiencing physically (i.e., knowing) the activity of riding bicycles. As a third instance, to elaborate on our comment above, even if the best possible lessons-learned documents and other media can be developed, it may be difficult to find the specific lesson or set of lessons most applicable to one's particular circumstances; this is the case in particular when time is of the essence (e.g., in the field). Consider if everyone in the agency recorded every lesson ever learned throughout his or her career. Depending upon the indexing and search schemes employed by the repository system, the metaphorical needle in a haystack may apply well here.

Storytelling represents another noteworthy knowledge-sharing approach described in the case. This is similar in many respects to capturing lessons learned. For instance: someone recognized as an expert is selected to share knowledge about a particular project; the knowledge of interest is tacit and experience-based in nature; people with less expertise are intended to benefit through some gap-filling and improve their performance. Alternatively, a key difference lies in the sharing activities. With lessons learned—as with formal training and expert systems too—a central task involves moving tacit knowledge to an explicit form and then making such formalized knowledge available organization-wide (e.g., via intranet). Through storytelling, on the other hand, the formalization step is omitted generally. Conversation represents the key activity associated with knowledge sharing, and instead of experts trying in advance to articulate through lessons learned all of the knowledge someone else might be expected to need one day, in a storytelling forum the experts interact directly with people in the audience, the latter of whom can ask focused questions and influence which "lessons" get articulated and at what level of detail.

The level of explicitness also differs in part between lessons learned and storytelling. The formalized knowledge captured via lessons-learned documents and other media is principally explicit. One can argue that storytelling involves making knowledge explicit as well, for the experts articulate through conversation the key contexts, events and decisions associated with a project, along with what they learned through the experience. Also, the storytelling session can be preserved via video and distributed for viewing by others at different times (This is essentially a lessons-learned video.), but a key difference lies in the interactive nature of the storytelling session. Arguably, with different people participating in a session and asking the questions they feel are most relevant personally and professionally, no two sessions would be the same. This reflects much more of a mentoring context of (tacit) knowledge sharing than formal training, lessons learned or other explicit-knowledge flows. Interpersonal bonding can also ensue from storytelling fora, and relatively inexperienced people can establish some trust and personal relationships with storytellers in a face-to-face setting, making potentially important contacts who can be consulted (e.g., in a mentoring role) later. Some of these same benefits may accrue as well through the recording and interfacing with lessons-learned documents and other media, but such documents and media detach the lessons from the storytellers, and they become the media of learning, not interactions with the experts directly. Hence storytelling involves some aspects of apprenticeship for (tacit) knowledge-sharing as well. These differences are subtler than those pertaining to many of the diverse and archetypical knowledge flows described and delineated above in this book.

The flows associated with storytelling are not completely tacit, but neither are they completely explicit. In Figure 3 we represent storytelling knowledge flows as a two-headed vector (points C-S: TIC ← → T'GS). This vector stems from the same Point C as above that reflects an expert's accumulated, experience-based tacit knowledge (TIC). It depicts also a flow to the group level through sharing, but notice this vector rises up from the tacit plane a bit: not as much as the lessons-learned vector, yet reflecting some explicitness in the knowledge sharing. Point S represents such group-level sharing of what we can refer to only as semi-tacit knowledge. We use an apostrophe in our coordinate shorthand (i.e., T'GS) to indicate the semi-tacit nature of such sharing. We also include a medium-thick line (i.e., denoting a blend of long and short flow times) and color it blue (i.e., denoting a mix of high and low knowledge power) but retain the dotted pattern (i.e., indicating that some knowledge dilution is likely to occur). Although knowledge sharing via lessons learned has many similarities to that via storytelling, the corresponding knowledge flow vectors delineate considerably different processes underneath, and the storytelling process appears to blend aspects of mentoring with those of classroom training as a hybrid.

We use this to induce our twenty-fourth leadership mandate from the practical application section of this book. Mandate 24. Systematic storytelling can increase the reach of this time-honored and effective approach to sharing tacit knowledge.

Leadership and Management Implications

This application case illustrates how knowledge management can be approached in a project environment, complete with a project manager and staff matrixed from home units within an organization. The tone of the application case is positive, suggesting successful progress toward enhancing knowledge flows in the focal organization, but one must question whether the project environment is matched well with the organization's stated goals such as "embedding KM processes into daily work." The use of a change agent such as the KM Task Force (i.e., Knowledge Management Officer, dedicated staff and budget) represents a time-proven approach to planning and effecting organizational change, but by its very nature the project represents a temporary undertaking, demarcated by a distinct project organization. Alternatively, daily work and organizational routines are perennial processes undertaken by ongoing line and staff organizations. The results remain to be seen, but the informed reader has good reason to question how well a KM project such as this can institutionalize enhanced knowledge flows over time.

The case illustrates also how KM-program evaluation factors such as preconditions for success and failure can be employed to assess KM projects in practice. The focal organization described in the case is reported in terms of a success story, but we observe how some preconditions for success appear to be missing and how some preconditions for failure appear to be present. Again, the results remain to be seen, but the informed reader has reason to question the likelihood and extent of success the focal organization will enjoy as its KM project continues to unfold and play out. Clearly other KM-program evaluation factors from the chapter above can be applied as well to practical projects such as this, but details presented in the case do not permit the same depth of evaluation that would be possible through analysis by experienced people onsite and interacting directly with organizational personnel.

The case illustrates further how the KM project involves more than just a narrow technological focus. Indeed, we describe organizational, personnel and processual initiatives, in addition to technological support. This is consistent with our principles above and can be considered as such to represent best principled practice. Moreover, the various organizational, personnel, processual and technological initiatives complement one another. Organizational initiatives such as appointing Knowledge Retention Managers combine with personnel and process initiatives such as encouraging and facilitating the development of cases and lessons learned. Technological initiatives such as maintaining an intranet and equipping a multimedia library enable the organization and sharing of such cases and lessons beyond the limits of interpersonal conversations and even paper documents. Hence the organization appears to be leveraging effectively its KM efforts through coordinated, complementary initiatives.

We describe in some detail from the case two noteworthy knowledge flows: 1) lessons learned, and 2) storytelling. These two flows share several similarities as well as differences. In particular, we highlight how the former involves movement of knowledge from tacit to explicit form to a greater extent than the latter does. Such greater explicitness supports broader reach and faster sharing through the organization than the more-tacit approach does, but some major part of the underlying experience-based tacit knowledge of the experts is lost through formalization into explicit knowledge. Through storytelling, the associated semi-tacit knowledge cannot be shared as broadly or as quickly through the organization as its explicit counterpart can. Alternatively, it can likely be shared more broadly and quickly than can tacit knowledge that remains embedded within an individual's professional expertise, and it carries some potential to at least partially mitigate the knowledge power dilution expected via lessons learned.

Other knowledge flows such as OJT are clearly prominent in this application case as well. Hence several alternate approaches to enhancing knowledge flows are available to the leader or manager. Each alternate approach has some common and some unique properties with respect to the others. An informed leader or manager can consider such common and unique properties when trying to determine which approaches will match relatively better or worse than others in terms of addressing any particular knowledge flow and/or clump. The kinds of knowledge flow diagrams delineated here can help managers visualize and understand the phenomena of knowledge flows. Hopefully such visualization and understanding can improve KM decision-making and implementation.

EXERCISES

5. Identify and describe three principles from earlier parts of the book that apply to this case. Can you induce additional principles from this application case that are not articulated in the earlier parts above?
6. Delineate vectors to describe knowledge flows corresponding to how the tacit knowledge possessed by a retired expert in the organization could be shared through part-time mentoring as described in the case.
7. Comment briefly on other approaches the agency could take to address its knowledge flow problems. What relative advantages and disadvantages apply to your suggestions when compared with the approach described in the case?
8. Describe briefly how your learning from this case can be related to an organization with which you are familiar. Include a knowledge flow diagram such as the one presented in the figure above.

PUBLIC SERVICE ORGANIZATION AND IT INTEGRATION PROJECT

We draw from Mueller and Dyerson (1999) for background of this case. We first summarize important events and issues for context. Visualization and analysis of key knowledge flows follow, with interpretation of leadership and management implications discussed subsequently. The section closes with exercises pertaining specifically to this application case.

Context

A medium-size government service agency is involved with a large-scale IT development and implementation project. This agency performs several financial services for the Government and has hundreds of branch offices distributed throughout the country (not the US). IT innovation has been sweeping for many years through the commercial finance sector of the host nation, but counterpart organizations in the public sector have been slow to adopt such innovation. This is attributed in part to conservatism inherent in government organizations and in part to the absence of competition to motivate service innovation.

Nonetheless, the time has come for large-scale automation in this agency, principally to address concerns about efficiency and service in a public organization. The organization plans for new-system development and implementation across its nation-wide branch network of 600 local offices. Automation is targeted to redesign a host of largely manual processes. Examples include financial collection, recording and processing activities. These processes are being redesigned also to transition from locally controlled, branch-based activities to centrally administered, automated processes.

The project involves IT development and implementation, which takes place over an extended period of more than five years. Although the IT implementation represents a one-shot project in many respects, the extended period of time devoted to the project also reflects an ongoing operation and continuous process. Indeed, the organization creates a new and separate division to develop, operate and maintain the new IT, as well as to perform the centralized process activities. Here we find the organization taking a long-term view of the process, both its IT development/implementation and its ongoing process operations. Hence the case illustrates aspects of a project-oriented organization along with those of an ongoing operational concern.

Employees in the new division are drawn from various branch offices and transferred to the centralized unit. Such employees reflect a mix of business analysts and technologists who work together on cross-functional teams. The business analysts are intended to restrain the technological zeal of computer programmers and systems analysts and to focus on business issues instead of just new technology. The technologists are intended to provide expertise necessary for effective system development. Teamwork is promoted broadly and formally in the organization. Not only does teamwork permeate the organizational culture, but the formal reward system (e.g., involving promotions and raises) emphasizes teamwork as well. For instance, many employees are compensated in large part based on *organizational performance*, not just individual efforts and accomplishments.

The organization's employee base is very stable. Turnover is noted as comparatively low (i.e., less than 5% annually). Promotion from within company ranks is predominant. Organization-specific expertise is considerable. For instance, most managers employed currently have been with the organization for multiple decades and have risen from the lowest-level professional and technical positions (e.g., business analysts, programmers). We learn from the case also that the organization has culture and processes centered on committee-based decision-making. Such factors suggest that the organization possesses considerable, experience-based tacit knowledge and is able to retain such knowledge, not only it its employees, but in its organizational routines also.

However, we learn further from the case that despite such considerable, organization-specific knowledge base, the employees possess collectively relatively little experience in terms of large-scale IT development and implementation (p. 246). As a result, the organization decides to engage external consultants to help with the integration. Yet the organization is concerned about the appropriability of knowledge by the consultants. It is common in public organizations, for instance, to have a great part of their expertise possessed and retained by consultants over time. One comment in the case suggests that consultants to some government agencies stay with such organizations for longer periods of time than employees do (p.248).

To address such potential appropriability problems, organization leaders decide to integrate the consultants directly into their line-management processes. For instance, consultants report individually to line managers, according to their function. This represents a vivid contrast to many consulting engagements, in which consultants report collectively (e.g., through a Partner in the consulting firm) at a relatively high level in the organization (e.g., Vice President, Director). Further, consultants are integrated expressly into cross-functional work teams with organization employees. Organization employees are further encouraged to shadow the consultants in their work areas, to observe what they do and how they do it. This too represents a vivid contrast to many consulting engagements, in which consultants work independently, accomplish their project objectives (or not), get paid handsomely, and then leave the organization. Many times, critical knowledge—both brought to the organization and learned from organizational work by consultants—leaves the organization at the end of the consulting contract.

Knowledge Flow Analysis

As in most of the cases discussed above, tacit knowledge flows are important in this application case. For instance, we learn about the organization's stable employee base and history of promotion from within. Organization-specific knowledge flows are notably sticky and require considerable time where tacit, experience-based knowledge is concerned. A stable employee base allows substantial time (e.g., years, decades) for workers to acquire organization-specific knowledge. Such substantial time allows also for workers to share, apply and refine their knowledge as well. Hence a stable employee base facilitates successive flows of knowledge through the life cycle, and successive flows through the life cycle are not limited to individual-level knowledge. Rather, groups also enjoy substantial time to work together on a variety of tasks and projects, and organizational routines likewise enjoy substantial time for creation, application and refinement.

We represent these stable and successive tacit knowledge flows in Figure 4 by using three interconnected cyclic vectors. The first cyclic vector is labeled "Individual OJT," reflects tacit knowledge, and cycles from creation through refinement along the life cycle. A parallel cyclic vector is labeled "Employee teamwork" and cycles tacit knowledge similarly along the life cycle. A third parallel cycle (i.e., labeled "Org routines") is delineated at the organization level of reach. Each cyclic vector is connected to another through two-headed knowledge-sharing vectors. These are labeled "Socialization" and "Acculturation," which depict individual-group and group-organization knowledge sharing, respectively. All of the vectors in this figure reflect thick, purple, solid arrows to depict the relatively slow, powerful flows associated with sticky, tacit knowledge. Technically, the flows corresponding to *knowledge application* on the life cycle axis could be represented more consistently with thinner arrows to contrast with their counterparts representing knowledge creation. However, all of the flows depicted in this case occur over extended time periods (i.e., years), which reflects relatively slow application overall. Nonetheless, knowledge flows appear to circulate well in this organization. Hence we label the diagram "Healthy" in Figure 4.

We use this to induce our twenty-fifth leadership mandate from the practical application section of this book. Mandate 25. Socialization, teamwork and acculturation must interconnect to enable healthy knowledge flow circulation.

Alternatively, with a less-stable employee base, a different set of flow patterns could be envisioned. For instance, consider if the socialization and acculturation flows did not form as well (e.g., only single-headed vectors) or did not form at all. Group teamwork and organizational routines similarly may not have ample time to form complete cycles, and with sufficient instability in the workforce, even individual OJT cycles may fail to form (e.g., knowledge may be created but never applied; knowledge may be applied but never refined). Hence the stable employee base enhances tacit knowledge flows at all levels of reach and is amplified across the complete life cycle.

The knowledge flows associated with the external consultants are particularly noteworthy in this application case. Figure 5 depicts two, separate, cyclic tacit knowledge flow vectors at the group level. One vector is labeled "Employee teamwork" as above and represents the cross-functional teams comprised of organizational employees. We repeat this cyclic vector here for reference and comparison, but we omit its individual and organizational

Figure 4. Healthy knowledge flow circulation

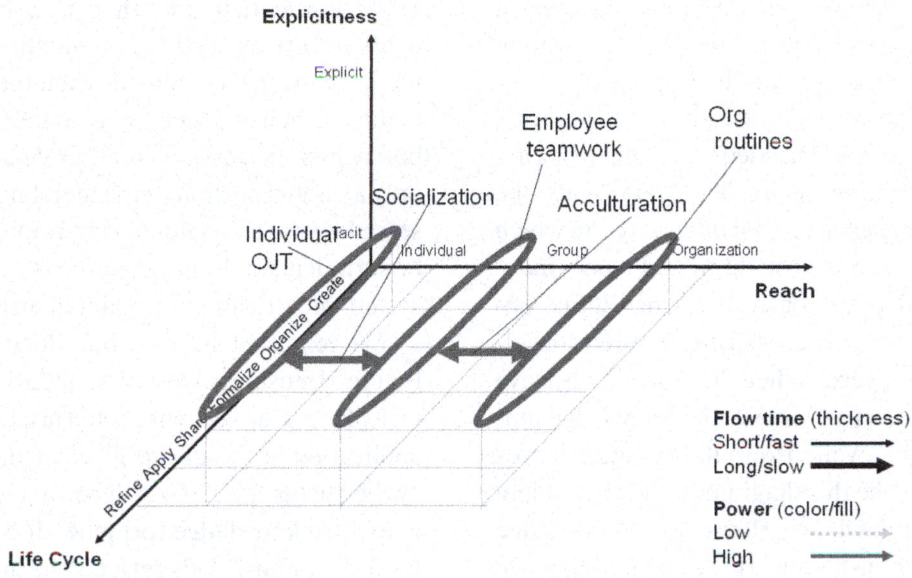

Figure 5. Unhealthy knowledge clumping

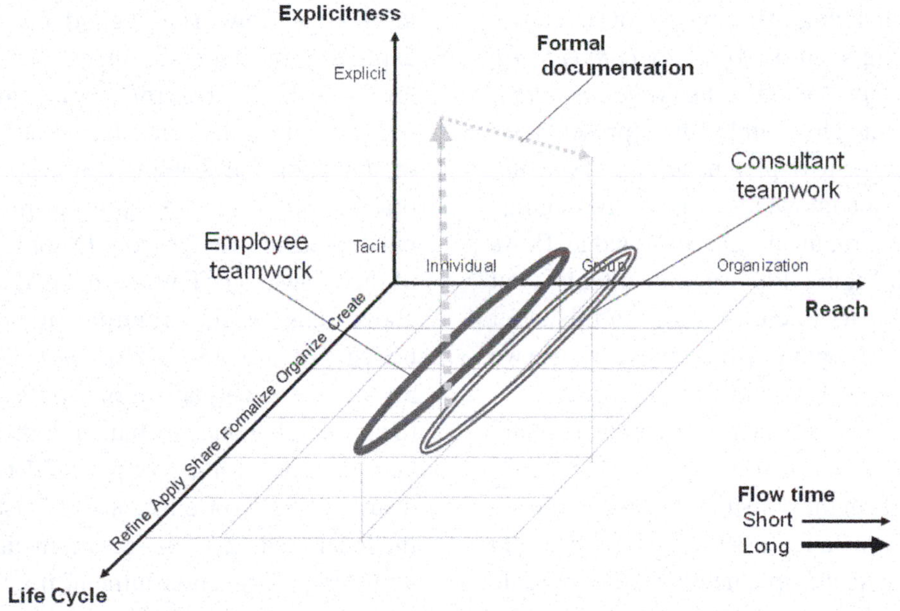

counterparts from above to reduce clutter in the diagram. The other vector in this figure is labeled "Consultant teamwork" and represents the teams of external consultants. This vector cycles similarly at the group level. Because external consultants tend to stay for extended periods (e.g., years) with large-scale IT-integration clients such as our focal organization, we use thick, purple, solid arrows here also to represent the relatively slow and powerful flows associated with sticky knowledge. To help distinguish the two, we place this cyclic consultant vector next to that used to delineate the flows for employee teamwork, and we use a different line style (e.g., double lines) to represent the knowledge flow of a different organization inserted (temporarily) into the focal agency.

Notice the two cyclic vectors are separate and have no single- or two-headed knowledge-sharing vectors connecting them. This represents the common approach *not taken in the case*, in which a consulting team is brought in and works independently. Such approach offers negligible opportunity for knowledge sharing between consultants and employees. When the consultants leave at the end of an engagement, the knowledge represented by the cyclic flows in the figure leaves with them. Hence this diagram depicts a problem in terms of knowledge flows: tacit knowledge clumps in the consultants' flows and fails to move into the client organization. Were we to overlay the individual- and organization-level cyclic flows from the figure above, we would include also the two-headed knowledge-sharing vectors as above, but such sharing vectors *would not connect with* the tacit flows represented by the *cyclic consultant teamwork* vector. The double-line representation is thus appropriate to depict the temporary nature of the consultant knowledge flows. In contrast with the tacit organizational knowledge flows represented in Figure 4 above, consultants' tacit knowledge appears to clump badly in this latter representation of organizational flows. Hence we label the diagram "Unhealthy" in Figure 5.

However, even with such an approach (again, not taken in the case), some knowledge would clearly move from the consultant group to the organization. For instance, assuming the consulting group is successful in implementing the large-scale IT system, knowledge embedded in the IT artifact would remain within the organization even after the consulting engagement terminated. Unfortunately, such embedded knowledge may not be accessible to the organization's employees (e.g., necessary to modify or maintain the system). As a related instance, the consulting organization would likely develop documentation and procedures for the IT system. Articulating their tacit knowledge in explicit form as such would ameliorate some of the knowledge gap created when the consultants complete their engagement with the organization, but such explicit documentation clearly represents only a diluted portion of the tacit knowledge possessed by the consultants, and it may or may not be sufficient for the organization's purposes (e.g., system modification or maintenance).

We represent such explicit documentation in Figure 5 by using a two-ray vector arising from the tacit plane. This vector is rooted in tacit knowledge application at the group level of the consultant cyclic vector (i.e., TGA). The first ray is headed to explicit knowledge formalization at the group level (i.e., EGF). This reflects the articulation of tacit knowledge via explicit documentation and is delineated as above via a thick, orange, dotted line to represent relatively a slow and diluted knowledge flow. The second ray is headed to explicit knowledge sharing at the organization level (i.e., EOS). This reflects the documentation being acquired by and shared across the focal organization and is delineated as above via a thin, orange, dotted line to represent relatively a fast but diluted knowledge flow. In contrast with some of the knowledge flows delineated in other cases above (e.g., formal training, lessons learned), notice that this vector *does not* include a third ray to represent organizational personnel learning the knowledge once formalized; that is, we show how the consulting group would formalize and distribute the knowledge, but we illustrate also how the focal organization—again, in an "unhealthy" knowledge flow environment, not the "healthy" environment described in the case—may not ever learn such knowledge. Other knowledge flows between external consultants and organizational employees are likely as well (e.g., conversations with management), but these are comparatively minor flows, which we omit from the diagram.

Importantly, the approach taken in the case differs from this knowledge flow representation (cf. Figure 4, Figure 5). Because of the manner in which external consultants are integrated in the case (e.g., at the line-management level, into cross-functional employee work teams), the disjoint cyclic vectors depicted in Figure 5 would not obtain. Rather, the two cyclic knowledge flow vectors (i.e., one representing employee teamwork, another representing the consulting group) delineated in Figure 4 would continue to apply instead. Indeed, the "healthy" diagram reveals how the employee and consulting knowledge flows are integrated into a single pattern. Integration of the consultants into the focal organization enables knowledge sharing over an extended period of time. Even though all individual consultants may retain higher levels of expertise than even the best organizational employees do, the group-level knowledge flows are more likely to resemble the integrated vectors delineated in Figure 4 than the counterpart, disjoint flows represented in Figure 5.

From a knowledge flow perspective, the approach taken in the case appears to be superior. It ameliorates the problem with knowledge clumping in the consulting organization. Of course other lenses (e.g., in terms of project cost or completion time) may reveal the opposite in terms of superiority; that is, enabling superior knowledge flows through a project may cost more and take longer to achieve than completing a project with less knowledge flow does. Moreover, given the rapid rate of IT change generally, one can question the extent to which it makes sense to internalize such deep system knowledge (esp. if the system will be replaced within a few years). This question reflects our tension from above between learning and doing. The "best" approach depends fundamentally upon the organizational leaders' and managers' preferences for exploration versus exploitation in the context of this project. We discuss this further below in terms of leadership and management implications.

Leadership and Management Implications

Knowledge appropriability is a serious concern, even for organizations in the public sector. Such organizations are not as concerned as their for-profit counterparts are with using knowledge for competitive advantage, but knowledge is key to performance, and serving constituents well represents a stated objective of most public-sector organizations. Further, dependence upon external consultants can be expensive, particularly where a mission-critical IT system is involved. Consultants enjoy knowledge asymmetries over clients, and they face powerful economic incentives to maintain such asymmetries. Unless a client organization can get important knowledge to flow from consultants, it risks the expensive proposition of becoming dependent. Additionally, the kinds of explicit reports, documents and procedures that are developed by consultants as work products fail to substitute for the rich tacit knowledge possessed. This is the case with most attempts to articulate tacit knowledge via explicit documents. Client organizations may develop a false sense of security when purchasing such explicit documentation.

This application case illustrates through two figures a contrast between comparatively healthy and unhealthy knowledge flows. The former flows are represented above in terms of complete, tacit flow cycles at all levels of reach, and such cyclic knowledge movements are interconnected richly with bidirectional sharing and acculturation flows. The pattern delineated in this former figure can be used by managers to illustrate at least one instantiation of healthy knowledge flows. Here the circulation of knowledge appears to be flowing smoothly. In contrast, the latter flows are represented above in terms of disjoint, tacit flow cycles at the group level of reach. The cyclic knowledge movements associated with the consulting group are separate and isolated from those associated with employee knowledge flows. Negligible knowledge sharing takes place within the tacit plane. Although a single vector arises from the tacit plane and flows to the organization in terms of explicit documentation, this represents a very poor substitute for tacit knowledge sharing. The pattern delineated in this latter figure can be used by managers to illustrate at least one instantiation of unhealthy knowledge flows. Here the circulation of knowledge appears to be constricted by a noticeable clump in the consultants' flows.

We close this section by addressing the question of cost. We note above how the approach taken in the case appears to be effective in terms of enhancing knowledge flows and ameliorating problems with knowledge clumping and appropriation by consultants. As a result of cross-functional, consultant-employee work teams, substantial technical knowledge is shared between consultants and employees, and many organizational processes improve their performance and retain collective knowledge through routines. From a knowledge flow perspective, this case reads like a success story. We can use knowledge flow diagrams such as the one presented in Figure 4 as a pattern reflecting healthy circulation.

Nonetheless, the informed reader must ask about the cost of such success. Engaging consultants represents a relatively expensive approach to obtaining expertise, and the longer the engagement, the greater the cumulative cost as a general rule. We do not know how expensive it would be to hire and train a technically proficient cadre of employees instead of engaging consultants. In particular, given the long time period associated with the project, it may be less expensive to hire and develop expertise from within the organization than to depend upon an external organization over a period of multiple years.

Additionally, assigning consultants and employees to work together on teams has its costs as well. Working with relative novices (i.e., employees) is likely to slow down the consultants, as they are in effect mentoring and teaching—or at least spending time explaining—as well as working. Likewise, encouraging employees to shadow consultants decreases the amount of time and energy they have for contributions to the organization's workflows. In particular, again, given the long time period associated with the project, a less-expensive approach may be to hire and develop expertise from within the organization. The experienced leader or manager may worry further about losing the organization's best people to the consulting firm; metaphorical poaching along such lines is common across many organizations in the public sector.

The aphorism about teaching someone to fish versus giving him or her a fish applies here; does the leadership and management wish for its people to learn how to implement and maintain IT along the lines of the implemented system, or is simply accomplishing such implementation and maintenance sufficient? The case does not provide sufficient information for us to assess this tradeoff, but the informed leader or manager would want to consider it. A model to help leaders and managers to balance such factors would be very helpful in circumstances like these—circumstances that confront nearly every knowledge-based organization. By measuring knowledge power (e.g., as described in Chapter 6), one can begin to quantify and assess tradeoffs such as this, but this remains an active topic of current research at the time of this writing.

EXERCISES

9. Identify and describe three principles from earlier parts of the book that apply to this case. Can you induce additional principles from this application case that are not articulated in the earlier parts above?

10. Delineate vectors to describe knowledge flows corresponding to how the tacit knowledge possessed by individual consultants could be shared with individual employees as described in the case.
11. Comment briefly on other approaches the agency could take to address its knowledge flow problems. What relative advantages and disadvantages apply to your suggestions when compared with the approach described in the case?
12. Describe briefly how your learning from this case can be related to an organization with which you are familiar. Include a knowledge flow diagram such as the one presented in the figure above.

REFERENCES

Bran, J. (2002). Five minutes with … NASA. *Knowledge Management Regular, 6*(3). Retrieved 1 November 2002, from http://www.kmmagazine.com/xq/asp/sid.0/articleid.338BAE9E-0E28-4B47-B090-55549E920A43/qx/display.htm

CALL. (2012). *Center for army lessons learned*. Ft. Leavenworth, KS: US Army Combined Arms Center. Retrieved from http://usacac.army.mil/cac2/call/index.asp

Goffman, E. (1961). *Asylums: Essays on the social situation of mental patients and other inmates*. Garden City, NY: Anchor.

Liebowitz, J. (2004). A knowledge management implementation plan at a leading US technical government organization: A case study. *Knowledge and Process Management, 10*(4), 254–259. doi:10.1002/kpm.184.

Mintzberg, H. (1980). Structure in 5's: A synthesis of the research on organization design. *Management Science, 26*(3), 322–341. doi:10.1287/mnsc.26.3.322.

Mueller, F., & Dyerson, R. (1999). Expert humans or expert organizations? *Organization Studies, 20*(2), 225–256. doi:10.1177/0170840699202003.

NASA. (2004). *Library past announcements*. Retrieved 19 August 2004, from http://km.nasa.gov/library/past_announcements.html

Nissen, M. E. (2002). *Understanding 'understanding' flow for network-centric warfare: Military knowledge flow mechanics* (NPS Technical Report NPS-GSBPP-02-001). Monterey, CA: Naval Postgraduate School.

Nissen, M. E. (2010). *CyberKM: Harnessing dynamic knowledge for competitive advantage through cyberspace* (Technical Report No. NPS-IS-10-006). Monterey, CA: Naval Postgraduate School.

Weick, K. E., & Roberts, K. H. (1993). Collective mind in organizations: Heedful interrelating on flights decks. *Administrative Science Quarterly, 38*(3), 357–381. doi:10.2307/2393372.

Chapter 9
Application Cases in Non-Profits

ABSTRACT

This chapter concentrates on knowledge flow diagnosis and intervention in the private, non-profit sector. The authors look at a national youth soccer organization. The discussion turns then to examine a local tennis club. The final case describes a nondenominational community church. In each case, they draw in part from secondary data sources for background. This should prove helpful to the reader who is interested in following up to consider more details than presented in this volume. The authors also draw considerably from their own research and personal experience to fill in missing information, and they apply principles and techniques of this book to contribute new insights through examination of knowledge flows in the cases. Each application case concludes with exercises to stimulate critical thought, learning, and discussion. In conjunction with the principles articulated in Section 1 of the book, the application cases explain how organizations from across a very wide range of sizes and domains both succeed and fail at harnessing dynamic knowledge; hence, through case-based reasoning, they provide both positive and negative examples for the leader and manager to use in comparison with his or her own organization.

NATIONAL YOUTH SOCCER ORGANIZATION

We draw from AYSO (2004) and Nissen (2004b) for background of this case. We first summarize important events and issues for context. Discussion and analysis of key knowledge flows follow, with interpretation of leadership and management implications discussed subsequently. The section closes with exercises pertaining specifically to this application case.

Context

Founded in 1964, a national organization provides a number of organized youth soccer programs. It is a non-profit organization, established to promote soccer for children between the ages of 5 and 18. The organization can be characterized well via multi-tier structure. A small national headquarters with a board of directors governs the overall organization. The national organization is divided geographically into multiple sections, which range

DOI: 10.4018/978-1-4666-4727-5.ch009

in area from collections of populous cities to the inclusion of multiple smaller states. Sectional organizations are divided further geographically into multiple areas, which are comprised in turn of multiple regions. The region represents the atomic, community-level, organizational unit.

This organization competes in a loose sense with other soccer enterprises, most of which are non-profits also. However, the competition is not based on profit, capital stock enhancement, market share, or like financial measure. Rather, the competition is based on philosophy—which differs appreciably across the various other soccer organizations—measured by the number of participating players and volunteers who adhere to the philosophy. At the time of this writing, the focal organization lists roughly 50,000 teams with 650,000 youth players nation-wide.

Volunteerism represents an important philosophical element of the organization. Indeed, the organization is practically all-volunteer. Only 50 paid employees on the headquarters staff are compensated for their time and effort. Another 250,000 parents, grandparents, siblings, business and community leaders, and other people serve as volunteers to organize, oversee and promote youth soccer throughout the sections, areas and regions. Indeed, volunteers are responsible for every aspect of the soccer organization below the headquarters level.

Primary staff roles include positions on sectional, area and regional boards of directors (e.g., Commissioner, Treasurer, Coach Administrator), but the operating core of the organization is comprised of volunteer coaches, referees, team parents, snack-shack operators, field maintainers and others. Local community businesses and like organizations donate time and money also to the soccer organization. Enlisting such volunteer family and community involvement enmeshes youth players in a culture of encouragement, participation and sharing. Additionally, many such volunteers are highly paid professionals (e.g., doctors, lawyers, business people). At current rates (e.g., $100,000/year including indirect and overhead costs), volunteers' time invested in this organization makes it comparable roughly to a multi-billion-dollar enterprise!

Many competing soccer organizations perform the same operational aspects of providing soccer opportunities for kids. However, several noteworthy differences with our focal organization pertain. For one, most such competing organizations do not rely upon volunteers to an extent anywhere near that of the focal organization. For instance, all people participating as coaches, referees and like official positions are compensated financially for their time and expertise in the competitive organizations. Further, these competing organizations tend to promote highly competitive soccer teams, players and games. For instance, children of all ages must try out for teams. This means that many lesser-skilled players are turned away, and those who make the teams must play the positions determined by coaches, often with little consideration of the children's desires. Indeed, many kids play the same positions, on the same teams, with the same coaches, year after year.

Moreover, children with the best skills are allowed to play the most in games. Less-advanced and –skilled teammates are confined to watch from the bench. Winning and the development of superior soccer skills is stressed in the competitive leagues. Teamwork represents the means toward an end of winning games. Unevenly matched teams and lopsided games represent a common and cherished occurrence in this soccer environment. Also, in great part because of its competitive environment, many of the teams and players in such soccer organizations exhibit greater skill levels than counterparts in the volunteer focal organization do. A great many children who progress to play collegiate and professional soccer emerge from these competitive organizations. Nonetheless, such primary emphasis on competition does not mesh well with the philosophy of the focal organization.

Alternatively, the focal soccer organization has a strong and unique philosophy that permeates its myriad community leagues and is embedded (albeit somewhat tenuously) within the culture. Organizing an environment in which children can play competitive soccer games is certainly part of the mission, and this organization shares such mission with other soccer federations and enterprises. However, competitive soccer represents only a minor part of the mission. Instead, the organization notes "dedication toward the development of responsible individuals" as its central mission focus (AYSO, 2004). Soccer represents the focal activity of the organization, but such activity is used as a vehicle to enhance the whole-life development of its youth players.

Five philosophical pillars support this central tenet, and organization-wide policies operationalize them. The first is, *everyone plays*. The program's goal is for all of its participating kids to play soccer, not just to perhaps be accepted onto a team and watch from the bench. The headquarters organization mandates that every player on every team must play at least half of every game, and teams are sized to enable most youth participants to play three quarters of every game, regardless of skill level. The second is, *balanced teams*. Program founders believe children develop best and have the most fun when teams of comparable ability play against one another. The national organization mandates that new teams form each year to ensure they are balanced as evenly as possible in terms of skill levels. The third is, *open registration*. The focal organization does not condone discrimination on any basis, not even soccer-playing ability. The youth soccer program is open to all children of age (i.e., 5 – 18) who want to register and play soccer. Interest and enthusiasm are the only criteria for playing, and players at any skill level, including beginners, are welcome at any age. The fourth is, *positive coaching*. The program founders believe that encouragement provides for greater enjoyment by the players and leads ultimately to better-skilled and better-motivated players, but more importantly, positive coaching is viewed as enhancing children's sense of self-worth and confidence. The fifth is, *good sportsmanship*. The organization strives to create a positive environment based on mutual respect rather than a win-at-all-costs attitude. The soccer program is designed to instill good sportsmanship in every facet of the organization.

Knowledge Flow Analysis

Knowledge is important for the performance of the youth soccer organization. In every region, one finds a mix of experienced and novice volunteers. One finds also a mix in terms of willingness to serve as a volunteer. Volunteers must know how to: recruit and register players; organize leagues, teams and games; enlist people to serve as coaches, referees, board members and other roles; set up and maintain playing fields; purchase soccer uniforms and equipment; and organize players' parents and like affiliated people to help accomplish the myriad operational activities required to be performed each season. Although numerous informative written procedures have been printed to articulate how each of these activities should be performed, it is unclear how many volunteers read them or even know they exist. Yet volunteers in thousands of community regions come together each weekend of every season to perform such operational activities, at widely varying efficacy levels.

Knowledge that enables such operational activities is possessed in great part through organizational routines. The knowing associated with such activities emerges also to a large extent. For instance, with negligible formal organization, in each of a thousand regions across the country, a cadre of people seems to show up on time for registration. A few people in each regional cadre may have some prior experience with registration, but most of the volunteers do not. The former gravitate to the critical activities, but few if any can articulate all of the registration tasks or perform all of the requisite activities themselves. The latter help out where they can, but many do not understand the significance of the actions they perform or where their efforts fit into the overall process. By the end of the day, however, an inexperienced collection of volunteers emerges somehow into a coherent group that whisks players and parents through the registration process with surprising efficiency. The enabling knowledge flows are principally experience-based, reflecting rich tacit knowledge held only in part by individuals. Through processes such as group interaction, observation and individual practice—along with trial and error—the knowing appears to emerge within each group of volunteers across a thousand regional soccer communities. Yet it reflects and effects—nation-wide and to various extents—the overarching philosophical principles of the focal organization as a whole.

In terms of knowledge flow processes, creation, sharing and application appear to predominate the dynamics of soccer-program operations (e.g., tasks noted above such as registration, forming teams, organizing coaches and referees). Creation takes place within each volunteer group—at the individual and group level alike—as inexperienced people learn how to perform unfamiliar tasks, and groups of people with negligible prior common experience learn how to work together as a group. As suggested above, trial and error accounts for a major portion of such knowledge flows. By learning through trial and error, individuals and groups can improve their performance gradually. Knowledge sharing plays a part also. The few people in each regional group with prior experience as volunteers in the organization generally set the agenda and organize the work tasks, sharing ideas for how each task may be accomplished in some orderly manner, but such volunteer groups are relatively small generally, and there appears always to be much more work required than resources available. Hence doing takes precedence over learning, and the amount of knowledge sharing within each community group (i.e., region) is relatively limited.

Some additional knowledge sharing takes place along hierarchical lines. Area volunteers, for instance, are generally quite experienced at all aspects of regional operations. Such volunteers are also generally quite willing to help regional volunteers to understand what needs to be accomplished. The same applies in terms of sectional volunteers assisting their area counterparts, and so forth up to the national headquarters, but regions are dispersed geographically, and the number of area volunteers is small. So is the volume of knowledge that flows in this manner. Another hierarchical vehicle for knowledge sharing is more formal in nature. Several training courses are offered at every level of the focal organization. However, few of the volunteers appear to take such courses. Hence the volume of knowledge that flows in this manner is small also. Although hierarchical knowledge flows may appear fluid and dynamic on paper, knowledge of soccer-program operations appears to be sticky and static in practice. Instead, slow but steady OJT via trial and error predominates, at the individual as well as the group level. In a departure from the application cases described above, here we omit graphical representations of these knowledge flows. Many archetypical and representative depictions of OJT knowledge flows included in the preceding chapters apply well here also.

Considerable individual knowledge is necessary for coaches and referees to perform their activities well. Here we discover a much more fluid collection of knowledge flows than those noted above pertaining to soccer-program operations. People who volunteer to perform in coach and referee roles tend to self-select to a great extent. For instance, many volunteer coaches and referees played youth soccer themselves, with a relatively small number having advanced to play at collegiate and even professional levels. Such experienced volunteers enter the season with an *a-priori* understanding of the game and how to coach players and/or officiate games. This represents a contrast with the comparatively inexperienced volunteers described above, who self-select for soccer-program operations. Even such comparatively inexperienced volunteers represent a further contrast with *the majority of people who do not volunteer at all.*

The knowledge flows associated with formal training of coaches and referees also appear to be more fluid and dynamic than those enabling soccer-program operations. Several levels (e.g., Beginner, Intermediate, Advanced) of coaching and refereeing courses are offered each season, and coaches as well as referees must be certified generally at the appropriate level before they can perform the corresponding duties. For instance, as one's children advance in age from one league to another (e.g., from leagues of 8/9 year olds to 10/11 year olds), the volunteer coaches must complete higher-level coaching courses (e.g., the Intermediate course). The same applies to advanced-level courses for older children (e.g., coaches of 14 – 18 year olds take the Advanced course). Alternatively, only the beginner-level courses are required to coach the younger children.

As a similar instance, the referees who officiate increasingly advanced games (e.g., played by 12/13 or 14 – 16 year olds) must take more-advanced refereeing courses than counterparts refereeing younger kids' (e.g., 6/7 or 8/9 year olds) games do. Mentoring plays a role here too. Many coaches with relatively more experience appear very willing to share tips with their less-experienced counterparts. Observation plays a role as well. Many teams share the same field on practice days, so coaches of different teams can observe how their counterparts work with the kids and conduct their drills. As above, we omit graphical representations of these knowledge flows. Many archetypical and representative depictions of formal-training and mentoring knowledge flows are included in the preceding chapters.

Perhaps the most noteworthy and challenging knowledge flows pertain to the organizational culture and philosophy. With only 50 paid employees to oversee a quarter million volunteers, clearly direct supervision would not represent an effective approach to acculturating organizational participants and instilling the organization's philosophy. Instead, the organization employs several other techniques in attempt to effect knowledge flows pertaining to culture and philosophy. For one, the concept *Kids' Zone* outlines the kinds of positive, supportive, good-sportsmanship behaviors expected of parents when they participate in games, practices and other official organizational soccer events. Every parent is asked to read and is required to sign a Kids' Zone Pledge, which outlines such expectations. Kids' Zone buttons and signs abound on people and fences, respectively, around soccer fields as well, but this approach appears to be limited. Many people can be observed signing pledges without reading them. Many parents wear buttons without being able to articulate what the Kids' Zone is. Many participants at soccer practices and games (i.e., within Kids' Zones) exhibit behaviors (e.g., criticizing referees, commenting negatively about coaches, encouraging unsportsmanlike play) that are inconsistent with the organizational philosophy. In this respect, knowledge flows associated with philosophical acculturation clump largely at the higher levels of the focal organization.

Alternatively, a number of people do appear to exhibit the kinds of behaviors encouraged formally by the focal organization. In great part, such people tend to be the same few, experienced volunteers described above who know how registration and other soccer-program operations should be conducted. They tend to be the more-experienced coaches and referees as well. They tend to volunteer to serve on boards of directors for their local community regions too. They tend to be a minority group. They definitely accomplish the majority of the work.

The formal training courses can account for some acculturation knowledge flows within this minority group. For instance, every training course—whether for coaching, refereeing, administration, or other volunteer activity—includes a section on the organization's philosophy. One can expect to take a test with questions pertaining to the five philosophical tenets in every course. Repetition of these philosophical tenets appears to have some effect—over considerable time—in terms of sharing the rich, tacit knowledge underlying the philosophy. The experienced volunteers appear to incorporate the philosophy into many decisions and actions pertaining to soccer practices, games and operations. When asked to explain "why" (e.g., why Johnny cannot play forward all of the time; why Suzie must sit out one quarter each game even though she is a better player than Amy is; why abusive parent spectators are asked by referees to leave games; why hyper-competitive coaches are not allowed to supervise youth players; and other similar questions), coaches, referees, board members and like people provide explanations often that reflect the focal organization's philosophy. By repeating the same explanations, again and again, to parent after parent, such coaches, referees, board members and like people appear—over considerable time—to influence the parents, spectators and others. In essence, these evangelical people are leading by example. They repeat the philosophical tenets to others and apply them to their own decisions and actions. Knowledge flows—albeit very slowly—tacitly via a blend of conversational repetition, mentoring, observation and more-subtle processes (e.g., evangelism) that defy explanation from the details available in this case.

Also as above, we omit graphical representations of these knowledge flows. Many archetypical and representative depictions of such knowledge flows are included in the preceding chapters. In many respects, we appear to be saturating our list of knowledge flow processes and corresponding vector diagrams. That is to say, the same set of processes and vectors appears to account well for a diversity of knowledge flows, across a variety of business, government and non-profit organizations. Little contribution is expected here from repeating the same diagrams again and again, and considerable confidence can be felt in our ability to explain a wide diversity of knowledge flow patterns.

Leadership and Management Implications

The environment of a non-profit organization shares both similarities and differences with that of business and government counterparts. Similarities include an organization of people that attempts to accomplish more than the disorganized collection of individuals could; a mission and set of workflow processes that define the organization's focus and activities; and a combination of formal and informal structures, communication channels and routines. Differences center on the organizations' profit motives and compensation schemes. Non-profit organizations generally require revenues to cover expenses and to function effectively, but they do not seek generally to return earnings for stakeholders. Government organizations (i.e., without profit motive) are more like non-profits than businesses in this regard. Many non-profit organizations compensate their employees at lower (e.g., below-market) wage rates—the extreme of this is depending upon (zero-wage) volunteers—than either business or government organizations do. Particularly in the kind of all-volunteer organization described in this case, participants who are responsible for accomplishing the organizational work are not interested in careers or even paid jobs with the organization. The kinds of processes that leaders and managers can employ successfully must vary accordingly; this is the case for non-profits in particular, where pecuniary incentives and extrinsic motivation are largely moot.

Nonetheless, knowledge enables action, and action drives performance. This applies to the non-profit organization as well as to other forms in the private and public sectors alike. People need to know what to do and how and why to do it well before they can accomplish effectively the organizational activities that are important. Hence knowledge needs to flow in non-profit organizations just as much as it does in their business and government counterparts. Many of the same kinds of knowledge flow processes described above pertain to non-profit organizations as well. Indeed, we find familiar processes such as OJT, formal training, mentoring and other archetypical patterns throughout the focal case.

We find also some less-familiar—or at least less-emphasized—knowledge flow processes in the focal organization. The role of conversational repetition, for instance, stands out. This process appears to be key in terms of acculturation, which involves very slow flows of rich and powerful tacit knowledge. Conversational repetition is likely to exist as well in the other kinds of organizations described above, but we do not find it emphasized to the same extent as it is in the focal organization. Leading by example and evangelism are similar. They clearly pertain to other kinds of organizations as well as to non-profits, but they are not emphasized as much as they are in the focal organization. For the business or government leader and manager, perhaps there is something important to be learned here from your non-profit counterparts.

We use this to induce our twenty-sixth leadership mandate from the practical application section of this book. Mandate 26. Leading by example and evangelism represent viable approaches to enhancing acculturation knowledge flows.

The point about saturation is noteworthy. A relatively small number of knowledge flow processes (e.g., OJT, formal training, mentoring, storytelling) appears to account for a relatively large variety of knowledge flows, across a diversity of different organizations. The number of combinations of such processes is practically uncountable, so the specific vectors and sequences that pertain to any particular organization are likely to be unique, but the underlying components used to form such combinations derive from a relatively small set. Hence once one understands this set of knowledge flow components, he or she can likely describe, visualize and analyze any knowledge flows—healthy or pathologic—in any organization. As noted in the beginning of the book, this represents an important factor in harnessing dynamic knowledge principles for competitive advantage in the technology-driven world.

We use this to induce our twenty-seventh leadership mandate from the practical application section of this book. Mandate 27. Once one understands a relatively small set of key knowledge flow processes, he or she can analyze any knowledge flows—healthy or pathologic—in any organization.

EXERCISES

1. Identify and describe three principles from earlier parts of the book that apply to this case. Can you induce additional principles from this application case that are not articulated in the earlier parts above?
2. Delineate vectors to describe knowledge flows corresponding to how the tacit knowledge associated with good sportsmanship flows to youth players as described in the case.
3. Comment briefly on other approaches the organization could take to address its knowledge flow problems. What relative advantages and disadvantages apply to your suggestions when compared with the approach described in the case?
4. Describe briefly how your learning from this case can be related to an organization with which you are familiar. Include a knowledge flow diagram such as the ones presented throughout this book.

LOCAL TENNIS CLUB

We draw from USTA (2004) and Nissen (2004c) for background of this case. We first summarize important events and issues for context. Discussion and analysis of key knowledge flows follow, with interpretation of leadership and management implications discussed subsequently. The section closes with exercises pertaining specifically to this application case.

Context

Founded in 1974, a small, private club provides tennis, swimming, fitness and other recreational facilities for use by its members. Like most private clubs, only members and their guests are allowed to use the facilities, and members pay both initiation fees and monthly dues to participate in the club. Unlike most private clubs, however, the focal organization is owned wholly by its 110 members, with each holding one share of voting stock. The club is notably non-profit. Its owner-members are interested in playing tennis, swimming, exercising and socializing through the club, not earning a profit. Yet as with the non-profit soccer organization described in the case above, the tennis club must earn revenues to cover expenses that are necessary to operate and provide services to its members.

The club has a board of directors, which meets monthly. The board consists of members elected for three-year terms. Board members serve on a volunteer basis. Their only compensation comes in the form of waived guest fees. All other members must pay nominal guest fees whenever non-members are brought into the club. Together board members meet to establish policy, oversee the club from a high level, and address novel or particularly challenging issues that arise from time to time. The board also hires a manager who is responsible for day-to-day operations of the club. The manager represents one of the few paid positions in the club. The manager, who is supported by a small cadre of part-time assistants, schedules tennis courts, organizes tournaments and social events, oversees club maintenance activities, and takes care of the modicum of paperwork associated with any non-profit organization. The other paid position is that of pro (i.e., Tennis Professional). The pro is paid a small stipend and allowed to use select courts for tennis instruction, from which he or she derives primary income. People of all ages come and pay for such instruction, and the pro also offers periodic clinics (e.g., for doubles partners to work together) on a fee basis. Unlike many tennis clubs, the focal organization has decided not to collect a portion of the pro's earnings in return for use of club facilities in instruction.

In contrast with the small group of people from above with official positions in the club, the majority of club participants are members, who have no official duties, and who use the club facilities for exercise and entertainment. A majority of club members use the tennis courts, but a sizeable fraction of members use only the swimming pool and fitness room. On any given hot afternoon or weekend, the pool may be filled with swimming kids, while the tennis courts are nearly empty. The converse may hold for any given cool day. At least one person is using the fitness room at nearly all times.

The tennis players have several avenues for arranging matches. The most common is person-to-person. Everyone in the club receives a list of members and telephone numbers, but tennis is a game that requires considerable time to develop skill, and players vary widely in their relative abilities. The club encourages members to have their skill levels rated (e.g., the United States Tennis Association has a standardized 7-point scale that is used commonly nation-wide). Unlike golf and like activities in which a person plays largely against him or herself, tennis is competitive, and matches between people with even marginally different skill levels can be very lopsided. Hence it is important for members to find others at roughly the same skill level. This takes time, as people watch one another play, ask about others who play at various levels, and play matches on a trial-and-error basis.

Tennis is a social game also to a large extent. People who are matched evenly in skill may be matched unevenly in disposition, and vice versa. Particularly with doubles (i.e., two people on each team) and mixed doubles (i.e., one man and one woman on each team), many tennis matches represent more of a social occasion than a competitive sporting event. In either case, once club members discover with whom they are matched evenly and enjoy playing, they call one another to set up playing dates, and many establish regular patterns of play (e.g., the Ladies' Tuesday/Thursday Morning Group, Men's Night).

Another avenue for arranging matches involves league play. Most tennis clubs organize teams by skill level to play against teams fielded by other local clubs. Each individual match (e.g., singles, doubles, mixed doubles) is played competitively against members of other clubs, but each club will field a team (e.g., two singles players, six doubles players) to compete against one another in a series of matches. Unlike the more-social approach above to arranging matches, members on a team have no input into whom they play against on other teams, and they have negligible input into whom they play with on their own team. Matches are also scheduled well in advance, on the home courts and away, so people on teams have little to say about when they play. Competitive matches are followed generally by social time, during which players from both teams interact over drinks and snacks. Signing up for and playing on a team represents a well-practiced approach to meeting other players at a member's skill level. Many person-to-person matches arranged during the off-seasons are between members who have met through team play, for instance.

The third avenue for arranging matches is through club tournaments and social events. Roughly every two months, the club will organize some kind of tennis event that is open to all of its members. Examples include the club singles and doubles tournaments—men and women compete in separate flights—mixed doubles and youth tournaments, and holiday occasions such as Valentine's Day, Independence Day, Thanksgiving Day and the like. The tournaments and social events provide another common approach to meeting other players at a member's skill level. Many person-to-person matches arranged during the off-seasons are between members who have met through such events, as another instance. A great many social activities that take place outside the club have their roots in people who have met through such events. People in the club share a number of common interests, and many establish friendships that carry through off the court as well as on it.

Knowledge Flow Analysis

Knowledge plays a central role in the tennis club. The most-obvious knowledge flows pertain to tennis playing. We note above how tennis requires considerable time to develop skill. Unlike many games that can be fun even for beginners and novices, tennis is not very enjoyable to most people until they develop a basic level of proficiency. Such basic level can take a year or more of lessons and/or routine practice to establish. Many intermediate and advanced players have devoted decades to developing and refining their games. Hence knowledge required for playing tennis—that is, knowing tennis—flows relatively slowly, on the order of years and decades. Like bicycle riding, such knowledge is largely tacit. Many books have been written that describe, in great detail, how to play tennis, but reading such books is insufficient for knowing tennis.

Tennis lessons represent a common learning approach taken by beginners (esp. youth players). Such lessons can be individual, group or class in nature, but generally a single individual such as the pro is providing instruction. Such instruction includes demonstrating techniques, observing and critiquing how students perform them, and offering guidelines for practice. Such instructional modes are limited in terms of the number of students who can be trained simultaneously. Indeed, most tennis instruction reflects more of a mentoring arrangement than formal training or classroom instruction.

Practice has a connotation of working on specific techniques to improve one's performance. Very few people practice tennis. The game requires considerable redundancy for one's muscle memory to develop (i.e., for knowing tennis). Many people describe such redundant activity as boring, and they prefer simply to play instead of practice. Practice can involve play as well, of course: the key is whether one is looking to learn from games that are played on the court or seeking instead simply to play the games. Hence the same activity—playing tennis—can take on different roles depending upon whether a person is focusing on the knowing activities of learning versus doing while playing games. Sometimes tennis coaches (e.g., from league play) and professionals (e.g., from lessons) will observe and comment on one's playing during matches. Some people find such critiques beneficial, and some find it annoying. Again, this appears to depend upon one's knowing focus (i.e., on learning vs. doing).

Of course playing contributes also to developing tennis skill. This is essentially OJT. A learning component is involved with every game played, but as with OJT in other knowledge domains, the contribution of OJT to learning is relatively small with respect to doing. Hence people who play but do not take lessons or practice tend to improve comparatively slowly. A great many such people are able to progress only so far before reaching a skill plateau. Such plateaus are similar in many respects to the kinds of competency traps discussed above in terms of organizational routines. People become somewhat proficient at a particular style of play, which is effective in common situations (e.g., against people at the same skill level), but such style of play is often ineffective against better players, who to continue the metaphor, have reached a higher plateau.

In addition to developing one's tennis-playing ability—whether in individual, dyadic or team matches—another knowledge flow is very important in the tennis club: socializing. We note above how enjoyment and social interaction represent important activities that members seek from their affiliation with the club. This local tennis club is not a professional tennis academy with a mission of developing professional players. Nor is it a collegiate or professional sports organization that exists exclusively for high-level competition. Rather, tennis represents both a physical and social activity that people enjoy. One need not be a particularly skilled tennis player in order to derive enjoyment through socialization in a club. Indeed, players at both extremes in terms of playing ability (i.e., beginning and advanced) are often less skilled socially than are club members in the middle of the distribution.

Socializing is in great part about finding people with common interests. Tennis represents clearly one interest that most club members share, but conversations about tennis do not seem to be self-sustaining. Many conversations begin with comments pertaining to a recent tennis match, but they tend to drift quickly to other sports, activities, people and events. Tennis is the *raison d'être* for a club such as our focal organization, but it is not the only reason the club exists. From an individual perspective, socializing is a process with which every reader is likely to be intimately familiar, but from an organization perspective, what models appear to apply?

Perhaps the community of practice can describe well the knowledge flows associated with socializing. People who engage in a common activity are able to exchange stories and ideas pertaining to such activity. Through such process, people become acquainted with one another, establish trust, and develop personal relationships that transcend activities of their "home" organizations (e.g., employers). Socializing in the kinds of guilds and like trans-organizational groups discussed above in connection with the film-production case offers similar insights. We examine above tacit knowledge flows associated with socializing and do not repeat such examination here, however.

Leadership and Management Implications

The local tennis club is owned wholly by its members. This makes it somewhat unique with respect to the other organizations examined above. The organization exists for the benefit of its members, who are its owners also. A board of directors, club manager and pro are elected, hired and commissioned, respectively, to oversee and effect the organizational activities required for the club to operate effectively, but the majority part of the club's activities involve members playing tennis and socializing with one another. In this sense, the workflows correspond to playing tennis and interacting socially. It does not matter that members derive enjoyment from such "work." Indeed, this represents a valuable lesson for leaders and managers: people will self-organize when they share activities in common and enjoy what they do.

We use this to induce our twenty-eighth leadership mandate from the practical application section of this book. Mandate 28. The key to self-organization is having people enjoy what they do together.

An important activity of the tennis club involves arranging matches between members. People are able to accomplish this for themselves once they know one another, but discovering which players exhibit various skill levels and social dispositions takes considerable time. The club facilitates such discovery by publishing a list of members' telephone numbers. It also includes ratings for various players to signal approximate skills levels. The club facilitates this discovery further by organizing league matches and a combination of club competitions and tennis socials. In any organization, different people will exhibit a variety of skill levels and areas of interest. Rating employees' skill levels and publishing such ratings may represent an approach with potential beyond the tennis club. In any organization also, different people will exhibit variety in terms of interpersonal compatibility. The ability of different people to work together on teams is important in business, government and non-profit organizations alike. The tennis club has established some organizational routines that facilitate self-organization based on compatibility as well as skill. Business and government alike may have something to learn here too.

We use this to induce our twenty-ninth leadership mandate from the practical application section of this book. Mandate 29. The ability of different people to work together on teams is just as important as the individual skills and experiences they bring individually.

In developing skill levels, we learn from the case how mentoring, OJT and practice all contribute toward tennis knowledge flows. We have discussed mentoring and OJT repeatedly through the cases above. Alternatively, through our analysis and discussion of the business and government sectors, the activity practice is unusual in the context of workflows and knowledge flows. Clearly tennis is a game, whereas new-product development, technology transfer, film production, warfare, public service, and like activities are serious endeavors. Nonetheless, tennis involves considerable skill development, and practice represents a disciplined approach to such development.

Within the business and government sectors, for instance, what would be the organizational equivalent (e.g., in the office) of practice? For one, simulation provides a venue for people to practice workflow activities virtually. Through repeated and varied, simulated work sessions, a person, team or organization can improve its skills. Pilots practice their flying skills regularly using flight simulators. Soccer and other sports teams practice their playing skills regularly using simulated game situations. Military units practice their warfare skills routinely through simulated battles. There may be a lesson here for organizations involved with new-product development, technology transfer and the like. Notice by simulation we include but do not limit our discussion to computer-based approaches.

EXERCISES

5. Identify and describe three principles from earlier parts of the book that apply to this case. Can you induce additional principles from this application case that are not articulated in the earlier parts above?
6. Delineate vectors to describe knowledge flows corresponding to how the tacit knowledge associated with socializing flows as described in the case.
7. Comment briefly on other approaches the organization could take to address its knowledge flow problems. What relative advantages and disadvantages apply to your suggestions when compared with the approach described in the case?
8. Describe briefly how your learning from this case can be related to an organization with which you are familiar. Include a knowledge flow diagram such as the ones presented throughout this book.

NONDENOMINATIONAL COMMUNITY CHURCH

We draw from Grace (2004) and Nissen (2004d) for background of this case. We first summarize important events and issues for context. Discussion and analysis of key knowledge flows follow, with interpretation of leadership and management implications discussed subsequently. The section closes with exercises pertaining specifically to this application case.

Context

Founded in 1956, a small community church provides worship, youth, mission and other faith-based services to people in a semi-rural, semi-suburban area. It is a non-profit, religious organization. This local church has a leader, a board of directors, officers who serve in various capacities (e.g., youth ministry, teaching, missionary), and a congregation of members and non-members. The church is nondenominational. Although it is interconnected richly with other similar churches worldwide, it remains independent. This represents something of a contrast with many local churches that represent "branch offices" of major national or international denominations. As a relatively independent organization, this church sets its own operating and governance guidelines, but as a richly interconnected organization, it conforms with others to a common set of theological principles and reference materials. The church includes *growth* among its mission elements, but in further contrast with many major denominational counterparts, it does not seek to become a large church. Indeed, as membership grows to 250 or so, the church guidelines suggest it will split off to form a "daughter church" (Grace, 2004) somewhere nearby, the latter of which will have its own, separate leader, board, officers and congregation. The church pastor prefers to term the church's primary mission element *health* (Pastor Bill, 2004).

From a congregational perspective, the church provides faith-based services. For instance, many adults and children participate in weekly educational programs on a weekend morning in addition to a worship service later the same morning. Times before, between and after these official events are designated for social conversation. As another instance, a youth group meets later in the evenings, and different groups of people meet also on a weekly basis outside of the weekend days. Other services such as counseling and support are provided by the organization as well, as are various larger scale social events such as bar-be-ques, trips and like occasions for extended interaction between members. From an organizational perspective, the church provides faith-based services. For instance, it seeks to help people develop spiritually and to provide guidance for living their daily lives. As another instance, it seeks to increase church membership selectively, accepting as members only people with a prescribed set of beliefs. Other activities include staffing and organizing the services above, various administrative tasks and other endeavors required to pursue the church mission.

Knowledge Flow Analysis

Knowledge is important in this church. As a religious organization, faith is stressed, and beliefs are made explicit. Reading and discussing common passages from reference materials represents a central knowledge flow activity. Much of the knowledge associated with the church's belief system has been articulated and collected through a canon of historical documents, but such documents are subject to a variety of interpretations, and applying such knowledge through action requires tacit internalization of knowledge principles. Notice this represents the reverse movement of knowledge formalization. Through formalization, tacit knowledge is made explicit. Through internalization of principles, explicit knowledge is made tacit.

An enduring series of separate and combined conversations serve to help people exchange ideas about what the various principles mean. Conversation represents a central knowledge flow process in this respect. Also, through the conduct of various faith-based services such as those noted above, the church leader provides regular guidance to facilitate interpretation of written principles. Such plenary services tend to be one-on-many and resemble the university lecture in many ways (e.g., including assignments from a common "textbook"). Independent reading and contemplation is noted also as a process for learning and interpretation. People are encouraged to read regularly passages from the reference materials. Formal "training" classes are offered as well to help people to learn about and to interpret the principles. Such classes are organized into smaller groups than those of the plenary sessions noted above. Continuing with the university metaphor, such one-on-not-so-many classes resemble lab sessions and are led often by the equivalents of teaching assistants.

Applying the knowledge acquired and interpreted as above requires also operationalization of principles. Instantiating the "knowing-doing gap" (i.e., a 'knowledge-knowing gap' or a knowledge 'potential-action gap') from above, simply knowing about the various principles is insufficient for knowing the principles through action. Such operationalization is accomplished through imitation of example in many respects. The reference materials are replete with examples of people who have performed in manners consistent with the principles. They are replete also with heuristic rules for performing as such, but many of the examples and rules are dated, and numerous people experience difficulty when trying to apply the principles to contemporary decisions and events in their lives.

This is addressed in part through the plenary and small-group conversations and interpretation activities described above, and it is addressed in part also through individual reading and contemplation, but a major share of the learning that enables principled application through the workflows of life entail knowledge flows of everyday experience. This is tantamount to OJT. Instead of learning by doing applied to some prescribed set of organizational work activities, however, the OJT in this sense consists of learning by doing applied to the everyday lives of church members. Considerable trial and error is involved, and discussing the various trials and errors with others represents another, conversation-based knowledge flow process.

Leadership and Management Implications

The local church shares aspects in common with other organizations described in application cases above. For instance: knowledge flows are important; the organization has a structure, leader, governing body, and set of members; the organization has a mission and executes processes to pursue organizational objectives. Further, as a non-profit organization, the church shares much in common with the two other application cases in this chapter. For instance: it relies heavily upon volunteers; it does not pursue profit and like pecuniary objectives; it exists in great part to provide services to its members. The local church is also quite small compared to several of the other application cases above. It is somewhat larger than the independent film-production company and the private tennis club, but it is much, much smaller than any of the business or government organizations examined in this book.

The church provides a set of services based upon faith. This is distinct in many respects from the other organizations, but it resembles in part the soccer organization and tennis club, which provide services based upon athletic activities, philosophy and social opportunities. Probably the most-defining difference of the church relative to the other organizations examined in this book condenses to a focus on members' beliefs. Leaders and managers of nearly every organization are interested clearly in members' beliefs to some extent. In business enterprises, for instance, employees' beliefs in the mission, organization and culture represent important concerns of leaders and managers, but the importance of such beliefs tends to pale in comparison with the performance of useful workflows. The same can be said for government agencies, as another instance.

Even more so in the soccer organization, as a third instance, philosophy plays a central role. Leaders and managers are concerned about acculturating participants, and this has many parallels with religious beliefs associated with the church. Even in the soccer organization, nonetheless, the purpose of shaping participants' beliefs is to enhance the developmental experience of its youth players. Likewise in the church, although beliefs themselves represent a central concern of its leaders and managers, the purpose of shaping participants' beliefs is to enhance their ordinary, daily lives. Leaders and managers with concerns about or problems with employees' beliefs can learn from the knowledge flow processes and priorities of this church.

The local church has the benefit of an explicit set of principles that underlie its system of beliefs. Many business, government and non-profit organizations have mission statements, codes of conduct, standard operating procedures, bylaws and like attempts to articulate their culture, but they seem to fall far short of those used by the local church. The church also has its workflow processes devoted to helping members learn about, interpret and apply the key principles of its belief system. Indeed, this represents a principal mission of the church organization. In other organizations, if any time and energy are invested in like learning and interpretation, it is comparatively minor in magnitude, emphasis and importance when compared with the focus on application. To the extent that leaders and managers in other types of organizations seek to address and shape the beliefs of its employees, customers, members or other stakeholders, much may be learned from the local church in terms of knowledge flows.

Of course, the local church does not have a product or service that it sells in the marketplace. As with the soccer organization and tennis club, church expenses are covered by fees collected from members, but members have an abundance of different churches from which to choose. So in a financial sense, the local church faces competition for "customers" (e.g., congregational members) in much the same way that other non-profit organizations do. In the process of shaping members' beliefs, the local church organization examined in this case provides a service to members that encourages them to belong to the organization and to contribute toward its goals through donation of time, talent and money. Additionally, this is accomplished without employment contracts, without membership fees, indeed without anything other than member volition and generosity. Again, in terms of shaping knowledge flows, leaders and managers in many different kinds of organizations have something to learn from the local church.

We use this to induce our thirtieth *leadership mandate* from the practical application section of this book. Mandate 30. Leaders who are concerned about acculturation knowledge flows must address participants' beliefs.

EXERCISES

9. Identify and describe three principles from earlier parts of the book that apply to this case. Can you induce additional principles from this application case that are not articulated in the earlier parts above?
10. Delineate vectors to describe knowledge flows corresponding to how the explicit knowledge associated with religious principles is internalized and interpreted by individuals as described in the case.
11. Comment briefly on other approaches the organization could take to address its knowledge flow problems. What relative advantages and disadvantages apply to your suggestions when compared with the approach described in the case?
12. Describe briefly how your learning from this case can be related to an organization with which you are familiar. Include a knowledge flow diagram such as the ones presented throughout this book.

REFERENCES

AYSO. (2004). *American youth soccer organization website*. Retrieved from http://www.soccer.org

Grace. (2004). *Grace community church*. Retrieved from http://www.redshift.com/~becbobtr/pgcc.html

USTA. (2004). *United States tennis association website*. Retrieved from http://www.usta.org

Chapter 10
Forward!

ABSTRACT

This chapter includes guidance for learning from Sections 1 and 2 of the book, for applying such learning to the emerging knowledge phenomena discussed in Section 3, and for continuing to develop new knowledge about how the power of dynamic knowledge principles can be harnessed for competitive advantage in the technology-driven world. The authors summarize the principles developed in Section 1 of the book. As noted above, this supports principles-based learning, reasoning, and application. They next summarize the leadership mandates induced in Section 2 of the book. As noted above, this supports case-based learning, reasoning, and application. As an editorial note, this tenth chapter could be placed quite logically at the very end of the book (e.g., Chapter 15) instead of placing it here to close Section 2. However, the authors prefer this placement closer to the principles and mandates articulated in Sections 1 and 2. Nonetheless, the authors close Section 3, at the end of Chapter 15, with an agenda for future research.

SUMMARY OF KNOWLEDGE FLOW PRINCIPLES

Recall from above the 30 knowledge flow principles developed in the first part of the book. We list these principles below for reference and summarize briefly the key points pertaining to each. This section can serve as a primer for how the power of dynamic knowledge principles can be harnessed for competitive advantage in the technology-driven world (e.g., for those people who prefer summaries to details). It can serve also as a pocket summary for the principled organizational knower and learner (e.g., for those people who prefer to print and post summaries).

1. In Chapter 1 we note first, distinguishing knowledge from information is important. One effective operationalization is, knowledge enables direct action (e.g., correct decisions, appropriate behaviors, useful work), whereas information provides meaning and context for such action (e.g., decision criteria, behavior norms, work specifications). As a Gedanken experiment, consider two people tasked to perform a knowledge-intensive activity. These could be captains on the bridge of a ship, surgeons at the operating table, managers at the negotiating table, professors in a classroom, attorneys in a courtroom, or many like situations requiring knowledge.

DOI: 10.4018/978-1-4666-4727-5.ch010

Provide these two people with exactly the same information (e.g., books to read, charts and reports to reference, instruments to monitor, direct views and sounds, advisors to consult, others), but say that one person has twenty years' experience, whereas the other has much less experience (or possibly none). Most informed leaders, managers and scholars would expect differential performance from these two people. Such differential performance can be attributed generally to differences in knowledge. Hence shuttling information around via computers, networks, reports and communications does not address the flow of knowledge, at least not directly or on the same time scale.

2. We note second, knowledge clumps in particular people, organizations, regions and times of application. Knowledge power through competitive advantage requires knowledge to flow, but tacit knowledge in particular is sticky, difficult to imitate, and slow to move. This same property, which enables knowledge-based competitive advantage to be sustainable, inhibits simultaneously sharing within the organization. Hence knowledge clumps need to be identified, and knowledge flows need to be enabled through the organization.
3. Third, explicit knowledge that can be articulated is distinct in many ways from the kind of tacit knowledge that accumulates, often slowly, through experience. Neither is individual expertise quite the same as knowledge shared across members of a group, team or other organization. Knowledge can also be quite situated, ephemeral and local, meaning a person on the "front lines" cannot always communicate the richness of what he or she knows to someone at headquarters. Yet people at headquarters tend to demand abundant information flows to support decision-making that is made better on location often. Of course, the person on the scene with detailed and local knowledge lacks the high-level integrative understanding of leaders and managers at headquarters often, and the need for functional specialists to share specific knowledge for complex problem solving is known well, but central to the point of knowledge power is, tacit knowledge supports greater appropriability than explicit knowledge does. Hence organizational leaders and managers may benefit from an emphasis on tacit knowledge flows.
4. Further, not all knowledge, not even tacit knowledge, is of equal value, and not all knowledge needs to be shared to effect performance. Indeed, there is a classic tension between exploration and exploitation. Because resources such as time, energy and attention are limited, investing in exploration of new knowledge and opportunities limits necessarily the resources available to exploit the knowledge and opportunities that exist, and vice versa. Further, to the extent that an organization focuses solely on exploitation, for instance, it can develop quickly competency traps and suffer from debilitations associated with single-loop learning; that is, an organization can learn to do the wrong thing very well and not realize that its competency is suited well to the environment no longer. Likewise, to the extent that an organization focuses solely on exploration, as a contrasting instance, it can see quickly its demise, as competitors capitalize upon current opportunities and take advantage of the organization's time away from task; that is, the organization can prepare itself well for a future environment but fail to survive until such future arrives. Similar tensions arise between learning and doing, sharing and hoarding knowledge, acquiring general versus specialized expertise, and like knowledge-oriented tradeoffs. Hence understanding the kinds of knowledge that are important in an organization's particular

environment is essential for promoting the most important knowledge flows.

5. Finally, it is known well that organizational personnel, work processes, structures and technologies are interconnected tightly and interact closely. When seeking to redesign and change organizations to identify knowledge clumps and to enhance knowledge flows, it is important to focus simultaneously upon all of these interconnected and interacting elements, together. Most people can identify quickly a technological "innovation" that failed to produce favorable results when implemented in an organization, for instance. Bringing in people or teams with different backgrounds in terms of education, training, skills and experience represents a similar instance (e.g., conjuring up memories of failed implementation), as does changing work processes or organizational reporting relationships and responsibilities without addressing personnel and technologies. Hence the elements people, processes, organizations and technologies operate as a cohesive system and should be addressed as an integrated design problem.
6. In Chapter 2 we note first, distinguishing knowledge from information and data is important. One effective operationalization is, knowledge enables direct action (e.g., correct decisions, appropriate behaviors, useful work). Alternatively, information provides meaning and context for such action (e.g., decision criteria, behavior norms, work specifications). Data reduce uncertainty or equivocality (e.g., supplying parameters to an equation, providing numbers for a formula, specifying states in a relationship). We identify also a fourth level for the knowledge hierarchy above: signals. One can say with confidence, "only signals flow across time and space," not knowledge, information, or even data. Signals (e.g., light reflecting from objects in the world or computer-generated images; sound waves propagating through a room; electrical currents alternating in discrete and analog patterns) are perceived by people and machines. Where they are interpretable, they can provide the basis for data; where uninterpretable, they constitute noise. Where in turn data are provided in context, they can inform. Where information enables direct action, knowledge exists. Hence understanding whether flows of data, information or knowledge are required in a particular situation depends upon what needs to be accomplished (e.g., resolving uncertainty, deriving meaning, enabling action, respectively).
7. We note second, data, information and knowledge are interrelated dynamically, yet distinct from one another, as mental and organizational processes. A number of Gedanken experiments and practical examples can be used to distinguish between the interrelated concepts, but all three involve mental and organizational (not physical) processes. Whether interpreting data from signals, deriving information from data, or learning knowledge from information, such processes take place in the minds of people and routines of organizations, not in computers, networks and databases. Hence people play the critical role in flows of data, information and knowledge.
8. Third, knowledge flows require flows of information, data and signals. Physically only signals flow. Data, information and knowledge flow via socio-cognitive processes, but such socio-cognitive processes of different people require communication. For knowledge to flow from a producer or sender, information is required to produce data, which are required to encode signals. In reverse sequence, for knowledge to flow to a consumer or receiver, signals must be interpreted into data, which must be placed into meaningful context to inform. Every

conversion (e.g., interpreting data from signals; ascribing meaningful information from data; learning knowledge from information) involves some kind of knowledge (e.g., language, context, physiology). Hence every flow (i.e., data, information and knowledge) from signal interpretation through knowledge creation, and back, requires some kind of knowledge.

9. Further, explicitness characterizes an important dimension of knowledge uniqueness. In particular, tacit knowledge can be distinguished along such dimension from its explicit counterpart. One's ability to articulate his or her knowledge provides an operationalization for explicitness: explicit knowledge has been articulated; tacit knowledge has not. Further, some kinds of tacit knowledge can be articulated into explicit form more easily than others can. Some kinds cannot be articulated at all. Most knowledge made explicit loses power in at least two important ways: 1) knowledge made explicit fails often to enable the same levels of performance corresponding to actions enabled by the tacit knowledge from which it is formalized; and 2) explicit knowledge shares many properties with information, which is more difficult to appropriate than tacit knowledge is. Hence moving knowledge through tacit versus explicit flows represents a leadership or management decision in many cases, a decision which has implications in terms of power.

10. Finally, IT support is limited principally to explicit knowledge flows—and information/data—but enables large amounts of such knowledge to be organized, aggregated, and disseminated broadly and quickly. Where knowledge is explicit—or can be formalized into explicit form—IT offers great power to enhance the corresponding flows, but where important knowledge is tacit—and cannot be formalized readily into explicit form—IT offers less potential to affect knowledge flows. Hence the nature of knowledge represents a critical factor for determining where IT can be expected to enhance knowledge flows.

11. In Chapter 3 we note first, knowledge at rest tends to stay at rest. If a leader or manager seeks to have knowledge flow, then something must be done to induce it to flow (e.g., formal training, OJT). Further, knowledge in motion tends to stay in motion in some cases (e.g., via employee defections). If a leader or manager seeks to cease or restrict knowledge flows in such cases, then something must be done to stem the flows. In contrast, if the leader or manager is content with such flows, then no action is required. In other cases, however, knowledge in motion (e.g., student learning through classroom interaction) appears to require additional action just to keep it in motion. If a leader or manager seeks to cease or restrict knowledge flows in such cases, then no action is required to stem its flow. In contrast, if the leader or manager wants such flows to propagate further, then something must be done to continue the flows. The organizational process represents the phenomenological analog to physical force in overcoming knowledge inertia. Hence knowledge flow processes represent direct focuses of leadership and management action.

12. We note second, workflows and knowledge flows interact, and various processes contribute in different magnitudes toward doing versus learning. If a leader or manager is interested in promoting knowledge flows in the organization, then it will be important for him or her to understand how the specific knowledge flows of concern interrelate with workflows of value to the organization. In some cases, workflows and knowledge flows are independent, so one can be changed without affecting the other. In most cases, however, workflows and knowledge flows

are interrelated tightly, so altering one will affect the other directly. Hence changes to workflows demand changes to knowledge flows, and vice versa.

13. Third, the activities associated with organizational processes are responsible for the phenomenon of knowledge flows. Knowledge flow processes represent the organizational analogs to physical forces. The different kinds of knowledge represent the organizational analogs to physical masses. Together the two determine the direction, rate and extent of knowledge flows. If a leader or manager is interested in inducing, enhancing, restricting or ceasing knowledge flows, then he or she should examine the associated organizational processes. Because processes are composed of activities, which have long been the focus of leadership and management attention, such a process focus should be quite natural. Also, there appears to be considerable opportunity for such a process focus to be supported by the same kinds of tools and techniques for the planning, organizing, monitoring and control of work (e.g., Gantt Charts, PERT networks, work/knowledge specifications). Indeed, in every case of knowledge-based action, knowledge flows lie on the critical paths of workflows and the associated organizational performance. Hence knowledge flows should be planned and managed like workflows are.
14. Further, knowledge flows and workflows vary in terms of timing. Some workflows require quick, precise and thorough activities that can be performed only by knowledgeable people. In such cases the enabling knowledge flows are prerequisite to their corresponding workflows. Other workflows afford greater tolerances in terms of timing and performance, which can be performed by people who learn over time and by trial and error. In such cases the enabling knowledge flows can be concurrent with (or even follow) their corresponding workflows. Indeed, in many cases such as OJT, the learning associated with knowledge flows takes place through the doing associated with workflows. Before deciding upon and implementing a particular approach to inducing, enhancing, restricting or ceasing knowledge flows, the leader or manager needs to consider how the target flows interact temporally with corresponding workflows of importance. Hence most knowledge flows must complete their course before critical and dependent workflows can begin.
15. Finally, explicit knowledge flows very quickly and broadly, but its relative power is diluted, whereas tacit knowledge flows comparatively slowly and narrowly, but at high power. In terms of decision-making heuristics, where knowledge inertia is relatively small (e.g., knowledge to be learned is not particularly difficult or complex), and it is important to distribute such knowledge broadly and quickly (e.g., across all parts of a global organization), it makes sense to focus on explicit knowledge flow processes for sharing. In contrast, where knowledge inertia is comparatively large (e.g., knowledge to be learned is quite difficult and complex), and it is important to sustain high knowledge power over time (e.g., for knowledge-based competitive advantage), it makes more sense to focus on tacit knowledge flow processes instead. Hence the dynamic nature of knowledge has great implication in terms of selecting the most appropriate organizational processes to effect knowledge flows.
16. In Chapter 4 we note first, IT plays an important role in supporting knowledge flows. In many cases IT is even necessary for knowledge to flow, but there is more to flows of knowledge than processing and flowing information and data, which is the principal domain of IT. Hence leaders and

managers need to employ non-technological interventions to enhance knowledge flows.

17. We note second, problems abound in terms of KM programs that rely heavily upon IT. Many leaders and managers expect naïvely that IT will improve knowledge flows. Looking at the "I" in IT, however, and understanding the distinctions and relationships between knowledge and information, it should be apparent why such expectations can be considered naïve. In particular, people—not information technology—are central to tacit knowledge flows. Hence one cannot manage tacit knowledge without managing people.
18. Third, the life cycle involves different kinds of knowledge activities, grouped broadly into classes to represent localized and expanded views of KM. We note above how IT supports activities in these two classes differently. For the localized activities, IT plays a supportive role and does so quite well. For the expanded activities, however, a performative role is called for, but few extant IT applications are capable of—or used for—playing such role. Hence most IT plays a supportive role in the organization, whereas people play most of the performative roles.
19. Further, expert systems, software agents, and like "intelligent" applications address knowledge directly, in addition to information and data. They also enable direct action, and hence can play some of the performative roles called for above. Specifically, once developed, an expert system can apply knowledge directly to perform knowledge work. Expert systems can also be distributed broadly through the organization and used in parallel, even by novices who can sometimes raise their performance to expert levels. Hence "intelligent" applications can play a performative role in the organization.
20. Finally, simulation technology can be used to enhance knowledge flows in addition to workflows. By using simulation models to learn about some systems or processes of interest in the real world, one can create new knowledge relatively quickly and safely. Knowledge associated with a simulation model can be shared and applied also, corresponding with multiple phases of the knowledge life cycle. Hence simulation represents a different class of IT, one that facilitates learning as well as doing through virtual practice.
21. In Chapter 5 we note first, knowing reflects knowledge in action. It is knowledge manifested through practice and involves doing (i.e., knowledge-based work). In most circumstances it is insufficient to simply know something. Whether to convince someone else that you know, to accomplish some objective associated with knowledge, or to otherwise make knowledge useful, some kind of action is required. Hence knowledge must be put to use through action in order to be useful.
22. We note second, learning reflects knowledge in motion. It represents the action associated with acquiring "new" knowledge (e.g., through scientific discovery or knowledge moving from one coordinate to another). Learning requires knowledge and is action oriented, so it constitutes a form of knowing, but the focus on acquiring knowledge distinguishes learning quite generally from other knowing activities (esp. doing). Hence learning both uses and increases knowledge.
23. Third, knowing and learning both take place at multiple levels of analysis. Individuals, groups, organizations, groups of organizations and so forth can know and learn, but whereas individuals can know and learn without being affiliated with groups or organizations, groups and organizations require individuals for knowing as well as for learning. Individuals are indispensable to groups and organizations, but there is more to groups and organizations than the collection

of associated individuals. The phrase, "the whole is greater than the sum of its parts," applies well here. Indeed, performance effects of knowledge flows can be amplified as they reach broadly through the organization. Hence the impact of leadership and management increases in direct proportion to the reach of knowledge flows through an organization.

24. Further, learning and doing are interrelated. Doing requires knowledge, which must be learned. Learning involves doing focused on acquiring new knowledge. Doing can also involve learning. Doing contributes to learning, and learning contributes to doing. Further, learning and doing involve tension and require decisions. Learning is associated with exploration and focuses on knowledge flows. Doing is associated with exploitation and focuses on knowledge stocks. Both serve important purposes, but constrained time and energy impose some degree of tradeoff between them. To the extent that an individual, group or organization focuses on one, then to some extent the other must suffer. Hence promoting doing can limit learning, and vice versa.
25. Finally, doing and learning involve action and potential. Doing reflects knowledge put to use through action, which requires knowledge to be acquired before such use. Learning reflects knowledge acquisition, which increases the potential range of actions enabled. Learning from experience (i.e., from action) represents a primary contributor to new knowledge and stems directly from doing, but doing is inhibited by what has been learned, and learning is inhibited by what experiences have been known. Hence an organization's knowledge inventory both enables and inhibits what actions it can take.
26. In Chapter 6 we note first, KM projects involve change. There is much to learn from the literature on change management in this regard. For instance, the leader and manager can assess an organization's preconditions for success as well as preconditions for failure. KM-specific factors such as knowledge representation, attention to tacit knowledge, and focus on organizational memory are important too and can be evaluated and addressed by the leader and manager. We find also how perceptual measures such as pessimism, affective commitment and normative commitment are important in KM projects as well. Hence the leader and manager have much to learn from change-management.
27. We note second, knowledge inventory can be used to assess an organization's readiness to perform its work processes effectively. The knowledge audit represents an approach to discovering and documenting sources, uses and sinks of knowledge in an organization. Generally executed via some kind of survey instrument, the knowledge audit is performed often by consultants and like professionals from outside the organization, but there is little reason why an organization should not be able to audit itself. In addition to articulating explicitly certain aspects of knowledge inventories and flows, conducting a knowledge audit can produce positive effects simply by inducing people within the organization to think about what knowledge is important, how it is used, and how it flows. Alternatively, knowledge audits consume precious time and energy. Perhaps the greatest potential in terms of a knowledge audit lies in the prospect of measuring knowledge inventory. This construct offers potential to assess an organization's readiness to perform its work processes effectively. Hence the leader and manager need to measure the knowledge inventory for every organization.
28. Third, knowledge power can be estimated and measured. The 5D model introduced above, combined with Knowledge Flow Theory, provides an approach to measuring,

analyzing and visualizing the dynamics of knowledge flows through an organization. With empirical analysis, one can leverage characteristics of organizational knowledge flows to predict the corresponding knowledge power effected via action. Although the 5D model and knowledge power analysis remain comparatively novel in terms of development and application, the technique reflects metaphorically the concept candle lighting: when in an environment without light, it is often better to light a candle than to curse the darkness (ancient Chinese proverb). Hence knowledge power measurement provides an approach to assessing the relative efficacy of knowledge flowing through various organizational processes.

29. Further, culture, trust and incentives affect organizational learning—and hence performance—as much as process, technology and training do. Learning rates can be measured and projected, and through the well-accepted and –established learning curve, the knowledge flow component of experiential knowing (i.e., learning) can be measured and related mathematically with the workflow component (i.e., doing). Several general rules of thumb provide guidance for application of learning curves. These include the well-studied roles of automation, calendar time, production rate, technology introduction and workforce capability, in addition to less-understood factors such as organizational culture, trust and incentives. Nonetheless, such latter factors can affect organizational learning and hence performance as much as the former ones do. Every organizational process involving repetition should experience performance improvement through learning at multiple levels of reach (e.g., individual, group, organization). Where such improvement may not obtain, this signals a problem with knowledge clumping and calls attention to the associated knowledge flows. Hence every organizational process should improve its performance over time, and every leader and manager should measure the dynamic performance of repetitive processes.

30. Finally, computational modeling can be used to learn about organizational knowing and learning. Computational models are used extensively in the physical sciences for the design of artifacts, and their use in the social sciences is increasing. Through advanced computational models that describe dynamic behaviors of knowledge flows in the organization, one can represent, simulate and analyze—virtually—many different organization designs to assess the relative strengths and weaknesses of alternate approaches to enhancing knowledge flows. By analyzing knowledge flows in different organization designs (e.g., alternate structures, workflows, personnel characteristics, technologies), one can gain insight into how different dynamic knowledge patterns affect organizational performance. One can gain insight also into how the knowing and learning that take place within an organization react to different leadership and management interventions (e.g., OJT, training, mentoring, simulation). This represents a risk-mitigation strategy for addressing the change aspect of KM projects: before deciding upon a specific KM approach and implementing a particular set of organizational, work, personnel and/or technological changes, one can assess computationally the relatively efficacy and efficiency of each alternative. Hence computational models of knowledge flows provide an approach to mitigating the risk inherent in KM programs.

HARNESSING KNOWLEDGE DYNAMICS IN YOUR ORGANIZATION

Not all of the knowledge flow principles from above will apply to or be compelling in every organization. Hence it is important for the leader and manager to understand the principles as a set and to assess the applicability of each to his or her organization. In this respect, the principles can be employed to guide a knowledge audit. For instance, using each of the 30 principles, one can assess the extent to which it applies, is relevant, and/or elucidates a problem area. Here we use the principles from above to organize suggestions for how leaders and managers may seek to accomplish such a principled audit. Notice in each case how this signals a need for leaders and managers to know and learn more about how their organizations know and learn.

1. Knowledge is distinct from information in enabling competitive advantage. Leaders and managers can look to understand better the basis of their organization's competition. Nearly every activity of modern work requires knowledge. Hence nearly every organization has potential for knowledge-based competition. An organization's strategic focus may merit review and possibly change to emphasize competitive advantage based on knowing and learning.
2. Knowledge is distributed unevenly and hence must flow for organizational performance. Leaders and managers can look to understand better where knowledge clumps in their organizations. Knowledge clumps are present in nearly every organization. The first problem is identifying such clumps. The second problem is dissolving them. The kinds of knowledge flow analysis and visualization techniques illustrated above can provide insight into addressing both problems.
3. Tacit knowledge supports greater appropriability for competitive advantage than explicit knowledge does. Leaders and managers can look to understand better where tacit knowledge resides and how it flows—indeed if it flows—through their organizations. Flows of tacit knowledge are particularly relevant in terms of promoting sustainable competitive advantage. The kinds of knowledge flow analysis and visualization techniques illustrated above can help focus attention on flows of tacit knowledge, at all levels of reach through the organization.
4. Knowledge flows must balance exploration through learning with exploitation through doing. Leaders and managers can look to understand better how their styles and priorities emphasize one versus the other. A great many people in operational organizations emphasize exploitation through doing over exploration through learning. Such emphasis is short sighted often. This is the case in particular where the organization seeks to compete on the basis of knowledge. Intervening to enhance knowledge flows can improve workflows, which can improve in turn organizational performance, but one must first make the investment in knowledge flows before expecting to reap any returns from workflows and performance.
5. Enhancing knowledge flows requires simultaneous attention to personnel, work processes, organizations and technologies. Leaders and managers can look to understand better how these four aspects of the enterprise interrelate. A great many organizations will find such aspects are at odds with one another. This can be the case in particular where changes are made in terms of inserting new information technology into unchanging people, organizations and work processes. The leader or manager should consider designing all four aspects of the enterprise, together, as an integrated system.

6. Knowledge enables action directly, whereas information provides meaning and context for such action. Leaders and managers can look to understand better the actions required for effective organizational performance. Such actions can point directly to the knowledge that enables their effective performance, and such knowledge can point directly in turn to the knowledge flows that may exhibit clumping or like circulation pathologies. Intervening to dissolve knowledge clumps and to remedy flow pathologies can improve organizational performance, by improving the knowledge-based activities they enable.
7. Data, information and knowledge flows are interrelated dynamically yet distinct mental processes. Leaders and managers can look to understand better how people come to know what they do in an organization. Whenever discussions turn to technologies in the context of knowledge flows, it is important to remember that flows of data, information and knowledge involve (individual, group and organizational) cognition. Technologies address flows of signals. It makes little sense to discuss new technologies in such context without discussing people (and organizations) also. Yet this is all too common of an occurrence.
8. Flows of knowledge require supplementary flows of information, data and signals. Leaders and managers can look to understand better which signals, data, information and knowledge are most important in their organizations. One should not lose sight of the complementary roles played at different levels of the knowledge hierarchy. Nor should one forget that the hierarchy points both ways, depending on whether one is viewing knowledge flows—along with corresponding flows of information, data and signals—from the perspective of producer/sender or consumer/receiver. Understanding the critical flows can inform important decisions in terms of people, work, organization and technology.
9. Explicitness represents a very discriminatory dimension for evaluating the uniqueness of knowledge. Leaders and managers can look to understand better how explicit versus tacit knowledge is viewed in an organization. Many organizations seem to prize explicit knowledge (esp. with its speed and reach) over tacit knowledge (esp. with its undiluted power). Yet we note above how tacit knowledge offers greater potential in terms of competitive advantage, although such potential is slower to be amplified through broader organizational reach. The kinds of knowledge flow analysis and visualization techniques illustrated above can provide insight into explicit versus tacit knowledge flows.
10. Information technology supports principally flows of explicit knowledge. Leaders and managers can look to understand better how IT can be employed to support tacit knowledge flows. In such role, IT and people must necessarily work together, and aside from very rare cases (e.g., enabled via increasingly sophisticated machine autonomy in the organization), the former should serve the latter, not vice versa. Interventions to enhance tacit knowledge flows will involve often non-technological approaches (e.g., pertaining to people, work processes, organizations), but buying a solution in a box represents a perennially easy way out for leaders and managers who are not informed well about knowledge flows.
11. Knowledge exhibits some properties of inertia such as tendency to remain at rest. This accounts for much of the knowledge clumping one finds in most organizations. Where such clumping is discovered, some kind of intervention is required. Where such

clumping pertains to tacit knowledge, technology represents an approach that, alone, is unlikely to be effective. The key point is, some action is required to move knowledge. Otherwise it remains static.

12. Experiential processes contribute principally toward workflows (i.e., doing), whereas educational processes contribute principally toward knowledge flows (i.e., learning). Leaders and managers can look to understand better how their alternate approaches to enhancing knowledge flows (e.g., OJT, formal training, mentoring) contribute toward learning versus doing. Different approaches are likely to apply relatively better or worse to various kinds of knowledge and organizational contexts; that is, one size is unlikely to fit all. It is important for the leader or manager to consider different approaches and to learn which approaches are relatively more or less effective in the various contexts of interest.
13. Knowledge flows lie always on the critical paths of workflows and hence organizational performance. Leaders and managers can look to understand better how important workflows are affected by knowledge flows. A great many leaders and managers plan and manage workflows meticulously yet ignore the knowledge flows that enable them. Extensions to popular leadership and management tools and techniques such as Gantt Charts, PERT networks and computational models to address flows of knowledge (i.e., in addition to flows of work) offer considerable promise in this light.
14. Time-critical workflows must wait for enabling knowledge flows to run their course. This point about managing enabling knowledge flows is particularly pertinent in cases of time-critical workflows. All requisite flows of knowledge must complete their trajectories before such workflows can begin effectively, and because knowledge—particularly tacit knowledge—flows on timescales that are qualitatively different than those of the workflows they enable, substantial, advance attention to and planning of knowledge flows is warranted in time-critical contexts.
15. Explicit knowledge flows very quickly and broadly, but its relative power is diluted, whereas tacit knowledge flows comparatively slowly and narrowly, but at high power. Leaders and managers can look to understand better how knowledge moves through their organizations, particularly in the context of their competitive environments. Understanding the dynamics of explicit knowledge enables leaders and managers to identify the most appropriate knowledge flows on which to concentrate when it is important to distribute important knowledge broadly and quickly. Likewise, understanding the dynamics of tacit knowledge enables leaders and managers to identify the most appropriate knowledge flows on which to concentrate when it is important to sustain high knowledge power over time.
16. Information technology is helpful and necessary but not sufficient for knowledge management. Leaders and managers can look to understand better how IT can support KM and where it falls short generally. In particular and as noted above, IT enables impressive performance in terms of transmitting signals (e.g., at great speeds, across great distances, to great numbers of people and machines), which are necessary for knowledge flows. IT enables people to manage data well. It supports pervasive, high-volume data flows. IT can help people to derive meaning from data and to appreciate the corresponding context, particularly at a distance. This is important for remote communication and information flows. IT can enable people to formalize and encode knowledge in explicit form and to share such knowledge quickly and broadly through an organization. This

represents a powerful application of IT for KM. Alternatively, most IT at present offers little to people interested in creating, sharing or applying tacit knowledge. The kinds of knowledge flow analysis and visualization techniques illustrated above can help differentiate tacit knowledge flows from counterpart flows of explicit knowledge, information, data and signals. Leaders and managers can rely upon such differentiation to identify where IT is comparatively more or less likely to support KM effectively.

17. People—not information technologies—are central to tacit knowledge flows. Leaders and managers can look to understand better how on-the-job experience, trial and error, direct observation, mentoring, shared interaction, reflective communication, contemplation and like dynamic processes account for most tacit knowledge flows in the organization. Most IT offers little support for such processes. It is important for leaders and managers to know which knowledge flow processes pertain to human-centric tacit knowledge and to appreciate how such flows center on people.
18. Information technology plays supportive roles for the most part in organizational work routines, whereas people play the performative roles generally. Leaders and managers can look to understand better how supportive and performative roles are played in their organizations and how IT contributes toward the corresponding knowledge-based activities. It is important for leaders and managers to know the central roles played by people, and the support roles played by IT, in flows of both tacit and explicit knowledge. The kinds of knowledge flow analysis and visualization techniques illustrated above can help leaders and managers to identify which roles apply to the various organizational routines of interest and importance to enterprise performance.
19. Expert systems, software agents, and like "intelligent" applications address and apply knowledge directly. Leaders and managers can look to understand better how software applications in this class work directly with knowledge, in addition to information and data. Although such knowledge is necessarily explicit, it enables effective, performative actions (e.g., informed decision-making, appropriate organizational behaviors, useful contributions to workflows) through machines. Leaders and managers may identify methods for integrating intelligent applications into the personnel systems, work processes and organizational structures of interest. It is important for work to be allocated on the basis of relative capability. People are much better at some activities (e.g., understanding social norms) than even the most-intelligent machines are; and even the least-intelligent machines can be much better at other activities (e.g., brute computation) than people are.
20. Simulation technology can enhance knowledge flows in addition to workflows. Leaders and managers can look to understand better how simulation enables virtual practice, by people in groups and organizations as well as individually. Such virtual practice can support learning through trial and error without the risks and consequences of mistakes and failures in operational organizations. Alternatively, virtual practice through simulation contributes only rarely and minimally—if at all—to workflows. Hence the focus is on knowledge flows through learning to a much greater extent than it is on workflows through doing. Through simulation, leaders and managers may find an effective balance between traditional knowledge flow processes such as formal training and OJT.
21. Knowing reflects knowledge in action and is required to realize a return on investment. Leaders and managers can look to under-

stand better how knowing contributes to capitalizing on investments in knowledge and how putting knowledge into action can help obviate the "knowing-doing gaps" (i.e., 'knowledge-knowing gaps' or knowledge 'potential-action gaps') in organizations. The knowing activity doing is associated often with overcoming such gaps, but formalizing, sharing, refining and other activities along the life cycle contribute toward knowledge in action as well. Leaders and managers may benefit by shifting their focus from knowledge (e.g., an emphasis on possession) to knowing (e.g., en emphasis on practice) in the organization.

22. Learning reflects knowledge in motion and is required for knowing. Leaders and managers can look to understand better how knowledge flows depend upon learning in the organizational context and how doing depends upon learning for the performance of knowledge-based activities. The knowing activity learning corresponds most closely with the creation stage of the knowledge life cycle, but learning takes place also through other activities such as formalizing (e.g., machines can learn explicit knowledge), sharing (e.g., people can learn from one another), application (e.g., people can learn from experience) as well. Leaders and managers need to appreciate the power of learning and may benefit by emphasizing learning activities to the same extent as—or possibly even greater extent than—their doing counterparts.
23. Amplifying knowing and learning beyond the individual (e.g., to groups, organizations, interorganizational collectivities) offers the greatest potential for knowledge superiority. Leaders and managers can look to understand better how knowledge-based performance can be amplified as knowledge flows across increasingly broad reaches of organizations. Examples from music, sports, business, military, politics and many other domains make clear how broadly reaching knowledge flows enable performance at levels superior to those enabled by narrowly flowing counterparts. In particular where leaders and managers seek knowledge superiority as a means to competitive advantage, promoting broadly flowing knowledge is key. The kinds of knowledge flow analysis and visualization techniques illustrated above can help leaders and managers to assess the breadth of knowledge flows—explicit and tacit, fast and slow, around the whole knowledge life cycle—through their organizations.
24. To the extent that an individual, group or organization focuses on knowing, then to some extent learning must suffer, and vice versa. Leaders and managers can look to understand better how learning is critical for acquiring the knowledge that enables knowing and how knowing in practice can contribute to learning. In particular, the more that is known in some domain, the faster is learning in that domain. This highlights the interaction between knowledge stocks and knowledge flows. The implications are strategic. Where one individual, group or organization can obtain a lead over its competitors in terms of knowledge, such leader can expect to learn more quickly than its competitors can. By learning more quickly, the leader can expect in turn to acquire more knowledge than its competitors can. This enables even faster learning, even more knowledge, and so forth through a virtuous cycle. It is important for leaders and managers to appreciate the dynamic nature of knowledge-based competition: especially how even a small lead can grow over time to an insurmountable edge.
25. Doing and learning involve action and potential. Leaders and managers can look to understand better how what has been learned to date, at any point in time, affects the ability to learn something new. They

can look to understand likewise how what is known, at any point in time, affects the ability to perform knowledge-based actions. The experiences of any organization contribute toward its knowledge inventory, and the associated learning can contribute toward its core competencies. Alternatively, the knowledge possessed by an organization also limits the relative ease and difficulty of learning something new in a particular domain, and the associated knowledge can contribute instead toward core rigidities. It is important for leaders and managers to appreciate the path-dependent nature of knowledge flows, and hence the corresponding knowledge-enabled workflows. When abrupt shifts in knowledge flows (e.g., to learn in a new domain) become necessary, the organization may benefit in particular by "forgetting" collectively (e.g., via personnel actions, work-process changes, organizational restructurings) knowledge that constrains new organizational learning.

26. Knowledge management involves organizational change. Leaders and managers can look to understand better how managing knowledge can entail considerable deviation from the stable routines of many organizations. Managing change has been studied considerably and practiced extensively. Hence substantial knowledge in terms of lessons learned, case experiences, heuristic principles, preconditions for success and failure, and other forms is available. It is important for leaders and managers to anticipate substantial change and to both prepare for and implement such change in an informed manner. Several of the techniques described in Part II of the book can help with such informed preparation and implementation.
27. Knowledge inventory can be used to assess an organization's readiness to perform its work processes effectively. Leaders and managers can look to understand better how various activities in terms of work experience, education, training, mentoring, social interaction, simulation, reflective contemplation, and other knowledge flow processes contribute toward the knowledge stocks or inventories of individuals, groups and organizations. Such inventories enable knowledge-based actions and facilitate within-domain learning. Where a set of critical knowledge-based actions can be identified in an organization, it may be possible to link such actions with the kinds of knowledge—and hence the corresponding knowledge flow processes—required to enable them. Where a person, group or organization possesses all of the requisite knowledge associated with a set of actions, one can infer a positive degree of readiness to perform such actions. In contrast, where all of the requisite knowledge is not possessed in current inventory, one can infer a negative degree of readiness and identify the knowledge flow processes appropriate to fill the corresponding knowledge gaps. Leaders and managers may benefit by working to measure knowledge inventories at various levels of reach in their organizations.
28. When estimating the value of knowledge, it is often better to light a candle than to curse the darkness. Leaders and managers can look to understand better how knowledge contributes toward workflows and hence performance in their organizations. Several aspects of leadership and management exhibit tensions between competing foci (e.g., learning vs. doing, exploration vs. exploitation) and require tradeoff decisions to be made (e.g., allocation of finite time and energy). Knowledge is inherently intangible and difficult to measure, particularly at broader reaches (e.g., teams, groups, departments, organizations), but its role is critical. Even crude measurements can be illuminating and informative. Several of the techniques discussed in Part II of the

book can help leaders and managers to measure knowledge. Much research remains to be conducted in this area to improve knowledge-measurement techniques, but it is important for leaders and managers to measure knowledge in their organizations. Even crude measurements are better often than no measurements.

29. Culture, trust and incentives affect organizational learning and hence performance as much as process, technology and training do. Leaders and managers can look to understand better how factors such as a culture of knowledge sharing, interpersonal trust, and incentivized knowledge hoarding can affect knowledge dynamics in the organizational context. In particular where problems with tacit, human-centered knowledge flows are discovered, organizational culture and interpersonal trust play key roles often. Incentives provide a well-recognized approach to changing behaviors. It is important for leaders and managers to assess the knowledge-creating and –sharing nature of their organizations in terms of culture and trust and to devise incentives for enhancing knowledge flows. Such incentives should necessarily complement other management interventions in terms of personnel systems, work processes, technologies and learning activities.
30. Computational modeling is useful for knowing and learning about organizational knowing and learning. Leaders and managers can look to understand better how computational models of organizations provide relatively high-fidelity representations of operational organizations in practice. Many different kinds of organizational behaviors can be examined through such models, and the relative efficacy of numerous alternate management interventions can be assessed via simulated performance. By learning about how different organizational processes interact, leaders and managers can know better how to diagnose knowledge flow pathologies and how to intervene more effectively to enhance knowledge flows. In turn by knowing their organizations better, leaders and managers can develop and refine higher fidelity computational models and can derive greater insight from them. Computational models of knowledge dynamics are emerging still from the research lab, but they offer considerable promise in terms of organizational knowing and learning. It is important for leaders and managers to know the capability and potential of computational models.

SUMMARY OF LEADERSHIP MANDATES

Recall from above the 30 leadership mandates developed through the second part of the book. We list these mandates below for reference, reemphasize how they derive from practical application, and exhort the leader and manager to leverage them for case-based reasoning.

Beginning with mandates derived in Chapter 6.

1. Realistic expectations, shared vision, and appropriate people participating full-time represent the preconditions for success that are absent or insufficient most often in KM projects.
2. Reliance upon external expertise, narrow technical focus, and animosity toward staff and specialists represent the preconditions for failure that are present or sufficient most often in KM projects.
3. Knowledge representation, attention to tacit knowledge, and focus on organizational memory represent unique considerations that merit particular attention in KM projects.
4. Knowledge audits can help organizations that do not know what they know.

5. In cases where quick results in short conflicts are important, the organization should focus on explicit knowledge flows, but where sustained results in long confrontations are required, tacit knowledge flows offer greater power.
6. Knowledge value analysis privileges tacit knowledge appropriately.
7. The greater the use of automation at the beginning of a process, the lower the improvement rate.
8. Performance improvement reflected by learning curves involves more than just individual knowing and learning.
9. Knowledge can be lost and found.
10. Trust cannot be bought.
11. Using computational models, organizations can be designed and tested virtually, in a manner similar to the design of airplanes, bridges and computers.
12. Specialist and generalist knowledge represent (imperfect) economic substitutes for one another.

Continuing with mandates derived in Chapter 7.

13. Knowledge flow vectors can be used to represent dynamic knowledge requirements.
14. It is essential to plan how knowledge technologies will be used by people.
15. The learning curve measures knowledge flows through OJT.
16. Socialization and acculturation represent viable approaches to enhancing tacit knowledge flows.
17. Trans-organizational collectivities (e.g., communities) may have greater influence over employee knowledge, culture and performance than leadership and management do.
18. Knowledge flows critical to enabling critical workflows center on tacit knowledge.
19. An organizational process without consistent improvement over time suffers from knowledge clumping.
20. Members of a team must learn to work with one another before knowing how to work together on a project.

Adding in mandates derived in Chapter 8.

21. Ten unique knowledge flow processes are required for military task force efficacy.
22. OJT involves knowledge flowing at two different speeds: knowledge application through doing is fast; knowledge creation through learning is slow.
23. Given the time-critical nature of warfare, most tacit knowledge must already be in place when the officer reports first for duty.
24. Systematic storytelling can increase the reach of this time-honored and effective approach to sharing tacit knowledge.
25. Socialization, teamwork and acculturation must interconnect to enable healthy knowledge flow circulation.

Including mandates derived in Chapter 9.

26. Leading by example and evangelism represent viable approaches to enhancing acculturation knowledge flows.
27. Once one understands relatively small set of key knowledge flow processes, he or she can analyze any knowledge flows—healthy or pathologic—in any organization.
28. The key to self-organization is having people enjoy what they do together.
29. The ability of different people to work together on teams is just as important as the individual skills and experiences they bring individually.
30. Leaders who are concerned about acculturation knowledge flows must address participants' beliefs.

Section 3
Emerging Phenomena

Scientia potentia est. – Sir Francis Bacon (or Thomas Hobbs)

The wise prevail through great power, and those who have knowledge muster their strength. – Solomon

The emerging phenomena part of this book builds upon the Knowledge Flow Theory presented in Section 1 and the practical application discussed in Section 2. Knowledge Flow Theory provides the intellectual basis for diagnosis and intervention of problems with knowledge flows. As such, the principles explain why dynamic knowledge phenomena behave as they do, and through principles-based reasoning, they inform the leader and manager on ways to harness dynamic knowledge for competitive advantage in the technology-driven world. They provide the intellectual foundation needed for practical application as addressed in Section 2 of the book.

Practical application provides tools and techniques for diagnosing problems with knowledge flows and for identifying appropriate leadership and management interventions. As articulated through the chapters in Section 2, we include general as well as specific tools and techniques for practical application. The application cases explain further how organizations from across a very wide range of sizes and domains both succeed and fail at harnessing dynamic knowledge; hence, through case-based reasoning, they provide both positive and negative examples for the leader and manager to use in comparison with his or her own organization.

In combination, the KFT principles and application cases enable insightful interpretation of emerging phenomena discussed here in Section 3. This discussion provides a current set of challenging issues to address through both theory and application and to help demonstrate further the broad and enduring applicability and utility of our ideas and techniques.

This third section of the book is organized into five chapters. Chapter 11, "Emerging Knowledge Phenomena," outlines an approach to harnessing the power of dynamic knowledge principles for competitive advantage in our current, technology-driven, and socially connected world. Chapter 12, "Cyberspace and Cloud Knowledge," focuses on the dynamics of knowledge associated with the ubiquitous and interconnected networks and computers comprising cyberspace and enabling cloud computing. Chapter 13, "Virtual Worlds Knowledge," delves more deeply into cyberspace to concentrate on the kinds of synthetic, artificial, or virtual worlds within which an ever-increasing number of people are spending time, money, and energy. Chapter 14, “Social Media Knowledge,” examines the phenomena associated with expanding interpersonal presence and interaction enabled by social media technologies. Chapter 15, “Leadership and Management Implications,” consolidates our learning through this book into a set of considerations that are essential for leaders and managers of today and tomorrow. We also include an aggressive agenda for future research to continue our contribution to new knowledge regarding the harnessing of dynamic knowledge principles for competitive advantage in the technology-driven world.

Chapter 11
Emerging Knowledge Phenomena

ABSTRACT

This introductory chapter outlines an approach to harnessing the power of dynamic knowledge principles for competitive advantage in our current, technology-driven and socially connected world. The authors begin their consideration of emerging phenomena here.

INTRODUCTION

Whenever using the term emerging in an enduring medium such as this book, one must be careful, for people are likely to read these words long after they have been written and published. Phenomena that may be emerging today are likely to have emerged already in the near future, and they may have even become conventional wisdom by sometime in the far future.

This pertains in particular to technological discussions, for the kinds of technologies associated most commonly with knowledge dynamics change relatively quickly (e.g., consider Moore's Law). I recall, for instance, a team of prominent researchers publishing an article in the 1990s that specified an advanced-at-the-time computer processor (i.e., xx486) used in their work; these researchers were trying to emphasize how "advanced" their research technology was. Reading this article today makes such emphasis laughable, however, for that specific technology has been obsolete for twenty years. I look back on the article today, saying, "pfffft: xx486; how quaint."

People and organizations, on the other hand, do not change anywhere nearly as quickly. The Bible and other ancient writings, for instance, have described most people as being self interested from time immemorial, yet such self interest remains the focus today of much current thinking in terms of how to organize, incentivize, lead and manage people effectively. Indeed, Adam Smith's famous Invisible Hand that underlies modern economics is predicated upon people pursuing their individual self interests (yet benefitting the economy as a whole; see McCreadie, 2009). As another instance, these and other ancient writings have characterized the Hierarchy as the most prominent organizational form since the first accumulations and concentrations of organizational power, yet the Hierarchy today remains the most common approach to organization still, particularly for

DOI: 10.4018/978-1-4666-4727-5.ch011

large collectivities. Because the emerging phenomena that we address in this third part of the book involve people and organizations, in addition to technologies, their corresponding knowledge dynamics affect a mix of both quickly and slowly changing elements.

It is helpful at this point to make a distinction between emerging technologies and emerging phenomena. Emerging technologies, for the most part, are the product of scientific discovery and engineering innovation. Emerging knowledge and information technologies, in particular, are also IT-centric and driven by market forces that fuel relatively short product life cycles. Other emerging technologies (e.g., pertaining to alternative energy, medical diagnosis, warfare)—although not (as) IT-centric or driven to (such) short product life cycles—are similar products of scientific discovery and engineering innovation.

For several instances of currently emerging technologies, considerable attention is beginning to focus on Cyberspace now, which exists solely within IT systems and artifacts, and which involves nearly incessant innovation to enable streams of different offensive and defensive technologies to surge past one another iteratively. As scientists discover new materials, architectures, algorithms and mechanics that enable faster, more powerful and more discrete network and computational effects, engineers apply the underlying knowledge to design, test and field innovative devices and systems that put such effects into practice. Cloud computing is emerging similarly as an IT-centric approach to pooling computational resources in third-party systems, which leverages likewise more capable network and computational discoveries, and which implements innovative devices and systems that put such discoveries into practice. Virtual worlds share much of this same IT focus too, as do social media applications, both of which are dependent fundamentally upon enabling IT, which is driven in turn by scientific discovery and engineering innovation. Within the socio-technical context of emerging phenomena, the technical part corresponding to emerging technologies is expected to continue changing relatively rapidly and unpredictably.

Alternatively, as noted above, emerging phenomena involve people and organizations too, albeit in conjunction with technology often. Hence even the IT-centric examples of emerging technologies from above are set within the socio-technical context of emerging phenomena. Cyberspace, for instance, may exist solely within IT systems and artifacts, but the phenomenon is important and emerging because people depend increasingly upon such systems and artifacts to perform both critical and everyday organizational knowledge and work processes. The same applies to cloud computing, which is shifting increasingly the manner in which people in organizations design and use information systems to perform knowledge and work processes. Virtual worlds, which are rooted likewise in IT, are emerging phenomenologically from the manner in which people and organizations are utilizing them as alternate realities (e.g., virtual social and game worlds), marketing channels (e.g., involving immersive consumer-product interactions), collaboration venues (e.g., virtual meeting spaces) and like, process-focused ends. Social media applications enable similarly novel ways for people and organizations to exchange ideas and experiences across geographical and temporal distances, but the social media phenomenon is centered on the people and organizations that utilize such applications, in addition to the knowledge, work and social processes enabled by them. Within the socio-technical context of emerging phenomena, the socio part corresponding to people and organizations is expected to continue changing comparatively slowly and anticipatably.

Notice how a process links each emerging technology from above with the people and organizations that use it. The process is where the socio and the technical parts come together: how people in organizations employ technologies to perform goal-oriented activities. Because the process provides an action-focused interface between fast-moving technologies and comparatively slow-moving people and organizations, it governs the proliferation and change of emerging phenomena. Hence the process represents an important lens for viewing, understanding and predicting emerging phenomena—whether driven by emerging technologies, non-technological innovation, or both. Thus, technologically enabled, organizational, knowledge and work processes in particular are likely keys in terms of leveraging emerging phenomena for competitive advantage. Where concentrating on how dynamic knowledge drives such phenomena, we use the term emerging knowledge phenomena.

THEORETICAL GUIDANCE

Here we select five particularly relevant theoretical principles from Part I of the book to guide our understanding of emerging knowledge phenomena. This helps both to elucidate important theoretical insights and to guide organizational leaders and managers seeking competitive advantage. Together, we can see emerging knowledge phenomena as continuities as opposed to exceptions, and by focusing on dynamic knowledge principles, we reveal an approach to harnessing their power for competitive advantage. We use this set of five principles in subsequent chapters to help discuss and characterize each emerging phenomenon, and we provide illustrative examples in this chapter to reveal the technique.

Principle 1: Knowledge is distinct from information in enabling competitive advantage. This first principle is particularly relevant when knowledge and information technologies are driving emerging phenomena in an organizational context. Two different organizations may implement the same, emerging, knowledge or information technologies at the same time, for instance, but outcomes in terms of competitive advantage may vary considerably. Because knowledge enables action, action drives performance, and performance supports competitive advantage, employing one or more technologies to enhance flows of knowledge through an organization would appear to lie on the critical path of guiding emerging knowledge phenomena to support and sustain competitive advantage.

The key to harnessing this principle centers on delineating the critical path and linking knowledge—through action and performance—to the competitive strategy selected by organizational leaders and managers. One can start anywhere along such path and work in either or both directions (e.g., forward or backward chaining in Artificial Intelligence (AI) parlance). For instance, say that organizational leaders have analyzed current rivals, potential new entrants, barriers to entry, power of customers and suppliers, and like aspects of their competitive arena (Porter, 1980), and say that a particular organization strategy (e.g., Prospector, Defender, Analyzer, or Reactor) has been selected to guide competitive efforts (Miles & Snow, 1978).

As one approach, this organization could begin by working backward from its chosen strategy (e.g., Prospector): identifying first the kinds and levels of performance required to effect the strategy efficaciously (e.g., locating and exploiting new product and market opportunities faster and better than competitors do); identifying next the actions required to drive such performance (e.g., innovating products and services, anticipating changing customer needs, creating new customer demands); and identifying in turn the kinds and levels of knowledge needed to enable necessary actions (e.g., fast-learning generalist, adaptive collaboration, and equivocality reducing knowledge).

The organization could then compare how its current performance measures up to required levels, which necessary actions are being accomplished sufficiently well, and the kinds and levels of extant possessed knowledge with respect those needed to enable the appropriate actions. Say, for instance, that the organization seeks to pursue the prospector strategy as above, and that it has consistent success at locating new product and market opportunities, but that it seems to trail competitors regularly in terms of exploiting such opportunities. In this case, actions driving the location of opportunities appear to be sufficiently powerful, but those required for exploitation are inadequate to pursue the prospector strategy effectively.

In this case, the organization could consider an alternate strategy that leverages its effective performance with respect to opportunity location, but which does not depend so heavily upon rapid exploitation and first-mover advantages (e.g., Analyzer), or it could look instead at enhancing or acquiring the kinds of knowledge required to accelerate opportunity exploitation (e.g., rapid prototyping, flexible IT architecture, organizational networking). This provides leaders and managers with a systematic approach to effecting strategy through analysis of requisite knowledge, action and performance. Other considerations such as organization structure, process and technology are clearly important too (Burton et al., 2006), and we consider them at a relatively high level below.

As an alternate approach, the organization could begin by working forward from its extant (or attainable) kinds and levels of knowledge (e.g., deep-specialist, functionally focused, and market-specific knowledge) and identify the actions enabled most productively by such knowledge (e.g., long-term innovation, operational efficiency, financial endurance). The kinds and levels of performance that could be driven effectively by such actions (e.g., cost leadership, market share expansion, customer loyalty) might suggest an alternate strategy (e.g., Defender). The organization could then compare how closely its current portfolio of actions match those enabled best by its extant knowledge stocks, and it could also consider realigning its action portfolio to concentrate more directly on driving performance to support this alternate strategy.

As still other approaches, the organizational analysis could begin with examination of actions or performance instead, and it could move backward toward knowledge as in the first case above, or it could move forward toward strategy as in the second case. Either way, linking knowledge with strategy provides a powerful approach to harnessing the power of this first, dynamic knowledge principle for competitive advantage. The other principles can be harnessed similarly.

Principle 5: Enhancing knowledge flows requires simultaneous attention to people, processes, organizations and technologies. This principle follows directly from our socio-technical-processual lens noted above, and it complements Principle 1. Two different organizations may achieve one or more of the same innovations individually in terms of people (e.g., via strategic recruiting, education, mentoring), processes (e.g., via radical redesign, tight customer-supplier linkages, load-surging and –shedding redundancies), organizations (e.g., via flexible structure, dynamic reconfiguration, interorganizational collaboration), or technologies (e.g., via emerging applications in Cyberspace, cloud computing, virtual worlds, social media), but outcomes in terms of competitive advantage may vary considerably. Because knowledge lies on the critical path to supporting and sustaining competitive advantage, an organization's treatment of people, process, organization and technology as an integrated design problem would appear central to leveraging innovation for competitive advantage.

The key to harnessing this principle centers on considering, simultaneously and complementarily, how all four resources (i.e., people, processes, organizations and technologies) can be balanced and integrated to enable the kinds and levels of knowledge to flow from when and where they are to when and where they're needed in order to enable necessary actions (e.g., to drive requisite kinds and levels of performance required to support competitive advantage through a particular strategy). One of the best ways to think about such balance and integration is through the inverse.

Consider, for instance, a business firm, government agency, non-profit or other collectivity that implements some new technology (e.g., cloud computing, virtual worlds, social media applications) but that does not do anything regarding people, process or organization. This should not be too difficult to imagine (or remember), for it happens all the time! Technological implementation is viewed by many as a relatively quick route to innovation, but technology-driven change has remained a substantial challenge for decades, if not centuries or millennia. Consider further that leaders and managers decide to introduce one or more social media applications (e.g., Facebook, Twitter, Wikis) into the organization. Although some people in the organization will likely have considerable knowledge about how to use such applications, some or perhaps even many others (at the time of this writing) will not possess such knowledge. As with the organizational implementation any new technology, at least a modicum of training (e.g., in-house courses, OJT, community college) will be required for unfamiliar people to even use it.

Moreover, many new technologies require substantial cultural shifts (e.g., information sharing vs. hording, teamwork vs. individual effort, crowd sourcing vs. information search) in order to leverage them to enable new actions, drive higher performance levels or sustain competitive advantage. As above, although some people in the organization are likely to reflect such culture already, and hence be able to leverage the new technology readily, others are comparatively unlikely to be culturally aligned. Unlike training courses that can be used to overcome technical unfamiliarity, most training approaches are relatively ineffective in terms of cultural change. Thus, an implementing organization will necessarily need to consider its current workforce with respect to the culture and skills required to leverage any new technology effectively. It may even find that an alternate workforce mix is needed, or conversely that implementation of this particular technology does not make sense at the current time and with the current mix of people's backgrounds, experiences and cultures.

Continuing this same example of introducing one or more social media applications into the organization, leveraging them effectively will require integration with the organization's key knowledge and work processes. If the technology sits outside of such key processes, then it's highly unlikely to produce benefits that outweigh its costs. Indeed, it's very likely to be more of a distraction than a resource. One needs to look no further than the introduction of Web technologies into the workplace over the past two decades. The people who use such technology to identify knowledge resources that support their work activities, to collaborate with geographically or temporally remote colleagues, to perform web-driven processes, and to accomplish like knowledge and work processes are likely to leverage the Web effectively; whereas those who use it to check personal stock quotations, update their relationship status, play online games, and perform similar activities are likely to waste most organizations' time and money. Where a new technology enables process innovation (e.g., consider the myriad online business models today), the corresponding processes must change to incorporate such technology, but where processes are too rigid or expensive to change (e.g., many organizations experience this via ERP implementation), the organization may benefit more by foregoing or deferring that particular technology implementation.

This social media example illuminates organizational issues as well. Consider first the kinds of activities enabled by this technology in terms of how an organization is structured. Many social media applications enable people to communicate through multiple media (esp. text, images, videos) and across both space and time. When used by knowledgeable people to perform important organizational processes, these applications offer potential to cross functional, spatial and temporal boundaries, but such potential may be at odds with an organization that seeks to maintain centralized authority, vertical information flows, functional division of labor, and like organizational characteristics common across many (esp. large and prominent) business firms, government agencies, non-profits and other collectivities. Indeed, leaders and managers may need to consider substantial organizational change in order for its people to leverage effectively the new technology through knowledge- and work-process integration. Where such leaders and managers are unwilling or unable to change, they may be better off foregoing or deferring the introduction of this technology.

This example begins above with the introduction of new technology and examines the impact on people, processes and organizations, and it elucidates the interconnected nature of these key resources. However, it could begin just as clearly with change in any resource. Where people, for instance, comprising the workforce shift in terms of knowledge, skill, culture and like characteristics (e.g., via generational progression), changes in process, organization and technology may be warranted, and they should certainly be considered over time. Likewise, where process change, as another instance, is needed to effect new actions or performance levels—or perhaps forced upon an organization by fiat, merger or acquisition—changes in organization, technology and people may be warranted, and they should certainly be considered over time. Similarly, where organization changes its structure and other characteristics, as a third instance, changes in technology, people and process may be warranted, and they should certainly be considered over time. Treating people, process, organization and technology as an integrated design problem would appear central to leveraging innovation for competitive advantage, and such integration provides a powerful approach to harnessing the power of this second, dynamic knowledge principle for competitive advantage. The other principles can be harnessed similarly.

Principle 8: Flows of knowledge require supplementary flows of information, data and signals. Despite our concentration in this book on flows of *knowledge*, it is important to remember that other flows are critical too. This is the case in particular where organizational people and processes are distributed geographically and temporally. Signals must flow quickly and reliably in order for data to flow similarly; data must flow quickly and reliably in order for information to flow similarly; information must flow quickly and reliably in order for knowledge to flow similarly; and knowledge must flow quickly and reliably in order support competitive advantage through knowledge-enabled action and performance. Two different organizations may implement one or more of the same emerging technologies, or pursue competitive advantage based on harnessing one or more of the same emerging knowledge phenomena, but outcomes in terms of competitive advantage may vary considerably. Because of tight linkages all along the Knowledge Hierarchy, effective integration and supplementation of dynamic knowledge, information, data and signals would appear central to enhancing knowledge flows for competitive advantage.

The key to harnessing this principle centers on linking and leveraging the bidirectional flows up and down the Knowledge Hierarchy. One can start anywhere along such flows and work in either or both directions. Recall in particular the irregular shape for the Knowledge Hierarchy introduced in Chapter 2 (delineated here again for reference via Figure 1). An important implication is that tacit knowledge is relatively abundant with respect to its explicit counterpart, the latter of which is comparatively the scarcest along the entire hierarchy. Despite the enormous abundance of explicit knowledge articulated via books, journals, reports, formulae, graphics, software and like artifacts, all such knowledge has to be articulated—generally through considerable time and energy invested by knowledgeable people and organizations—from tacit to explicit form. Presuming that at least some tacit knowledge remains unarticulated, the

Figure 1. Knowledge hierarchy with irregular shape for tacit knowledge

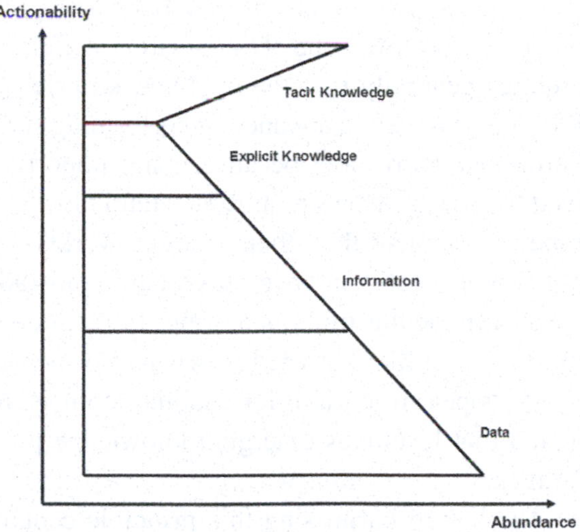

abundance of knowledge in tacit form should necessarily exceed that in the explicit.

Indeed, as illustrated figuratively here, the relative abundance of tacit knowledge approximates that of information, both of which exceed that of explicit knowledge. Yet there is a qualitative difference between knowledge and information: knowledge enables action, whereas information provides meaning and context for action. Even everyday colloquial expressions reflect such qualitative difference. Consider, for example, the common term information overload, which afflicts many (esp. decision making) people in organizations. This term implies that too much information can degrade performance, an implication supported by innumerable laboratory experiments as well as personal observations. The similar term drowning in data is common in organizational contexts and supported via both experiment and observation as well. Alternately, at the other end of the hierarchy we have tacit knowledge, which is collected broadly by experience and organized naturally within people's minds and organizations' routines. When is the last (or first) time that you recall someone in an organization complaining about having too much tacit knowledge or simply being too smart?

Many organizations go to great lengths and expenses to induce flows of data and information into explicit knowledge, and such flows lie at the center of most KM programs today still. Many other organizations value the importance of tacit knowledge carried by their people and routines, and an increasing number of KM programs are emphasizing tacit knowledge sharing instead of explicit knowledge creation, storage and dissemination. Still other organizations understand that both tacit and explicit knowledge are important, but few organizations today appear to be viewing tacit and explicit knowledge—in addition to information, data and signals—along a continuum that can be traversed according to circumstance.

Consider, for instance, an organization with express emphasis on creating, organizing and sharing explicit knowledge to enable action, drive performance and support competitive advantage. The Knowledge Hierarchy suggests that such explicit knowledge has two primary sources: 1) knowledgeable people can employ their experience to convert information into actionable form (e.g., synthesizing information from different sources to identify coherent patterns), or 2) knowledgeable people can articulate their experience to convert tacit knowledge into explicit form (e.g., writing instructional materials). Once in explicit form, such knowledge can be organized quickly and shared broadly, which represents its principal allure. Nonetheless, in either case, the process begins with the experiences of knowledgeable people. Hence the accumulation of experience by knowledgeable people lies at the root of explicit knowledge creation, organization and sharing.

Consider, as another instance, an organization with express emphasis on creating, organizing and sharing tacit knowledge to enable action, drive performance and support competitive advantage. The Knowledge Hierarchy suggests that such tacit knowledge has two, different, primary sources: 1) people can learn from explicit knowledge (e.g., reading instructional materials), or 2) they can learn through direct experience with other people (e.g., via conversation) and the world (e.g., via observation) around them. Once learned tacitly, such knowledge can be applied quickly and powerfully, which represents its principal allure. Nonetheless, in either case, the process begins with learning. Hence learning lies at the root of tacit knowledge creation, organization and sharing.

From these two instances that emphasize explicit and tacit knowledge, respectively, flows along the Knowledge Hierarchy can come from either direction (i.e., up or down), and the flow directions can be either high-to-low-abundance (e.g., information to explicit knowledge, tacit to explicit knowledge) or the reverse (e.g., explicit knowledge to information, explicit to tacit knowledge). One could extend these examples further to focus on the creation, organization and sharing of information (e.g., by placing data into context, by expressing explicit knowledge through coherent English sentences), data (e.g., by interpreting signals, by decomposing English sentences into individual words) or even signals (e.g., by transmitting signals via protocol, by encoding English words into digital form), but we wish to focus on knowledge in this book, for it enables action, which drives performance and supports competitive advantage in turn. We wish further to note the differences discussed above between knowledge in explicit and tacit forms, particularly in terms of its characteristics (e.g., rapid organization and broad sharing vs. slow but powerful application). We discuss such differences in greater detail below.

Principle 14: Time-critical workflows must wait for enabling knowledge flows to run their course. This principle accentuates the dynamic nature of knowledge and work as they flow through the organization. This is the case in particular for critical workflows that require quick, precise and thorough activities that can be performed by only knowledgeable people. In most such cases, the enabling knowledge flows are prerequisite to their corresponding workflows. Two different organizations may seek to capitalize upon one or more of the same emerging knowledge phenomena—even implementing one or more of the same innovations regarding people, processes, organizations or technologies—but outcomes in terms of competitive advantage may vary considerably. Because highly competent performance of time-critical activities requires generally that the enabling knowledge become tacit well in advance of performing such knowledge work, and because many important tacit knowledge flows require substantially more time to complete than their enabled workflows do, allowing for—and even insisting upon—adequate experiential time, mentoring effort, training expense, and like knowledge-oriented priorities would appear important for enabling competent action that leverages emerging knowledge phenomena.

The key to harnessing this principle centers on evaluating the relative flow rates of specific knowledge and work that is important in an organization, in addition to assessing an organization's knowledge and work stocks. Where knowledge flows quickly and work flows slowly through an organization, the dynamics of knowledge are unlikely to become a major issue, provided that adequate knowledge stocks can be developed and maintained. Even where knowledge stocks become depleted, sufficiently rapid knowledge flows—with respect to the workflows enabled by such knowledge—can mitigate performance problems. Alternatively, where knowledge flows slowly and work flows rapidly through an organization, the dynamics of knowledge may become prohibitive, unless adequate knowledge stocks can be developed and maintained. Even where knowledge stocks can be maintained, work processes that shift knowledge requirements abruptly or knowledge that becomes obsolete quickly can render such stocks ineffectual.

Consider, for instance, a work process such as picking strawberries. The flow of this work is relatively slow (e.g., picking in a particular field may take place over several days), and it requires relatively little knowledge in order to perform at least competently. (This instance is not intended to belittle fruit pickers in any sense; the work is very demanding, and experienced pickers have undoubtedly acquired much knowledge.) Say that an organization loses its best strawberry picker in the middle of a hot, humid, picking day. The slow pace of picking work would likely enable even an inexperienced picker to replace his or her more-experienced counterpart within minutes, and although the replacement worker may not pick as many strawberries at peak ripeness as the expert picker did, even the loss of such expert seems unlikely to thwart the process as a whole. Here the requisite knowledge can flow very quickly (e.g., within minutes), whereas the work progresses at a comparatively slow pace. The corresponding organization would likely invest negligibly in terms of employee education, training or mentoring, and it would probably pay little attention to knowledge stocks or flows; access to a pool of unskilled laborers willing to do the fieldwork may suffice. Here an organization could schedule (and conceivably begin) the picking process and wait to recruit a sufficient number of laborers until the process is underway already; there is little need to delay workflows on the basis of their enabling knowledge flows.

Consider now, as a contrasting instance, a work process such as brain surgery. The flow of this work is relatively fast (e.g., surgery on a particular patient takes place over several hours at most), and it requires abundant knowledge—tacit and explicit alike—to perform at least competently. (This instance is not intended to glorify brain surgeons in any sense; the work is very demanding, and even novice surgeons have undoubtedly acquired much knowledge.) Say that an organization loses a competent brain surgeon in the middle of a complex, risky surgery. The fast pace of surgery work would challenge even an expert surgeon—much less a novice—to replace his or her competent counterpart within the time required to complete the surgery successfully, and although even a novice surgeon may have considerable knowledge and experience, attempting to replace the original surgeon may thwart the process. Here the requisite knowledge can flow only very slowly, whereas the work progresses at a comparatively fast pace. The corresponding organization would likely invest highly in terms of employee education, training and mentoring, and it would probably pay great attention to knowledge stocks and flows; scheduling a competent backup surgeon to stand by, observe (e.g., learn by observation) or at least be on call may be required. Here an organization could not even schedule (much less begin) the surgery process until a sufficient number of competent surgeons were available; there is little sense in starting workflows until their enabling knowledge flows have completed.

These represent relatively extreme cases that help to illustrate the principle and its implications. In the first, we find slow process workflows and fast process knowledge flows; in the second, we find comparatively fast process workflows and slow process knowledge flows. Mixed cases in between (e.g., processes with fast workflows and fast knowledge flows, processes with slow workflows and slow knowledge flows) will not be so extreme or straightforward to analyze, but comparing the relative pace of knowledge flows and workflows will be important. This point resurfaces repeatedly in our subsequent chapters as we examine emerging knowledge phenomena in detail.

Principle 15: Explicit knowledge flows very quickly and broadly, but its relative power is diluted, whereas tacit knowledge flows comparatively slowly and narrowly, but at high power. This principle complements those above by differentiating between two, important classes of knowledge flow and by distinguishing them in terms of dynamic flow characteristics. Two different organizations may seek to attain competitive advantage by enhancing either explicit or tacit knowledge flows, but outcomes in terms of competitive advantage may vary considerably. Because the dynamics of knowledge in tacit and explicit forms differ markedly, emphasizing one or the other, at the most appropriate times and on the most appropriate occasions, would appear important for leveraging emerging knowledge phenomena for competitive advantage.

The key to harnessing this principle centers on understanding an organization's competitive arena. Where such arena favors activities to seize ephemeral opportunities in one or more short competitions, the organization focusing on the quick and broad flows of explicit knowledge may outperform counterparts emphasizing tacit knowledge instead, and such organization may gain first-mover advantages as a result. However, where opportunities are more enduring or competitions are more extended, even such first-mover organization may not be able to sustain competitive advantage gained through explicit knowledge flows. Indeed, the comparatively diluted power of explicit knowledge may give way relatively quickly to competitive advantage won through long and sustained commitment to deep and shared tacit knowledge flows.

Consider, for instance, two, relatively well-matched organizations engaged in a competitive struggle, and say that—given appropriate circumstances, timing and first-mover advantages—either organization possesses the capability to dominate its rival in such engagement. Say further that opportunities to dominate as such tend to be ephemeral; hence the organizations spend most of their time struggling in a metaphorical stalemate. This situation is common in many military engagements, but companies in fast-paced industries, politicians in close campaigns, organizations competing to recruit talented people, computer network attackers and defenders, and numerous other competitive arenas experience similar conditions also.

Were one organization able to identify an exploitable weakness of its rival, share knowledge about how to exploit such weakness quickly and broadly, and then act coherently to exploit it, that organization would likely benefit from accentuating and sharing explicit knowledge. In the military case, a weakness along these lines could manifest itself, for example, via an adversary's defensive systems (e.g., air defense, perimeter defense, network defense) shutting down or degrading in capability (e.g., due to unscheduled maintenance, power failure, sabotage) sufficiently long to be penetrated. In this military case, such penetration could be followed by destruction of the adversary's capability to strike back or perhaps even continue to defend itself, at which point it would be dominated, and first-mover advantages (esp. destruction of an adversary's offensive and defensive capabilities) may enable competitive advantage to obtain. Explicit knowledge, once articulated—and particularly when encoded in digital form on a network—can be shared very quickly and broadly (e.g., around the world in seconds via network), and it offers potential, if sufficiently powerful, to enable the kind of dominating action noted above. Where such power is insufficient, however, the speed and breadth of knowledge flows may be irrelevant.

Consider further, to continue this instance, that the competitive struggle between these organizations involves many skirmishes along the lines of our military example above, but that neither victory nor defeat in any single skirmish is sufficient for either organization as a whole to gain or lose competitive advantage. This could be the case in our current example where many other organizational units come to the aid of any one that is being dominated, and where together such many units bring sufficient power to repel the adversary and restore balance in the competitive struggle. Similarly, one company in a fast-paced industry could lose first-mover advantages for some particular new product but become the first mover for another product; one politician in a close campaign could fall behind in polls and popularity following some particular publicized debate but regain the lead following a subsequent debate; one organization competing to recruit talented people could fail to hire a particularly strong candidate for a job in one division but succeed at hiring strategically in another division; one computer network defender may be unable to foil a novel attack but follow in turn with a crippling counter-attack; and similar examples in other competitive arenas could obtain likewise.

Now, instead of relying upon victory or defeat in any particular skirmish, say that one organization is able to develop techniques to achieve victory (or defeat) across all potential skirmishes simultaneously. Doing so (or not) could render the losing organization incapable of responding in kind, and it could lead to sustainable competitive advantage for the victor. However, this may require extended and detailed observation, analysis and testing across all areas of conflict (i.e., all places for potential skirmishes), and the specific approach employed in any particular conflict area may necessarily have to be unique. As such, distributing the kind of explicit knowledge noted above would not appear to have comparable power in this circumstance. It would not be so important to share the same knowledge across all organization participants (e.g., across all conflict areas), for different, local knowledge will be needed for each individual skirmish. This places a premium on local, tacit knowledge, which may take considerable time to develop, and which may not flow either quickly or broadly from its situated context. Nonetheless, such local, tacit knowledge could carry great power, and with sufficient knowledge and information systems to enable an attack to be coordinated across all skirmishes simultaneously, competitive advantage may obtain in ways unattainable via explicit knowledge flows. Where such local, tacit knowledge must be shared quickly and broadly, however, the corresponding knowledge power may be irrelevant.

Similar power of tacit knowledge for competitive advantage could pertain to other competitive arenas as well. One company in a fast-paced industry could develop a core competency, for instance, in terms of rapid product or service innovation. Such competency would reflect tacit knowledge carried in the minds of its key people and through organizational routines, and it may be sufficiently inimitable that rival companies are rendered unable to compete. Similarly, one politician in a close campaign could develop an important, experienced-based skill, for instance, in terms of communicating compelling visions for the future. Such skill would reflect tacit knowledge embodied in the politician, and it may be sufficiently inimitable that campaign rivals are rendered unable to compete. Likewise, one organization competing to recruit talented people could help its personnel to develop an attractive and unique culture of caring, support and commitment with respect to employees. Such culture would reflect tacit knowledge expressed through the beliefs of people in the organization, and it may be sufficiently inimitable that rival recruiters are rendered unable to compete. Further, one computer network defender could develop a set of exploits and attacks capable of crippling the network infrastructure of any rival. Such exploits and attacks would have their basis in the tacit knowledge of the organization's people—although enabled by technology clearly—and it may be sufficiently inimitable that other network organizations are rendered unable to compete.

Through all of these examples, the dynamics of explicit and tacit knowledge favor unique conditions in terms of seeking competitive advantages. Explicit knowledge flows quickly and broadly, but with diluted power; this favors short and ephemeral competitive encounters. Tacit knowledge, in contrast, flows comparatively slowly and narrowly, but at high power; this favors long and extended competitive struggles. Hence explicit knowledge is in no way "better" than tacit knowledge is, nor vice versa; each has its relative advantages and disadvantages, and each has it opportune times and circumstances for emphasis and use. Harnessing the power of these dynamic knowledge principles for competitive advantage in our current, technology-driven and socially connected world follows accordingly.

EXERCISES

1. In the discussion of Principle 1 above, we learn that two different organizations may implement the same, emerging, knowledge or information technologies at the same time, but with different outcomes in terms of competitive advantage. Consider an organization that you're familiar with, and describe a situation in which this maxim could be observed.
2. In the discussion of Principle 5 above, we learn that two different organizations may achieve one or more of the same innovations individually in terms of people, processes, organizations, or technologies, but with different outcomes in terms of competitive advantage. Consider an organization that you're familiar with, and describe a situation in which this maxim could be observed.
3. In the discussion of Principle 15 above, we learn that two different organizations may seek to attain competitive advantage by enhancing either explicit or tacit knowledge flows, but with different outcomes in terms of competitive advantage. Consider an organization that you're familiar with, and describe a situation in which this maxim could be observed.
4. Describe one of the emerging phenomena noted in this chapter (i.e., Cyberspace, cloud computing, virtual worlds, social media) that you're familiar with, and how it can be used to enhance your knowledge (cf. information).

REFERENCES

Burton, R. M., DeSanctis, G., & Obel, B. (2006). *Organizational design: A step by step approach*. Cambridge, UK: Cambridge University Press. doi:10.1017/CBO9780511812415.

McCreadie, K. (2009). *Adam Smith's the wealth of nations: A modern-day interpretation of an economic classic*. Oxford, UK: Infinite Ideas.

Miles, R. E., & Snow, C. (1978). *Organizational strategy, structure, and process*. New York: McGraw-Hill.

Porter, M. E. (1980). *Competitive strategy*. New York: Free Press.

Chapter 12
Cyberspace and Cloud Knowledge

ABSTRACT

Cyberspace and cloud computing represent emerging phenomena that are commanding tremendous interest and generating immense activity across organizations—corporate, government, military, non-profit, and others—today. Understanding how knowledge flows influence and are influenced by these phenomena is important for harnessing the power of dynamic knowledge principles for competitive advantage in our current, technology-driven and socially connected world. As discussed in Chapter 11, these phenomena have both technical (esp. involving information technology) and non-technical (esp. involving people and organizations) aspects, which come together through the process for productive and goal-oriented action. Indeed, the process is where the socio and the technical parts come together: how people in organizations employ technologies to perform goal-oriented activities. Because the process provides an action-focused interface between fast-moving technologies and comparatively slow-moving people and organizations, it governs the proliferation and change of emerging phenomena. As such, technologically enabled, organizational, knowledge, and work processes in particular are key to leveraging emerging phenomena for competitive advantage. In this chapter, the authors employ familiar principles for understanding and analysis of cyberspace and cloud computing as emerging knowledge phenomena.

CYBERSPACE

Cyberspace as a term has changed considerably from consensual hallucination (Gibson, 1984; 2004) over the past three decades, and it continues to carry different meanings across a variety of contexts, communities and circumstances (Kuehl, nd). The US Military, for instance, offers a relatively current, unclassified definition emphasizing a largely infrastructural role for Cyberspace: "A global domain within the information environment consisting of the interdependent network of information technology infrastructures, including the Internet, telecommunications networks, computer systems, and embedded processors and controllers" (JP1-02, 2011). Arguably, from this definition Cyberspace would include all networked computers and associated networking equipment; hence it's difficult to conceive of anything in the networked world that's not part of Cyberspace. The implications might surprise some people.

DOI: 10.4018/978-1-4666-4727-5.ch012

Consider the venerable land-line telephone, for instance, which like the telegraph before it has played an instrumental role in remote human communication for over a century. Many people would not consider the telephone as part of Cyberspace, particularly because most people using land-line telephones pick up and use telephone handsets, not computers. Nonetheless, telecommunications texts dating back to the mid-Nineties (e.g., Beyda, 1996; Goldman, 1995; Rowe, 1995) reveal how most aspects of a telephone conversation take place via networked computers. Indeed, voice data are digitized early in the process of each conversation and carried as such through a part of Cyberspace owned and operated largely by large telephone companies, and of course some telephony is accomplished via computer directly (e.g., VOIP, Vonage, Skype).

This and like examples help to illustrate the breadth of Cyberspace as viewed through the infrastructural lens from above, and such lens focuses principally upon technological phenomena. Because Cyberspace exists solely within IT systems and artifacts, its enabling technological infrastructure changes quickly and frequently. Scientists discover continually new materials, architectures, algorithms and mechanics that enable faster, more powerful and more discrete network and computational effects. Engineers then follow quickly to apply the underlying knowledge to design, test and field innovative devices and systems that put such effects into practice. In this respect, despite the considerable current attention being drawn to Cyberspace, not much is new. Technology changes quickly and requires flexible architectures to accommodate such frequent change. We've understood this for several decades. From a purely infrastructural perspective, even as an emerging knowledge phenomenon, Cyberspace is neither new nor particularly interesting.

Alternatively, the people and organizations using Cyberspace within a socio-technical context change comparatively slowly. Cyberspace may exist solely within IT systems and artifacts, but the phenomenon is important and emerging because people depend increasingly upon computer and network systems and artifacts to perform both critical and everyday organizational knowledge and work processes. The enabling technology may change very rapidly, but it's not until such technology is put to novel and productive uses that the emerging knowledge phenomenon Cyberspace appears to be new or interesting.

The militaries of many nations, for instance, are working currently to integrate Cyberspace into their strategies, operations and tactics as a fifth domain of warfare—along with land, sea, air and space (e.g., see Lynn, 2010). This involves much more than technological infrastructure: the same kinds of computational and networking equipment that support military operations in the other four warfare domains are starting to be used differently today, but this takes time. People are developing new skills—for example, those that enable exploitation of vulnerabilities to attack networks offensively (e.g., STUXNET; see Milevsky, 2011; Zetter, 2011)—but the knowledge enabling many such skills is being developed largely through trial and error, an understandably slow process. Organizations are planning new operations—for example, those that use Cyberspace to facilitate kinetic operations in the physical world, and those that use kinetic operations to facilitate cyber operations (Miller & Kuehl, 2009; Clarke & Knake, 2010), but the organization design is changing only minimally, impeding efforts to integrate complementary cyber-kinetic operations for combined effects. Knowledge and work processes are shifting—for example, to identify new technical capabilities quickly—but incorporating them into both offensive and defensive actions requires redesign and adaptation of highly entrenched processes, which govern proliferation and change via Cyberspace.

Albeit without the term Cyberspace, technological innovation that emerged with the World Wide Web (Web) in the 1990s required process integration similarly, which in turn paced the dot-com phenomenon. Although the metaphorical bubble burst in the late Nineties, and a great many dot-coms became insolvent, the phenomenon revolutionized business, and the underlying knowledge remains both compelling and commonplace today (Savitz, 2013). Hence a quick re-examination of dot-com history can shed metaphorical light on Cyberspace as an emerging knowledge phenomenon. This is the case in particular, because much of the technology that enabled the dot-com phenomenon nearly 20 years ago remains at the center of Cyberspace today, and because successful organizations had to look well beyond the enabling technology to achieve, much less sustain, competitive advantage (Cronin, 1995).

At first, the new Web technology was a novelty. Select technologists in organizations, along with myriad technophiles at home, simply experimented and gained familiarity with the Web. Then, so called brick-and-mortar businesses (i.e., no Web presence; e.g., a bookstore selling only paper books from within a physical building) began using prototype Web applications in the workplace. Their fundamental business models had not changed, but their suite of technological capabilities had expanded marginally, and some internal knowledge and work processes were augmented by primitive Web applications. Knowledge flowed principally via trial and error, and Web-experimenting firms did not gain competitive advantage necessarily through their experimentation. Nonetheless, knowledge continued to accumulate, and ideas for process integration began to emerge.

Over time, Web applications continued to advance, and people became increasingly adept at integrating such applications into business processes (e.g., Web-database integration). Potential for large increases in both efficiency and efficacy fostered organizational change, and Web applications became woven into an increasing fraction of firms' knowledge and work processes. On the B2C[1] (i.e., business-to-consumer) side, the so called click-and-mortar companies (i.e., Web applications replicating extant knowledge and work processes; e.g., a bookstore selling paper books from within a physical building and ebooks via the Web) emerged. Their fundamental business models had not changed, but many firms operated online marketing, sales, processing and delivery channels in parallel with those continuing to take place as usual within physical buildings. Knowledge continued flowing principally via trial and error, but Web-implementing firms were gaining some competitive advantage, in part because their Web use was viewed by consumers as progressive, and in part because their parallel marketing channels were reaching new markets and customers without alienating existing ones.

Then we witnessed so called pure-play enterprises (i.e., Web presence only; e.g., a bookstore selling only ebooks via the Web), with business models based exclusively upon Web-enabled operations. The associated companies had negligible physical presence, and their knowledge and work processes centered on integrated Web applications, yet they competed effectively in many product, service and (especially) information markets. Knowledge continued flowing principally via trial and error, but Web-based firms gained competitive advantage in some markets, and some of these firms have managed to sustain such advantage for more than a decade now.

With the shift to new business models and online operations, many changes were required of successful organizations. Because an increasing fraction of knowledge and work processes were being performed online, the enabling networks, computers and other technological infrastructure had to become more reliable. Investments in higher capability and redundant hardware became necessary, and high-wage technical personnel needed to ensure network reliability became increasingly prevalent in such firms. Re-organization to integrate technical people with those in marketing, sales, operations, logistics, accounting and other business functions followed, with some entirely new organization designs emerging (e.g., Network Organizations [Miles & Snow, 1978], Clans

[Ouchi, 1980], Virtual Organizations [Davidow & Malone, 1992], Platform Organizations [Ciborra, 1996]). Most of the important knowledge (esp. enabling competitive advantage) was tacit, having been acquired over multiple years and largely via trial and error, and difficult for competitors to imitate quickly.

After five to ten years, however, nearly everyone in such business functions had become Web savvy; software and other tools (e.g., common word processing applications) facilitated work with Web-enabled systems, decreasing the expertise level required to use them effectively; customers learned to use and trust online business processes increasingly; financial institutions adapted their business processes to support speedy online transactions; firms modified their hiring practices and began seeking employees with technical skills, even for "non-technology" jobs; organizations became noticeably flatter, with fewer hierarchical levels, abundant cross-functional interaction, and even some aspects of self-organization; the novelty of online business faded, and today only the rare, anachronistic firm is left bereft of at least some online presence and process. Nonetheless, some of the firms that made early competitive gains are managing to sustain dominance still. Hence we see how—over time—people in organizations, integrating technology to enable new knowledge and work processes, enabled the dot-com phenomenon to emerge in the first place and to alter business as we know it today, and we see the central role played by (esp. tacit) knowledge, even as it accumulated relatively slowly and largely via trial and error.

Returning to our example from above, the military is in the metaphorical brick-and-mortar stage with respect to Cyberspace, with much to learn, a long way to go, and a host of competitors accumulating knowledge via trial and error also. Even for other organizations that are pursuing Cyberspace with current interest today, competitive advantage seems unlikely to result from technology alone. Indeed, with an infrastructural lens, most of the technology associated with Cyberspace is very familiar and far from novel. Alternately, with a view toward integrating people, processes and organizations with technologies, the novelty and emerging potential of Cyberspace illuminate. Promising organizational leaders and managers may find it useful to reread the relatively recent history describing the dot-com phenomenon.

CLOUD COMPUTING

Cloud computing as a term is relatively new with respect to computer networking, and it lies at the center of the emerging cloud knowledge phenomenon. Of course the Internet has been depicted for decades in network diagrams as a simple cloud shape (e.g., with no details, implying that internal activities take place effectively, comparable to the black box shape used historically to depict systems with details abstracted away), and lore suggests that this is the key intent behind the term. In short, networked computing takes place in "the cloud," meaning that designers, users and administrators do not concern themselves with details regarding how, where or what technology. Instead of an organization architecting, owning, securing and managing its own databases, servers, computers and like computing apparati—and hence being responsible for their procurement, development, administration and maintenance—such systems are architected, owned, secured and managed by others, in the cloud, who charge fees for such services.

Although the cloud computing term is relatively new and the phenomenon is emerging, the concept of abstracting away from design and operational details is not. Even with "conventional computing" (i.e., not in the cloud), a great many end users, for instance, would have difficulty articulating exactly where the various databases, servers, networking equipment and like infrastructural elements are located physically. It matters little to them how databases are organized and synchronized, whether servers are running Linux or Windows, or what bandwidth and service levels networking equipment supports; it matters instead that they're able to accomplish their work reliably and with service levels necessary to do so consistently.

Indeed, we have observed a steady trend over many years toward thinner clients. This implies that—despite ever increasing computational speed, memory and bandwidth available overall—end users' computational machines are becoming decreasingly capable (e.g., with fewer software applications installed, with fewer configuration options available, smaller processors and memories), with the computational power moving instead to centralized facilities, equipment and operations (esp. via server racks, arrays and farms). Such client-server architecture became popular in the Nineties as an approach to reducing total cost, and it has remained popular because such thin-client networks are easier to maintain (e.g., in terms of security, software updates, policy).

This trend reverses the preceding pattern toward thicker clients, in which end user machines became increasingly capable, and end users acquired increasing control over machine configuration and operation. The thick client arose with the personal computer in the Eighties, as end users were able to obtain increasing computational power through desktop machines, and organizations were able to save on mainframe computer operations and maintenance costs. Of course, when considering the preceding era of mainframe computing from today's perspective, one can see that such era represented a clear predecessor to the thin clients of today: end users' machines had negligible internal computational power and were capable of little more than communicating (textually) with a centralized (mainframe) host located in the basement of some building (cf. in a "cloud"?).

Hence the client-server architecture represents a swing back toward mainframe-like computing with thinner clients. Cloud computing can be seen in turn as an extension of such swing, but with organizational servers becoming thinner or disappearing altogether. With cloud computing, the end users' organizations do not even own the host mainframe computers, servers or other computational machinery; they are owned, operated and maintained by third-party organizations "in the cloud." As always, there's a bit more to the phenomenon than this (e.g., progression from software as a service, through platform as a service, to infrastructure as a service), but infrastructurally this should provide sufficient grist for our purposes here.

As noted in terms of Cyberspace above, because cloud computing takes place solely within IT systems and artifacts, its enabling technological infrastructure changes quickly and frequently. Scientists discover continually new materials, architectures, algorithms and mechanics that enable faster, more powerful and more transparent network and computational effects. Engineers then follow quickly to apply the underlying knowledge to design, test and field innovative devices and systems that put such effects into practice. In this respect, despite the considerable current attention being drawn to cloud computing, not much is new. Computational power inherent within end user client machines remains limited; host mainframes, servers and other computational machinery are aggregated to reduce total costs; and end users are happy so long as they're able to accomplish their work reliably and with service levels necessary to do so consistently. We've understood this for several decades. From a purely infrastructural perspective, even as an emerging knowledge phenomenon, cloud computing is neither new nor particularly interesting.

Alternatively, the people and organizations using cloud computing within a socio-technical context change comparatively slowly. Cloud computing may take place solely within IT systems and artifacts, but the phenomenon is important and emerging because people depend increasingly upon computer and network systems and artifacts—in the cloud—to perform both critical and everyday organizational knowledge and work processes. The enabling technology may change very rapidly, but it's not until such technology is put to novel and productive uses that the emerging knowledge phenomenon cloud computing appears to be new or interesting.

For instance, people may be changing slowly, but their patterns of work behavior and technology usage are shifting. The working professional is becoming increasingly mobile and expected increasingly to remain productive while on the move. This affects technology usage, as such professional can afford no longer to have computational power limited to a desktop terminal or client machine in a physical office. Instead, he or she requires nearly constant and ubiquitous access to computational power from virtually anywhere in the world and at practically any time of day or night. In addition to computational support, this professional requires nearly constant and ubiquitous access to other people also, as team projects represent the norm, and knowledge work depends increasingly upon transactive memory via coworkers, colleagues, friends and even anonymous sources. These are some driving reasons behind the continued proliferation of ever more-capable smart phones and social media applications, for example. With some thought, one can see that the services provided to such phones and applications come from the cloud (e.g., beyond cell towers).

As another instance, organizations may be changing slowly, but their patterns of interaction and governance are shifting. Different organizations (e.g., with different stakeholders, serving different markets, reflecting different designs) are becoming increasingly interdependent and expected increasingly to interoperate seamlessly and in near real-time. This affects organization design, as leaders and managers in any particular organization find themselves increasingly without centralized authority over the other people and organizations that are critical to their success. Instead, they require rich lateral communications, interactions and mechanisms for managing knowledge and work processes that cross multiple organizational boundaries. Strategic alliances, network organizations, inter-organizational supply chains and webs, and like organizational forms have been replacing some centralized hierarchies and multi-divisional organizational structures for many years now, but most (particularly large) organizations have changed only negligibly in terms of design. Many leaders and managers struggle at present to lead and manage effectively via interorganizational processes without (inter) organizations designed to accommodate such processes. With some thought, one can see that the multiple, unpredictable and variable electronic interactions between different sets of organizations, as they work together with changing intensities and on diverse occasions, are facilitated by cloud computing.

As a third instance, knowledge and work processes are changing at rates that mediate between the relatively fast pace of technological change and the comparatively slow change exhibited by people and organizations. Even where people are slow to learn about new technologies, knowledge and work processes supported by cloud computing abstract the associated technological change away from them. Even where organization designs are slow to accommodate fluid interorganizational interactions, knowledge and work processes supported by cloud computing obviate the need to modify computer and network architectures, configurations and operations internally. So long as network-supported knowledge and work processes are sufficiently malleable to accommodate change—yet not require rapid turnover of people's skill sets or frequent organization design change—many organizations are able to keep pace with technological innovation. With some thought, one can see that the ability to link together diverse knowledge and work processes across different and variable sets of interorganizational participants, but abstracting away the need for internal process or organizational change, is facilitated by cloud computing.

Reconsidering our military example from above, we find a concerted effort to move IT infrastructure and services into the cloud today. As with other military, government and commercial organizations expending similar efforts, promises of decreased costs, increased performance and even enhanced security abound. With multiple, different organizations such as these all moving toward cloud computing, however, competitive advantage seems unlikely to result from such movement alone. Indeed, with an infrastructural lens, most of the technology associated with cloud computing is very familiar and simply extends the idea of thin clients further, essentially entailing thin organization-owned servers and hosts or possibly even none at all. Alternately, with a view toward integrating people, processes and organizations with technologies, the novelty and emerging potential of cloud computing may illuminate. Promising organizational leaders and managers may find it useful to reread the relatively recent history describing the client-server phenomenon.

APPLIED PRINCIPLES

To consider the emerging Cyberspace and cloud computing phenomena further, we select five particularly relevant theoretical principles from Part I of the book to guide our understanding. These are the same five principles discussed in Chapter 11 above, which we use to focus on dynamic knowledge principles and elaborate the corresponding approach to harnessing their power for competitive advantage. By using these same five principles, we reinforce both their power and versatility, illustrating in this case how they apply well to Cyberspace and cloud knowledge knowledge.

Principle 1: Knowledge is distinct from information in enabling competitive advantage. The key to harnessing this principle centers on delineating the critical path and linking knowledge—through action and performance—to the competitive strategy selected by organizational leaders and managers. One can start anywhere along such path and work in either or both directions. In the case of the dot-com phenomenon, for instance, most companies started with the development of new knowledge pertaining to Web technologies. As such knowledge advanced, even primitive Web prototype applications could be seen over time to enable novel actions.

Knowledge to integrate a B2C firm's external Web presence with internal databases, for example, enabled potential customers to see for themselves which items were for sale and in stock, without consulting a product catalog or contacting a company representative. This reduced the time required for a potential customer to receive product information; it reduced the company's expenses for printing and mailing product catalogs; and it allowed the firm to operate with fewer telephone lines and company representatives to field calls and respond to product inquiries. These novel actions enhanced the performance of potential customers (e.g., by reducing the time required to find products of interest) and selling firms (e.g., by reducing expenses) alike. Such performance effects supported competitive advantage by some firms, as many pleased customers chose to become more loyal (e.g., supporting a differentiation strategy; see Porter, 1985), and many cost-saving firms could beat rival firms' prices (e.g., supporting a cost strategy; see Porter, 1996).

Additional knowledge to integrate financial transactions and initiate shipping activities, as another example, enabled potential customers to purchase and receive items of interest, without traveling to a physical store or contacting a company representative. This reduced the time required for a potential customer to purchase and receive a product; it reduced the company's expenses for physical stores and sales personnel; and it allowed the firm to operate with faster knowledge and work processes. As above, these novel actions enhanced the performance of potential customers and selling firms alike, and such performance effects supported competitive advantage, ultimately even through new business models and organization designs.

Notice that the novel Web technologies, themselves, were insufficient to produce competitive advantage. People in these organizations required knowledge about how to leverage such technologies through new actions that enable faster and lower cost business processes. The organizations required knowledge about how to increase performance for potential customers, as well as for company operations, and organizational leaders and managers required knowledge about how to link such external and internal performance gains with strategy to obtain competitive advantage.

Principle 5: Enhancing knowledge flows requires simultaneous attention to people, processes, organizations and technologies. The key to harnessing this principle centers on considering, simultaneously and complementarily, how all four resources (i.e., people, processes, organizations and technologies) can be balanced and integrated to enable the kinds and levels of knowledge to flow from where and when they are to where and when they're needed in order to enable necessary actions (e.g., to drive requisite kinds and levels of performance required to support competitive advantage through a particular strategy). We discuss some aspects of this principle above with reference to the dot-com phenomenon of the Nineties and its bearing on Cyberspace today.

There is, however, a relatively unique aspect of Cyberspace today that differs from the Internet and Web infrastructure that helped to enable the dot-com phenomenon two decades before: offensive operations. In past years, computer hackers and occasional criminals represented a minor nuisance to dot-com firms, and companies competed for customers, market share, publicity, funding and like gains in competitive arenas centered on business, finance and economics. Only very rarely, it seems, would one dot-com company deliberately attack and attempt to destroy a competitor's network infrastructure via cyber, and relatively stiff civil and criminal penalties served to diminish the likely gains from doing so.

Today's military, in contrast, faces daily network attacks by nation states, organized crime syndicates, hacktivists and others, and the increasingly sophisticated knowledge and tools used to attack appear to be outpacing those available to defend increasingly prolific, vulnerable and interconnected networks and computers (Brenner, 2011). Moreover, the complexity of Cyberspace today, exacerbating the sophistication of attack knowledge and tools, makes attribution to attackers very difficult to accomplish reliably. Further, the stakes associated with nation states are arguably much higher than the economic consequences of one (dot-com or other) firm gaining some competitive advantage over a business rival.

Beyond military targets, even civilian institutions (e.g., power plants, financial firms, Internet providers, telephone companies) appear to be increasingly interconnected and vulnerable to attack. This adds a whole new dimension to competitive advantage: one rival can gain advantage by disabling or even destroying the very Cyberspace infrastructure used by other rivals to compete. Industrial espionage is becoming increasingly sophisticated and discrete too, with some competitors able to appropriate at negligible cost the results of rivals' huge investments in research and development.

Nonetheless, again, there is much more to such dimension than the enabling technology: people with new skills, organizations with new missions, and processes with new knowledge and work flows, in addition to new technological capabilities, all come together to enable competition via Cyberspace.

Principle 8: Flows of knowledge require supplementary flows of information, data and signals. The key to harnessing this principle centers on linking and leveraging the bidirectional flows up and down the Knowledge Hierarchy. One can start anywhere along such flows and work in either or both directions. As above, we discuss some aspects of this principle with reference to the dot-com phenomenon of the Nineties and its bearing on Cyberspace today.

During the dot-com revolution, knowledge was key to competitive advantage, and it accumulated largely via trial and error. As noted above, particularly important was knowledge about how to employ rapidly advancing Web technologies to enable radical change to business processes. Nonetheless, many of the dot-com organizations' people and processes were distributed geographically and temporally. Signals had to flow quickly and reliably in order for data to flow similarly. This required increasingly prolific and high capacity network infrastructure, for instance, to shunt signals appropriately, which in turn required an expanded workforce of people with network skills and opened up an increased number of business opportunities in terms of network security, monitoring, equipment sales, consulting and other areas attendant to signals.

Likewise, data had to flow quickly and reliably in order for information to flow similarly. This required increasingly prolific and high capacity database infrastructure, for instance, to support reliable knowledge and work processes, which in turn required an expanded workforce of people with database skills and opened up an increased number of business opportunities in terms of database design, development, administration, maintenance and Web-process integration. The same applied to information, which had to flow quickly and reliably in order for knowledge to flow similarly, and knowledge had to flow quickly and reliably also in order to support competitive advantage through knowledge-enabled action and performance. Notice how each level of the Knowledge Hierarchy (i.e., signals, data, information, knowledge) involved increasing knowledge (e.g., network knowledge to enable quick and reliable signal flows, database knowledge to enable Web-process integration).

The same applies to the emerging Cyberspace knowledge phenomenon today. However, computing power has increased many-fold, network bandwidth has exponentiated, mobile devices have enabled access on the move, many internal processes now operate via cloud computation, and as discussed above, many organizations (e.g., military, government, corporate) expend increasing resources on defending their networks. Distributed, reliable, 24x7 network connectivity has become critically important to an ever increasing fraction of organizations. To the chagrin of many organizational leaders and managers, an extended network attack from a rival organization can be sufficient to achieve competitive advantage. The extent to which any such advantage can be sustained depends largely upon the resilience of the defending organization's Cyberspace infrastructure, the redundancy of its knowledge and work processes, the maneuverability of its organization design, and the skill of its people. Hence Cyberspace attack can be thought of today as a relatively novel strategy for seeking competitive advantage, and an increasing fraction of organizations will find their competitive arenas involving Cyberspace strategies, operations and tactics.

Principle 14: Time-critical workflows must wait for enabling knowledge flows to run their course. The key to harnessing this principle centers on evaluating the relative flow rates of specific knowledge and work that is important in an organization, in addition to assessing an organization's knowledge and work stocks. We note above how much knowledge during the dot-com revolution accumulated relatively slowly via trial and error. Many startup firms and ventures failed while attempting novel business models, strategies and operations before accumulating requisite knowledge (e.g., pertaining to computer-network infrastructure, Web-database integration, online marketing).

The pace of technological innovation appeared to be staggering during this period. Indeed, many people were challenged just to keep up with the myriad new ideas and implementations pervading organizations. Not all such ideas and implementations were equally viable, however, and many organizations backing or adopting the nonviable experienced stunning failures. Alternatively, first-mover advantages appeared to be great during this period, and many organizations hesitating and watching rivals from afar were left behind competitively. This produced a conundrum for organizational leaders and managers: how to balance the risk of implementation failure as an early adopter with the risk of competitive disadvantage as a slow mover.

This produced a conundrum in terms of organizational design also. Many relatively small, flat and agile startups demonstrated great maneuverability during the turbulent times of the dot-com revolution. They were able to change people's skill sets, alter business processes, shift organization designs, and incorporate new technologies quickly and inexpensively. However, such nimble firms were fragile often, unable to withstand and survive even relatively short periods of market setbacks or financial losses. Alternatively, many comparatively large, hierarchical and rigid enterprises demonstrated great stability during this same period. They were able to endure even long periods of market setback and financial loss. However, such solid firms were immovable often, unable to effect even relatively minor changes to people's skills, business processes, organization designs, or technological infrastructure at a pace required to leverage advancing technologies and business models effectively. This reflects an inherent tradeoff between organizational stability and maneuverability (Nissen & Burton, 2011).

Of course, we witnessed many organizational hybrids too. Numerous large organizations created or spun off small "entrepreneurial" units, for instance. Where the parent organizations were too stingy with financial backing, however, their entrepreneurial children organizations suffered the same fate as the maneuverable startups from above. Similarly, where the parent organizations were too meddlesome in business and operations, their enterprise children organizations suffered the same problems as their unmaneuverable parents. Many relatively small organizations sought to overcome their fragility by forming strategic alliances, participating in organizational networks, integrating inter-organizational supply chains, and like measures as well. Similarly, many comparatively large organizations sought to overcome their immovability by purchasing maneuverable firms that had demonstrated themselves and survived the startup stages of business growth.

Indeed, during this period, organization design became more important strategically than the advancing technologies enabling new business models and processes to succeed. Many long-standing rules of organization appeared to be challenged—and violated—effectively, and considerable time was required for organization researchers, leaders and managers to learn and apply the new rules. Those able to learn and apply such rules comparatively quickly—and especially possessing the organizational stability and financial resources to permit new knowledge processes to catch up to corresponding work processes—helped to exemplify this Principle 14. As above, learning from the dot-com revolution—when viewed through our lens focused on dynamic knowledge—illuminates the emerging Cyberspace knowledge phenomenon.

Principle 15: Explicit knowledge flows very quickly and broadly, but its relative power is diluted, whereas tacit knowledge flows comparatively slowly and narrowly, but at high power. The key to harnessing this principle centers on understanding an organization's competitive arena. We continue using the dot-com revolution for insight into Cyberspace. A great part of Web-database integration, for instance, required considerable time and effort for people to learn—largely via trial and error as noted above.

Recall, for example, how Perl and other, relatively primitive scripting languages were used painstakingly to integrate stateless Web pages to dynamic databases. For quite some time (e.g., a relative eternity according to "Internet Time") Perl scripting was an art, people possessing the corresponding skill and experience commanded a salary premium, and firms able to employ such people effectively to develop integrated Web-database implementations enjoyed competitive advantages in this market niche. The underlying knowledge was principally tacit, and it flowed relatively slowly, making imitation difficult for rival organizations to compete in this arena. Once the scripts were written, however, and integrated Web-database implementations began to proliferate, much of the key knowledge had been made explicit via code, and such knowledge was distributed broadly as such. Scripting artisans replaced artists, and soon the process of scripting itself was implemented via code. The persistent competitive advantage enjoyed by Perl scripters in labor markets, along with such advantage enjoyed by Web-database integration firms in product and service markets, waned, and Web-database integration today has been reduced nearly to drag and drop.

While scripting knowledge remained principally tacit, it was highly appropriable and powerful in terms of enabling relatively persistent competitive advantage. As such knowledge was articulated and disseminated increasingly via explicit code, its power to develop integrated Web-database applications remained high. Indeed, one could say that this knowledge power increased when Web-database integration became sufficiently automated to support drag and drop. However, articulation of the integration knowledge via explicit code caused its appropriability to decline, and the power of such knowledge to support competitive advantage diluted to the point of becoming trivial.

We can see some parallels with the emerging Cyberspace phenomenon. For many years, the technical skills required to hack into, exploit and otherwise attack networks were relatively rarified, and the art was enabled by highly tacit and appropriable knowledge. Comparatively small communities of like-minded people would share knowledge and exchange information about their largely self-taught tools and techniques, and the associated knowledge and information were held relatively closely, preserving their appropriability. Over time, however, such knowledge became increasingly explicit, and the once-small and close-knit community grew and was unable to keep it private.

Now, a great many of the tools and techniques are well-known and widely available (Andress & Winterfeld, 2011), to the point where the term script kiddies is used somewhat pejoratively to describe how even technologically ignorant kids can accomplish the same kinds of network attacks reserved formerly for technologically savvy hackists, where anti-malware programs can identify and neutralize many known issues, and networks can defend themselves automatically against previously unstoppable threats. Hence keeping secrets surfaces as an important aspect of leveraging the emerging Cyberspace knowledge phenomenon for competitive advantage. Any number of organizations today continue to develop new knowledge about how to exploit vulnerabilities in opponents' networks (e.g., zero-day exploits), but in many cases they're not sharing such knowledge. Indeed, the US Military, as one instance, retains knowledge and information regarding such exploits among its most highly guarded secrets.

REFERENCES

Andress, J., & Winterfeld, S. (2011). *Cyber warfare: Techniques, tactics and tools for security practitioners*. Waltham, MA: Elsevier.

Beyda, W. (1996). *Data communications: From basics to broadband* (2nd ed.). Upper Saddle River, NJ: Prentice Hall.

Brenner, J. (2011). *America the vulnerable: Inside the new threat matrix of digital espionage, crime, and warfare*. New York, NY: Penguin Press.

Ciborra, C. U. (1996). The platform organization: Recombining strategies, structures, and surprises. *Organization Science*, *7*(2), 103–118. doi:10.1287/orsc.7.2.103.

Clarke, R. A., & Knake, R. (2010). *Cyber war: The next threat to national security and what to do about it*. New York, NY: HarperCollins.

Cronin, M. (1995). *Doing more business on the internet: How the electronic highway is transforming American companies*. New York, NY: Van Nostrand Reinhold.

Davidow, W. H., & Malone, M. S. (1992). *The virtual corporation: Structuring and revitalizing the corporation for the 21st century*. New York: Edward Burlingame Books/HarperBusiness.

Gibson, W. (1984). *Neuromancer*. New York: ACE Books.

Gibson, W. (2004). Neuromancer: 20th anniversary Ed. New York: ACE Books.

Goldman, J. (1995). *Applied data communications: A business-oriented approach*. New York, NY: Wiley.

JP1-02. (2011). Department of Defense dictionary of military and associated terms. *Joint Publication 1-02* (8 November 2010, amended through 15 August 2011). Washington, DC: Joint Chiefs of Staff.

Kuehl, D. (n.d.). *From cyberspace to cyberpower: Defining the problem*. (Information Resources Management College/National Defense University Working Paper). Washington, DC: National Defense University.

Lynn, W. J. III. (2010, September/October). Defending a new domain: The Pentagon's cyberstrategy. *Foreign Affairs*, 97–108.

Miles, R. E., & Snow, C. (1978). *Organizational strategy, structure, and process*. New York: McGraw-Hill.

Milevski, L. (2011). STUXNET and strategy: A special operation in cyberspace? *Joint Forces Quarterly*, *63*, 64–69.

Miller, R. A., & Kuehl, D. T. (2009). *Cyberspace and the first battle in 21st century war* (working paper). Washington, DC: National Defense University, Information Resources Management College.

Nissen, M. E., & Burton, R. M. (2011). Designing organizations for dynamic fit: System stability, maneuverability and opportunity loss. *IEEE Transactions on Systems. Man and Cybernetics – Part A*, *41*(3), 418–433. doi:10.1109/TSMCA.2010.2084569.

Ouchi, W. G. (1980). Markets, bureaucracies, and clans. *Administrative Science Quarterly*, *25*(1), 129–141. doi:10.2307/2392231.

Porter, M. E. (1985). Technology and competitive advantage. *The Journal of Business Strategy*, *5*(3), 60–77. doi:10.1108/eb039075.

Porter, M. E. (1996). What is strategy? *Harvard Business Review*, *74*(6), 61–78. PMID:10158474.

Rowe, S. (1995). *Telecommunications for managers* (3rd ed.). Englewood Cliffs, NJ: Prentice Hall.

Savitz, E. (2012, October 23). Gartner: Top 10 strategic technology trends for 2013. *Forbes CIO Network*. Retrieved from http://www.forbes.com/sites/ericsavitz/2012/10/23/gartner-top-10-strategic-technology-trends-for-2013/

Zetter, K. (2011, July 11). How digital detectives deciphered Stuxnet, the most menacing malware in history. *Wired*.

ENDNOTES

1 We omit discussion of the equally exciting B2B (i.e., business-to-business) progression here.

Chapter 13
Virtual Worlds Knowledge

ABSTRACT

Virtual worlds represent emerging phenomena that continue to proliferate through military, government, corporate, and non-profit organizations as well as tens of millions of households. In addition to supporting immersive entertainment and online social interaction, virtual worlds are home to myriad serious applications that are changing the way people think about and work in organizations. Understanding how knowledge flows influence and are influenced by these phenomena is important for harnessing the power of dynamic knowledge principles for competitive advantage in our current, technology-driven, and socially connected world. As discussed in Chapter 11, these phenomena have both technical (esp. involving information technology) and non-technical (esp. involving people and organizations) aspects, which come together, through the process, for productive and goal-oriented action. Indeed, the process is where the socio and the technical parts come together: how people in organizations employ technologies to perform goal-oriented activities. Because the process provides an action-focused interface between fast-moving technologies and comparatively slow-moving people and organizations, it governs the proliferation and change of emerging phenomena. As such, technologically enabled, organizational, knowledge, and work processes in particular are key to leveraging emerging phenomena for competitive advantage. In this chapter, the authors employ familiar principles for understanding and analysis of virtual worlds as emerging knowledge phenomena.

VIRTUAL ENVIRONMENT

Virtual environment as a term has expanded markedly over the years as progressively greater computational speed and power have enabled the development of exponentially advanced, immersive and engaging interfaces and experiences. Indeed, some virtual worlds today enable users to sense social presence, co-presence, psychological engrossment and affective experience reminiscent of direct, physical and face-to-face (F2F) interaction on multiple levels (Short, 1976; Witmer, 1998).

Not all virtual environments possess these characteristics, however. Indeed, it is useful to make an operational contrast between virtual worlds and virtual environments. When using the term virtual world, we refer to the kinds of immersive, psychologically engrossing, computer-mediated environments that participants experience with

DOI: 10.4018/978-1-4666-4727-5.ch013

affect characteristic of F2F interactions in the real world. Alternatively, when using the term virtual environment, we refer to any technology enabled application. Clearly virtual world is a subset of virtual environment, as are emailing, texting, social networking, microblogging, and the kinds of other social media applications discussed in the next chapter. Further, virtual environments are enabled and supported by Cyberspace infrastructure; they are used increasingly via cloud computing; and many would say that one is inside Cyberspace whenever using a virtual environment. Hence we see how many of the knowledge phenomena emerging currently are interrelated tightly.

This tight interrelation helps to illustrate the breadth of virtual environments as viewed through the infrastructural lens from above, and such lens focuses principally upon technological phenomena. Because the virtual environment exists solely within IT systems and artifacts, its enabling technological infrastructure changes quickly and frequently. Scientists discover continually new materials, architectures, algorithms and mechanics that enable faster, more powerful and more engaging computational and interface effects. Engineers then follow quickly to apply the underlying knowledge to design, test and field innovative devices and systems that put such effects into practice. In this respect, despite the considerable current attention being drawn to virtual environments, not much is new. Virtual environments represent another metaphorical step forward along a long path of technological advance. We've understood this for several decades. From a purely infrastructural perspective, even as an emerging knowledge phenomenon, virtual environments are neither new nor particularly interesting.

Alternatively, the people and organizations using virtual environments within a socio-technical context change comparatively slowly. Virtual environments may exist solely within IT systems and artifacts, but the phenomenon is important and emerging because people are able to accomplish knowledge and work processes in ways never possible before, in addition to wholly novel process capabilities that are possible only within virtual environments. The enabling technology may change very rapidly, but it's not until such technology is put to novel and productive uses that the emerging knowledge phenomenon virtual environment appears to be new or interesting. Moreover, because the virtual world represents a relatively extreme manifestation of virtual environment—one being put to exceptionally novel and productive uses today—we examine it more closely in this chapter.

Virtual World

Drawing heavily from Nissen and Bergin (2013), the term virtual world means many things to many people, and there is little general agreement regarding what constitutes, much less defines, a virtual world. Some see virtual worlds in the background, for instance, reflecting little or no difference with commonplace technology applications (Lehdonvirta, 2010; McLennan, 2008; Porter, 1997; Sicart, 2010) via virtual environments. Others, as a contrasting instance, view virtual worlds in the foreground, as unique and distinct from the real world (Chidambaram & Zigurs, 2001; Ellaway & Topps, 2010). Blending and balancing these views (Castronova, 2005; Lehdonvirta, 2010; Wankel & Malleck, 2010; Yee, 2006b), we see virtual worlds through a middle ground lens: as computer-mediated environments that participants perceive to be distinct from the real world, but that immerse users affectively in such environments, and that exhibit spillover effects (e.g., cultural, economic, perceptual, social) between the real and virtual worlds.

For instance, organizations are spawning wholly within in virtual worlds (Chidambaram & Zigurs, 2001). Here the organization and its environment exist solely within technological artifacts (Castronova, 2005), within Cyberspace. More than simply metaphor for organization (Morgan, 1997; Morgan, 2006), organizational environment and technology meld into one, confluent experience that blurs the line between what we consider real and virtual (Castronova, 2005; Lehdonvirta, 2010; Wankel & Malleck, 2010; Yee, 2006b). For instance, teams and organizations within such virtual worlds are real in the sense that collectivities of people band together to accomplish (at least partially) shared goals (Scott, 1995), but they are virtual in the sense that they have no presence or counterparts outside of their graphically rendered environments. They are real in the sense that participating people perceive them as functioning teams and organizations, subject to structuration (Giddens, 1984), "… as socially constructed entities, with various aspects of organizational life being negotiated through organizational policies and through everyday interaction among individuals" (Chidambaram & Zigurs, 2001, p. 134), but they are virtual in the sense that such teams, organizations, policies and interactions take place only within technology enabled virtual worlds.

Further, many serious organizations (e.g., marketing, architecture, real estate) are emerging within virtual worlds (Oravec, 2001), and the "population" (Wankel & Malleck, 2010, p. 2) and per capita "gross domestic product" (Castronova, 2005, p. 19) in some virtual worlds exceed those of major nations across Europe, Asia and elsewhere. Also, virtual worlds have few physical constraints (e.g., teleportation is a common mode of transportation; death is inconvenient but temporary; altering one's appearance unrecognizably requires only a few mouse clicks) on what organizations can accomplish (Teigland, 2010), and "money" within many virtual worlds is traded continuously via active (albeit mostly underground) markets with ready exchange rates to major real world currencies (e.g., US dollars).

Moreover, advances in graphics technology and cinematic engagement enable unparalleled levels of immersiveness that can induce sustained psychological engrossment in virtual worlds (Ellaway & Topps, 2010). More than computers as theater (Laurel, 1991), users in many virtual worlds write and enact their own scripts, constitute the audience as well as the cast, and come to think of computational representations of themselves (e.g., via computer avatars) in emotional and personally identifiable ways (Castronova, 2005; Yee, 2006b). As one of several, multiple realities (Schutz, 1971) or frames of experience (Goffman, 1974), a virtual world has meaning to its inhabitants (Fine, 1983, p. 217), as the real world does.

Indeed, time investments made by people in some virtual worlds are comparable to or exceed those in real world organizations. For instance, tens of millions of people spend 20 – 30 hours a week (i.e., equivalent to part-time employment) in virtual worlds (Yee, 2006a), and these are not just kids playing video games after school; virtual worlds are inhabited by people of all ages, with the average participant's age estimated between 27 and 31 (Castronova, 2005; Chidambaram & Zigurs, 2001; Yee, 2006a) but reflecting considerable variation (e.g., including grandchildren and grandparents alike). Plus, emotional commitments to organizations in virtual worlds can exceed those associated with physical organizations in the real world. For several instances: roughly 20% of participants in one survey report a virtual world as their "real world" (Castronova, 2005, p. 2); nearly a third of participants in another survey report that experiences in virtual worlds are more rewarding, satisfying and frustrating than counterparts in the real world are; and nearly half report that participation in virtual worlds improves their real world leadership skills (Yee, 2006a, pp. 322-323). Many participants characterize time spent in virtual worlds "as a second job," and for some, participation in virtual worlds is "more stressful and demanding than their actual jobs" (Yee, 2006b, pp. 69-70).

This has real economic and organizational consequences. Quite distinct from most organizations in the physical world, which must pay employees (handsomely often) to participate, people in such virtual worlds pay real money voluntarily for the privilege of engaging in them. Beyond just fantasy worlds (Fine, 1983) or unproductive environments—like the mythical islands of lotus eaters encountered by Odysseus (Homer, 2008)—virtual worlds have many attributes that make them real, and serious organizations emerging within them merit serious examination (Baym, 2000).

Virtual World Instance

To provide greater insight, here we draw from continuing ethnographic work (Nissen, 2010a) and describe one very popular virtual world instance to provide more detailed insight into this class of social media applications: SecondLife (SL). SL claims a population of roughly 20 million inhabitants (Linden Labs, 2010) and appears to be the most popular virtual world social media application; hence it enjoys broad usage and provides good general insight into immersive virtual worlds for this discussion.

SL is a persistent, massively multi-user, virtual social world that is rendered in three dimensions with motion and that permits users to represent themselves within such world via computer avatars. Users are able to create and dress relatively elaborate avatars to resemble nearly any humanoid, move them freely throughout the environment, and use them to interact with other users via their corresponding avatars. Most people create avatars that resemble themselves in appearance, and they come to identify personally with their avatars, referring to them in first-person (e.g., "I went to the mall yesterday."), for instance (Castronova, 2005; Yee, 2006b).

The SL virtual world as visualized from the perspective of a user's avatar is immense: very many orders of magnitude greater than what can be "seen" through any one avatar's eyes at one time (e.g., equivalent to land extending well beyond the horizon). In terms of geography, this world is comprised of myriad "islands," which can be reached by flying (e.g., avatars can fly, run, walk, stand and sit) or more commonly teleporting (e.g., one can input the map coordinates of a destination and travel there instantaneously).

Once at a destination, users can maneuver their avatars through 3D virtual renderings of buildings, streets, malls, buses, rivers, lakes, oceans, skies, fields, mountains, valleys and like representations of artifacts common in the real world. Users can move and look around in all directions within this virtual world; they see their avatar and those of other users within a viewing distance and perspective that looks very similar to what we experience daily in the real world. Most artifacts within this virtual world resemble equivalent artifacts in the real world, and many artifact builders seek to replicate the real world closely.

As with most popular virtual environments, users communicate principally through text chat, and one can incorporate links to webpages, images, music, videos, social media applications and other online resources outside of SL. Indeed, one can use most popular social media applications, for instance, from within SL. In this sense it can be viewed as subsuming many other such applications. It is also straightforward to overlay voice communication (e.g., VOIP) on top of these other modalities, and SL avatars come with a rich set of emotive actions (e.g., laughing, shrugging, yawning) and body language (e.g., turning one avatar's back to another's, walking away, standing closely during a conversation). Hence this is a very media-rich application (Daft & Lengel, 1986), and the sensations of presence and copresence develop readily when immersed within this virtual world and interacting with other users through such rich, multiple communication modes.

The sensations of presence and copresence can be compelling in this virtual world. One is aware of course that the world is virtual and that interaction with other people via avatars is not the same as F2F conversation, but the rich, immersive, 3D experience is psychologically convincing and engrossing on several levels. Being able simultaneously to view avatars that look like recognizable people in the real world, move at will to interact via avatar with different users, engage in conversations via voice and text, express emotions via avatar body language, travel with others through the virtual world, participate in group activities, and experience jointly in-world multimedia interactions (e.g., including social networking and online video) creates convincing sensations of presence and copresence (Nissen, 2010a).

Like many virtual worlds, SL is persistent, and as a massive multiplayer online environment it enables interaction between millions of users. Buildings, yards, malls, pools, streets, fire hydrants, rivers, buses and like virtual world artifacts are rendered equivalently to all users (i.e., every user, from every computer, and in every location around the real world visualizes the same artifacts in the same way) and available to all users at all times, whether or not any particular user is logged on and accessing the environment or not. Each user is able to change his or her avatar at will, so the corresponding user's avatar will appear differently to others, but the shared, graphically rendered environment inhabited by avatars does not change as a result. Such persistence and massive interaction serve to differentiate SL and like virtual worlds from most console, single-player and like games and environments that are instantiated and viewable only when a particular user is engaged; persistence along these lines—albeit via much richer and more immersive 3D virtual environment—is similar to the manner in which the content of a social networking application (e.g., Facebook) remains online and can be viewed the same way by myriad users regardless of whether the author or any particular viewer of such content is online or not.

Although persistent, such environment is dynamic, however. For instance, users have the ability to purchase and build upon "land" on one or more "islands" (i.e., with real world currency such as US Dollars; although basic access to SL is free, some more advanced capabilities such as buying land require real world money to be spent outside of the virtual world.) and build artifacts such as those listed above. If a particular user views an open field on a Friday, and a different user constructs a building in that area over the weekend, then the former user will see a building in that field when he or she returns to the environment on Monday. Hence this virtual world is persistent yet dynamic.

Further, there can be considerable spillover between the SL virtual world and the physical world, spillover which enables SL to effectively subsume many popular virtual environment applications. Indeed, we set up an SL account, purchase virtual land, construct virtual buildings, and create virtual tables, chairs, computer monitors, white boards, projection screens and like appurtenances common to office and classroom environments in the physical world. Within these virtual world creations, user avatars can enter, move around in, and move between such buildings, and within any particular room, one's avatar can sit in chairs, view common content on white boards (e.g., user-written notes) and projection screens (e.g., online content from outside SL). Moreover, one can even use the virtual computer monitors to access, in-world, the same social networking, microblogging, collaborative projects and like social media applications available in the physical world[1]. Thus, our SL virtual world instance embeds common social media applications within an immersive 3D experience that induces affective engrossment through immersive presence and copresence.

APPLIED PRINCIPLES

To consider the emerging virtual world phenomena further, we select five particularly relevant theoretical principles from Part I of the book to guide our understanding. These are the same five principles discussed in Chapter 11 above, which we use to focus on dynamic knowledge principles and elaborate the corresponding approach to harnessing their power for competitive advantage. By using these same five principles, we reinforce both their power and versatility, illustrating in this case how they apply well to virtual worlds knowledge.

Principle 1: Knowledge is distinct from information in enabling competitive advantage. The key to harnessing this principle centers on delineating the critical path and linking knowledge—through action and performance—to the competitive strategy selected by organizational leaders and managers. One can start anywhere along such path and work in either or both directions, but in the case of virtual worlds, most organizations will likely find it best to start with knowledge of how to work within virtual worlds. Although the "population" of such worlds continues to grow, it remains very small with respect to that of people in real world organizations. Until one understands what can be accomplished within them, it is difficult to envision how they may be leveraged for competitive advantage.

For instance, one needs to become accustomed to participating and interacting with others through in-world avatars. This is similar in some respects to interacting with colleagues, coworkers and clients via email, or interacting with friends, family and others via social networking sites, in that interactions are constrained by the communication media available. With email, for example, interactions are asynchronous, and communication is limited principally to text (e.g., with opportunities to attach files, embed images and insert links to other resources). Most interactions via social networking sites, as another example, are asynchronous also, and communication is likewise limited principally to text (accompanied by images and links to videos and like resources). However, the sites themselves enable considerably broader information access (e.g., with sufficient permissions, one can see other people's pictures, read about their lives, hobbies and activities, access their networks of 'friends' connected through the site, and see a persistent accumulation of many postings over time), so one may be able to get a greater sense of knowing someone through site interaction than through email exchange solely, particularly for people who do not know one another well already. Indeed, social networking sites enable people to find and meet one another virtually, whereas one must generally discover someone's email address through some means beyond the email system itself.

Consistent with these examples, a great part of communication within virtual worlds is accomplished textually as well, but (generally) interactions within such virtual environment tend to be more synchronous than those accomplished through email and social networking sites. Hence virtual world textual interactions tend to be more like cell phone texting in this respect. Further consistent with the social networking example, virtual world interactions come with visual images of other participants, but (generally) virtual world visualization is dynamic and in 3D through controllable avatars, as opposed to generally static photos and other images that provide considerable grist for social networking sites.

Moreover, in addition to looking at other people's avatars (and vice versa), two or more people can move their avatars together to look at and interact with other aspects of the virtual world, seeing and experiencing the same sites and events jointly, from the same perspective, at the same time, and in the same way. This is much more like interacting with another person F2F, and it carries a more encompassing—and potentially confusing—set of cultural expectations. In some respects, via avatar communication and interaction, two or more participants may be expected culturally to respect boundaries and customs similar to those accepted broadly for real world interactions. However, without physical boundaries, barriers or risks associated with real world interaction, many such boundaries and customs appear (generally) to be relaxed within virtual worlds. This requires time and experience for most people to learn simply how to interact and communicate with others in-world.

Plus, there's voice in many virtual worlds. As with the telephone, for example, in-world voice communications are synchronous generally (cf. exchanging voice mail messages), but virtual world participants can see directly that intended recipients of voice communications are "home" (e.g., their avatars are online and 'awake'). More like a VTC, Skype or like multimedia conversation, participants can see and talk to one another at the same time, but unlike such multimedia conversation, many in-world interactions can occur randomly and without advance planning. Indeed, one need not perform any planning or setup before seeing and speaking with another participant, as they may simply encounter one another's avatars in sufficiently close proximity to encourage and enable a conversation. This is much more like encountering and interacting with people via F2F in an office, mall or party setting than making a (visual or not) phone call. Hence communications and interactions within virtual worlds tend to be richer and to involve many simultaneous media, stimuli and cues, and knowledge of how to communicate and interact effectively within such worlds is important for all users to develop. This knowledge can be taught in part, but as with F2F conversation and interaction in the real world, most is acquired informally through experience and experimentation (i.e., OJT).

This begins to hint at a somewhat different (or at least complementary) skill set for people who will be expected to leverage virtual worlds for competitive advantage. They must be capable of communicating and interacting effectively in-world, and as in the real world, their behaviors must adjust to different situations (e.g., speaking with organizational subordinates vs. seeking to sell some product or service vs. introducing oneself to and getting to know another participant). Since most if not all communications and interactions occur within virtual worlds, participants need to be comfortable spending time within them, and they must be capable of performing required in-world actions effectively. This brings us to the next step along the knowledge flow sequence: knowledge enabled actions.

Many actions that can be accomplished within virtual worlds are straightforward proxies for their real world counterparts. Where someone needs to have an effective business conversation with an important client in a virtual office, for instance, this can be accomplished—albeit via avatar and with multiple communication modes—using techniques very similar to those that one would employ F2F (e.g., sitting around a virtual table, viewing presentation slides on a virtual screen, taking turns talking). Likewise where an organization has a sales representative attending to a virtual representation of a store within a virtual world, as another instance, such representative can interact with and try to sell products and services to potential customers—again, albeit via avatar and with multiple communication modes—using techniques very similar to those that one would employ F2F (e.g., approaching with, "Can I help you to find something?").

Alternatively, the virtual office needs to be designed and built, as does the virtual store, using entirely different skills and techniques for architecture and construction than are required in the real world. Yet virtual world designers and builders work generally in the real world, not in-world, and their design and building actions require very different knowledge (e.g., computer programming, human-computer interface, presence) than is needed typically for real world architecture and construction (e.g., drafting, building codes, laying tile). Hence as above we find a somewhat different skill set required for people who will be expected to leverage virtual worlds for competitive advantage.

Further, even within seemingly familiar settings (e.g., inside virtual offices and stores), one needs to understand how immersion within a dynamic 3D virtual world affects the strategies, tactics and actions that are effective in the real world. Given the sensations of presence, copresence and emotional engrossment reported by many virtual world participants, one would think initially that all of the same real world strategies, tactics and actions would be equally appropriate in corresponding virtual worlds. However, most virtual worlds do not support tactile interactions (e.g., a sincere look into another person's eye, a firm handshake, touching a product) well. To the extent that tactile interactions are important, one or more proxies must be found; that is, new knowledge is required to enable new actions to replace, mediate or obviate those that are infeasible within virtual environments.

Consider the world's oldest profession, for instance. Regardless of how attractive, witty, attentive and desirable a seller's avatar may be to a potential client, or how reasonable the fees for services may be set, or how visually and aurally realistic and compelling dynamic 3D in-world interactions may be accomplished, without tactile interaction, the client is unlikely to have a service experience that is considered to be as "effective" in a virtual world as in the real world. This brings us to the next level along the knowledge flow sequence: knowledge enabled performance.

Indeed, few potential virtual world clients are likely to consider service performance in terms of the world's oldest profession to be comparable to that achievable in the real world. This is not to imply that a profitable market for such virtual world services cannot be developed, captured and sustained; rather, it could probably not compete on a head-to-head basis with the same services performed in the real world. Appropriate knowledge enables desired actions, and desired actions drive capable performance, but such performance is inadequate in many circumstances to compete with that achievable via people, organizations and processes in the real world.

Alternatively, performance driven by other knowledge enabled actions in virtual worlds may be superior to those achievable via people, organizations and processes in the real world. Consider, for instance, where a potential client or customer desires to customize some new product, but that such client or customer is unsure of exactly how he or she wishes to customize it (e.g., a great many iterations may be required), and that repeated customization of the product in the real world would be prohibitively time-consuming or expensive (e.g., a novel design for a car, house or nanobot machine).

Notwithstanding the widespread availability of artists' sketches, scale models, computer diagrams and like objects, interactions with such objects would not be the same as sitting inside each of a potentially long series of new car design alternatives, walking down the staircase inside each of a potentially long series of new house alternatives, or observing directly mechanical interactions between the physical components inside each of each of a potentially long series of new machine design alternatives. Were such a potential client or customer able instead to immerse him or herself within a suitably convincing virtual world representation of that new car, house or nanobot, however, and able to customize the design quickly and iteratively with the push of a key or click of the mouse, the corresponding virtual world performance in terms of customer satisfaction and purchase likelihood may exceed that of its real world process counterpart many fold.

Imagine, for instance, being able to "see" and "move" through an adversary's computer network from within it, looking for exploitable vulnerabilities, and potentially even using avatars to plant logic bombs, install eves dropping devices, and undertake like offensive and exploitative actions. As above, different knowledge and skill sets—and the actions that they enable—may be required to create, operate and interact through such virtual world representations, but with large performance gains possible, the differential performance may create an opportunity for competitive advantage. This brings us to the final step along the knowledge flow sequence: knowledge enabled competitive advantage.

Performance differences along the lines suggested above could potentially support competitive advantage in terms of either a cost or differentiation strategy. In terms of the former, it may be much, much less costly to iterate product design points repeatedly in a virtual world than in the real world, for instance; hence the implementing organization could potentially sell its design services and products at lower cost than competitors could. In terms of the latter, it may be much, much more compelling for customers to change and experience different product designs directly in a virtual world than to observe artist, architect or computer renderings of such designs in the real world; hence the implementing organization could potentially charge higher prices for its design services and products than competitors could.

Principle 5: Enhancing knowledge flows requires simultaneous attention to people, processes, organizations and technologies. The key to harnessing this principle centers on considering, simultaneously and complementarily, how all four resources (i.e., people, processes, organizations and technologies) can be balanced and integrated to enable the kinds and levels of knowledge to flow from where and when they are to where and when they're needed in order to enable necessary actions (e.g., to drive requisite kinds and levels of performance required to support competitive advantage through a particular strategy). We discuss some aspects of this principle above with reference to the SecondLife virtual world and work to integrate counterterrorism intelligence work.

For more than a decade since the tragic terrorist attacks on the US World Trade Center, Pentagon and elsewhere, considerable, sustained effort has been expended around the world to improve counterterrorism knowledge sharing, analysis and intervention. Not surprisingly, most such effort has focused on technological tools (esp. larger and faster databases, more intuitive and faster search algorithms, tools to fuse and integrate diverse intelligence sources and media). However, following what is viewed broadly as an intelligence failure on a national scale, we also note some recognition that technology alone is insufficient (National Commission on Terrorist Attacks, 2004).

One effort along these lines has sought to identify ways in which virtual environments may help to improve counterterrorism intelligence work, and such effort examines knowledge sharing and work within virtual worlds (Bergin et al., 2010; 2011; Nissen & Bergin, 2013). Toward this end, a sophisticated virtual world is constructed within SecondLife to support the kinds of knowledge and work processes common to counterterrorism intelligence. Analysts work within this immersive virtual world via avatars and interact with other people as well as with virtual systems and tools that are common in the physical world (e.g., intelligence databases, knowledge sharing systems, secure computer networks). Given that analysts working within virtual worlds do not face all of the same constraints as their counterparts in the physical world, this effort examines people's different skill sets, experiments with different organization structures, and analyzes different processes in terms of knowledge and work flows. In short, the effort seeks to view counterterrorism intelligence work as a design effort that can balance people, processes, organizations and technologies (i.e., along the lines of this principle).

Interestingly, people's experience with virtual worlds themselves proves to be important to their counterterrorism intelligence performance. Those with prior experience with immersive virtual worlds appear to carry out their knowledge-based actions very smoothly and quickly, but those with negligible or no prior experience appear instead to be distracted by the interface and disoriented by their immersion within the virtual world. Despite the sophistication of the technology, the skill and experience of people using such technology is critically important.

Also, the knowledge and work processes are set up specifically to encourage and incentivize knowledge sharing and collaboration between analysts, and such team-oriented incentives appear to help obviate the kinds of parochial, stove-piped, knowledge-hoarding activities for which the Intelligence Community is decried broadly. Still, the prior virtual worlds experience noted above has a noticeable effect in terms of people's ability to accomplish the knowledge-enabled actions required for effective performance of the counterterrorism intelligence tasks. Analysts can be observed striving to share knowledge, but some are able to do so considerably better than others are, and with knowledge distributed so broadly across the participants, even one metaphorical weak link is sufficient to impede the effort as a whole. For instance, if even one important aspect of a suspected terrorist plot fails to be shared (e.g., due to the corresponding analyst's preoccupation with and distraction by the virtual world interface), then the plot as a whole may not be anticipated and interrupted in time.

Further, the organization structure is varied greatly from the traditional hierarchy that forms the predominant basis of organizing intelligence work today. For instance, the Edge Organization (Alberts & Hayes, 2003) is examined to assess how its flat, leaderless and open structure compare to intelligence business as usual via hierarchical, centralized and functional organization. As above, people's experience with alternate organization structures appears to have some initial effect on their performance, but such effect appears to be transient; those in the Edge Organization overcome their initial unfamiliarity and uncertainty relatively quickly, and different leaders emerge at different times in ways that encourage prolific knowledge sharing. Indeed, participants in the Edge Organization outperform counterparts in hierarchies consistently and across many different examinations.

In order to balance and integrate people, processes, organizations and technologies in terms of immersive virtual worlds, these examinations point in particular to the people's skills and experiences as critical. Once participants are able to overcome their unfamiliarity with and distraction by the virtual world interface, the complementary processes that encourage knowledge sharing, the complementary organization that enables leadership to emerge, and the complementary virtual environment that supports prolific horizontal knowledge sharing can offer considerable potential to improve performance. With sufficient performance improvement, with respect to adversaries, the Intelligence Community may be able to attain—and possibly even sustain—competitive advantage.

Principle 8: Flows of knowledge require supplementary flows of information, data and signals. The key to harnessing this principle centers on linking and leveraging the bidirectional flows up and down the Knowledge Hierarchy. One can start anywhere along such flows and work in either or both directions. As above, we discuss some aspects of this principle with reference to virtual worlds.

Continuing with the examination discussed above regarding counterterrorism intelligence work, one can see this principle in action. The various intelligence analysts are distributed geographically as a general rule, yet they require fast and reliable access to data and one another via computer network. The signals traveling across networks need to be reliable in order to enable access to various databases, information repositories, explicit knowledge sources and people who possess tacit knowledge. Likewise, the data scattered across different databases need to be intelligible and reliable, so that analysts can understand and have confidence in their veridicality, and such data need to flow and be accessible to analysts at different times and in different locations. Likewise also, the information that arises as people put diverse data into context (e.g., names of various terrorist organizations, locations of suspected targets, movements of known terrorist operators) needs to flow to whichever analysts are working on anticipating the associated terrorist plots. In the end, people need to use their background skill and experience with counterterrorism intelligence—but also to learn from various patterns suggested by the diverse information flowing between them, and to share and build upon one another's partial formulations and incomplete hypotheses—to identify likely terrorist plots. Once identified, the details of such likely plots represent actionable knowledge that can enable a counterterrorist action team to disrupt them. If any set of flows along the Knowledge Hierarchy (i.e., signal, data, information, knowledge) were to fail, slow or become unreliable, then the entire process would likely fail.

Principle 14: Time-critical workflows must wait for enabling knowledge flows to run their course. The key to harnessing this principle centers on evaluating the relative flow rates of specific knowledge and work that is important in an organization, in addition to assessing an organization's knowledge and work stocks. Our discussion above pertaining to analysts' diverse skills and experience levels with immersive virtual worlds exemplifies this principle nicely. When working within the immersive virtual world discussed above, the pace of work processes is very rapid. People are sharing data, information and knowledge in real-time, and time is of the essence: likely terrorist plots have to be identified sufficiently far in advance in order to provide time to be countered. In contrast, an important component of requisite knowledge, namely tacit knowledge of how to work effectively within virtual environments, is comparatively slow to flow. Indeed, observations prove that such tacit knowledge fails to flow sufficiently quickly to enable analysts without prior virtual world experience to perform effectively in-world.

This highlights the importance of personnel selection and training to match the technology used to support knowledge and work processes. If an organization intends to rely upon some technology that is relatively uncommon in the workplace—at the time of this writing, virtual worlds clearly qualify as being relatively uncommon in the workplace—then the organization will need to pay particular attention to the skills and experiences of the people that it recruits and assigns. Indeed, the case could arise in which an existing cadre of people may need to be replaced by others with corresponding technological skills. Of course, this could be disruptive, so people with corresponding technological skills could instead be assigned to supplement the existing cadre of people, but this creates the kind of mixed experience team discussed above, one that could potentially fail due to weak links. Training is an alternative also, but it tends to be relatively expensive, and substantial time can be required for inexperienced people to gain proficiency with immersive work within virtual worlds; most analysts are also unable to work on their counterterrorism tasks while participating in training courses, which distracts them from their fast paced work processes. A simple answer to the question and solution to the problem remains elusive, but understanding the underlying knowledge principle illuminates the key characteristics and highlights alternatives for leaders and managers to consider.

Principle 15: Explicit knowledge flows very quickly and broadly, but its relative power is diluted, whereas tacit knowledge flows comparatively slowly and narrowly, but at high power. The key to harnessing this principle centers on understanding an organization's competitive arena. The observations discussed above regarding experiments with different organization schemes helps to shed metaphorical light on this principle. Explicit knowledge in the counterterrorism intelligence domain can be shared, via the numerous networked information systems, very quickly and broadly. Indeed, once articulated in explicit form and distributed to known network sites, all analysts—all around the world—can access the same explicit knowledge, immediately, with a single mouse click. Nonetheless, knowing simply that one or more particular terrorist organizations has become increasingly active, that one or more particular terrorist leaders have traveled recently, that one or more particular foreign embassies, financial institutions or civilian gathering points are being considered for terrorist attack, or any other, disconnected chunk of explicit knowledge is insufficient generally to identify a likely terrorist attack. In other words, some knowledge-based actions can be taken (e.g., increase monitoring of an organization that is becoming more active; alert airport authorities regarding movements of a traveling terrorist leader; recommend increased security at increasingly likely targets) on the basis of each disconnected knowledge chunk, but the larger goal of disrupting the terrorist plot as a whole may not be possible without knowledge integration.

Alternatively, an experienced analyst, who has accumulated tacit knowledge over many years, may be able to synthesize various chunks of knowledge into one or more coherent plans likely to be considered by a particular terrorist organization at a particular time and place. Such analyst's tacit knowledge may be sufficiently powerful to enable action on the terrorist plot as a whole, whereas the disconnected explicit knowledge noted above appears to lack the same power level. However, not all analysts possess the same experience and tacit knowledge power, nor may the one analyst be able to teach or otherwise share his or her tacit knowledge effectively with others within the time required to identify a particular plot. Nonetheless, over considerable time, other analysts can indeed learn from the experienced analyst—in addition to learning via training, mentoring, trial and error, and other sources—but the flows of such tacit knowledge tend to be relatively narrow (e.g., involving individuals, dyads and small groups of people) and slow (e.g., requiring months, years or even decades). Of course, one can combine the speed and breadth of explicit knowledge flows (e.g., via IT) with the power of their tacit counterparts (e.g., via experienced people), but this principle highlights how both explicit and tacit knowledge flows exhibit distinct and complementary strengths and weaknesses.

REFERENCES

Alberts, D. S., & Hayes, R. E. (2003). *Power to the edge: Command and control in the information age*. Washington, DC: Command and Control Research Program.

Baym, N. K. (2000). *Tune in, log on*. Thousand Oaks, CA: Sage.

Bergin, R. D., Adams, A. A., Andraus, R., Hudgens, B., Lee, J. G. C. Y., & Nissen, M. E. (2010). Command & control in virtual environments: Laboratory experimentation to compare virtual with physical. In Proceedings International Command & Control Research & Technology Symposium. Santa Monica, CA: Academic Press.

Bergin, R. D., Hudgens, B., & Nissen, M. E. (2011). Examining work performance in immersive virtual environments versus face-to-face physical environments through laboratory experimentation. In Proceedings Hawaii International Conference on System Sciences. Koloa, HI: IEEE.

Castronova, E. (2005). *Synthetic worlds: The business and culture of online games*. Chicago, IL: University of Chicago Press.

Chidambaram, L., & Zigurs, I. (Eds.). (2001). *Our virtual world: The transformation of work, play and life via technology*. Hershey, PA: Idea Group.

Daft, R. L., & Lengel, R. H. (1986). Organizational information requirements, media richness and structural design. *Management Science*, *32*(5), 554–571. doi:10.1287/mnsc.32.5.554.

Ellaway, R. H., & Topps, D. (2010). Preparing for practice: Issues in virtual medical education. In Wankel, C., & Malleck, S. (Eds.), *Emerging ethical issues of life in virtual worlds*. Charlotte, NC: Information Age Publishing.

Fine, G. A. (1983). *Shared fantasy: Role-playing games as social worlds*. Chicago, IL: University of Chicago Press.

Giddens, A. (1984). *The constitution of society: Outline of the theory of structuration*. Berkeley, CA: University of California Press.

Goffman, E. (1974). *Frame analysis*. Cambridge, MA: Harvard University Press.

Homer. (2008). *The odyssey. (D. Stevenson* (Butler, S. (Trans. Ed.)). Cambridge, MA: Internet Classics Archive.

Laurel, B. (1991). *Computers as theatre*. Reading, MA: Addison-Wesley.

Lehdonvirta, V. (2010). Virtual worlds don't exist: Questioning the dichotomous approach in MMO studies. Game Studies, 10(1). Retrieved from http://gamestudies.org/1001/articles/lehdonvirta

Linden Labs. (2010). Second life. Retrieved from http://secondlife.com/

McLennan, K. J. (2008). *The virtual world of work: How to gain competitive advantage through the virtual workplace*. Charlotte, NC: Information Age.

Morgan, G. (1997). *Images of organization* (2nd ed.). Thousand Oaks, CA: Sage Publications.

Morgan, G. (2006). Images of organization (updated ed.). Thousand Oaks, CA: Sage Publications.

National Commission on Terrorist Attacks upon the United States. (2004). The 9/11 commission report: Final report of the national commission on terrorist attacks upon the United States. Washington, DC: US Government Printing Office.

Nissen, M. E. (2010). Command and control in virtual environments: Using contingency theory to understand organization in virtual worlds (Technical Report No. NPS-IS-10-005). Monterey, CA: Naval Postgraduate School.

Nissen, M. E., & Bergin, R. D. (2013). Knowledge work through social media applications: Team performance implications of immersive virtual worlds. *Journal of Organizational Computing and Electronic Commerce*, *23*(1-2), 84–109. doi :10.1080/10919392.2013.748612.

Oravec, J. A. (2001). Online recreation and play in organizational life: The internet as virtual contested terrain. In Chidambaram, L., & Zigurs, I. (Eds.), *Our vitual world: The transformation of work, play and life via technology*. Hershey, PA: Idea Group. doi:10.4018/978-1-878289-92-6.ch008.

Porter, D. (1997). *Internet culture*. New York, NY: Routeledge.

Schutz, A. (1971). *Collected papers I: The problem of social reality*. The Hague, The Netherlands: Martinus Nijhoff.

Scott, W. R. (1995). *Institutions and organizations*. Thousand Oaks, CA: Sage.

Short, J. (1976). *The social psychology of telecommunications*. Academic Press.

Sicart, M. (2010). This war is a lie: Ethical implication of massively multiplayer online game design. In Wankel, C., & Malleck, S. (Eds.), *Emerging ethical issues of life in virtual worlds*. Charlotte, NC: Information Age Publishing.

Teigland, R. (2010). What benefits do virtual worlds provide charitable organizations? A case study of peace train--A charitable organization in Second Life. In Wankel, C., & Malleck, S. (Eds.), *Emerging ethical issues of life in virtual worlds*. Charlotte, NC: Information Age Publishing.

Wankel, C., & Malleck, S. (Eds.). (2010). *Emerging ethical issues of life in virtual worlds*. Charlotte, NC: Information Age Publishing.

Witmer, B. G. (1998). Measuring presence in virtual environments: A presence questionnaire. *Presence (Cambridge, Mass.)*, *7*(3), 225–240. doi:10.1162/105474698565686.

Yee, N. (2006a). The demographics, motivations, and derived experiences of users of massively multi-user online graphical environments. *Presence (Cambridge, Mass.)*, *15*(3), 309–329. doi:10.1162/pres.15.3.309.

Yee, N. (2006b). The labor of fun: How video games blur the boundaries of work and play. *Games and Culture*, *1*(1), 68–71. doi:10.1177/1555412005281819.

ENDNOTES

1 Consider, for instance, how someone could use an avatar within SL to enter SL *within SL* and use a more deeply embedded avatar within SL; that is, an avatar within SL could use an avatar within SL within SL, which could in turn use an avatar within SL within SL within SL, and so forth.

Chapter 14
Social Media Knowledge

ABSTRACT

Social media represents emerging phenomena that proliferates through military, government, corporate, and non-profit organizations, as well as tens of millions of households around the world. Politicians, entertainers, revolutionaries, grandparents, and grandchildren alike are all participating in various aspects of the social media phenomena. Understanding how knowledge flows influence and are influenced by these phenomena is important for harnessing the power of dynamic knowledge principles for competitive advantage in our current, technology-driven, and socially connected world. As discussed in Chapter 11, these phenomena have both technical (esp. involving information technology) and non-technical (esp. involving people and organizations) aspects, which come together, through the process, for productive and goal-oriented action. Indeed, the process is where the socio and the technical parts come together: how people in organizations employ technologies to perform goal-oriented activities. Because the process provides an action-focused interface between fast-moving technologies and comparatively slow-moving people and organizations, it governs the proliferation and change of emerging phenomena. As such, technologically enabled, organizational, knowledge, and work processes in particular are key to leveraging emerging phenomena for competitive advantage. In this chapter, the authors employ familiar principles for understanding and analysis of social media as emerging knowledge phenomena.

SOCIAL MEDIA

Social media as a term is relatively new (at the time of this writing). Nonetheless, emerging with Web 2.0 capabilities, predictions suggest that social media will account for nearly half of the roughly $5B market for Web 2.0 products when this book is published (Liebowitz, 2012). Moreover, social media phenomena are being considered actively now in terms of knowledge-based competitive advantage, particularly because the social reach of knowledge is deemed by many to amplify its power in terms of organizational performance (Nonaka, 1994). Indeed, many social media applications extend such reach effectively (Nahapiet & Ghoshal, 1998), and because they facilitate knowledge exchange (Kaplan & Haenlein, 2010) through technological intermediation also, they are expected broadly to improve the performance of organizational work (Becerra-Fernandez & Sabherwal, 2001; Choi, Lee, & Yoo, 2010; Martínez-Moreno, González-Navarro, Zornoza, & Ripoll, 2009; Maznevski & Chudoba, 2000; Montoya, Massey, & Lockwood, 2011; Samarah, Paul, & Tadisina, 2007).

DOI: 10.4018/978-1-4666-4727-5.ch014

Drawing from Nissen and Bergin (2013), for several instances, without central coordination of their activities or interactions, social networking (e.g., Facebook), microblogs (e.g., Twitter) and collaborative projects (e.g., Wikis) enable geographically and temporally distributed people to communicate and collaborate, in near-real-time often (Goel, Junglas, & Ives, 2009; Palen, Hiltz, & Liu, 2007; Sandelowski, 2000); demonstrative and instructional videos (e.g., YouTube) allow unknown (to the content creators) participants to learn by reviewing knowledge-based activities being performed, in addition to reading and hearing explanations about them, all via persistent media; simulation and game technologies that facilitate knowledge transfer (e.g., for training aircraft pilots to fly, for instructing business managers on decision making, for teaching people to play chess and other board games), although not considered by all as "Web 2.0" or "social media" applications per se, enable people to experience directly and practice knowledge work first hand, albeit in synthetic environments; and as we discuss in Chapter 13 above, immersive, 3D environments supporting virtual social (e.g., SecondLife) and game (e.g., World of Warcraft) worlds, which represent social media applications also (Kaplan & Haenlein, 2010), enable users to sense social presence, co-presence, psychological engrossment and affective experience reminiscent of direct, physical and face-to-face (F2F) interaction on multiple levels (Short, 1976; Witmer, 1998).

Because social media applications exist solely within IT systems and artifacts (i.e., Cyberspace), their enabling technological infrastructure changes quickly and frequently. Scientists discover continually new materials, architectures, algorithms and mechanics that enable faster, more powerful and more inclusive and compelling computational and communication effects. Engineers then follow quickly to apply the underlying knowledge to design, test and field innovative devices and systems that put such effects into practice. In this respect, despite the considerable current attention being drawn to social media applications, not much is new. Technology changes quickly and enables consistently novel communication capabilities through such frequent change. Social media applications represent another metaphorical step forward along a long path of technological advance. From a purely infrastructural perspective, even as emerging knowledge phenomena, social media applications are neither new nor particularly interesting.

Alternatively, the people and organizations using social media within a socio-technical context change comparatively slowly. Social media applications may exist solely within IT systems and artifacts, but the phenomena are important and emerging because groups, teams and organizations of people are able to accomplish knowledge and work processes in ways never possible before, in addition to wholly novel process capabilities that are enabled by social media. The enabling technology may change very rapidly, but it's not until such technology is put to novel and productive uses that the emerging knowledge phenomena social media appear to be new or interesting. As a particularly compelling example, the use of social media in support of widespread protest and regime change in the Arab Spring of 2011 is examined more closely in this chapter.

Arab Spring

Although the general discontent of a restive populace had proliferated across North Africa and the Middle East for some time, the widespread protest and regime change fomented in 2011—referred to widely as the Arab Spring—is noted broadly as beginning in December 2010 when a Tunisian man executed an extreme protest through self-immolation (Blight et al., 2012). This act triggered civil disobedience locally, followed by roughly ten days of sometimes violent protest, in a nation where dissent had been comparatively rare but where widespread unemployment had left much of the population without work. Protests spread and intensified, turning increasingly violent and leading to several protestors' deaths, for several weeks afterward. In January 2011 the Tunisian President stepped down from power and fled to Saudi Arabia.

Contemporaneous protests and demonstrations in Algeria, Egypt, Jordan, Lebanon, Palestine and Yemen began also, including a self-immolation in Cairo to protest economic conditions there. The Yemeni President responded to continued protest by vowing to step down from power in 2013 and institute electoral reform. Pursuing a different tactic, the Egyptian Government clashed violently with protestors, but in February the Egyptian President vowed similarly to step down from power. Protestors in Bahrain, Iran, Iraq, Libya, Morocco, Saudi Arabia and Syria joined the ranks soon after, with civil disobedience spreading broadly. The following months passed with violent revolution in Libya that led ultimately to the overthrow of its longtime leader and the formation of a revolutionary government. A year later, protest and demonstration in Syria had progressed to civil war, with the Government using military tanks, helicopters and jets against its populace.

Many people have ascribed an enabling and empowering role to social media in support of the Arab Spring (Norton, 2011; Petit, 2012; Staff, 2012). Social networking, microblogs, online videos and collaborative sites are noted as particularly influential, with each class of application serving its own purpose (Gerkin, 2012). Social networking sites, for instance, provided alternate channels for news regarding events, channels which were not controlled readily by the governments in power and under protest. Moreover, such channels were somewhat exclusive (e.g., involving mostly online "friends"), with filtered content (e.g., including mostly content of specific interest) and frequent updating by myriad "reporters" (e.g., protestors) in the field. Many people felt as though they could place greater trust in information conveyed via social networking than via broadcast or print media. This is not to imply that such information was free from bias or without agenda. Indeed, emergent leaders and promoters of the civil disobedience and protest were able to utilize this alternate channel to communicate their own propaganda. Hence we make no value judgment regarding the bias or veracity of information communicated via social networking; rather, we highlight the capability for comparatively exclusive, filtered and current content provided by many people outside of immediate state control.

Microblogs, as another instance, provided similar capabilities (e.g., comparatively exclusive, filtered and current content provided by many people outside of immediate state control), but via mobile phones that did not require Internet connections. Indeed, people could use such microblogs to find—any particular day and time—where reliable Internet connections could be accessed, where state police and other authorities had been seen, where sympathizers were gathering currently, where safe exits from community squares and like public places could be found in case of police intervention, where people were being jailed, and other tailored, pertinent and timely information. In military terms, microblogs enabled a considerable degree of effective command and control (C2) among dissidents in "leaderless revolutions" (Petit, 2012, p. 25).

Online video, as a third instance, lacked the capability for content exclusivity noted above, and it required relatively high bandwidth Internet connectivity, but like other social media its searchable content could be filtered, kept current and provided by many people outside of immediate state control. Moreover, the video content was conveyed via rich media, through which users could watch and listen to people and events, and through which actionable knowledge (e.g., what to do when tear gas is shot into crowds; see Staff, 2012) could be conveyed. The rich video media could serve to convey much more emotion and urgency than text and static images could, and considerable knowledge can be embedded into an instructional video.

Collaborative sites, to continue, enabled collaboration to occur without regard for time or place. Someone in New York, Frankfurt, Hong Kong or anywhere with an Internet connection and an invitation could participate at any time of day in the population of one or more common websites devoted to an issue. Those people in the midst of chaotic protest and demonstration, for example, could benefit—possibly hours, days or weeks later—from the explicit knowledge shared by others well out of Harm's way. Such knowledge could include revolutionary tactics, motivational approaches, media hacking techniques and like action-oriented content shared via collaborative sites (Norton, 2012).

These social media technologies themselves are not particularly interesting. For several instances, social networking simply links self-selected and like-minded people together via largely static web pages, which enable them to share information via text, image and video; microblogging only links similar people together via very short text messages on mobile phones; online videos just allow interested people to find and view short, homemade movie clips; collaborative sites solely support multiple people contributing content to common websites. Alternatively, the manner in which people with comparatively little official power were able to self-organize, self-synchronize, amass and disperse through coordinated protest and demonstration—that is, how the technology was used to perform knowledge and work processes—was very interesting, and it reveals how competitive power can be leveraged through the emerging social media knowledge phenomena: in this case, such power was sufficient to topple longstanding governments.

APPLIED PRINCIPLES

To consider the emerging social media phenomena further, we select five particularly relevant theoretical principles from Part I of the book to guide our understanding. These are the same five principles discussed in Chapter 11 above, which we use to focus on dynamic knowledge principles and elaborate the corresponding approach to harnessing their power for competitive advantage. By using these same five principles, we reinforce both their power and versatility, illustrating in this case how they apply well to social media knowledge.

Principle 1: Knowledge is distinct from information in enabling competitive advantage. The key to harnessing this principle centers on delineating the critical path and linking knowledge—through action and performance—to the competitive strategy selected by organizational leaders and managers. One can start anywhere along such path and work in either or both directions. In the case of the social media phenomena, for instance, competitive strategy emerging during the Arab Spring centered on massive and highly publicized civil disobedience to exert pressure on unpopular leaders. The corresponding social movements were able to grow rapidly and gain support via positive media attention and demonstrate—to the world, to the leaders, and to their participants—that such leaders had only limited de-facto power. Whether leaders reacted with submission (e.g., in Tunisia), assurance (e.g., in Yemen), violence (e.g., in Egypt) or other responses, protestors were able to defy the leaders, ignore both requests and demands to stop protesting, and reflect to the world a viable alternative to extant rule. This in turn attracted more protestors to the cause, garnered more media attention, and exerted more pressure on embattled leaders to step down. In many of the affected nations, the competitive strategy succeeded, and the revolutionary governments have continued to maintain competitive advantage over the proponents and followers of displaced regimes.

The performance required to effect such competitive advantage centered initially on demonstrating en masse, attracting positive media attention, and both defying and frustrating embattled leaders' wishes and demands. Corresponding knowledge-based actions pertaining to demonstrations involved the publication, recruiting and coordination of mass protests. Movement leaders were emergent, not appointed or elected, and had to organize many thousands of generally unaffiliated people (e.g., sharing little more than general geographical location, political dissatisfaction and economic status). Much of the underlying knowledge is explicit, as civil disobedience and protest are long-practiced approaches to exerting pressure for political reform and regime change, which has been documented abundantly in books, movies, stories and other explicit media.

Every regime, culture and protest is different, however, so abundant tacit knowledge had to be learned, in real-time, during the demonstrations. Emergent leaders had to learn how to motivate and organize masses of people, the vast majority of whom they neither knew personally nor controlled organizationally. Protestors had to learn how to demonstrate together in relative harmony, despite internal differences in culture, ethnic background, political ideology and like dimensions. Each emergent protest organization as a whole had to learn which kinds of activities would attract positive versus negative media attention and hence both popular and (foreign) political support, within its local, situated, and often-unique context. These protest leaders and organizations as a whole had to learn effective means of coordination and demonstration tactics.

Their cause was aided by demonstrating in relative peace, for instance, and avoiding catastrophic casualties in the face of violent opposition. Social media technologies proved to be useful in these regards, as people were able to communicate freely—in advance and in real-time—share intelligence, and synchronize their activities. It is difficult to find textbooks describing the how-to knowledge behind such actions; most of it was learned through direct experience (OJT) with developing and refining processes to integrate technological change with the people and organizations comprising the various individual movements within the broader Arab Region.

Principle 5: Enhancing knowledge flows requires simultaneous attention to people, processes, organizations and technologies. The key to harnessing this principle centers on considering, simultaneously and complementarily, how all four resources (i.e., people, processes, organizations and technologies) can be balanced and integrated to enable the kinds and levels of knowledge to flow from where and when they are to where and when they're needed in order to enable necessary actions (e.g., to drive requisite kinds and levels of performance required to support competitive advantage through a particular strategy). We discuss some aspects of this principle above with reference to the Arab Spring.

We note above how these four resources were all involved in the protests. The social media technologies were clearly useful and enabling, but people had to learn and know how to use them, and in particular, they had to learn and know how to employ them in support of civil disobedience. People had to learn and know how to tolerate and overcome cultural, ethnic, political and economic differences, and they had to believe that their cause was worth protesting—and in many cases even dying—for. Without people willing to protest physically (e.g., filling large public squares beyond capacity, defying orders to disperse, subjecting themselves to arrest, aggression and violence), the underlying technologies (esp. used to convey textual and graphic information via words and images) would likely have little comparative effect.

Similarly, the processes that emerged to organize, coordinate and publicize mass protests required people to utilize technologies without an express organization. Emergent leaders utilized processes to influence people's attitudes and behaviors in ways that contributed toward the revolutionary cause. Separate processes were employed to organize mass demonstrations, coordinate (loosely) the movements and activities of participants, and enable people to obviate, escape and mitigate many of the violent reactions of embattled political leaders. Still different processes were developed to attract and retain positive media attention and to recruit an ever increasing number of participants and outsiders sympathetic to the cause. The corresponding Edge organization (Alberts & Hayes, 2003) proved to be highly agile and effective, relying upon shared goals, political dissent and mutual adjustment to organize people, equip them with compatible technologies, coordinate the processes outlined above, and engage in the actions more generally that produced the desired performance effects leading to competitive advantage and goal attainment. The people, processes, organizations and technologies all came together, in balance and with synergy, to enable the Arab Spring.

Principle 8: Flows of knowledge require supplementary flows of information, data and signals. The key to harnessing this principle centers on linking and leveraging the bidirectional flows up and down the Knowledge Hierarchy. One can start anywhere along such flows and work in either or both directions. As above, we discuss some aspects of this principle with reference to the Arab Spring.

Starting with signals, the social media technologies and underlying infrastructure enabled people to use devices to communicate. Principally mobile telephones, for instance, relied upon common technological standards to send and receive interpretable signals through cell towers and other telephone company equipment. Of course, interpretable is the key term here. Unless one could read Arabic, for instance, even such signals received successfully would likely be ineffective. Hence intelligible data were required to be discernible from the signals.

Likewise with mobile applications like microblogs, for instance, that enabled large numbers of people to follow emergent leaders without such leaders becoming overwhelmed by the associated coordination burden. [in Arabic] "Protest at 4:00 PM." "Police coming from the south." "Television cameras behind the palace." "Regroup at same time and place tomorrow." Even short messages such as these, when distributed instantaneously to many thousands of people sharing a common purpose, could be highly useful in terms of informing people of the emergent leaders' plans and intentions. More than just data that were discernible in Arabic or whichever other, common language, the context of civil disobedience provided such data with meaning to recipients, which enabled emergent leaders to inform large masses of people regarding protest locations, publicity opportunities, violence risks and like aspects of their movements.

Similarly with social networking sites, as another instance, that enabled large numbers of people to communicate via common websites regarding their beliefs, frustrations and plans. A huge amount of information could be exchanged—efficiently and without the risk of public exposure outside the relative privacy and security of people's own homes—so that myriad people could learn about and keep up with events, both as they were being planned and as they unfolded. Videos of previous demonstrations, civil disobedience taking place in other countries and regions, revolutionary propaganda and other cause-serving topics could be distributed quickly and broadly through such sites.

This gets to the knowledge that enabled action. Knowledge of how to employ social media technologies in motivational ways enabled emergent leaders to recruit new participants to their causes. Such knowledge in isolation, however, could not have been put into action (or at least not as quickly, readily or effectively) without the capability for broad, rapid and uncensored information dissemination, which relied fundamentally upon the capability to communicate in common language, which is based in turn on the ability to send and receive electromagnetic signals reliably and without interference. Hence the signals, data, information and knowledge all worked inextricably together to enable the key actions, which drove protestors' performance to levels that enabled (and in many cases have sustained) competitive advantage.

Principle 14: Time-critical workflows must wait for enabling knowledge flows to run their course. The key to harnessing this principle centers on evaluating the relative flow rates of specific knowledge and work that is important in an organization, in addition to assessing an organization's knowledge and work stocks. We note above how much knowledge regarding civil disobedience, protest and demonstration was developed and shared quickly, in real-time often, as people individually and en masse learned largely via OJT what kinds of techniques, tactics and procedures produced comparatively more versus less desirable actions. In some contrast to application of this principle in previous chapters, many aspects of the workflows were not particularly time-critical or rapid. So long as many thousands of people occupied a common public location at roughly the same time, and so long as they remained there for an extended period of time to demonstrate power and determination to the embattled political leaders and onlookers throughout the world, time did not appear to represent a critical performance factor.

Hence knowledge could flow relatively slowly and still keep pace with the workflows. Individual demonstrations would last for many hours and even several days, and protestors would continue their civil disobedience for days, weeks and even months on end. This provided ample time for both tacit and explicit knowledge to develop and flow through the emergent organization. The workflows were also highly visible and relatively easy to understand. Mass gatherings of people in one's town are hard to miss; making signs and yelling slogans to condemn embattled leaders is technologically very simple and straightforward to learn through observation and imitation; reacting to avoid police attacks comes naturally to most people, and observing fellow demonstrators as they get arrested, beaten and even killed serves to accelerate such learning. Patience, persistence and popularity turned out to be key factors in the Arab Spring. The associated workflows are neither rapid nor knowledge-intensive for the masses. Indeed, given the relative spontaneity underlying many activities across the Arab Region during this time, it appears that much of the knowledge flowed contemporaneously with its corresponding work.

Principle 15: Explicit knowledge flows very quickly and broadly, but its relative power is diluted, whereas tacit knowledge flows comparatively slowly and narrowly, but at high power. The key to harnessing this principle centers on understanding an organization's competitive arena. We continue using the Arab Spring for illustration. Explicit knowledge shares many dynamic properties and behaviors with information. Particularly once encoded in digital form, explicit knowledge and information can be shared broadly and rapidly (e.g., around the world in seconds).

Emergent leaders could, for instance, share knowledge pertaining to atrocities committed by embattled leaders with a very broad audience—comprised of potential new recruits and foreign political supporters as well as active participants—which influenced many people to join and continue contributing to a common cause, despite its inherent dangers. They could, as another instance, explain and disseminate plans for specific demonstrations, which would enable participants to understand the purpose and focus of any particular demonstration, and which would enable them to group en masse at intended times and locations. These leaders could further, as a third instance, instruct participants regarding likely reactions of and interventions to be taken by authorities, teach them about civil disobedience in general, and even help them to justify their actions in terms of deep-seeded cultural and religious beliefs, all of which enabled performance-enhancing actions of the social movement organizations as wholes.

Alternatively, explicit knowledge along these lines was highly unlikely to substitute for many aspects of tacit knowledge that contributed toward the people's success through the Arab Spring. Cultural mores are learned very slowly (e.g., over a lifetime), for instance, and are highly resistant to change. When subjected to an apparent conflict between one's deep-seeded cultural beliefs and experiences, for instance, and emergent leaders' rationale for engaging in civil disobedience, explicit knowledge associated with the latter can lose considerable efficacy with respect to its tacit counterpart in the former. Acculturation is a notably very slow knowledge flow, and it represents a key institutional pillar (Nissen, 2007). Techniques to accelerate such flow (Adams et al., 2010) offer promise, but the power of cultural knowledge makes it highly robust to conflicting knowledge and perspectives (e.g., as conveyed explicitly).

Protestors also had to overcome some inherent mistrust toward one another. Far from a single, homogeneous and coherent organization, demonstrations were comprised of many separate factions—often with long-running animosity between them—united principally by dissatisfaction with the current political regime. These people had to learn to trust—or at least work and coexist peacefully with—one another in order for their collective actions to produce the desired performance effects. Trust is a delicate phenomenon (Powley & Nissen, 2012). Notwithstanding near-infinite explicit knowledge shared to explain and encourage participants from diverse groups and factions to trust and work with one another, tacit knowledge—developed slowly and often through small trust-based interactions at first—needed to trust someone comes principally through experience. Once people and their factions learn to trust one another, they can unify, cooperate and take action in huge aggregate, which is critical for social movements. This highlights the power of tacit knowledge in our current context, and the relatively slow, experience-based development of trust also helps to explain why large social movements can require considerable time to amass participants and gather metaphorical momentum. The ultimate results, nonetheless, outpower any knowledge-based actions enabled by explicit knowledge. This helps to explain why patience and persistence are key to the efficacy of nonviolent social movements.

REFERENCES

Adams, A. A., Lee, J. G. C. Y., & Nissen, M. E. (2010). Tacit knowledge flows and institutional theory: Accelerating acculturation. In Proceedings Hawaii International Conference on System Sciences. Koloa, HI: IEEE.

Alberts, D. S., & Hayes, R. E. (2003). *Power to the edge: Command and control in the information age*. Washington, DC: Command and Control Research Program.

Becerra-Fernandez, I., & Sabherwal, R. (2001). Organizational knowledge management: A contingency perspective. *Journal of Management Information Systems*, *18*(1), 23–55.

Blight, G., Pulham, S., & Torpey, P. (2012). Arab spring: An interactive timeline of Middle East protests. The Guardian. Retrieved from http://www.guardian.co.uk

Choi, S. Y., Lee, H., & Yoo, Y. (2010). The impact of information technology and transactive memory systems on knowledge sharing, application, and team performance: A field study. *Management Information Systems Quarterly*, *34*(4), 855–870.

Gerkin, K. (2011). Word of click: Social networking and the Arab spring revolutions. Retrieved from http://www.bad.eserver.org/issues/2011/Word-of-Click.html 02/13/2012

Goel, L., Junglas, I., & Ives, B. (2009). Virtual worlds as platforms for communities of practice. In Sharda, R., Voß, S., & King, W. R. (Eds.), *Knowledge Management and Organizational Learning. New York*. Springer, US. doi:10.1007/978-1-4419-0011-1_12.

Kaplan, A. M., & Haenlein, M. (2010). Users of the world unite! The challenges and opportunities of social media. *Business Horizons*, *53*(1), 59–68. doi:10.1016/j.bushor.2009.09.003.

Liebowitz, J. (2012). *Knowledge management handbook: Collaboration and social networking* (2nd ed.). Boca Raton, FL: CRC Press. doi:10.1201/b12285.

Martínez-Moreno, E., González-Navarro, P., Zornoza, A., & Ripoll, P. (2009). Relationship, task and process conflicts on team performance: The moderating role of communication media. *The International Journal of Conflict Management*, *20*(3), 251–268. doi:10.1108/10444060910974876.

Maznevski, M. L., & Chudoba, K. M. (2000). Bridging space over time: Global virtual team dynamics and effectiveness. *Organization Science*, *11*(5), 473–492. doi:10.1287/orsc.11.5.473.15200.

Montoya, M. M., Massey, A. P., & Lockwood, N. S. (2011). 3D collaborative virtual environments: Exploring the link between collaborative behaviors and team performance. *Decision Sciences*, *42*(2), 451–476. doi:10.1111/j.1540-5915.2011.00318.x.

Nahapiet, J., & Ghoshal, S. (1998). Social capital, intellectual capital, and the organizational advantage. *Academy of Management Review*, *23*(2), 242–266.

Nissen, M. E. (2007). Knowledge management and global cultures: Elucidation through an institutional knowledge-flow perspective. *Knowledge and Process Management*, *14*(3), 211–225. doi:10.1002/kpm.285.

Nissen, M. E., & Bergin, R. D. (2013). Knowledge work through social media applications: Team performance implications of immersive virtual worlds. *Journal of Organizational Computing and Electronic Commerce*, *23*(1-2), 84–109. doi :10.1080/10919392.2013.748612.

Nonaka, I. (1994). A dynamic theory of organizational knowledge creation. *Organization Science*, *5*(1), 14–37. doi:10.1287/orsc.5.1.14.

Norton, Q. (2012, January 11). 2011: The year Anonymous took on cops, dictators and existential dread. Wired.

Palen, L., Hiltz, S. R., & Liu, S. B. (2007). Online forums supporting grassroots in emergency preparedness and response. *Communications of the ACM*, *50*(3), 54–58. doi:10.1145/1226736.1226766.

Petit, B. (2012, April-June). Social media and UW. Special Warfare, 20-28.

Powley, E. H., & Nissen, M. E. (2012). If you can't trust, stick to hierarchy: Structure and trust as contingency factors in threat assessment contexts. *Journal of Homeland Security and Emergency Management*, *9*(1), 1–19. doi:10.1515/1547-7355.1986.

Samarah, I., Paul, S., & Tadisina, S. (2007). Collaboration technology support for knowledge conversion in virtual teams: A theoretical perspective. In Proceedings Hawaii International Conference on System Sciences. IEEE.

Sandelowski, M. (2000). Combining qualitative and quantitative sampling, data collection, and analysis techniques in mixed-method studies. *Research in Nursing & Health*, *23*(3), 246–255. doi:10.1002/1098-240X(200006)23:3<246::AID-NUR9>3.0.CO;2-H PMID:10871540.

Short, J. (1976). *The social psychology of telecommunications*. Academic Press.

Staff. (2012). World development book case study: The role of social networking in the Arab spring. New Internationalist. Retrieved from http://www.newint.org/books/reference/world-development/case-studies/social-networking-in-the-arab-spring/

Witmer, B. G. (1998). Measuring presence in virtual environments: A presence questionnaire. *Presence (Cambridge, Mass.)*, *7*(3), 225–240. doi:10.1162/105474698565686.

Chapter 15
Leadership and Management Implications

ABSTRACT

This final chapter consolidates the learning through the book into a set of implications that are essential for the leaders and managers of today and tomorrow. The authors begin with a summary of the most important key ideas articulated in the book. These ideas are targeted toward leaders and managers for action and attention. A focused agenda of future research along these lines is outlined in turn. This agenda is targeted toward researchers to develop new knowledge that will guide leaders and managers seeking to harness dynamic knowledge principles for competitive advantage in the technology-driven world. They conclude with a concise summary of summaries: sage aphorisms that can be committed to memory, written on index cards, and scrolled across organization social media feeds as a reminder of where to focus time, money, and talent.

MOST IMPORTANT KEY IDEAS

Part I of the book outlines its intellectual basis centering on Knowledge Flow Theory (KFT), which encompasses a large body of research articulating principles of knowledge dynamics to understand and explain how knowledge "moves" through an organization. As understood within such principled rubric, knowledge enables action; action drives performance; and performance supports competitive advantage. Leaders and managers need to focus on knowledge, because it lies on the critical path of organizational action, performance and competitive advantage through the work that it enables.

The first chapter focuses on how the power of dynamic knowledge principles can be harnessed for competitive advantage in the technology-driven world. In it we look at how knowledge enables competitive advantage and discuss the nature of knowledge flows. Succinctly it is difficult to find an organization that is not interested in competitive advantage in today's dynamic, global, highly competitive environment. Many organizations seek to compete still on the basis of traditional economic inputs (e.g., land, labor, capital), but any competitive advantage that can be obtained therethrough is likely to be ephemeral; substitution of such inputs enables imitation by competitors. Likewise with competition based on IT; where others can

DOI: 10.4018/978-1-4666-4727-5.ch015

buy, build and integrate IT similarly, imitation by competitors can ensue readily. Information and explicit knowledge suffer from this same dilemma too; unless they can be kept secret, there is little to prevent imitating competitors from erasing any competitive advantage that may obtain.

Alternatively, tacit knowledge, particularly knowledge that is specific to a particular person, organization, market or domain, is not as susceptible to loss. Gained principally through experience and accumulated over time, personal and organizational capabilities based upon tacit knowledge are difficult to imitate, even if observed directly by competitors. This makes such tacit knowledge highly appropriable, and hence the associated knowledge-based competitive advantage is more likely to be sustainable.

The implication for leaders and managers should be clear. Like hygiene factors (Herzberg et al., 1959), land, labor, capital, IT, information and explicit knowledge are all necessary to compete, but they are unlikely to be sufficient, at least in the long term. Organizations will need to acquire, develop, manage and integrate all of these bases of competition effectively in order to simply not lose in competitive arenas and fall behind competitors, but such bases are not highly appropriable, and imitation will make any competitive advantage that obtains ephemeral. Hence the organization should invest sufficient time, money and talent in these bases to match the performance of competitors, but anything more is likely to be unproductive in terms of competitive advantage. In contrast, leaders and managers should invest all additional time, money and talent in appropriable tacit knowledge—of individual people, cross-functional teams and whole organizational units.

The second chapter focuses on how flows of knowledge differ, importantly, from flows of information and data. Clearly each layer of the Knowledge Hierarchy is important individually. One must have reliable signals in order to manage data proficiently; one must have reliable data in order to manage information proficiently; and one must have reliable information in order to manage knowledge proficiently.

Additionally, it is important to develop and support the knowledge processes for moving vertically, up and down this hierarchy, through what we describe as vertical knowledge flows. Converting signals to data, through information, to knowledge is critical to individual, group and organizational learning, but converting tacit knowledge to information, through data, to signals is equally critical to individual, group and organizational teaching. Moreover, since effective teaching can accelerate effective learning, the value of flows in both directions, up and down the hierarchy, should be clear. Leaders and managers need to invest in vertical flows up and down the Knowledge Hierarchy.

The third chapter focuses phenomenologically on the dynamics of knowledge flows, examining the organizational processes responsible for knowledge flows, their dynamic patterns, and temporal interactions between knowledge flows and workflows. Thinking of knowledge with a Physics lens as having inertia and requiring work for movement is useful. Organizational analogs to mass, friction, energy and like concepts affect how fast and how far knowledge will move, and how much time, money and talent need to be invested in order to effect its movement. Such investments focus on knowledge flow processes, which cause knowledge to move from where and when it is to where and when it's needed. If a knowledge flow process is not performed (or not performed well), then the associated knowledge does not flow (well). Examples of knowledge flow processes include educating, training, researching, contemplating, discussing, mentoring, observing, reading, working via trial and error, and others. In addition to processes associated with flows of work (e.g., marketing, designing, engineering, manufacturing, supporting), leaders and managers need to focus on and invest in processes associated with flows of knowledge. In a great many cases—particularly those associated with the kind of rich, experience-based tacit knowledge offering potential for sustainable competitive advantage—such investments must be made often well in advance of the workflows that they enable.

The fourth chapter surveys several classes of technologies and indicates which kinds of knowledge flows are enabled and supported relatively better and worse by such technologies. We see how Class 1 technologies (e.g., used for organizing, formalizing and sharing knowledge), representing a localized view of KM, play principally a supportive role in the organization, whereas their Class 2 counterparts (e.g., used for creating, applying and refining knowledge), representing an expanded view of KM, play a performative role. It becomes readily apparent that most IT plays a supportive role in KM. Building upon our discussion above, such supportive IT is vitally important; for knowledge to flow well, information, data and signals—all facilitated by supportive IT—must flow well also. Such supportive IT, however, only provides the potential for knowledge to flow; performative IT contributes to knowledge flows directly.

We single out expert system and simulation technologies in particular to exemplify and to help illustrate performative IT. Many expert systems are capable of performing knowledge-based actions as well or better than people can, and many simulation systems enable people, groups and organizations to practice key knowledge-based actions without exposure to the risks and perils inherent in their real-world performance. We discuss this further in Part III of the book (and its corresponding summary in this chapter), but leaders and managers need to invest in both the automation (e.g., via expert, autonomous and robotic systems) and practice of knowledge work (e.g., via simulation), for such automation and practice can enhance knowledge flows via performative IT and help support competitive advantage.

The fifth chapter discusses the concepts knowing, which involves knowledge in action, and learning, which involves knowledge in motion, and the knowledge-based activity doing, which interconnects them tightly and weaves together many of their dynamic interrelations in the organizational context. This discussion differentiates between knowledge stocks or inventories, which offer potential for action, and knowledge flows or applications, which effect action directly. Leaders and managers must put knowledge into action via knowing in order to generate returns on their investments of time, money and talent.

This discussion also highlights reach as a powerful lever for knowledge-based action and performance. Knowing can reach well beyond the knowledge and actions of individuals in an organizational context, and the power of knowledge put to use through action amplifies as organizational reach increases. Coordinated (e.g., via leadership and management) knowledge-based actions of groups, teams, organizations and even larger social aggregations offer huge potential for competitive advantage, for the underlying, aggregate tacit knowledge can make such actions exceptionally difficult for competitors to imitate. This elucidates the critical role of dynamic knowledge in the organization: dynamic knowledge that flows well through the organization contributes directly to appropriability and sustainable competitive advantage. Leaders and managers will find their greatest returns in knowledge flowing dynamically within and between people, groups, organizations and larger social aggregations.

KFT provides the intellectual basis for diagnosis and intervention of problems with dynamic knowledge. Harnessing dynamic knowledge requires understanding flow principles well enough to identify and correct pathologies. Further, it requires anticipating where and when future flow problems are likely to occur, and it depends upon designing work processes, organizations, technologies and personnel systems to address such problems before they become manifest.

The sixth chapter begins Part II of the book, which focuses on practical application of the principles articulated via the chapters from Part I. Chapter 6 focuses in particular on tools and techniques for identifying problems with flows of knowledge and includes a general set of management interventions that apply across several broad classes of organizations. Chapters 7 – 9, respectively, summarize application cases in the business, government and not-for-profit sectors. The key implication for leaders and managers is that dynamic knowledge principles are not just academic theory; they apply to serious organizational work, and they apply broadly across all kinds of organizations, from the family, church and bowling team to multinational corporations, alliances and networks.

The application cases explain further how organizations from across a very wide range of sizes and domains—from the largest corporations and government agencies to the smallest non-profit clubs and groups—both succeed and fail at harnessing dynamic knowledge; hence through case-based reasoning, they provide both positive and negative examples for the leader and manager to use in comparison with his or her own organization. Chapter 10 summarizes 30 principles applied to and 30 leadership mandates induced from knowledge-based practice.

Part III of the book addresses emerging phenomena that provide a current set of challenging issues to address through both theory and application and that help demonstrate further the broad and enduring applicability and utility of our ideas and techniques. Chapter 11 outlines an approach to harnessing the power of dynamic knowledge principles for competitive advantage in our current, technology-driven and socially connected world. We see how technology, particularly information technology, changes rapidly over time; this technical part of harnessing knowledge is thus highly dynamic. Alternatively, people and the organizations they comprise change comparatively very slowly; this socio part of harnessing knowledge is thus relatively static. Yet these socio and technical parts must come together and co-operate in harmony for competitive advantage to be attainable.

The process is where these socio and technical parts come together: how people in organizations employ technologies to perform goal-oriented activities. Because the process provides an action-focused interface between fast-moving technologies and comparatively slow-moving people and organizations, it governs the proliferation and change of emerging phenomena. Hence the process represents an important lens for viewing, understanding and predicting emerging phenomena—whether driven by emerging technologies, non-technological innovation, or both. Thus, the leader and manager need to concentrate on technologically enabled, organizational, knowledge and work processes in particular to leverage emerging phenomena for competitive advantage.

Also in this eleventh chapter we select five particularly relevant theoretical principles from Part I of the book to guide our understanding of emerging knowledge phenomena. This helps both to elucidate important theoretical insights and to guide organizational leaders and managers seeking competitive advantage. Together, we can see emerging knowledge phenomena as continuities as opposed to exceptions, and by focusing on dynamic knowledge principles, we reveal an approach to harnessing their power for competitive advantage. We use this same set of five principles in Chapters 11 – 14 to help discuss and characterize each emerging phenomenon, and we recapitulate them here for reference. If people today must focus on only a subset of the 30 principles and 30 leadership mandates outlined in this book, then these five principles should represent the predominant object of leadership and management attention when seeking to obtain and sustain competitive advantage.

Principle 1: Knowledge is distinct from information in enabling competitive advantage. This first principle is particularly relevant when knowledge and information technologies are driving emerging phenomena in an organizational context. Two different organizations may implement the same, emerging, knowledge or information technologies at the same time, for instance, but outcomes in terms of competitive advantage may vary considerably. Because knowledge enables action, action drives performance, and performance supports competitive advantage, employing one or more technologies to enhance flows of knowledge through an organization would appear to lie on the critical path of guiding emerging knowledge phenomena to support and sustain competitive advantage. The key to harnessing this principle centers on delineating the critical path and linking knowledge—through action and performance—to the competitive strategy selected by organizational leaders and managers. One can start anywhere along such path and work in either or both directions (e.g., forward or backward chaining).

Principle 5: Enhancing knowledge flows requires simultaneous attention to people, processes, organizations and technologies. This principle follows directly from our socio-technical-processual lens noted above, and it complements Principle 1. Two different organizations may achieve one or more of the same innovations individually in terms of people (e.g., via strategic recruiting, education, mentoring), processes (e.g., via radical redesign, tight customer-supplier linkages, load-surging and –shedding redundancies), organizations (e.g., via flexible structure, dynamic reconfiguration, interorganizational collaboration), or technologies (e.g., via emerging applications in Cyberspace, cloud computing, virtual worlds, social media), but outcomes in terms of competitive advantage may vary considerably. Because knowledge lies on the critical path to obtaining and sustaining competitive advantage, an organization's treatment of people, process, organization and technology as an integrated design problem would appear central to leveraging innovation for competitive advantage. The key to harnessing this principle centers on considering, simultaneously and complementarily, how all four resources (i.e., people, processes, organizations and technologies) can be balanced and integrated to enable the appropriate kinds and levels of knowledge to flow from when and where they are to when and where they're needed in order to enable necessary actions (e.g., to drive requisite kinds and levels of performance required to support competitive advantage through a particular strategy).

Principle 8: Flows of knowledge require supplementary flows of information, data and signals. Despite our concentration in this book on flows of knowledge, it is important to remember that other flows are critical too. This is the case in particular where organizational people and processes are distributed geographically and temporally. Signals must flow quickly and reliably in order for data to flow similarly; data must flow quickly and reliably in order for information to flow similarly; information must flow quickly and reliably in order for knowledge to flow similarly; and knowledge must flow quickly and reliably in order support competitive advantage through knowledge-enabled action and performance. Two different organizations may implement one or more of the same emerging technologies, or pursue competitive advantage based on harnessing one or more of the same emerging knowledge phenomena, but outcomes in terms of competitive advantage may vary considerably. Because of tight linkages all along the Knowledge Hierarchy, effective integration and supplementation of dynamic knowledge, information, data and signals would appear central to enhancing knowledge flows for competitive advantage. The key to harnessing this principle centers on linking and leveraging the bidirectional flows up and down the Knowledge Hierarchy. One can start anywhere along such flows and work in either or both directions.

Principle 14: Time-critical workflows must wait for enabling knowledge flows to run their course. This principle accentuates the dynamic nature of knowledge and work as they flow through the organization. This is the case in particular for critical workflows that require quick, precise and thorough activities that can be performed by only knowledgeable people. In most such cases, the enabling knowledge flows are prerequisite to their corresponding workflows. Two different organizations may seek to capitalize upon one or more of the same emerging knowledge phenomena—even implementing one or more of the same innovations regarding people, processes, organizations or technologies—but outcomes in terms of competitive advantage may vary considerably. Because highly competent performance of time-critical activities requires generally that the enabling knowledge become tacit well in advance of performing the corresponding knowledge work, and because many important tacit knowledge flows require substantially more time to complete than their enabled workflows do, allowing for—and even insisting upon—adequate experiential time, mentoring effort, training opportunity, and like knowledge-oriented priorities would appear important for enabling competent action that leverages emerging knowledge phenomena. The key to harnessing this principle centers on evaluating the relative flow rates of specific knowledge and work that is important in an organization, in addition to assessing an organization's knowledge and work stocks.

Principle 15: Explicit knowledge flows very quickly and broadly, but its relative power is diluted, whereas tacit knowledge flows comparatively slowly and narrowly, but at high power. This principle complements those above by differentiating between two, important classes of knowledge flow and by distinguishing them in terms of dynamic flow characteristics. Two different organizations may seek to attain competitive advantage by enhancing either explicit or tacit knowledge flows, but outcomes in terms of competitive advantage may vary considerably. Because the dynamics of knowledge in tacit and explicit forms differ markedly, emphasizing one or the other, at the most appropriate times and on the most appropriate occasions, would appear important for leveraging emerging knowledge phenomena for competitive advantage. The key to harnessing this principle centers on understanding an organization's competitive arena.

Chapter 12 focuses on the dynamics of knowledge associated with the ubiquitous and interconnected networks and computers comprising Cyberspace and enabling cloud computing, which represent emerging phenomena that are commanding tremendous interest and generating immense activity across organizations—corporate, government, military, non-profit and others—today. Understanding how knowledge flows influence and are influenced by these phenomena is important for harnessing the power of dynamic knowledge principles for competitive advantage in our current, technology-driven and socially connected world.

Building upon the approach and principles outlined in Chapter 11 and recapitulated above, we understand how Cyberspace and cloud computing have both technical (esp. involving information technology) and non-technical (esp. involving people and organizations) aspects, which come together, through the process, for productive and goal-oriented action. Indeed, the process is where the socio and the technical parts come together: how people in organizations employ technologies to perform goal-oriented activities. From a purely infrastructural perspective, even as an emerging knowledge phenomenon, neither Cyberspace nor cloud computing is new or particularly interesting.

Alternatively, when one examines either of these emerging phenomena through a broader, socio-technical lens—where people, processes, organizations and technology come together as an integrated whole—it becomes apparent that it's not until Cyberspace, cloud computing or like technology is put to novel and productive uses that the emerging knowledge phenomena appear to become new and interesting. To appreciate, anticipate and react to Cyberspace and cloud computing, leaders and managers should reread the relatively recent histories describing, respectively, the dot-com and client-server phenomena. History tends to repeat itself in socio-technical terms; familiarity breeds understanding, whereas ignorance breeds repetition of mistakes.

Chapter 13 delves more deeply into Cyberspace to examine virtual environments and worlds, which represent emerging phenomena that continue to proliferate through military, government, corporate and non-profit organizations as well as tens of millions of households. In addition to supporting immersive entertainment and online social interaction, virtual worlds are home to myriad serious applications that are changing the way that people think about and work in organizations. Understanding how knowledge flows influence and are influenced by these phenomena is important for harnessing the power of dynamic knowledge principles for competitive advantage in our current, technology-driven and socially connected world.

As above, building upon the approach and principles outlined in Chapter 11 and recapitulated here, we understand how virtual worlds have both technical (esp. involving information technology) and non-technical (esp. involving people and organizations) aspects, which come together, through the process, for productive and goal-oriented action. Indeed, from a purely infrastructural perspective, even as an emerging knowledge phenomenon, neither the virtual environment nor world is new or particularly interesting.

Alternatively, when one examines either of these emerging phenomena through a broader, socio-technical lens—where people, processes, organizations and technology come together as an integrated whole—it becomes apparent that it's not until virtual environments and worlds are put to novel and productive uses that the emerging knowledge phenomena appear to become new and interesting. Virtual worlds in particular witness new organizations spawning wholly within them, organizations that are capable of activities that are impossible or infeasible in the real world and yet have social and economic spillover effects comparable to those of organizational counterparts in the real world.

Moreover, advances in graphics technology and cinematic engagement enable unparalleled levels of immersiveness that can induce sustained psychological engrossment in virtual worlds, making participation in such worlds approach the kinds of presence, copresence and affect associated more broadly with face-to-face social interaction. Virtual world organizations have the potential to incur lower costs for comparable products and especially services offered by competitors, and they have the potential likewise to charge higher prices through extreme product and service differentiation. Leaders and managers should look to this double-positive effect of lower costs and higher prices enabled by virtual worlds in terms of supporting competitive advantage.

Finally, Chapter 14 elaborates on the social media emerging phenomena that continue to proliferate through military, government, corporate and non-profit organizations as well as tens of millions of households around the world. Politicians, entertainers, revolutionaries, grandparents and grandchildren alike are all participating in various aspects of the social media phenomena. Understanding how knowledge flows influence and are influenced by these phenomena is important for harnessing the power of dynamic knowledge principles for competitive advantage in our current, technology-driven and socially connected world.

Building familiarly upon the approach and principles outlined in Chapter 11 and recapitulated here, we understand how social media have both technical (esp. involving information technology) and non-technical (esp. involving people and organizations) aspects, which come together, through the process, for productive and goal-oriented action. Indeed, from a purely infrastructural perspective, even as emerging knowledge phenomena, social media are not new or particularly interesting.

Alternatively, when one examines these emerging phenomena through a broader, socio-technical lens—where people, processes, organizations and technology come together as an integrated whole—it becomes apparent that it's not until social media are put to novel and productive uses that the emerging knowledge phenomena appear to become new and interesting. As a particularly compelling example, the use of social media in support of widespread protest and regime change in the Arab Spring of 2011 is examined more closely in the chapter. Many people have ascribed an enabling and empowering role to social media in support of the Arab Spring, with social networking, microblogs, online videos and collaborative sites noted as particularly influential, and with each class of application serving its own purpose yet integrating together to enable effects nothing short of revolutionary.

Nonetheless, individual, groups and organizations of people must learn to employ social media technologies effectively—via knowledge and work processes—in order to accomplish productive results. This highlights some generational differences and signals a particularly pressing need for dynamic knowledge to flow. In particular, albeit stereotyping, many people (and hence groups and organizations comprised thereof) from younger generations (e.g., Generation Y and Millennials) tend to be much more familiar and comfortable with social media than their counterparts from older generations (e.g., Generation X and Baby Boomers) are. This can establish separate communication and interaction webs in groups and organizations, which can combine and ossify in ways that effectively preclude the most important, tacit knowledge flows from occurring.

The younger generations have much to learn from the rich, tacit experiences of their older counterparts, and the older generations have much to learn from the deft social media habits and culture of their younger counterparts. The young must be willing to learn from the old—in many circumstances even modifying their habits and routines—and the old must be willing similarly to learn from the young—and likewise even modifying their habits and routines in many circumstances. Because most leaders and managers represent the older generations, learning from the young must begin necessarily with them, but they must be willing and patient teachers also.

FUTURE RESEARCH

Through the Knowledge Flow Theory articulated in this book, we can understand the dynamics of knowledge better than at any point in history. More than simple or colorful metaphors, knowledge flows represent important phenomena. Through attribution to the processes responsible for knowledge flows, we can identify and explain increasingly well how knowledge moves through an organization. Through the kind of multidimensional coordinate system illustrated above, we can classify and visualize myriad diverse dynamic knowledge flow trajectories. Through the kinds of knowledge flow propositions developed in these pages, we can understand how the power of dynamic knowledge principles can be harnessed for competitive advantage in the technology-driven world to unprecedented extent.

Additionally, through the kinds of application cases studied here, we can learn from the (positive and negative) experiences of others and examine directly how various knowledge flow principles and management interventions apply and contribute to a diversity of organizations. Through our extension of dynamic knowledge principles to develop guidance for leaders and managers to assess their own organizations, we can translate theory into practice and inform practice with theory. Through the kinds of leadership mandates induced from application, knowledge about knowledge flows can be applied directly. Through knowing what we know about knowledge flows, we can identify important knowledge gaps. Through continued research on knowledge flows, we can seek to discover new interventions to fill such gaps. Through the ongoing research processes of creating, sharing and applying the associated knowledge, we can improve further our ability to understand how the power of dynamic knowledge principles can be harnessed for competitive advantage in the technology-driven world. This final section outlines an agenda for such continued research on knowledge flows.

The agenda outlined here makes no claim of completeness. Space prohibits us from articulating a complete agenda. Such complete agenda will necessarily change through time anyway. Hence what may be complete today will become incomplete tomorrow. Further, so many important deficiencies remain in the field of knowledge science that, as above, space prohibits us also from articulating an agenda of even the most important topics. Such agenda is unlikely to generate agreement from our community of scholars and practitioners as to its content anyway. Hence what may represent our list of most important topics will probably vary from yours.

Instead, the agenda outlined here seeks to articulate the hard problems. It challenges researchers to stop following practitioners around and to stop describing knowledge management as it is practiced today. It exhorts researchers instead to investigate ever more deeply the dynamics of knowledge flows and to extend both theory and practical application through new phenomenological knowledge. It follows the study of dynamic flows in multiple domains of the physical sciences and seeks to understand and model the mechanics of knowledge flows. It follows likewise the engineering of dynamic artifacts in multiple physical domains and seeks to design organizations and processes to enhance knowledge flows. These represent hard problems. Here we ask some of the questions but do not have all of the answers.

First, to re-iterate, researchers need to stop following practitioners around and to stop describing knowledge management as it is practiced today. By most measures—qualitative and quantitative alike—the current practice of KM remains ineffective and uninformed across myriad organizations and industries, despite over two decades (at least) of practice. Learning from failure can provide important lessons, but such provision depends critically upon knowing what causes failure (e.g., preconditions) and learning how it can be prevented. Little of the current KM research even poses research questions along these lines or employs research methods appropriate for answering such questions. Researchers need to depart from description and move toward measurement, explanation and prediction. Descriptive theory is important, but to understand the mechanics of knowledge, one must be able to measure diverse knowledge flows under various conditions and to explain how such mechanics work. To engineer knowledge flows, one must be able to predict the effects of alternate designs, under various conditions and in diverse environments. Little of the current KM research addresses measurement, explanation or prediction.

Explanation requires rich, deep, interpretive research methods to answer research questions posed in terms of "how" and "why," instead of just "what," "who," "where," "how many," and the like. This is the case in particular with tacit knowledge flows, which are necessarily human centric. Researchers need to immerse themselves in operational organizations in the field and to investigate how people as individuals, in groups, in organizations, and in even larger collectivities know and learn. They need to identify and understand the processes responsible for the corresponding knowledge flows. They need to identify and distinguish the contextual factors that affect the efficacy of various knowledge flow processes. They need to build upon one another's research and to compare knowledge dynamics across a breadth of different organizations. They need to develop rich theoretical and computational models of knowledge flows that characterize well the fundamental dynamics of such flows. They need to stop focusing on technologies and flows of data and information. This will require a shift in the research (and practice) foci and methods of most people involved with KM.

Particularly important in this regard is the research topic Knowledge Measurement. Measurement remains a very important topic of current and future knowledge research. This is the case especially in terms of dynamic knowledge. Even measuring static knowledge is sufficiently challenging to defeat most people's and organizations' efforts. Measuring knowledge dynamics is even harder. Most techniques for gauging static knowledge concentrate on examining knowledge stocks. People's education, training and experience levels, for instance, serve as proxies for tacit knowledge, and organizational procedures, knowledge repositories and IT tools provide venues for accessing explicit knowledge. Alternatively, techniques for gauging dynamic knowledge must concentrate instead on examining knowledge flows. We understand that knowledge is distributed unevenly through organizations, and hence must flow quickly and reliably from where and when it is to where and when it's needed in order to support competitive advantage. Important future research will need to focus on knowledge flow processes, particularly those associated with powerful tacit knowledge. Processes such as education, mentoring, socialization, acculturation and even OJT are central to tacit knowledge dynamics. Researchers need to identify and calibrate techniques for measuring dynamic knowledge through these and like processes.

Second, KM researchers need to learn from their counterparts in the physical sciences who have investigated, very successfully, dynamic phenomena for decades and even centuries. Clearly knowledge flows involve people and organizations—not molecules and forces—and are not represented well at present by precise models and mathematical formulae. Nonetheless, several principles from the physical sciences (e.g., inertia) appear to have application to dynamic knowledge flows, and many others (e.g., energy, entropy, density) offer promise as well. Even if such principles remain metaphorical, they can provide insights into the mechanics of knowledge flows. For the many researchers not knowing where to begin a phenomenological investigation of knowledge flows, seeking to falsify metaphorical relations with physical principles in the domain of knowledge dynamics (e.g., identify their applicability, limits breaking points: where the metaphors inform and where they break down) provides a place to start. One may find that some aspects of various principles pertain well to knowledge flows (i.e., among the many that do not) and that such aspects can guide further the investigation.

More importantly, KM researchers have much to learn from their counterparts in the physical sciences in terms of research methods and communicating results. Research in the physical sciences is inherently positivistic, and reductionistic experimentation predominates many fields. Such research is distinct qualitatively from the kinds of interpretive, constructivist field and survey work that is practiced broadly in KM today. Despite this qualitative distinction, however, the two epistemic views and approaches to inquiry are complementary, not conflicting. The positivist can learn from the interpretivist, and vice versa. Experimentation can inform ethnography, and vice versa. Theoretical and computational models can help guide fieldwork, and fieldwork can help inform theory and model development. Hard problems need to be approached across multiple fronts. Understanding how the power of dynamic knowledge principles can be harnessed for competitive advantage in the technology-driven world remains a hard problem, but researchers are concentrated still within just a few, narrow lines of inquiry.

Particularly important in this regard is the research topic Tacit-Explicit Knowledge Power. The dynamics of tacit and explicit knowledge differ in important and understandable ways. Tacit knowledge is powerful but flows slowly and narrowly, whereas explicit knowledge flows quickly and broadly but carries diluted power. Neither is necessarily "better" than the other; rather, they're both complementary and important. Where circumstances call for quick and broad flows, and where the diluted power of explicit knowledge is sufficient, then leaders and managers should place their organizations' emphasis there. Where circumstances call instead for high-power tacit knowledge, and where the knowledge-enabled actions can wait for the correspondingly slow and narrow flows to complete, then leaders and managers should place their organizations' emphasis there. Tacit and explicit knowledge comprise therefore a trade space for leadership and management consideration and decision making. Researchers need to delineate the tacit-explicit trade space and articulate analytic and decision rules to guide leadership and management action.

Third, effective design requires principled knowledge and accurate analysis. Most engineered artifacts benefit from canons of principles developed through the physical sciences. They benefit also from the application of advanced mathematics and more recently of computational methods. Knowledge Flow Theory is nowhere near as complete in terms of principled knowledge as theory from any of the physical sciences is, but it provides an intellectual basis for informed research as well as practical application, and the 5D vector space enables measurement of dynamic knowledge to an unprecedented extent. Knowledge flow principles can be used as propositions for different personnel, work-process, organizational and technological designs, and 5D measurements can be used to test empirically such propositions. This provides an excellent start, but few KM researchers (or practitioners) to date are taking advantage of the growing number of such principles and measurement capabilities.

Although the application of advanced mathematics remains challenging in the domain of knowledge dynamics, and it is doubtful that knowledge flows will ever lend themselves to mathematical representation to the degree that counterpart physical flows (e.g., fluids, heat, electricity, radiation) do, nearly all analytic representations of physical flows employ multidimensional coordinate systems, within which vector mathematics, phase spaces, spectral analyses and like techniques are hugely informative. Elaborating on the 5D measurement capability noted above, knowledge flows can be described, quantified and compared within multidimensional coordinate systems as well. We illustrate this kind of description repeatedly throughout the book—in terms of theory and practice alike. Researchers need to begin applying—theoretically and empirically alike—these and like techniques necessary for representing, manipulating and measuring knowledge flow vectors and trajectories in analytically meaningful ways that can bear down upon design problems in organizations.

The use of computational methods can help. Simulation, for instance, is used in the domain of organization studies today to assess the performance of systems that defy mathematical representation and analysis. Knowledge flows can be represented via computational models (e.g., with POWer), through which dynamic behaviors can be emulated. Computational methods in the physical sciences are employed widely to address problems in which exact, analytical solutions are unobtainable, and many computational methods employ brute processing power and speed to effect iterative-approximation algorithms to approach hard physical problems in dynamics. Researchers need to embrace computational methods—despite their comparatively primitive level of current development in the social sciences—and work to enhance such methods to address hard problems in the domain of knowledge dynamics.

Particularly important in this regard is the research topic Dynamic Knowledge and Organization. Leaders and managers have organized around knowledge from time immemorial—at least where knowledge stocks are concerned. Nearly every organization today has one or more divisions of labor, for instance, based on people's domain or functional knowledge. This is why most organizations group engineers with engineers, accountants with accountants, marketers with marketers and so forth. Even in product, process and matrix organizations, where cross-domain and –functional people work together on common product lines, process bundles and like foci, they tend to cohere based upon knowledge stocks accumulated through education, training and experience. Given the critical importance of knowledge flows, however, one can argue that organizations may serve their stakeholders better by dividing labor according to dynamic as opposed to static knowledge. Such emphasis on flows as opposed to stocks of knowledge will likely make organizations look different than they do today, and such organizations may themselves need to become more dynamic, changing structure and behavior agilely and routinely to both facilitate and correspond with shifting dynamic knowledge needs. How to do this is unclear, but people, processes, organizations and technologies will be involved inevitably. Researchers need to help leaders and managers understand how to address dynamic knowledge and organization.

These represent hard research problems. Addressing them effectively will require considerable change on the part of many KM researchers. Perhaps such change will be too great for the current cadre. Perhaps a new field called Knowledge Science will emerge and carve out a niche left addressed poorly by researchers in Information Science, Computer Science, Organization Science, Cognitive Science, Economics, Strategy and other fields. Such new science will be populated undoubtedly by researchers from the physical sciences, for the agendas and methods are similar, but such new science will need to be populated also by researchers from the social sciences too, for people—in an organizational context—are central to knowledge dynamics. Knowledge Science, whether it emerges as a niche discipline or not, will need to reflect multidisciplinary work. Knowledge is central to everything that we as people do, regardless of discipline; hence its study has a place in every science.

The prospect of knowledge science emerging from the confusion of current KM research is exciting, and the potential of the knowledge developed through such science is awesome. The power to harness knowledge dynamics at quantum new levels awaits. The knowledge required for principled organizational knowing and learning is here today, and we understand better now than ever before in history how the power of dynamic knowledge principles can be harnessed for competitive advantage in the technology-driven world.

Although the representation through this book is explicit—and the authors clearly know more about this than they can tell—it articulates a substantial volume of knowledge about how the power of dynamic knowledge principles can be harnessed for competitive advantage in the technology-driven world. Because knowing and learning are mutually reinforcing, path-dependent processes, leaders and managers who learn the dynamic knowledge principles today—and who apply them to their own organizations—can take a lead over competitors. The more that we know about dynamic knowledge, the faster that we learn about it; and the faster that we learn about dynamic knowledge, the more that we know about it; and so forth, over time. Through knowledge-based competition, such lead may become insurmountable. Hence this book offers a contribution toward, as well as insight into, sustainable competitive advantage based on the power of dynamic knowledge principles in the technology-driven world. This strikes us as highly appropriate for a book on the power of dynamic knowledge principles in the technology-driven world.

SUMMARY OF SUMMARIES

As promised, here we summarize concisely the dozen most important key summaries articulated above, through which we offer sage aphorisms that can be committed to memory, written on index cards and scrolled across organization social media feeds as a reminder of where to focus time, money and talent.

1. Leaders and managers need to focus on knowledge, because it lies on the critical path of organizational action, performance and competitive advantage through the work that it enables.
2. The organization should invest sufficient time, money and talent in these bases to match the performance of competitors but invest all additional time, money and talent in appropriable tacit knowledge.
3. Leaders and managers need to invest in vertical flows up and down the Knowledge Hierarchy.
4. In addition to processes associated with flows of work (e.g., marketing, designing, engineering, manufacturing, supporting), leaders and managers need to focus on and invest in processes associated with flows of knowledge.
5. Leaders and managers need to invest in both the automation (e.g., via expert, autonomous and robotic systems) and practice of knowledge work (e.g., via simulation).
6. Leaders and managers must put knowledge into action via knowing in order to generate returns on their investments of time, money and talent.
7. Leaders and managers will find their greatest returns in knowledge flowing dynamically within and between people, groups, organizations and like social aggregations.
8. The key implication for leaders and managers is that dynamic knowledge principles are not just academic theory; they apply to serious organizational work, and they apply broadly across all kinds of organizations.
9. The leader and manager need to concentrate on technologically enabled, organizational, knowledge and work processes in particular to leverage emerging phenomena for competitive advantage.
10. Leaders and managers should reread the relatively recent history describing, respectively, the dot-com and client-server phenomena.
11. Leaders and managers should look to the double-positive effect of lower costs and higher prices enabled by virtual worlds in terms of supporting competitive advantage.
12. Because most leaders and managers represent the older generations, learning from the young must begin necessarily with them, but they must be willing and patient teachers also.

Organizational leaders and managers are busy people with challenging jobs to do. Hence most of them lack the means to conduct systematic research to examine difficult phenomena such as knowledge dynamics, and they need help from researchers. Drawing from our agenda above, here we recapitulate the three most important future research topics challenging us at present.

1. Researchers need to identify and calibrate techniques for measuring dynamic knowledge.
2. Researchers need to delineate the tacit-explicit trade space and articulate analytic and decision rules to guide leadership and management action.
3. Researchers need to help leaders and managers understand how to address dynamic knowledge and organization.

We have learned much about knowledge flows, particularly about how to harness dynamic knowledge principles for competitive advantage in the technology driven world. The principles, applications and attention to emerging phenomena articulated in this book should prove helpful for organizational leaders and managers with active organizations to guide them through their competitive arenas. Likewise, the knowledge articulated through this book should prove helpful for technological and organizational researchers alike with challenging research agendae to pursue. If we accept that we do not know everything—yet understand that we're not relegated to knowing nothing—and we commit to learning—as individuals, groups and organizations—then our futures are likely to shine brightly with wisdom. If not, then those who do will be the ones to give us orders and trample our organizations competitively. I've made my choice! Now how about you?

REFERENCES

Herzberg, F., Mausner, B., & Snyderman, B. B. (1959). *The motivation to work*. New York, NY: John Wiley.

Appendix

EXPERT SYSTEM RULES

This appendix is included for reference to help the interested reader to see the complete set of rules used to develop the small expert system described in Chapter 4. This appendix includes the whole file in textual form, which should facilitate the reader's understanding of the components that comprise a simple expert system. The interested reader can use this appendix further to build his or her own simple expert system as well.

As a guide, the expert system code below is divided into several parts, which each part beginning with the symbol "%" followed by a short descriptor of its content. For instance, the third line below is, "% folder". This starts the first part, which is the folder section. This particular expert system does not utilize extensively the folder feature of the shell tool.

The second part begins with "% knowledgebase". This is where the problem-solving goal (i.e., "goals = [technology_use]") is expressed, where the main action of the expert system is specified, and where some HTML formatting is accomplished.

The third part begins with "% fact". This is where declarative, factual information is stored. If this expert system had been loaded with pre-existing facts, then such declarative chunks would be included here. Such facts are used in many systems for aspects of the world that remain constant or at least very stable. This particular expert system does not utilize facts. The reason is twofold. First, few aspects of asynchronous instructional tools remain constant, so facts entered in this section would have to be updated frequently. But second and more importantly, this small, simple, illustrative application gathers all of its necessary factual information from users, and it was programmed with many facts "hardwired" into the rules that follow. This does not represent first-class programming practice. But it suffices to development the expert system for demonstration.

The fourth part begins with "% question". This is the part that guides the expert system's interrogative interaction with the user and hence where it acquires factual information to use for inference and decision-making. For instance, the first question, labeled "prompt = text("5. What computer skills do you expect students to have?")," is asking about student computer skills. Notice the program offers a predetermined set of choices, labeled: "choices = ["none", "browsing", "programming"]". Of course alternate approaches can be pursued as well.

The sixth part begins with "% sql". This small, simple, illustrative expert system does not utilize the SQL feature.

The seventh part begins with "% rule_set". This is where procedural, explicit knowledge is stored. The two rules included in the figure discussed in Chapter 4 are taken from this part. This is where the inferential problem solving and decision making logic of the expert system is programmed.

The eighth and ninth parts begin with "% rules_table" and "% data_table", respectively. As noted above in connection with some other parts, this small, simple, illustrative expert system does not utilize these features.

The tenth part begins with "% text". This is where prescripted textual messages are included. As with the questions above, such textual messages are presented interactively with the user.

***

```
knowledgewright_jig(basic, 11).
knowledgewright_license(academic_personal, '[]').
% folder
:- indexed folder(1,0,0).
% knowledgebase
:- indexed knowledgebase(1,0,0).
knowledgebase(main, /, [
description = "Implements part of the Bates & Poole (2003) SECTIONS Model for
selecting and using education technology.",
goals = [technology_use],
date_format = 'm/d/y',
odbc = "",
charset = "",
question_separator = "<P>",
menu_separator = "<BR>",
value_separator = "<P>",
question_top = text("<HTML><HEAD></HEAD><BODY><FORM METHOD=""POST"" ACTION=""/
cgi-bin/kwcgibasic.exe" + system(cgi_parameters) + """>"),
question_bottom = text("<P><INPUT NAME=""Submit"" TYPE=""Submit""
VALUE=""Submit""></INPUT> <INPUT TYPE=""Reset"" VALUE=""Reset""></INPUT></
FORM></BODY></HTML>"),
output_top = text("<HTML><HEAD></HEAD><BODY>"),
output_continue = text("<FORM METHOD=""POST"" ACTION=""/cgi-bin/kwcgibasic.
exe" + system(cgi_parameters) + """><INPUT NAME=""Submit"" TYPE=""Submit""
VALUE=""Continue""></INPUT></FORM>"),
output_bottom = text("</BODY></HTML>")
]).
% fact
:- indexed fact(1,0,0).
% question
:- indexed question(1,0,0).
question(student_skills, /, [
prompt = text("5. What computer skills do you expect students to have?"),
question_type = menu_single_choice,
question_style = listbox,
choices = ["none", "browsing", "programming"],
```

```
'rule-display_choices' = [["rule_text", "display_text"]],
answer_type = text,
length = 20,
height = 1,
default = "",
ask_also = '[]'
]).
question(student_priorDL, /, [
prompt = text("7. What prior approaches to learning are students likely to
have?"),
question_type = menu_single_choice,
question_style = listbox,
choices = ["classroom only", "classroom and VTE", "classroom and media",
"classroom and webbased"],
'rule-display_choices' = [["rule_text", "display_text"]],
answer_type = text,
length = 20,
height = 1,
default = "",
ask_also = '[]'
]).
question(student_demographics, /, [
prompt = text("2. What are the likely demographics of the students you will be
teaching?"),
question_type = menu_single_choice,
question_style = listbox,
choices = ["resident students", "professionals ashore", "officers at sea"],
'rule-display_choices' = [["rule_text", "display_text"]],
answer_type = text,
length = 20,
height = 1,
default = "",
ask_also = '[]'
]).
question(equipment_cost, /, [
prompt = text("6. Will students be able to justify the marginal cost of tech-
nology required for the course?"),
question_type = menu_single_choice,
question_style = listbox,
choices = ["no", "yes"],
'rule-display_choices' = [["rule_text", "display_text"]],
answer_type = text,
length = 20,
```

```
height = 1,
default = "",
ask_also = '[]'
]).
question(student_access, /, [
prompt = text("3. To which technologies are students likely to have regular
access?"),
question_type = menu_single_choice,
question_style = listbox,
choices = ["T1+", "DSL or cable", "modem", "other", "none"],
'rule-display_choices' = [["rule_text", "display_text"]],
answer_type = text,
length = 20,
height = 1,
default = "",
ask_also = '[]'
]).
% sql
:- indexed sql(1,0,0).
% rule_set
:- indexed rule_set(1,0,0).
rule_set(access, /, [
description = "",
type = single_value,
rules = [[conditions, value], [student_access = "modem", text("low band-
width")], [student_access = "DSL or cable", text("high bandwidth")], [student_
access = "T1+", text("high bandwidth")], [student_access = "other", text("low
bandwidth")], [student_access = "none", text("no bandwidth")]]
]).
rule_set(cost, /, [
description = "",
type = single_value,
rules = [[conditions, value], [equipment_cost = "no", text("not cost-effec-
tive")], [equipment_cost = "yes", text("cost-effective")]]
]).
rule_set(feasible, /, [
description = "",
type = single_value,
rules = [[conditions, value], [cost = "not cost-effective",
text("infeasible")], [access = "low bandwidth" and cost = "cost-effective",
text("feasible")], [access = "high bandwidth" and cost = "cost-effective",
text("feasible")], [access = "no bandwidth" and cost = "cost-effective",
text("feasible")]]
```

```
]).
rule_set(technology, /, [
description = "",
type = single_value,
rules = [[conditions, value], [feasible = "feasible" and access = "low band-
width", text("use minimal graphics & interaction via technology")], [feasible
= "feasible" and access = "high bandwidth", text("use full graphics & interac-
tion via technology")], [default, text("current technology does not appear to
support your plan")]]
]).
rule_set(class_type, /, [
description = "",
type = single_value,
rules = [[conditions, value], [student_demographics = "resident students",
text("an enhanced, mediated, or web-based course")], [student_demograph-
ics = "professionals ashore" and access \= "no bandwidth", text("a web-based
course")], [student_demographics = "officers at sea" and access \= "no band-
width", text("a web-based course")], [default, text("your current course plan
appears infeasible")]]
]).
% rules_table
:- indexed rules_table(1,0,0).
% data_table
:- indexed data_table(1,0,0).
% text
:- indexed text(1,0,0).
text(technology_use, /, [
description = "",
type = text,
file = "",
text = text("Given the information you have provided, SECTIONS Advisor recom-
mends: " + class_type + "; " + technology + ".
Key factors in this recommendation include: " + access + ", " + student_demo-
graphics + " and " + cost + ". Thank you for using SECTIONS Advisor.
")
]).
```

Glossary

This glossary is included to facilitate ready reference to terms and concepts presented in the book that may be unfamiliar to the reader. Clearly, definitions and interpretations other than those included here exist and make sense as well, but the definitions and interpretations below are consistent with the presentation throughout the book, and almost every item below includes a pointer to the chapter in which the associated terms and concepts are discussed.

Abundance: One of two dimensions used to characterize the Knowledge Hierarchy (see Ch. 2). In any organization, data are more abundant than information is, which is in turn more abundant than (explicit) knowledge is.

Action: The manifest accomplishment of some mental, social or physical activity such as decision-making, communication or work (see Ch. 1). The term *action* is used to differentiate the concept *knowledge* from *information*: knowledge enables direct action (e.g., correct decisions, appropriate behaviors, useful work), whereas information provides meaning and context for such action (e.g., decision criteria, behavior norms, work specifications).

Actionability: One of two dimensions used to characterize the Knowledge Hierarchy (see Ch. 2). In any organization, knowledge is more actionable than information is, which is in turn more actionable than data are.

Apprentice: A person who works with a skilled master or craftsman to learn a skill or craft. Apprenticeship represents a technique for experts to share tacit knowledge (see Ch. 1).

Appropriation: A term connoting one's ability to assert ownership over some asset, generally with the intent to extract *economic rent* (e.g., monetary payment) from it. The term *appropriation* is used to differentiate tacit knowledge from its explicit counterpart in terms of greater competitive advantage. Speaking generally, as used in this book, tacit knowledge confers greater appropriability than explicit knowledge, for actions enabled by the former are less imitable than the latter, and hence easier for the lead firm to maintain its exclusive ownership over and right to exploit such knowledge (see Ch. 1).

Articulable Knowledge: Knowledge that can be described through words, diagrams, formulae, computer programs and like means. The term *articulable* is used to differentiate explicit knowledge from its tacit counterpart (see Ch. 2).

Articulation: The action of describing knowledge through words, diagrams, formulae, computer programs and like means. Tacit knowledge resists articulation and transfer (see Ch. 1).

Artificial Intelligence: This field of Computer Science focuses on developing computational devices (e.g., expert systems, software agents, robots) that emulate the behaviors of people who are considered to be intelligent. Unlike most information technologies, many artificial intelligence applications address knowledge—as opposed to information—directly and are performative in nature (see Ch. 4).

Backcasting: A modification of forecasting techniques through the process of "predicting," *ex-post*, known organizational outcomes using only information that was available at the beginning of a project. This technique is used to validate computational models (see Ch. 6).

Barrier to Market Entry: An impediment that makes it difficult for some rival firm to compete in a particular market. Barriers to market entry can be financial (e.g., high capital costs), positional (e.g., large market share and brand loyalty), geographical (e.g., the best location), knowledge-based (e.g., inimitable knowledge), and based on other advantages (see Ch. 1).

Business Process Re-Engineering: A philosophy and set of tools and methods conceived originally as an approach for radical change to effect dramatic performance improvements in organizations. This organizational phenomenon in the Nineties provided a broad-based impetus and set of techniques to enable organizations to perform better with fewer resources (see Ch. 1). Re-engineering research has addressed several important questions pertaining to managing change (see Ch. 6). As with most knowledge management projects today, the abundance of re-engineering projects focused on information technology.

Case-Based Reasoning: An Artificial Intelligence technique that uses aspects of stored case descriptions to guide inference pertaining to problem solving associated with similar cases. Organizational applications such as technology help desks demonstrate benefits of this approach (see Ch. 4), and our discussion of applications cases in business (see Ch. 7), government (see Ch. 8) and non-profits (see Ch. 9) supports case-based reasoning through both positive and negative examples of managing knowledge and promoting knowledge flows.

Chat: The common name for the *Internet relay chat protocol* that enables users to exchange near-synchronous, near-duplex, textual messages between computers. This information technology application is used for distributed, synchronous, text-based communications, often in the place of telephone or radio conversations. Chat differs from e-mail in that it supports synchronous communication, whereas e-mail messages are asynchronous (see Chs. 2 and 4).

Competency Trap: This term *competency trap* is used to describe a situation in which an organization develops considerable competency in some area, only to find itself unable to develop one or more alternate competencies when necessitated by either management strategy or environmental shifts (see Ch. 1). Competency traps can develop through unbalanced focus on exploitation of extant knowledge over exploration to develop new knowledge (see Ch. 5).

Competitive Advantage: This concept is discussed generally in economic terms such as earning superior rents, gaining larger market share, raising barriers to market entry, locking out competitors, and locking in customers (see Ch. 1). It pertains more generally to the ability of one organization to outperform its competitors.

Competitive Disadvantage: This is the opposite of competitive advantage. It pertains generally to the ability of an organization's competitors to outperform it. Where knowledge fails to flow well, even to enable ordinary workflows, the organization may experience competitive disadvantage, as it fails to perform even its routine work effectively (see Ch. 1).

Competitive Potential: This refers to the potential for competitive advantage. By the term *potential*, we imply that a firm has the capability to attain competitive advantage but may not have done so yet through manifest action (see Ch. 1).

Competitive Resource: In a resource-based view, an organization competes on the basis of the unique set of resources it possesses and puts to use. Economic inputs such as *land, labor* and *capital* represent traditional resources employed in this view. *Knowledge* represents more than just another resource along these lines, because its tacit form can enable sustainable competitive advantage (see Ch. 1).

Computational Modeling: This information technology application represents an extension of simulation (see Ch. 4). Computational models are used extensively in the physical sciences (e.g., to represent the dynamics of phenomena such as fluid flows, heat transfers and resilience of structures) and progressively more often in the social sciences (e.g., to represent the dynamics of money flows, economic transfers and communication structures). Models from both sciences provide a basis for designing physical artifacts (e.g., airplanes, bridges, computers) and for making decisions about social systems (e.g., finance, trade, broadcasting) by representing such artifacts and systems via models and by simulating their dynamic behaviors under various conditions (see Ch. 6).

Context: Context refers to the situation, environment and perspective of actions such as cognition, conversation and work. Context can make data intelligible and enable them to convey meaning as information (see Ch. 2). The term *context* is used along with *meaning* to operationalize the concept *information*.

Core Competencies: The capabilities that can enable competitive advantage for an individual, group or organization. Many organizations shed peripheral capabilities to focus their attention on the core set that is most relevant strategically (see Ch. 5).

Core Rigidities: The duality associated with core competencies that restrict the range of activities that can be performed well by an organization (see Ch. 5).

Critical Path: The sequence of tasks, activities and/or events in a project that determine the shortest possible schedule for completion. The *critical path* concept is used extensively in Project Management for planning and analysis. Because knowledge is required for the performance of work, knowledge flows can be viewed clearly as lying on the critical paths of the workflows they enable (see Ch. 1).

Data: Data are operationalized best as interpreted signals that can reduce uncertainty or equivocality. Relationships and distinctions between *data, information* and *knowledge* are important (see Ch. 2).

Database: A class of information technology applications for the organized storage and retrieval of data. Databases can be massive and sophisticated. As conveyed by their name, databases address data, not information or knowledge (see Chs. 2 and 4).

Database Query: The use of interactive techniques for a user to extract desired subsets and summaries of data from a database. Database queries are used often to answer factual or statistical questions.

Data Mining: The use of statistical and inferential pattern-matching techniques to identify regularities in databases that are imperceptible to most people. This is the main idea behind the *big data* movement today. The discovery of new patterns and regularities in data represents a form of knowledge creation (see Chs. 2 and 4).

Data Warehouse: A very large, generally decision-support database that is used to collect, organize and retrieve data from multiple, generally operational databases. Data warehouses are used often in conjunction with data mining (see Ch. 4).

Declarative Knowledge: The class of knowledge that is expressed as facts or assertions. The term *declarative knowledge* is used often in contrast with *procedural knowledge* (see Ch. 2).

Diagnose: The deductive sequence of tasks associated with identifying a problem or pathology. The term *diagnose* is used often in a medical context of identifying diseases. This term makes sense also in the context of identifying problems or pathologies suffered by an organization. *Knowledge clumping* represents one such pathology addressed in particular in this book (see Ch. 1).

Discussion Board: An information technology application that enables multiple, simultaneous, asynchronous, textual conversations between geographically distributed participants. Generally each unique conversation is labeled with a title and separated from other conversations as distinct *threads*. This groupware application offers infrastructural support for knowledge work and enhances the environment in which knowledge artifacts are created and managed (see Ch. 2).

Discussion Thread: A unique, segmented and labeled conversational topic associated generally with discussion boards, network news groups and e-mail lists (see Ch. 2).

Document Repository: An information technology application for the organized storage and retrieval of documents. A document repository is equipped generally with some kind of search engine that uses keyword matching and like techniques to locate and retrieve documents of potential interest to users. The document repository is analogous to the database in terms of function and use. However, the document repository addresses informational documents, whereas the database addresses data (see Chs. 2 and 4).

Doing: A form of knowing focused on accomplishing work activities (see Ch. 1). The term *doing* is used often for contrast with *learning* (see Ch. 5).

Education: A formal approach to knowledge flow in which students enroll in organized courses offered by institutions such as universities, colleges and vocational schools. Generally an instructor leads the course, which consists of prearranged readings, assignments, lectures, laboratory experiments, discussions and other learning activities. The term *education* is used often in the same context as *training* (see Ch. 1) and for contrast with other knowledge flow processes such as *on-the-job training (OJT), trial and error, direct experience* and others that connote the informal accumulation of experience-based knowledge (see Ch. 3).

E-Mail: Electronic mail is an information technology application that enables the asynchronous exchange of textual messages across computer networks. The e-mail application complements its chat counterpart, the latter of which enables synchronous, networked communication (see Chs. 2 and 4).

Ephemeral Competitive Advantage: Competitive advantage that can be obtained but not sustained over time. The term *ephemeral competitive advantage* is used often for contrast with *sustainable competitive advantage* (see Ch. 1).

Ephemeral Knowledge: Knowledge that can be created or acquired but not retained or preserved over time (see Ch. 1).

Equivocality: A state of ignorance pertaining to context, in which the causes of observable or putative effects or results cannot be identified, or in which decision makers lack sufficient knowledge of their situation to even know which questions to ask. The terms *equivocality* and *uncertainty* are used often in the context of data (see Ch. 2).

Experience: The accumulation of knowledge associated with direct interaction with some object, process or system in the world (see Ch. 1). The term *experience* is used often in connection with the performance of work activities. The performance of people and organizations improves generally as a result of experience and can be measured often using learning curves (see Ch. 6).

Experience-Based Knowledge: Knowledge created and accumulated through experience (see Ch. 1). Such knowledge is tacit generally and slow to accumulate (see Ch. 3).

Expert: A person recognized as possessing qualitatively higher levels of skill and experience in some, generally narrow domain than most people possess. The term *expert* is used often to describe a person who has accumulated very large stocks of knowledge and for contrast with *novice* (see Chs. 1, 4, and 5).

Expert System: An information technology application from the field of Artificial Intelligence that seeks to emulate the performance of human experts. Expert system applications address knowledge directly and are performative in nature. This provides a contrast with the supportive nature of most information technologies (see Ch. 4).

Explicit Knowledge: Knowledge that has been articulated through words, diagrams, formulae, computer programs and like means. The term *explicit knowledge* is used widely for contrast with *tacit knowledge*, the latter of which cannot be or has not been articulated, and with *implicit knowledge*, which can be but has not been articulated (see Ch. 2).

Explicitness: The degree to which knowledge has been articulated. *Explicitness* describes the nature of knowledge along a dimensional construct with tacit and explicit endpoints. It represents one of the five dimensions used in this book to classify and visualize knowledge flows (see Ch. 3).

Exploitation: The application of extant knowledge for organizational performance and pursuit of competitive advantage (see Ch. 1). The term *exploitation* is used often for contrast with *exploration*. Exploitation involves principally the form of knowing called *doing* and the application or refinement of existing knowledge, whereas exploration involves principally the form of knowing called *learning* and the creation or acquisition of new knowledge (see Ch. 5).

Exploration: The search for new knowledge for organizational performance and pursuit of competitive advantage (see Ch. 1). The term *exploration* is used often for contrast with *exploitation*. Exploration involves principally the form of knowing called *learning* and the creation or acquisition of new knowledge, whereas exploitation involves principally the form of knowing called *doing* and the application or refinement of existing knowledge (see Ch. 5).

Externalization: One of four knowledge flow processes associated with the Spiral Model of knowledge flows. The term *externalization* refers generally to knowledge formalization from tacit to explicit form (see Ch. 3).

Flow Principles: Systematic and general principles pertaining to fluid movements such as exhibited by water, air, heat and electricity. Flow principles are used to describe, explain and predict the dynamics of such fluids. Flow principles can be used also to describe, explain and predict the dynamics of knowledge (see Ch. 3).

***Gedanken* Experiment:** *Gedanken* means, "thought." Gedanken experiments refer to mental simulations (see Chs. 1, 2 and 4).

Generalist Knowledge: Knowledge that pertains more to high-level patterns and relationships than to low-level details. The term *generalist knowledge* is used often for contrast with *specialist knowledge*. To some extent, generalist and specialist knowledge can be substituted for one another, but they may exhibit some complementation also (see Ch. 6).

Groupware: A class of information technology applications that offer infrastructural support for knowledge work and enhance the environment in which knowledge artifacts are created and managed. Common organizational applications include e-mail, chat, discussion boards and like technologies (see Ch. 4).

Hindcasting: A modification of forecasting techniques through the process of "predicting," *ex-post*, known organizational outcomes using only information that was available at the beginning of a project. This technique is used to validate computational models (see Ch. 6).

Ignorance: The lack of knowledge in some domain or area. The adjective *ignorant* is used often for contrast both with both *knowledgeable* and with *stupid*. The former contrast connotes that the ignorant person lacks knowledge (see Ch. 1). The latter contrast connotes that the ignorant person is capable of learning to overcome ignorance (see Ch. 5). Groups and organizations can be ignorant, knowledgeable or stupid too.

Imitable: Capable of imitation. Where knowledge-based action that enables some kind of competitive advantage is imitable, the corresponding advantage is likely to be ephemeral. Competitors will try to imitate the organizational processes, technologies, products and services that provide for competitive advantage. Organizational capabilities predicated on explicit knowledge are more imitable generally than those predicated on tacit knowledge are (see Ch. 1).

Implicit Knowledge: Knowledge that is articulable but has not been articulated yet through words, diagrams, formulae, computer programs and like means. The term *implicit knowledge* is used widely for contrast with *tacit knowledge*, the latter of which cannot be or has not been articulated, and with *explicit knowledge*, which can be and has been articulated (see Ch. 2).

Information: Information is operationalized best as providing meaning and context for action. Relationships and distinctions between *data, information* and *knowledge* are important (see Ch. 2).

Inimitable: Incapable of imitation. Where knowledge-based action that enables some kind of competitive advantage is inimitable, the corresponding advantage is likely to be sustainable. Competitors may try but will fail to imitate the organizational processes, technologies, products and services that provide for competitive advantage. Organizational capabilities predicated on tacit knowledge are more inimitable generally than those predicated on explicit knowledge are (see Ch. 1).

Instruction: This knowledge flow process is associated with formal classroom education or training (see Ch. 1). It focuses more on the knowing activity *learning* than on *doing* and is used often for contrast with informal, experience-oriented knowledge flow processes such as *on-the-job training (OJT), trial and error* and the like (see Ch. 5).

Intelligent Tutoring: An information technology application from Artificial Intelligence that uses models of students to facilitate and tailor pedagogical decisions and actions such as lesson plans, tests and reinforcement activities (see Ch. 4).

Internalization: One of four knowledge flow processes associated with the Spiral Model of knowledge flows. The term *internalization* refers generally to knowledge refinement from explicit to tacit form (see Ch. 3).

Intranet: An information technology application comprised of computer networks and services that are based on Internet standards and protocols but that are restricted to use by people within an organization. Most such applications are Web-based (see Ch. 4).

Knower: The entity associated with knowing, either learning or doing (see Chs. 2 and 5).

Knowing: Knowing involves knowledge in action. Learning and doing represent two forms of knowing (see Ch. 5).

Knowing-Doing Gap: (We would refer to this as a 'knowledge-knowing gap' or a knowledge 'potential-action gap'.) A knowing-doing gap manifests itself in part when organizations "know better" than to do what they do and in part when organizations "know how" to do something they do not do (see Ch. 5).

Knowledge: Knowledge is operationalized best as enabling direct action. Relationships and distinctions between *data, information* and *knowledge* are important (see Ch. 2).

Knowledge Acquisition: Gaining new knowledge through learning. Knowledge acquisition represents a form of knowledge creation. The knowledge acquired need not be "new" to the entire world (e.g., knowledge developed through scientific discovery). Rather, such knowledge needs only to be new in the situated context of its coordinates (e.g., to an individual or organization, at a particular point in space or time; see Ch. 5).

Knowledge Application: Using existing knowledge through doing. Knowledge application involves putting knowledge into action. *Knowledge application* represents the fifth stage of the knowledge life cycle (see Ch. 3).

Knowledge Audit: The Knowledge Audit is a diagnostic activity focused on identifying organizational problems with potential to be addressed via knowledge management (see Ch. 6).

Knowledge-Based Theory of the Firm: An extension of the resource-based view that privileges the power of knowledge for competitive advantage (see Ch. 1).

Knowledge Capture: Gaining new knowledge through learning. Knowledge capture represents a form of knowledge creation. The knowledge acquired need not be "new" to the entire world (e.g., knowledge developed through scientific discovery). Rather, such knowledge needs only to be new in the situated context of its coordinates (e.g., to an individual or organization, at a particular point in space or time; see Ch. 5).

Knowledge Chunks: Discrete units of knowledge acquired through learning. A chunk can be a low-level unit such as a fact, a medium-level unit such as a procedure, or a high-level unit such as a pattern. The psychological term *chunking* refers to the cognitive process associated with memory and recall. The accumulation of many knowledge chunks is associated with expertise (see Ch. 1) and expert systems development (see Ch. 4).

Knowledge Clump: Knowledge that collects at some isolated coordinate (e.g., in an individual or organization, at a particular point in space or time; see Ch. 3). Knowledge clumps are symptoms of flow pathologies in the organization.

Knowledge Consumer: A person or organization on the receiving end of knowledge flows and that is learning new knowledge. The term *knowledge consumer* is used synonymously often with *knowledge receiver* and for contrast with *knowledge producer/source* (see Ch. 2).

Knowledge Creation: Gaining new knowledge through learning. *Knowledge creation* represents the first stage of the knowledge life cycle (see Ch. 3). The knowledge created need not be "new" to the entire world (e.g., knowledge developed through scientific discovery). Rather, such knowledge needs only to be new in the situated context of its coordinates (e.g., to an individual or organization, at a particular point in space or time; see Ch. 5).

Knowledge Differential: The difference in levels of knowledge stocks between two or more, different individuals or organizations. Knowledge differential can provide a basis for competitive advantage (see Ch. 1).

Knowledge Directionality: A vector representation of dynamic knowledge, in which the corresponding flow has a distinguishable source and receiver (see Ch. 2).

Knowledge Dissemination: Sharing knowledge broadly. Knowledge dissemination represents a form of knowledge sharing, associated generally with explicit knowledge and broad organizational reach (see Ch. 3).

Knowledge Dynamics: The study of how knowledge moves with respect to time. Phenomenological research methods are most prevalent in this study at present.

Knowledge Engineer: A technological intermediary responsible for the development of expert systems (see Ch. 4).

Knowledge Flow: A dynamic movement of knowledge between coordinates (e.g., between individuals or organizations, or points in space or time; see Ch. 3).

Knowledge Flow Process: The sequence of organizational activities responsible for producing and propagating knowledge flows (see Ch. 3).

Knowledge Flow Theory: The canon of principles and techniques from Knowledge Dynamics pertaining to the phenomenology of knowledge flows.

Knowledge Flow Time: The amount of time required for knowledge to flow between coordinates (e.g., individuals or organizations, or points in space or time). *Knowledge flow time* represents one of the five dimensions used in this book to classify and visualize knowledge flows (see Ch. 3).

Knowledge Flow Vector: A graphical representation of knowledge flows in which arrows are used to depict magnitude and direction of dynamic motion (see Ch. 3).

Knowledge Flow Visualization: The graphical representation of knowledge flows that uses a multidimensional vector space to delineate dynamic movements of knowledge (see Ch. 3). The five dimensions *explicitness, reach, life cycle, flow time* and *power* are used in this book for visualization of knowledge flows.

Knowledge Formalization: Articulating tacit knowledge into explicit form. *Knowledge formalization* represents the third stage of the knowledge life cycle (see Ch. 3).

Knowledge Hierarchy: The Knowledge Hierarchy provides a conceptualization of interrelations between knowledge, information and data (see Ch. 2).

Knowledge Hoarding: The practice of not sharing knowledge (see Ch. 1).

Knowledge Inertia: The tendency of knowledge at rest to remain at rest. Knowledge that has clumped will remain clumped unless some kind of managerial intervention is taken (see Ch. 3).

Knowledge Inventory: A construct to measure the level of knowledge stock in a person or organization. An organization's knowledge inventory both enables and inhibits what actions it can take (see Chs. 1 and 5). The term *knowledge inventory* is used synonymously often with *knowledge level*.

Knowledge Level: A construct to measure the knowledge inventory possessed by a person or organization (see Chs. 1 and 5). The term *knowledge level* is used synonymously often with *knowledge inventory*.

Knowledge Life Cycle: A dimensional construct to characterize the kind of activity associated with knowledge flows. *Knowledge life cycle* represents one of the five dimensions used in this book to classify and visualize knowledge flows (see Ch. 3).

Knowledge Management: The practice of leveraging knowledge for competitive advantage. Most knowledge management programs to date have focused on technology (see Ch. 4).

Knowledge Management System: A suite of information technology applications and organizational routines employed for knowledge management. Most knowledge management systems employed to date have focused on technology (see Ch. 4).

Knowledge Management Tools: A set of information technology applications employed for knowledge management (see Ch. 4).

Knowledge Power: The capability of harnessing dynamic knowledge for competitive advantage (see Ch. 1). *Knowledge power* represents one of the five dimensions used in this book to classify and visualize knowledge flows (see Ch. 3).

Knowledge Producer: A person or organization on the sending end of knowledge flows and that is sharing existing knowledge. The term *knowledge producer* is used synonymously often with *knowledge source* and for contrast with *knowledge consumer/receiver* (see Ch. 2).

Knowledge Receiver: A person or organization on the receiving end of knowledge flows and that is learning new knowledge. The term *knowledge receiver* is used synonymously often with *knowledge consumer* and for contrast with *knowledge producer/source* (see Ch. 2).

Knowledge Refinement: Learning over time from experience. *Knowledge refinement* represents the sixth stage of the knowledge life cycle. It connects *knowledge application* with *knowledge creation* to complete a cycle of knowledge flows (see Ch. 3).

Knowledge Sharing: Inducing knowledge to flow between different people, organizations, places or times. *Knowledge sharing* represents the fourth stage of the knowledge life cycle (see Ch. 3).

Knowledge Source: A person or organization on the sending end of knowledge flows and that is sharing existing knowledge. The term *knowledge source* is used synonymously often with *knowledge producer* and for contrast with *knowledge consumer/receiver* (see Ch. 2).

Knowledge Stocks: A concept to characterize the level of knowledge accumulated by a person or organization. *Knowledge inventory* and *knowledge level* represent two measures intended to operationalize the concept *knowledge stocks*. Knowledge flows and knowledge stocks interrelate tightly and dynamically (see Ch. 5).

Knowledge Technology: Technology used for knowledge management. Information technologies are employed most widely at present for knowledge management (see Ch. 4).

Knowledge Transfer: Sharing knowledge locally. Knowledge transfer represents a form of knowledge sharing, associated generally with tacit knowledge and broad organizational reach (see Ch. 3).

Knowledge Uniqueness: The strong distinction between the concepts *knowledge* and *information/data* (see Ch. 2).

Knowledge Value Analysis: Knowledge Value Analysis employs principles such as *information entropy* in attempt to measure the return on investments in acquiring and sharing knowledge (see Ch. 6).

Learning: Learning refers to knowledge in motion. It is used most often to characterize the creation or acquisition of new knowledge. The term *learning* is used often for contrast with *doing* (see Ch. 5).

Learning Curves: An empirical technique that blends theory with practice to measure knowledge flows (see Ch. 6). Knowledge-based performance at the individual, group and organizational levels improves at measurable and predictable rates through task repetition and refinement.

Learning Rate: The speed at which learning is accomplished. *Learning rate* is inversely proportional to *knowledge flow time* (see Ch. 1).

Local Knowledge: Knowledge of proximal conditions. Much tacit knowledge is situated and local in nature, meaning it can be difficult to share broadly (see Ch. 3).

Locking out Competitors: Raising barriers to entry that prohibit new competitors from challenging an organization (see Ch. 1).

Locking in Customers: Raising switching costs that prohibit customers from pursuing products or services from rival competitors (see Ch. 1).

Management Interventions: Actions taken by leaders and managers to change aspects of an organization that are seen as problematic or pathological (see Ch. 1).

Market Share: The fraction of a market segment that is controlled by a particular competitor (see Ch. 1).

Meaning: The significance of information. *Meaning* implies that a message has caused some cognitive change in the receiver's understanding. This term is used along with *context* to operationalize the concept *information* (see Ch. 2).

Mentoring: A knowledge flow process in which an experienced or otherwise-knowledgeable person helps a less-experienced or -knowledgeable person to learn in a work setting. Mentoring is a part of apprenticeship and contrasts with both the knowledge flow processes *on-the-job training/trial and error* and *formal education/training* (see Ch. 3).

Meta-Data: Data about data in a database. Meta-data are used to describe characteristics of the data that are organized and stored within a database. Examples include the names of fields, types of values various data can take on, and relationships between different database tables (see Ch. 2).

Multimedia: An information technology application that enables textual, graphical, audio and other modes of data to flow across a network and to be presented simultaneously, in an integrated manner (see Ch. 2).

Novice: A person recognized as possessing qualitatively lower levels of skill and experience in some domain than most people possess. The term *novice* is used often to describe a person who has accumulated very small stocks of knowledge and for contrast with *expert* (see Chs. 1, 4 and 5).

Observation: Watching physically some task, activity or process being performed, often with the intent of learning how to perform such task, activity or process (see Ch. 2).

On-the-Job Training: Direct experience with some work task, activity or process, generally with the implication that some kind of experience-based learning is taking place. *On-the-Job Training (OJT)* is used widely as a euphemism for *trial and error*, a relatively slow and error-prone but pervasive knowledge flow process employed by organizations (see Chs. 1 and 3).

Organization: A collectivity of people who coordinate their actions for some common purpose.

Organizational Change: A program of planned alteration of the structure, processes, technologies or other aspects of an organization (see Ch. 6).

Organizational Learning: Learning at the organizational level of reach. Organizational learning is a form of knowing that relates most closely with knowledge flows and is oriented principally toward exploration. In contrast, organizational memory is a form of knowing that relates more closely with knowledge stocks or inventories and is oriented principally toward exploitation (see Ch. 5).

Organizational Memory: Memory and retrieval at the organizational level of reach. Organizational memory is a form of knowing that relates most closely with knowledge stocks or inventories and is oriented principally toward exploitation. In contrast, organizational learning is a form of knowing that relates more closely with knowledge flows and is oriented principally toward exploration (see Ch. 5).

Organizational Performance: How closely the results of an organization's actions fit its goals. Performance of one organization can be absolute in terms of its internal goals or can be relative in terms of competitors' performance (see Ch. 1).

Organizational Reach: A dimensional construct to characterize the level of social aggregation associated with knowledge flows. *Organizational reach* represents one of the five dimensions used in this book to classify and visualize knowledge flows (see Ch. 3).

Organizational Routines: Systems, procedures, habits and patterns of activity in organizations that produce outputs and represent knowledge application at the organizational level of reach (see Ch. 3).

Path-Dependent: The longitudinal nature of organizational experience that results from making choices. Once one metaphorical path has been chosen, one or more alternate paths cannot be taken at the same time. An organization develops a set of capabilities based on activities it has experienced over time. However, it also fails to develop alternate sets of capabilities based on activities it has not experienced over time. Path-dependency relates to both *core competencies* and *core rigidities* in terms of organizational learning (see Ch. 5).

Pathology: A serious problem or illness. *Knowledge clumping* represents a common organizational pathology (see Ch. 1).

Performative Applications: A class of information technology applications that focus directly on knowledge and are able to perform work in lieu of people. The term *performative* is used often for contrast with *supportive* applications (see Ch. 1).

Precedence Relations: A necessary sequential ordering. Various knowledge flows are interrelated tightly through precedence relations; that is, some chunks of knowledge must complete their flows before others can begin effectively. Workflows are related by precedence as well (see Ch. 3), and many knowledge flows are precedent to the workflows they enable (see Ch. 1).

Procedural Knowledge: The class of knowledge that is expressed as processes or procedures. The term *procedural knowledge* is used often in contrast with *declarative knowledge* (see Ch. 2).

Qualitative Reasoning: A class of information technology applications from Artificial Intelligence that seek to represent and support inference pertaining to commonsense knowledge. This represents a contrast with expert systems, which seek to represent and support inference pertaining to expert knowledge (see Ch. 4).

Redesign: Planned organizational change, generally on a relatively large scale. The term *redesign* is used often to describe the key analytical activity associated with Business Process Re-engineering (see Ch. 6).

Research: A knowledge flow process focused on systematic discovery of new knowledge. Research focuses on exploration through learning new knowledge but also involves exploitation through application of existing knowledge (see Ch. 3).

Resource-Based View: In a resource-based view, an organization competes on the basis of the unique set of resources it possesses and puts to use. Economic inputs such as *land, labor* and *capital* represent traditional resources employed in this view. *Knowledge* represents more than just another resource along these lines, because its tacit form can enable sustainable competitive advantage (see Ch. 1).

Search Engine: An information technology application that uses keyword matching and like techniques to locate and retrieve documents of potential interest to a user. Search engines accompany commonly document repositories, intranets and Web portals, and they are invaluable for finding information on the Internet (see Ch. 2).

Semantic: Having to do with meaning. Knowledge is required to establish a semantic structure to represent information (see Ch. 2). The term *semantic* is used frequently to distinguish information technologies that focus on information from those that focus on data (see Ch. 4).

Semantic Web: A class of information technology applications, many involving Artificial Intelligence, that combine and integrate diverse techniques to enable computers to accomplish autonomously many information work tasks that can be accomplished at present only by people (see Ch. 4).

Shell Tools: A class of information technology applications involving Artificial Intelligence that are used to develop expert systems (see Ch. 4).

Shopping Bots: A class of information technology applications, many involving Artificial Intelligence, that are used to automate several aspects of information work associated with shopping (see Ch. 4).

Signals: Physical patterns (e.g., pressure variations, photon reflections, electromagnetic changes) that may be interpreted to constitute data. All flows of knowledge, information, and data reduce ultimately to signals in the physical realm (see Ch. 2).

Single-Loop Learning: Single-loop learning represents organizational learning that focuses on improving performance with respect to a static goal; that is, an organization can learn to do the wrong thing very well and not realize that its competency is suited well to the environment no longer. The term *single-loop learning* is used synonymously often with *competency traps* often and for contrast with *double-loop learning*, the latter of which pertains to learning how and when to adjust organizational goals (see Ch. 1).

Situated Knowledge: Knowledge that is proximal to the knower and local context. Situated knowledge implies that one must be at a particular space-time coordinate to learn. Such knowledge tends to be tacit and local, making it difficult to share broadly (see Ch. 1).

Socialization: One of four knowledge flow processes associated with the Spiral Model of knowledge flows. The term *socialization* refers generally to knowledge sharing in tacit form (see Ch. 3).

Software Agents: A class of information technology applications, many involving Artificial Intelligence, which are used to automate several aspects of information work. Shopping bots represent a kind of software agent. Software agents play a prominent role in the Semantic Web (see Ch. 4).

Specialized Expertise: Knowledge that pertains more to low-level details than to high-level patterns and relationships. The term *specialist knowledge* is used often for contrast with *generalist knowledge*. To some extent, generalist and specialist knowledge can be substituted for one another, but they may exhibit some complementation also (see Ch. 6).

Standard Operating Procedure: A formal, generally written routine for performing a set of work tasks in the organizational context. Standard operating procedures reflect explicit knowledge used to support organizational routines (see Ch. 1).

Sticky Knowledge: Sticky knowledge represents tacit experience that is difficult to transfer across organizational units (see Ch. 1).

Supportive Applications: A class of information technology applications that focus indirectly on knowledge to support people who perform work tasks. The term *supportive* is used often for contrast with *performative* applications (see Ch. 1).

Sustainable Competitive Advantage: Competitive advantage that can be obtained and sustained over time. The term *sustainable competitive advantage* is used often to contrast with *ephemeral competitive advantage* (see Ch. 1).

Tacit Knowledge: Knowledge that cannot be or has not been articulated through words, diagrams, formulae, computer programs and like means. The term *tacit knowledge* is used widely for contrast with *explicit knowledge*, the latter of which has been articulated in explicit form, and with *implicit knowledge*, which can be but has not been articulated (see Ch. 2).

Tactic: A set of actions based upon knowledge. The term *tactic* is used often when describing competitive military combat actions (see Ch. 1).

Taxonomy: An organized hierarchy of concepts. Taxonomies are used broadly to classify concepts such as different kinds of life, different kinds of rocks, and like tangible concepts. Taxonomies are used also to classify different kinds of knowledge, information and data (see Ch. 2).

Teaching: This knowledge flow process is associated with formal classroom education or training (see Ch. 1). It focuses more on the knowing activity *learning* than on *doing* and is used often for contrast with informal, experience-oriented knowledge flow processes such as *On-the-Job Training (OJT)*, *trial and error* and the like (see Ch. 5).

Tradeoff: The requirement for a decision maker to give up some of one thing of value in order to obtain more of another valued item. Tradeoffs manifest themselves broadly in decision-making when resources are constrained (see Ch. 3).

Training: A formal approach to knowledge flow in which students enroll in organized courses offered by human resource departments and like units within organizations. Generally an instructor leads the course, which consists of prearranged readings, assignments, lectures, laboratory experiments, discussions and other learning activities. The term *training* is used often in the same context as *education* (see Ch. 1) and for contrast with informal, experience-oriented knowledge flow processes such as *on-the-job training (OJT), trial and error, direct experience* and the like (see Ch. 3).

Trial and Error: Direct experience with some work task, activity or process, generally with the implication that some kind of experience-based learning is taking place. The term *trial and error* is used sparingly as a substitute for its euphemism *on-the-job training (OJT)*, a relatively slow and error-prone but pervasive knowledge flow process employed by organizations (see Chs. 1 and 3).

Uncertainty: A state of ignorance pertaining to fact, in which the values of particular states or variables are unknown, but in which decision makers have sufficient knowledge of their situation to know which questions to ask. The terms *uncertainty* and *equivocality* are used often in the context of data (see Ch. 2).

Video Teleconferencing: An information technology application enabling synchronous, remote, multimedia communications, generally through multiplexed audio and visual channels (see Ch. 2).

Web Portal: An information technology application that organizes data and information in an intranet environment. Web portals include generally multiple tools and services such as databases, document repositories, search engines and like facilitators of information work. Web portals are very prominent at the present in knowledge management projects (see Chs. 2 and 4).

Work: The context of purposeful action in an organization. Work drives performance and depends upon knowledge (see Ch. 1).

Work Process: The sequence of activities associated with a workflow and required to produce work in the organization (see Ch. 1).

Workflow: A dynamic movement of work through an organization. Workflows drive performance dynamically and depend upon knowledge flows (see Ch. 1).

Workflow System: An information technology application focused on supporting information workflows (see Chs. 1 and 4).

Compilation of References

Adams, A. A., Lee, J. G. C. Y., & Nissen, M. E. (2010). Tacit knowledge flows and institutional theory: Accelerating acculturation. In Proceedings Hawaii International Conference on System Sciences. Koloa, HI: IEEE.

Alberts, D. S., Garstka, J. J., & Stein, F. P. (1999). *Network centric warfare: Developing and leveraging information superiority* (2nd ed.). Washington, DC: CCRP Publication Series.

Alberts, D. S., & Hayes, R. E. (2003). *Power to the edge: Command and control in the information age*. Washington, DC: Command and Control Research Program.

Andress, J., & Winterfeld, S. (2011). *Cyber warfare: Techniques, tactics and tools for security practitioners*. Waltham, MA: Elsevier.

Andrews, D. C., & Stalick, S. K. (1994). *Business reengineering: The survival guide*. New York, NY: Yourdon Press Computing Series.

Argote, L., Beckman, S. L., & Epple, D. (1990). The persistence and transfer of learning in industrial settings. *Management Science*, *36*(2), 140–154. doi:10.1287/mnsc.36.2.140.

Argyris, C., & Schon, D. A. (1978). *Organizational learning*. Reading, MA: Addison-Wesley.

AYSO. (2004). *American youth soccer organization website*. Retrieved from http://www.soccer.org

Barney, J. B. (1986). Strategic factor markets: expectations, luck, and business strategy. *Management Science*, *32*(10), 1231–1241. doi:10.1287/mnsc.32.10.1231.

Barney, J. B. (2002). *Gaining and sustaining competitive advantage*. Upper Saddle River, NJ: Prentice Hall.

Bashein, B. J., Markus, M. L., & Riley, P. (1994). Preconditions for BPR success: And how to prevent failures. *Information Systems Management*, *11*(2), 7–13. doi:10.1080/10580539408964630.

Baym, N. K. (2000). *Tune in, log on*. Thousand Oaks, CA: Sage.

Becerra-Fernandez, I., & Sabherwal, R. (2001). Organizational knowledge management: A contingency perspective. *Journal of Management Information Systems*, *18*(1), 23–55.

Bergin, R. D., Adams, A. A., Andraus, R., Hudgens, B., Lee, J. G. C. Y., & Nissen, M. E. (2010). Command & control in virtual environments: Laboratory experimentation to compare virtual with physical. In Proceedings International Command & Control Research & Technology Symposium. Santa Monica, CA: Academic Press.

Bergin, R. D., Hudgens, B., & Nissen, M. E. (2011). Examining work performance in immersive virtual environments versus face-to-face physical environments through laboratory experimentation. In Proceedings Hawaii International Conference on System Sciences. Koloa, HI: IEEE.

Beyda, W. (1996). *Data communications: From basics to broadband* (2nd ed.). Upper Saddle River, NJ: Prentice Hall.

Blight, G., Pulham, S., & Torpey, P. (2012). Arab spring: An interactive timeline of Middle East protests. The Guardian. Retrieved from http://www.guardian.co.uk

Bogner, W. C., & Bansal, P. (2007). Knowledge management as the basis of sustained high performance. *Journal of Management Studies*, *44*(1), 165–188. doi:10.1111/j.1467-6486.2007.00667.x.

Bran, J. (2002). Five minutes with ... NASA. *Knowledge Management Regular, 6*(3). Retrieved 1 November 2002, from http://www.kmmagazine.com/xq/asp/sid.0/articleid.338BAE9E-0E28-4B47-B090-55549E920A43/qx/display.htm

Brenner, J. (2011). *America the vulnerable: Inside the new threat matrix of digital espionage, crime, and warfare*. New York, NY: Penguin Press.

Brown, J. S., & Duguid, P. (1991). Organizational learning and communities-of-practice: Toward a unified view of working, learning, and innovation. *Organization Science, 2*(1), 40–57. doi:10.1287/orsc.2.1.40.

Burton, R. M., DeSanctis, G., & Obel, B. (2006). *Organizational design: A step by step approach*. Cambridge, UK: Cambridge University Press. doi:10.1017/CBO9780511812415.

CALL. (2012). *Center for army lessons learned*. Ft. Leavenworth, KS: US Army Combined Arms Center. Retrieved from http://usacac.army.mil/cac2/call/index.asp

Carpenter, S., & Rudge, S. (2003). A self-help approach to knowledge management benchmarking. *Journal of Knowledge Management, 7*(5), 82–95. doi:10.1108/13673270310505403.

Castillo, J. (2003). Challenging the knowledge management mystique: An exploratory study on the performance of knowledge managing companies. *Journal of Management Research, 3*(3), 152–172.

Castronova, E. (2005). *Synthetic worlds: The business and culture of online games*. Chicago, IL: University of Chicago Press.

Chaharbaghi, K., & Lynch, R. (1999). Sustainable competitive advantage: towards a dynamic resource-based strategy. *Management Decision, 37*(1), 45–50. doi:10.1108/00251749910252012.

Cheng, C. H. F., & Levitt, R. E. (2001). Contextually changing behavior in medical organizations. In *Proceedings of the 2001 Annual Symposium of the American Medical Informatics Association*. Washington, DC: AMIA.

L. Chidambaram, & I. Zigurs (Eds.). (2001). *Our virtual world: The transformation of work, play and life via technology*. Hershey, PA: Idea Group.

Choi, S. Y., Lee, H., & Yoo, Y. (2010). The impact of information technology and transactive memory systems on knowledge sharing, application, and team performance: A field study. *Management Information Systems Quarterly, 34*(4), 855–870.

Christiansen, T. R. (1993). *Modeling efficiency and effectiveness of coordination in engineering design teams*. (Unpublished doctoral dissertation). Department of Civil and Environmental Engineering, Stanford University, Palo Alto, CA.

Ciborra, C. U. (1996). The platform organization: Recombining strategies, structures, and surprises. *Organization Science, 7*(2), 103–118. doi:10.1287/orsc.7.2.103.

Clarke, R. A., & Knake, R. (2010). *Cyber war: The next threat to national security and what to do about it*. New York, NY: HarperCollins.

Cleland, D. I., & Ireland, L. R. (2002). *Project management: Strategic design and implementation* (4th ed.). New York: McGraw-Hill.

Clemons, E. K., Thatcher, M. E., & Row, M. C. (1995). Identifying sources of reengineering failures: A study of the behavioral factors contributing to reengineering risks. *Journal of Management Information Systems, 12*(2), 9–36.

Cohen, G. P. (1992). *The virtual design team: An object-oriented model of information sharing in project teams*. (Unpublished doctoral dissertation). Department of Civil Engineering, Stanford University, Palo Alto, CA.

Cohen, W. M., & Levinthal, D. A. (1990). Absorptive capacity: A new perspective on learning and innovation. *Administrative Science Quarterly, 35*, 128–152. doi:10.2307/2393553.

Cook, S. D. N., & Brown, J. S. (1999). Bridging epistemologies: The generative dance between organizational knowledge and organizational knowing. *Organization Science, 10*(4), 381–400. doi:10.1287/orsc.10.4.381.

Cronin, M. (1995). *Doing more business on the internet: How the electronic highway is transforming American companies*. New York, NY: Van Nostrand Reinhold.

Czarniawska, B., & Joerges, B. (1996). Travels of ideas. In B. Czarnaiwska & G. Sevon (Eds.), Translating organiztional change, (pp. 13-48). Berlin: de Gruyter.

Daft, R. L., & Lengel, R. H. (1986). Organizational information requirements, media richness and structural design. *Management Science*, *32*(5), 554–571. doi:10.1287/mnsc.32.5.554.

Daghfous, A. (2004). Organizational learning, knowledge and technology transfer: A case study. *The Learning Organization*, *11*(1), 67–83. doi:10.1108/09696470410515733.

Darr, E. D., Argote, L., & Epple, D. (1995). The acquisition, transfer, and depreciation of knowledge in service organizations: Productivity in franchises. *Management Science*, *41*(11), 1750–1762. doi:10.1287/mnsc.41.11.1750.

Darroch, J. (2005). Knowledge management, innovation and firm performance. *Journal of Knowledge Management*, *9*(3), 101–115. doi:10.1108/13673270510602809.

Davenport, T. H. (1993). *Process innovation: Re-engineering work through information technology*. Boston, MA: Harvard University Press.

Davenport, T. H., De Long, D. W., & Beers, M. C. (1998, Winter). Successful knowledge management projects. *Sloan Management Review*, 43–57.

Davenport, T. H., & Stoddard, D. B. (1994). Reengineering: Business change of mythic proportions? *Management Information Systems Quarterly*, *18*(2), 121–127. doi:10.2307/249760.

Davidow, W. H., & Malone, M. S. (1992). *The virtual corporation: Structuring and revitalizing the corporation for the 21st century*. New York: Edward Burlingame Books/HarperBusiness.

DeFillippi, R. J., & Arthur, M. B. (1998). Paradox in project-based enterprises: The case of film making. *California Management Review*, *40*(2), 125–139. doi:10.2307/41165936.

Dierickx, I., & Cool, K. (1989). Asset stock accumulation and sustainability of competitive advantage. *Management Science*, *35*(12), 1504–1511. doi:10.1287/mnsc.35.12.1504.

Drucker, P. F. (1995). *Managing in a time of great change*. New York, NY: Truman Talley.

Ellaway, R. H., & Topps, D. (2010). Preparing for practice: Issues in virtual medical education. In C. Wankel, & S. Malleck (Eds.), *Emerging ethical issues of life in virtual worlds*. Charlotte, NC: Information Age Publishing.

Epple, D., Argote, L., & Devadas, R. (1991). Organizational learning curves: A method for investigating intra-plant transfer of knowledge acquired through learning by doing. *Organization Science*, *2*(1), 58–70. doi:10.1287/orsc.2.1.58.

Fahey, J. (2002). A resource-based analysis of sustainable competitive advantage in a global environment. *International Business Review*, *11*(1), 57–77. doi:10.1016/S0969-5931(01)00047-6.

Fine, G. A. (1983). *Shared fantasy: Role-playing games as social worlds*. Chicago, IL: University of Chicago Press.

Galbraith, J. R. (1977). *Organization design*. Reading, MA: Addison-Wesley.

Gateau, J. B., Leweling, T. A., Looney, J. P., & Nissen, M. E. (2007). Hypothesis testing of edge organizations: Modeling the C2 organization design space. In *Proceedings International Command & Control Research & Technology Symposium*. Newport, RI: Academic Press.

Gerkin, K. (2011). Word of click: Social networking and the Arab spring revolutions. Retrieved from http://www.bad.eserver.org/issues/2011/Word-of-Click.html 02/13/2012

Gibson, W. (2004). Neuromancer: 20th anniversary Ed. New York: ACE Books.

Gibson, W. (1984). *Neuromancer*. New York: ACE Books.

Giddens, A. (1984). *The constitution of society: Outline of the theory of structuration*. Berkeley, CA: University of California Press.

Goel, L., Junglas, I., & Ives, B. (2009). Virtual worlds as platforms for communities of practice. In R. Sharda, S. Voß, & W. R. King (Eds.), *Knowledge Management and Organizational Learning. New York*. Springer, US. doi:10.1007/978-1-4419-0011-1_12.

Goffman, E. (1961). *Asylums: Essays on the social situation of mental patients and other inmates*. Garden City, NY: Anchor.

Goffman, E. (1974). *Frame analysis*. Cambridge, MA: Harvard University Press.

Goldman, J. (1995). *Applied data communications: A business-oriented approach*. New York, NY: Wiley.

Goldstein, D. K. (1986). *Hallmark cards*. Boston: Harvard Business School.

Grace. (2004). *Grace community church*. Retrieved from http://www.redshift.com/~becbobtr/pgcc.html

Grant, R. M. (1996). Toward a knowledge-based theory of the firm. *Strategic Management Journal*, *17*, 109–122.

Grover, V., Jeong, S. R., Kettinger, W. J., & Teng, J. T. C. (1995). The implementation of business process reengineering. *Journal of Management Information Systems*, *12*(1), 109–144.

Hammer, M., & Champy, J. (1993). *Reengineering the corporation: A manifesto for business revolution*. New York, NY: Harper Business Press. doi:10.1016/S0007-6813(05)80064-3.

Hansen, P. A. (1995). Publicly produced knowledge for business: When is it effective? *Technovation*, *15*(6), 387–397. doi:10.1016/0166-4972(95)96599-O.

Hargadon, A., & Fanelli, A. (2002). Action and possibility: Reconciling dual perspectives of knowledge in organizations. *Organization Science*, *13*(3), 290–302. doi:10.1287/orsc.13.3.290.2772.

Harrington, H. J. (1991). *Business process improvement: The breakthrough strategy for total quality, productivity, and competitiveness*. New York, NY: McGraw-Hill.

Herzberg, F., Mausner, B., & Snyderman, B. B. (1959). *The motivation to work*. New York, NY: John Wiley.

Holsapple, C. W., & Jones, K. G. (2007). Knowledge chain activity classes: Impacts on competitiveness and the importance of technology support. *International Journal of Knowledge Management*, *3*(3), 26–45. doi:10.4018/jkm.2007070102.

Holsapple, C. W., & Singh, M. (2001). The knowledge chain model: Activities for competitiveness. *Expert Systems with Applications*, *20*(1), 77–98. doi:10.1016/S0957-4174(00)00050-6.

Holsapple, C. W., & Wu, J. (2011). An elusive antecedent of superior firm performance: The knowledge management factor. *Decision Support Systems*, *52*(1), 271–283. doi:10.1016/j.dss.2011.08.003.

Holt, D. T., Bartczak, S. E., Clark, S. W., & Trent, M. R. (2007). The development of an instrument to measure readiness for knowledge management. *Knowledge Management Research & Practice*, *5*(2), 75–82. doi:10.1057/palgrave.kmrp.8500132.

Homer. (2008). *The odyssey. (D. Stevenson* (S. Butler (Trans. Ed.)). Cambridge, MA: Internet Classics Archive.

Housel, T. J. (2004). *Where to invest in information systems: A CRM case study* (Working paper). Monterey, CA: Naval Postgraduate School.

Housel, T. J., El Sawy, O., Zhong, J. J., & Rodgers, W. (2001). Measuring the return on knowledge embedded in information technology. In *Proceedings International Conference on Information Systems*. IEEE.

Housel, T. J., & Bell, A. H. (2001). *Measuring and managing knowledge*. Boston, MA: McGraw-Hill.

Ingram, P., & Simons, T. (2002). The transfer of experience in groups of organizations: Implications for performance and competition. *Management Science*, *48*(12), 1517–1533. doi:10.1287/mnsc.48.12.1517.437.

Jayasingam, S., Ansari, M. A., Ramayah, T., & Jantan, M. (2012). *Knowledge management practices and performance: are they truly linked?* Knowledge Management Research & Practice. doi:10.1057/kmrp.2012.5.

Jennex, M. E., & Olfman, L. (2004). Assessing knowledge management success/effectiveness models. In *Proceedings Hawaii International Conference on System Sciences*. Hawaii, HI: IEEE.

Jin, Y., & Levitt, R. E. (1996). The virtual design team: A computational model of project organizations. *Computational & Mathematical Organization Theory*, *2*(3), 171–195. doi:10.1007/BF00127273.

Johansson, H. J., McHugh, P., Pendlebury, A. J., & Wheeler, W. A. III. (1993). *Business process reengineering: Breakpoint strategies for market dominance*. Chichester, UK: Wiley.

JP1-02. (2011). Department of Defense dictionary of military and associated terms. *Joint Publication 1-02* (8 November 2010, amended through 15 August 2011). Washington, DC: Joint Chiefs of Staff.

Kaplan, A. M., & Haenlein, M. (2010). Users of the world unite! The challenges and opportunities of social media. *Business Horizons*, *53*(1), 59–68. doi:10.1016/j.bushor.2009.09.003.

Kettinger, W. J., Guha, S., & Teng, J. T. C. (1995). The process reengineering life cycle methodology: A case study. In V. Grover, & W. Kettinger (Eds.), *Business Process Change: Reengineering Concepts, Methods and Technologies*. Hershey, PA: Idea Publishing.

King, J. L., & Konsynski, B. (1990). *Singapore tradenet: A tale of one city*. Boston: Harvard Business School.

King, W. R., & Ko, D. G. (2001). Evaluating knowledge management and the learning organization: An information/knowledge value chain approach. *Communications of the Association for Information Systems*, *5*(14), 1–27.

KnowledgeWright. (2004). *KnowledgeWright expert system development shell*. Retrieved 2004, from http://www.amzi.com/products/knowledgewright.html

Kramer, F. D., Starr, S. H., & Wentz, L. (2011). *Cyberpower and national security*. Dulles, VA: Potomac.

Kuehl, D. (n.d.). *From cyberspace to cyberpower: Defining the problem*. (Information Resources Management College/National Defense University Working Paper). Washington, DC: National Defense University.

Kulkarni, U., & Freeze, R. (2004). Development and validation of a knowledge management capability assessment model. In *Proceedings of the Twenty-Fifth International Conference on Information Systems*. IEEE.

Kulkarni, U., & Freeze, R. (2006). Measuring knowledge management capabilities. In *Encyclopedia of Knowledge Management*. Hershey, PA: Idea Group. doi:10.4018/978-1-59140-573-3.ch079.

Kunz, J. C., Levitt, R. E., & Jin, Y. (1998). The virtual design team: A computational simulation model of project organizations. *Communications of the ACM*, *41*(11), 84–92. doi:10.1145/287831.287844.

Laurel, B. (1991). *Computers as theatre*. Reading, MA: Addison-Wesley.

Law, A. M., & Kelton, W. D. (1982). *Simulation modeling and analysis*. New York, NY: McGraw-Hill.

Leavitt, H. J. (1965). Applying organizational change in industry: structural, technological and humanistic approaches. In J. March (Ed.), *Handbook of Organizations*. Chicago, IL: Rand McNally.

Lehdonvirta, V. (2010). Virtual worlds don't exist: Questioning the dichotomous approach in MMO studies. Game Studies, 10(1). Retrieved from http://gamestudies.org/1001/articles/lehdonvirta

Levitt, B., & March, J. G. (1988). Organizational learning. *Annual Review of Sociology*, *14*, 319–340. doi:10.1146/annurev.so.14.080188.001535.

Levitt, R. E., Thomsen, J., Christiansen, T. R., Junz, J. C., Jin, Y., & Nass, C. (1999). Simulating project work processes and organizations: Toward a micro-contingency theory of organizational design. *Management Science*, *45*(11), 1479–1495. doi:10.1287/mnsc.45.11.1479.

Liebowitz, J. (2004). *Addressing the human capital crisis in the federal government: A knowledge management perspective*. Amsterdam: Elsevier.

Liebowitz, J. (2012). *Knowledge management handbook: Collaboration and social networking* (2nd ed.). Boca Raton, FL: CRC Press. doi:10.1201/b12285.

Liebowitz, J., Rubenstein-Montano, B., McCaw, D., Buchwalter, J., Browning, C., Newman, B., & Rebeck, K. (2000). The knowledge audit. *Knowledge and Process Management*, *7*(1), 3–10. doi:10.1002/(SICI)1099-1441(200001/03)7:1<3::AID-KPM72>3.0.CO;2-0.

Linden Labs. (2010). Second life. Retrieved from http://secondlife.com/

Loch, C. H., Pich, M. T., Terwiesch, C., & Urbschat, C. (2001). Selecting R&D projects at BMW: A case study of adopting mathematical programming models. *IEEE Transactions on Engineering Management*, *48*(1), 70–80. doi:10.1109/17.913167.

Looney, J. P., & Nissen, M. E. (2006). Computational modeling and analysis of networked organizational planning in a coalition maritime strike environment. In *Proceedings Command & Control Research & Technology Symposium*. San Diego, CA: Academic Press.

Lynn, W. J. III. (2010, September/October). Defending a new domain: The Pentagon's cyberstrategy. *Foreign Affairs*, 97–108.

March, J. G. (1991). Exploration and exploitation in organizational learning. *Organization Science*, *2*(1), 71–87. doi:10.1287/orsc.2.1.71.

March, J. G., & Simon, H. A. (1958). *Organizations*. New York: Wiley.

Markus, M. L. (2001). Toward a theory of knowledge reuse: Situations and factors in reuse success. *Journal of Management Information Systems*, *18*(1), 57–93.

Marques, D. P., & Simon, F. J. G. (2006). The effect of knowledge management practices on firm performance. *Journal of Knowledge Management*, *10*(3), 143–156. doi:10.1108/13673270610670911.

Martínez-Moreno, E., González-Navarro, P., Zornoza, A., & Ripoll, P. (2009). Relationship, task and process conflicts on team performance: The moderating role of communication media. *The International Journal of Conflict Management*, *20*(3), 251–268. doi:10.1108/10444060910974876.

Massey, A. P., Montoya-Weiss, M. M., & O'Driscoll, T. M. (2002). Performance-centered design of knowledge-intensive processes. *Journal of Management Information Systems*, *18*(4), 37–58.

Massey, A. P., Montoya-Weiss, M. M., & O'Driscoll, T. M. (2002). Knowledge management in pursuit of performance: Insights from Nortel networks. *Management Information Systems Quarterly*, *26*(3), 269–289. doi:10.2307/4132333.

Matusik, S. F., & Hill, C. W. L. (1998). The utilization of contingent work, knowledge creation, and competitive advantage. *Academy of Management Review*, *23*(4), 680–697. doi:10.2307/259057.

Maznevski, M. L., & Chudoba, K. M. (2000). Bridging space over time: Global virtual team dynamics and effectiveness. *Organization Science*, *11*(5), 473–492. doi:10.1287/orsc.11.5.473.15200.

McCreadie, K. (2009). *Adam Smith's the wealth of nations: A modern-day interpretation of an economic classic*. Oxford, UK: Infinite Ideas.

McLennan, K. J. (2008). *The virtual world of work: How to gain competitive advantage through the virtual workplace*. Charlotte, NC: Information Age.

Miles, R. E., & Snow, C. (1978). *Organizational strategy, structure, and process*. New York: McGraw-Hill.

Milevski, L. (2011). STUXNET and strategy: A special operation in cyberspace? *Joint Forces Quarterly*, *63*, 64–69.

Miller, R. A., & Kuehl, D. T. (2009). *Cyberspace and the first battle in 21st century war* (working paper). Washington, DC: National Defense University, Information Resources Management College.

Mintzberg, H. (1980). Structure in 5's: A synthesis of the research on organization design. *Management Science*, *26*(3), 322–341. doi:10.1287/mnsc.26.3.322.

Montoya, M. M., Massey, A. P., & Lockwood, N. S. (2011). 3D collaborative virtual environments: Exploring the link between collaborative behaviors and team performance. *Decision Sciences*, *42*(2), 451–476. doi:10.1111/j.1540-5915.2011.00318.x.

Morgan, G. (2006). Images of organization (updated ed.). Thousand Oaks, CA: Sage Publications.

Morgan, G. (1997). Images of organization (2nd ed.). Thousand Oaks, CA: Sage Publications.

Mueller, F., & Dyerson, R. (1999). Expert humans or expert organizations? *Organization Studies*, *20*(2), 225–256. doi:10.1177/0170840699202003.

Nahapiet, J., & Ghoshal, S. (1998). Social capital, intellectual capital, and the organizational advantage. *Academy of Management Review*, *23*(2), 242–266.

NASA. (2004). *Library past announcements*. Retrieved 19 August 2004, from http://km.nasa.gov/library/past_announcements.html

National Commission on Terrorist Attacks upon the United States. (2004). The 9/11 commission report: Final report of the national commission on terrorist attacks upon the United States. Washington, DC: US Government Printing Office.

Nissen, M. E. (2002). *Understanding 'understanding' flow for network-centric warfare: Military knowledge-flow mechanics* (NPS Technical Report NPS-GSBPP-02-001). Monterey, CA: Naval Postgraduate School.

Nissen, M. E. (2004). *Dynamic knowledge patterns to inform design: A field study of knowledge stocks and flows in an extreme organization*. Working paper.

Nissen, M. E. (2010). Command and control in virtual environments: Using contingency theory to understand organization in virtual worlds (Technical Report No. NPS-IS-10-005). Monterey, CA: Naval Postgraduate School.

Nissen, M. E. (2010). *CyberKM: Harnessing dynamic knowledge for competitive advantage through cyberspace* (Technical Report No. NPS-IS-10-006). Monterey, CA: Naval Postgraduate School.

Nissen, M. E. (1998). Redesigning reengineering through measurement-driven inference. *Management Information Systems Quarterly*, *22*(4), 509–534. doi:10.2307/249553.

Nissen, M. E. (2002). An extended model of knowledge-flow dynamics. *Communications of the Association for Information Systems*, *8*, 251–266.

Nissen, M. E. (2005). Toward designing organizations around knowledge flows. In K. Desouza (Ed.), *New frontiers in knowledge management*. New York: Palgrave McMillian.

Nissen, M. E. (2006). *Harnessing knowledge dynamics: Principled organizational knowing & learning*. Hershey, PA: IGI Global.

Nissen, M. E. (2007). Knowledge management and global cultures: Elucidation through an institutional knowledge-flow perspective. *Knowledge and Process Management*, *14*(3), 211–225. doi:10.1002/kpm.285.

Nissen, M. E. (2011). Measuring dynamic knowledge flows: Implications for organizational performance. In G. Schiuma (Ed.), *Managing Knowledge Assets and Business Value Creation in Organizations*. Hershey, PA: IGI Global.

Nissen, M. E., & Bergin, R. D. (2013). Knowledge work through social media applications: Team performance implications of immersive virtual worlds. *Journal of Organizational Computing and Electronic Commerce*, *23*(1-2), 84–109. doi:10.1080/10919392.2013.748612.

Nissen, M. E., & Burton, R. M. (2011). Designing organizations for dynamic fit: System stability, maneuverability and opportunity loss. *IEEE Transactions on Systems. Man and Cybernetics – Part A*, *41*(3), 418–433. doi:10.1109/TSMCA.2010.2084569.

Nissen, M. E., Kamel, M. N., & Sengupta, K. C. (2000). Integrated analysis and design of knowledge systems and processes. *Information Resources Management Journal*, *13*(1), 24–42. doi:10.4018/irmj.2000010103.

Nissen, M. E., & Levitt, R. E. (2004). Agent-based modeling of knowledge dynamics. *Knowledge Management Research & Practice*, *2*(3), 169–183. doi:10.1057/palgrave.kmrp.8500039.

Nissen, M. E., & Levitt, R. E. (2005). Knowledge management research through computational experimentation. In D. Schwartz (Ed.), *Encyclopedia of Knowledge Management*. Hershey, PA: Idea Group. doi:10.4018/978-1-59140-573-3.ch008.

Nissen, M. E., Orr, R., & Levitt, R. E. (2008). Streams of shared knowledge: Computational expansion of organization theory. *Knowledge Management Research & Practice*, *6*(2), 124–140. doi:10.1057/kmrp.2008.1.

Nogueira, J. C. (2000). *A formal model for risk assessment in software projects*. (Unpublished doctoral dissertation). Department of Computer Science, Naval Postgraduate School, Monterey, CA.

Nold, H. A. (2012). Linking knowledge processes with firm performance: organizational culture. *Journal of Intellectual Capital*, *13*(1), 16–38. doi:10.1108/14691931211196196.

Nonaka, I. (1994). A dynamic theory of organizational knowledge creation. *Organization Science*, *5*(1), 14–37. doi:10.1287/orsc.5.1.14.

Nonaka, I., & Takeuchi, H. (1995). *The knowledge-creating company: How Japanese companies create the dynamics of innovation*. New York: Oxford University Press.

Norton, Q. (2012, January 11). 2011: The year Anonymous took on cops, dictators and existential dread. Wired.

O'Dell, C., Ostro, N., & Grayson, C. (1998). *If we only knew what we know: The transfer of internal knowledge and best practice*. New York: Simon & Schuster.

OPM. (2008). *An analysis of federal employee retirement data*. Washington, DC: US Office of Personnel Management.

Oravec, J. A. (2001). Online recreation and play in organizational life: The internet as virtual contested terrain. In L. Chidambaram, & I. Zigurs (Eds.), *Our vitual world: The transformation of work, play and life via technology*. Hershey, PA: Idea Group. doi:10.4018/978-1-878289-92-6.ch008.

Ouchi, W. G. (1980). Markets, bureaucracies, and clans. *Administrative Science Quarterly*, *25*(1), 129–141. doi:10.2307/2392231.

Palen, L., Hiltz, S. R., & Liu, S. B. (2007). Online forums supporting grassroots in emergency preparedness and response. *Communications of the ACM*, *50*(3), 54–58. doi:10.1145/1226736.1226766.

Petit, B. (2012, April-June). Social media and UW. Special Warfare, 20-28.

Pfeffer, J., & Sutton, R. I. (1999). Knowing 'what' to do is not enough: Turning knowledge into action. *California Management Review*, *42*(1), 83–108. doi:10.2307/41166020.

Pindyck, R. S., & Rubinfeld, D. L. (1998). *Microeconomics* (4th ed.). Upper Saddle River, NJ: Prentice-Hall.

Polanyi, M. (1966). *The tacit dimension*. Garden City, NY: Doubleday.

Polanyi, M. (1967). *The tacit dimension*. Garden City, NY: Anchor Books.

Porter, D. (1997). *Internet culture*. New York, NY: Routeledge.

Porter, M. E. (1980). *Competitive strategy*. New York: Free Press.

Porter, M. E. (1985). Technology and competitive advantage. *The Journal of Business Strategy*, *5*(3), 60–77. doi:10.1108/eb039075.

Porter, M. E. (1996). What is strategy? *Harvard Business Review*, *74*(6), 61–78. PMID:10158474.

Postrel, S. (2002). Islands of shared knowledge: Specialization and mutual understanding in problem-solving teams. *Organization Science*, *13*(3), 303–320. doi:10.1287/orsc.13.3.303.2773.

POWer. (2013). *Edge center*. Retrieved from http://www.nps.edu/Academics/Centers/CEP/

Powley, E. H., & Nissen, M. E. (2012). If you can't trust, stick to hierarchy: Structure and trust as contingency factors in threat assessment contexts. *Journal of Homeland Security and Emergency Management*, *9*(1), 1–19. doi:10.1515/1547-7355.1986.

Rowe, S. (1995). *Telecommunications for managers* (3rd ed.). Englewood Cliffs, NJ: Prentice Hall.

Samarah, I., Paul, S., & Tadisina, S. (2007). Collaboration technology support for knowledge conversion in virtual teams: A theoretical perspective. In Proceedings Hawaii International Conference on System Sciences. IEEE.

Sameulson, P. A. (1974). Complementarity: An essay on the 40th anniversary of the Hicks-Allen revolution in demand theory. *Journal of Economic Literature*, *12*(4), 1255–1289.

Sandelowski, M. (2000). Combining qualitative and quantitative sampling, data collection, and analysis techniques in mixed-method studies. *Research in Nursing & Health*, *23*(3), 246–255. doi:10.1002/1098-240X(200006)23:3<246::AID-NUR9>3.0.CO;2-H PMID:10871540.

Saviotti, P. P. (1998). On the dynamics of appropriability, of tacit and of codified knowledge. *Research Policy*, *26*, 843–856. doi:10.1016/S0048-7333(97)00066-8.

Savitz, E. (2012, October 23). Gartner: Top 10 strategic technology trends for 2013. *Forbes CIO Network*. Retrieved from http://www.forbes.com/sites/ericsavitz/2012/10/23/gartner-top-10-strategic-technology-trends-for-2013/

Schutz, A. (1971). *Collected papers I: The problem of social reality*. The Hague, The Netherlands: Martinus Nijhoff.

Scott, W. R. (1995). *Institutions and organizations*. Thousand Oaks, CA: Sage.

Senge, P. M. (1990). *The fifth discipline: The art and practice of the learning organization*. New York: Doubleday.

Short, J. (1976). *The social psychology of telecommunications*. Academic Press.

Sicart, M. (2010). This war is a lie: Ethical implication of massively multiplayer online game design. In C. Wankel, & S. Malleck (Eds.), *Emerging ethical issues of life in virtual worlds*. Charlotte, NC: Information Age Publishing.

Silvi, R., & Cuganesan, S. (2006). Investigating the management of knowledge for competitive advantage: A strategic cost management perspective. *Journal of Intellectual Capital*, *7*(3), 309–323. doi:10.1108/14691930610681429.

Snyman, R., & Kruger, C. J. (2004). The interdependency between strategic management and strategic knowledge management. *Journal of Knowledge Management*, *8*(1), 5–19. doi:10.1108/13673270410523871.

Spender, J. C. (1996). Making knowledge the basis of a dynamic theory of the firm. *Strategic Management Journal*, *17*, 45–62.

Staff. (2012). World development book case study: The role of social networking in the Arab spring. New Internationalist. Retrieved from http://www.newint.org/books/reference/world-development/case-studies/social-networking-in-the-arab-spring/

Stein, E. W., & Zwass, V. (1995). Actualizing organizational memory with information systems. *Information Systems Research*, *6*(2), 85–117. doi:10.1287/isre.6.2.85.

Stoddard, D. B., & Jarvenpaa, S. L. (1995). Business process redesign: Tactics for managing radical change. *Journal of Information Management Systems*, *12*(1), 81–107.

Stoddard, D. B., & Meadows, C. J. (1992). *Capital holding corporation - Reengineering the direct response group*. Boston: Harvard Business School.

STSC. (2000). *Guidelines for successful acquisition and management of software intensive systems (version 3.0). Hill AFB*. UT: Software Technology Support Center.

Szulanski, G. (1996). Exploring internal stickiness: Impediments to the transfer of best practice within the firm. *Strategic Management Journal*, *17*, 27–43.

Szulanski, G., & Winter, S. (2002). Getting it right the second time. *Harvard Business Review*, *80*(1), 62–69. PMID:12964468.

Talebzadeh, H., Mandutianu, S., & Winner, C. F. (1995). Countrywide loan-underwriting expert system. *AI Magazine*, *16*(1), 51–64.

Teece, D. (2009). *Dynamic capabilities and strategic management*. Oxford, UK: Oxford University Press.

Teece, D., Pisano, G., & Shuen, A. (1997). Dynamic capabilities and strategic management. *Strategic Management Journal*, *18*(7), 509–533. doi:10.1002/(SICI)1097-0266(199708)18:7<509::AID-SMJ882>3.0.CO;2-Z.

Teigland, R. (2010). What benefits do virtual worlds provide charitable organizations? A case study of peace train--A charitable organization in Second Life. In C. Wankel, & S. Malleck (Eds.), *Emerging ethical issues of life in virtual worlds*. Charlotte, NC: Information Age Publishing.

Thompson, J. D. (1967). *Organizations in action: Social science bases in administrative theory*. New York: McGraw-Hill.

Thomsen, J. (1998). *The virtual team alliance (VTA): Modeling the effects of goal incongruency in semi-routine, fast-paced project organizations.* (Unpublished doctoral dissertation). Department of Civil and Environmental Engineering, Stanford University, Palo Alto, CA.

Tuomi, I. (1999). Data is more than knowledge: Implications of the reversed knowledge hierarchy for knowledge management and organizational memory. *Journal of Management Information Systems*, *16*(3), 103–117.

Turban, E., & Aronson, J. (1998). *Decision support systems and intelligent systems*. Upper Saddle River, NJ: Prentice-Hall.

USTA. (2004). *United States tennis association website*. Retrieved from http://www.usta.org

VDT. (2004). *The virtual design team research group website*. Retrieved from http://www.stanford.edu/group/CIFE/VDT/ 2004

von Hippel, E. (1994). Sticky information and the locus of problem solving: Implications for innovation. *Management Science*, *40*(4), 429–439. doi:10.1287/mnsc.40.4.429.

von Krogh, G., Ichijo, K., & Nonaka, I. (2000). *Enabling knowledge creation: How to unlock the mystery of tacit knowledge and release the power of innovation*. New York, NY: Oxford University Press. doi:10.1093/acprof:oso/9780195126167.001.0001.

Walsh, J. P., & Ungson, G. R. (1991). Organizational memory. *Academy of Management Review*, *16*(1), 57–91.

C. Wankel, & S. Malleck (Eds.). (2010). *Emerging ethical issues of life in virtual worlds*. Charlotte, NC: Information Age Publishing.

Weick, K. E., & Roberts, K. H. (1993). Collective mind in organizations: Heedful interrelating on flights decks. *Administrative Science Quarterly*, *38*(3), 357–381. doi:10.2307/2393372.

Witmer, B. G. (1998). Measuring presence in virtual environments: A presence questionnaire. *Presence (Cambridge, Mass.)*, *7*(3), 225–240. doi:10.1162/105474698565686.

Wolf, P. (2011). Balanced evaluation: Monitoring the success of a knowledge management project. *Historical Social Research (Köln)*, *36*(1), 262–287.

Wright, T. (1936). Factors affecting the cost of airplanes. *Journal of the Aeronautical Sciences*, *4*(4), 122–128.

Yee, N. (2006). The demographics, motivations, and derived experiences of users of massively multi-user online graphical environments. *Presence (Cambridge, Mass.)*, *15*(3), 309–329. doi:10.1162/pres.15.3.309.

Yee, N. (2006). The labor of fun: How video games blur the boundaries of work and play. *Games and Culture*, *1*(1), 68–71. doi:10.1177/1555412005281819.

Yelle, L. E. (1979). The learning curve: Historical review and comprehensive survey. *Decision Sciences*, *10*(2), 302–328. doi:10.1111/j.1540-5915.1979.tb00026.x.

Zack, M., McKeen, J., & Singh, S. (2009). Knowledge management and organizational performance: An exploratory analysis. *Journal of Knowledge Management*, *13*(6), 392–409. doi:10.1108/13673270910997088.

Zetter, K. (2011, July 11). How digital detectives deciphered Stuxnet, the most menacing malware in history. *Wired*.

About the Author

Mark E. Nissen is Professor of Information Science and Management, and Edge Center Director, at the Naval Postgraduate School. His research focuses on dynamic knowing and organizing. He views work, technology, organization, and people as an integrated design problem, and he's concentrated for some time on the disparate dynamics of tacit and explicit knowledge flows, looking in particular at their measurement and at (re)designing organizations that balance stability with maneuverability. Mark's 150+ publications span information systems, project management, organization studies, knowledge management, and related fields. In 2000, he received the Menneken Faculty Award for Excellence in Scientific Research, the top research award available to faculty at the Naval Postgraduate School. In 2001, he received a prestigious Young Investigator Grant Award from the Office of Naval Research for work on Knowledge Flow Theory. In 2002 – 2003, he was Visiting Professor at Stanford, integrating Knowledge Flow Theory into agent-based tools for computational modeling and experimentation.

Index

P

R

S

T

U

V

W

Z

CPSIA information can be obtained
at www.ICGtesting.com
Printed in the USA
BVOW04*0754150917
494394BV00022B/57/P